D1205727

# Current Issues in Public-Utility Economics

# Current Issues in Public-Utility Economics

## Essays in Honor of James C. Bonbright

Edited by

**Albert L. Danielsen**
**David R. Kamerschen**
The University of Georgia

**LexingtonBooks**
D.C. Heath and Company
Lexington, Massachusetts
Toronto

**Library of Congress Cataloging in Publication Data**

Main entry under title:
   Current issues in public-utility economics.

   Includes index.
   1. Public utilities—United States—Addresses, essays, lectures.  2. Bonbright, James Cummings, 1891—Addresses, essays, lectures.  I. Bonbright, James Cummings, 1891.  II. Danielsen, Albert L.  III. Kamerschen, David R.
HD2766.C87     1982      338.4'3636      81-48612
ISBN 0-669-05440-2

Published simultaneously in Canada

Printed in the United States of America

International Standard Book Number: 0-669-05440-2

Library of Congress Catalog Card Number: 81-48612

*This book is dedicated to Dean William C. Flewellen, Jr., College of Business Administration, University of Georgia, for his enthusiastic support of the Public Utilities in Economics Program at the university. Under his administration, the department has been awarded a Chair of Public Utility Economics, initiated the annual Current Issues in Public Utility Economics Conference, and expanded programs in public-utility economics and regulation at both the graduate and undergraduate levels. It is through his efforts that these advances have been made in a field of ever-increasing importance and concern.*

# Contents

# Preface and Acknowledgments

This book is a tribute to one of the most respected academic and business economists of the twentieth century, the former Columbia University professor, James Cummings Bonbright. He was born December 5, 1891, in Evanston, Illinois, the son of Daniel Bonbright and Alice D. (Cummings). He married Martha Jane Earnest in 1933 and has three children: Alice Vivian B. Merrified; James C., Jr.; and Daniel I. Professor Bonbright and his wife now reside in Athens, Georgia, near the University of Georgia campus. Bonbright received the B.S. (1913) and L.L.D. degrees (1950) from Northwestern University and the Ph.D. from Columbia University in 1920. From 1920 to 1960 he rose from instructor of economics to professor in finance in the graduate school of business at Columbia. In 1960 he was appointed professor emeritus and was selected for the Ames Award of Harvard University Law School. During his career Bonbright was also selected to be a Ford Foundation faculty Fellow and was a member of the American Economic Association (vice-president and member of the executive committee), American Philosophical Association, American Academy of Arts and Sciences, Phi Beta Kappa, and Men's Faculty Club of Columbia University.

During the early part of his career Bonbright was associated with Bonbright & Company, investment bankers in New York. He was a U.S. delegate to the 1933 World Power Conference in Stockholm and a trustee to the Power Authority of the state of New York (1931-1946). From 1941 to 1946 he was chairman of the Power Authority. In 1959 he was named a member of the Governor's Committee on New York State's Power Resources. Bonbright was also a trustee for Teachers' Insurance and Annuity Association (1943-1946), and a consultant to the President's Inquiry Commission on the Committee on Interstate and Foreign Commerce and to the U.S. House of Representatives in their investigations of railway holding companies. His published works include *Railroad Capitalization, Principles of Public Utility Rates, Valuation of Property, Public Utilities and the National Power Policies,* as well as many other contributions presented in the bibliography. He has written for the *American Economic Review, Quarterly Journal of Economics, Public Utilities Fortnightly,* and many other professional economic and legal journals. His 1961 *Principles of Public Utility Rates* is considered a classic and continues to be one of the most cited works in the field. Bonbright has also been recognized in *Who's Who in America, Contemporary Authors,* and *Who's Who Among English and European Authors.*

Many leading professionals in the public-utilities field have contributed to this book. We are indebted to them for their perseverance and prompt submission of material, even when this required the sacrifice of other deadlines.

Eight of the twenty-one chapters are based on papers presented at the first Annual University of Georgia Public Utilities Conference held in Atlanta, Georgia, July 15 to 17, 1981. The conference, like this book, was dedicated to Bonbright. Thus, we are doubly indebted to the following individuals for their contributions to the conference and this book: John B. Legler, Leigh H. Hammond, John R. Marks III, and Ford B. Spinks (chapter 5); Jim J. Tozzi (chapter 8); Ronald P. Wilder (chapter 10); Milton Z. Kafoglis (chapter 13); Chris W. Paul II (chapter 14); Anthony D. Osbon (chapter 16); William R. Nusbaum (chapter 17); and Larry R. Weber (chapter 18); Hunter E. Harvey, Jr. (chapter 19). The remaining chapters were solicited from other prominent individuals in the public-utilities field. Their enthusiasm made an otherwise arduous editorial task a pleasure. We are especially indebted to Harry M. Trebing (chapter 1); Charles F. Phillips, Jr. (chapter 2); Roger Sherman (chapter 3); and Robert G. Uhler (chapter 4) for their efforts to explain Bonbright's unique contributions and the changes that have occurred in utility regulation since his more active involvement ended in the 1960s. Similarly, Alfred E. Kahn (chapter 6); J. Robert Malko and Gregory B. Enholm (chapter 7); and Edward H. Clark (chapter 8) were kind enough to supplement the work of our conference participants by discussing the changing structure and functions of the regulatory commissions. We are also indebted to William G. Shepherd (chapter 9); William J. Baumol (chapter 11); David R. Kamerschen and Donald C. Keenan (chapter 12); C. Lowell Harriss (chapter 15); Joe D. Pace (chapter 20); and William R. Hughes (chapter 21) for their contributions to this book. These contributions are intended more for the working professional and student of regulation than for the armchair philosopher. The final result is a celebratory book of unusual scope, imagination, and relevance.

# Part I
# Tribute to
# James C. Bonbright

# 1

# James C. Bonbright's Contributions to Public-Utility Economics and Regulation

*Harry M. Trebing*

James C. Bonbright is one of the legendary pioneers in the field of public-utility economics. In a career that spanned more than four decades, he addressed virtually all of the problems that confronted policymakers from the early 1920s to the mid-1960s. In an impressive list of publications and studies, he dealt with valuation of the rate base, determination of the rate of return under regulation, pricing and rate design, holding-company abuses, and regulatory reform. In each of these areas his contribution had a significant impact upon the work of academics and practitioners alike, as well as on public-policy formulation.

It would be difficult to find a major study of public-utility pricing that did not acknowledge its indebtedness to Bonbright's "Criteria of a Sound Rate Structure."[1] Similarly, almost every state and federal commission has been influenced, directly or indirectly, by his continued defense of the original-cost standard for valuation. At a time when the courts, industry spokesmen, and such well-known academics as Harry Gunnison Brown championed fair value, Bonbright argued on behalf of original cost, and its eventual acceptance by forty-five commissions was a tribute to the scholarly support that he provided.

Bonbright had a special affinity for regulatory reform at the state and federal levels. His participation in the hearings of the New York Commission on the Revision of the Public Service Commission's Law in 1930, and his critical evaluation of holding-company abuses in 1932 (coauthored with Gardner C. Means) provide a fascinating insight into a reformist's efforts to delineate a role for public-interest regulation while at the same time strengthening the ability of government to act. A juxtaposition of his views with those of the conservative Arthur T. Hadley in the New York hearings provides, in striking contrast, the case for and against economic regulation—this debate occurred at least thirty years before the topic was to become popular in the economic literature. Furthermore, the Bonbright-Means analysis of the holding-company problem certainly influenced the drafters of the Public Utility Holding Company Act of 1935, and it should be read by those who urge its repeal in 1982.

Bonbright's involvement in the solution of real-world regulatory problems clearly reflects the spirit of institutional economics which prevailed at Columbia University for much of his tenure. John Maurice Clark, Wesley Clair Mitchell, and Joseph Dorfman, all members of the Columbia faculty, stood in the forefront of this movement. It is significant to note that the other great proponent of public-interest regulation and public-utility economics during this same period, Professor Martin G. Glaeser, came out of a similar setting at the University of Wisconsin. At Wisconsin, John R. Commons and Richard T. Ely were among the founders of the institutionalist movement and, together with Glaeser, they enlisted a strong commitment on the part of the state government toward regulatory activism and reform.

The instructionalists were disenchanted with the ability of market forces to reconcile the complex problems confronting society. Instead of relying on imperfect markets, they viewed government intervention, or social control, as the more appropriate means for inducing change and achieving public-interest objectives. In this context, social control would be dynamic and oriented toward the future. It was not perceived as a static phenomenon or as a means of maintaining the status quo.

Of course it would be an oversimplification to argue that all institutionalists of this period held the same view of economic regulation. For the most part, Bonbright and Glaeser shared similar views on the importance of cost-of-service and original-cost valuation as the basis for determining revenue requirements and the components of rate-basis regulation. But Glaeser was also interested in incorporating public utilities within a larger context of planning and regional development, while Bonbright was particularly interested in marginal cost-pricing. Another prominent institutionalist, Horace M. Gray, took a more critical position on the viability of the commission system than either Bonbright or Glaeser. For Gray, the regulation of privately owned monopoly had been a failure, so it would be necessary to create new institutional forms, such as cooperatives and public-power authorities, to achieve social objectives. Nevertheless, Bonbright's work serves as the quintessential model of much of the institutionalist and reformist thought of the period. For this reason, it is especially appropriate that his views on price-earnings regulation and market structure be summarized and appraised in light of the changes that have taken place in the public-utility industries.

**The Bonbright Model of Economic Regulation**

Bonbright's perception of the role of social control clearly places him in the camp of those who support the public-interest theory of regulation. He believes that "the primary purpose of . . . regulation must be . . . the protection of the public in the role of consumers rather than in the role either of producers or of taxpayers."[2] Further, he argues that "what must justify public utility regulation . . . is the necessity of the regulation and not merely the necessity of the product."[3] The need for regulation, according to Bonbright, rests on significant production economies and on the localized and restricted nature of the markets for utility services which establish a uniquely close connection between utility plant and the consumers' premises. While noting that economies of scale may exist, he apparently does not hold them to be a prerequisite for regulation.

Bonbright believes that one of the major objectives of regulation is to assure that prices will be cost-based. To achieve this goal, he places great emphasis on cost-of-service as the appropriate standard of reasonableness, with costs defined in terms of "cost reasonably or prudently incurred."[4] For Bonbright, rates based on costs will serve to keep demand within economic bounds and attract the necessary resources for the provision of service.

In the institutionalist tradition, Bonbright is concerned more with the development of workable principles for the establishment of reasonable rates than with highly abstract models. He finds theoretical welfare economics to be of limited usefulness. On the other hand, he believes strongly that "public utility services are designed to be sold at cost, or at cost plus a fair profit."[5] Therefore, Bonbright is also critical of those who, like Horace Gray, would design public-utility prices to achieve social objectives.

As a proponent of a cost-of-service/original-cost approach to rate making, one would expect Bonbright to take a critical view of value-of-service and fair-value standards. Among other faults, he points to a special weakness of the value-of-service approach, notably its highly subjective nature. To illustrate, he cites the long-established foundation of the Bell system's approach to exchange rate making: the value of service rises directly with an increase in the size of the exchange. But he observes that telephone companies "offer no evidence of the amounts of these values, city by city. The relative 'values', if such they can be called, would seem to have merely ordinal, not cardinal, magnitudes."[6]

In his search for standards, Bonbright provides an imaginative analysis of the shortcomings of efforts to superimpose competitive market criteria on regulatory criteria. This includes "the popular assumption that a strictly competitive price is a price equal to replacement cost (which) must be rejected, even as a rough approximation."[7] Further, he notes the formal difficulties of making price equal to both average cost and marginal cost, and the real-world difficulties that would arise whenever utilities sought to attract capital if highly variable rates of profit and loss were to be introduced by regulatory action. Instead of emulating the competitive market, he would accept a normal profit approach. Similarly, he believes that highly flexible prices would impose a special burden on consumers as they sought to adapt to such changes. Bonbright concludes: "What I am trying to emphasize . . . is that the very nature of a monopolistic public utility is such as to preclude an attempt to make the emulation of competition very close."[8]

What emerges from Bonbright's effort to establish revenue requirements and price on a cost basis is an *actual-cost* or net-investment standard in which the rate base represents the actual cost of plant plus interest during construction and an allowance for working capital, with an appropriate deduction for accrued depreciation. A rate of return reflecting the capital-attraction test is then applied to this base, and the result, together with expenses, determines the revenues for the firm and the amount to be recovered through a structure of cost-based prices.

His commentary on individual aspects of the actual-cost standard provides a valuable insight into Bonbright's thought on the implementation of public-interest regulation. The allowance for accrued depreciation under this standard represents the amortized cost of the assets in the sense that this portion has been charged to previous periods of operation. Accrued depreciation is not viewed as a measure of the loss in value actually sustained by the assets since their date of acquisition. The net rate base represents that portion of the investment which the firm is still entitled to recoup and on which it is allowed to earn a return.

Construction work in progress would be excluded from the rate base until used and useful, but Bonbright feels that the longer the gestation period, the greater the uncertainty. Therefore, as construction periods lengthen and future uncertainty increases, the appropriate interest during construction (IDC) rate on construction work in progress (CWIP) would more closely approximate the firm's overall return than the short-term borrowing rate or the rate earned on a secure loan.[9]

With respect to the debate over normalization versus flowthrough of accelerated depreciation tax benefits, Bonbright adopts a rather cautious approach by accepting normalization with a deduction of the deferred tax reserve from the rate base.[10] On the question of the premature retirement of plant, he notes that the application of the actual-cost standard will require a choice between the enforcement of the used and useful test or the amortization of the cost of retired plant as an operating expense against future customers. Apparently he would favor the latter option.[11] He also notes that the strict application of the reproduction-cost/fair-value standard to premature retirements would deny the regulated firm any compensation at all for such retirements or for accelerated obsolescence. On the question of the appropriate level of capacity, he deals only with the existence of insufficient capacity: "As long as plant capacity is inadequate . . . rates will yield excess profits—profits that will fall to normal . . . as soon as the plant . . .

[is] enlarged to proper size."[12] To bring this about, regulators may have to compel new investment in capacity. The problems associated with redundant plant are not explicitly treated.

The overall rate of return would reflect the historical cost of debt, the current cost of equity, and a weighting reflecting the actual capital structure. There is relatively little discussion by Bonbright of the different measures of the cost of equity capital; however, this is not unexpected since his analysis predates much of the debate over the relative merits of the discounted cash-flow and capital-asset pricing models. Interestingly, Bonbright rejects the proposition that the market-to-book (M/B) ratio should be maintained at unity (or about 1.05 to 1.10) as a test of the adequacy of the return on equity. Instead, he would let the M/B ratio exceed unity in prosperous times, which apparently means that it should also be allowed to fall below unity during recessions.

On the question of incorporating incentive allowances into the rate of return, Bonbright is cautious, noting that "until more headway . . . has been made, proposals for the systematic use of efficiency differentials in rate-of-return allowances would probably be premature."[13] He is equally cautious in endorsing formal inflation allowances for the rate of return.[14]

In moving from the determination of total revenue requirements to the design of price structures, the actual-cost standard is maintained by insisting upon cost-based rates. However, this requires that a choice be made between a fully distributed or a marginal-cost approach to cost analysis. This is particularly true in attempting to determine the revenue contribution for individual classes of service or classes of customers, and in efforts to assign costs to peak and off-peak users. Bonbright clearly favors a marginalist approach. In discussing cost assignment by class of customer (which Bonbright calls intermediate cost coverage), he observes that the appropriate test is the incremental cost of serving a particular group. For Bonbright, the really important analysis is not the apportionment of total capital and operating costs to classes of customers or units of output, but rather the examination of differential, incremental, marginal, or escapable costs.[15]

In testimony on behalf of American Telephone & Telegraph (AT&T) before the Federal Communications Commission in 1966, Bonbright argued that the incremental cost of a class of users was the appropriate criterion for evaluating the presence or absence of discriminatory pricing.[16] This supported AT&T's position that the seven-way cost study did not disclose cross-subsidization despite the fact that the overall return was 7.5 percent and the monopoly services [MTS (message toll service) and WATS (wide-area telephone service)] earned over 10 percent, while the competitive Telpak offering earned only 0.3 percent. Proponents of fully distributed cost, on the other hand, believe that the results were a valid testimonial to the subsidization of competitive services by monopolistic services and that the Bell system had turned the risk/return relationship upside down. The Bonbright position was ultimately incorporated into AT&T's burden test, which was rejected by the commission in Docket 18128.[17] In the transition from overall revenue requirements, it was clear that the determination of what constituted an appropriate cost standard had become a highly contested issue.

On the matter of peak pricing, Bonbright argued that the allocation of capacity costs was essentially a matter of joint-product pricing. The peak is the main product, and the off-peak is the byproduct; the price of the latter should cover only separable, noncapacity costs.

The Bonbright model for price/earnings regulation is complemented by a perception of the appropriate market structure for the public-utility industries. The desired form of structural organization emerges from the Bonbright and Means criticism of holding-company abuses, combination companies, and utility-diversification programs.

In 1932 Bonbright and Means faulted the holding-company systems because they were conducive to social waste and inefficiency, financial manipulation (for example, the issuance of watered stock), secrecy and the manipulation of operating properties (for example, rate-base inflation and artificial write-ups), and excessive service-company fees that would be shifted forward to consumers. Combination companies were faulted because they contained a potential for cross-subsidization,[18] while diversification by utilities into nonutility activities was held to be potentially damaging to the ratepayer because of the "menace to the credit of the public utilities."[19]

The solutions proposed involved extending federal regulation to the holding companies, discouraging the formation of holding companies that did not yield demonstrable engineering and economic gains through improved performance, and the divestment of nonutility enterprises. It would appear that the desired structural format as seen by Bonbright and Means involved autonomous operating entities-unencumbered by needlessly complicated holding-company affiliations and diversification programs.

### Public Utilities in Transition: Departures from Cost-Based Rate Making

No one would doubt that the Bonbright view of price/earnings regulation will have a permanent place in the literature of public-utility economics, but an increasing number of persons question whether this form of rate-base/rate-of-return regulation is still relevant in view of the structural and technological changes that have taken place in recent years. Furthermore, critics of regulation point out that the public-interest theory of regulation has been severely shaken by the growing series of attacks which cast doubt on the ability of commissions to exercise independence and apply the tools of regulation without imposing substantial burdens on society and biasing income redistribution.[20]

There is little doubt that the energy and communications industries have undergone a significant transformation in the years since 1968 to 1969. Prior to that time, the comfortable assumption could be made that all public utilities were characterized by economies of scale, technological advance, and a stable rate of growth in demand which would combine to produce a continuous improvement in performance. During 1968 to 1969, however, there were unmistakable signs that these conditions were about to change. The rate of growth in total-factor productivity for the electric utilities flattened out and for many firms began to decline. At the same time, average price per kilowatt-hour (kwh) began to rise, indicating the end of an era of falling real prices which had prevailed for more than eighty years. In natural gas, the ratio of additions-to-reserves to annual production fell below unity for the first time, indicating that the era of abundant gas supplies was over. In telecommunicatins, the FCC's Carterfone decision (1968)[21] and Microwave Communications, Inc., (MCI) decision (1969)[22] were manifestations of a new technology that threatened the status quo by creating new sources of supply to meet the needs of the rapidly expanding voice and data markets.

In the post-1968 to 1969 period, the prophetic nature of these signals has become increasingly apparent. In electricity supply, sharply higher fuel costs, continued inflationary pressures, diminished economies of scale in generation, poor reliability records for some of the largest generating units, and environmental restrictions have led to successively higher retail rates, reduced rates of growth in demand, excess capacity, and poor earnings. For public-utility management, the plight of the industry calls for drastic changes, including a general relaxation of rate-base regulation. Strict adherence to the traditional model, it is argued, will destroy the industry. The remedy requires liberalized passthroughs, CWIP in the rate base, trended original-cost valuation of plant and equipment, a forecasted test year, and a higher rate of return. The latter could possibly be accomplished by turning to the $q$ ratio as the appropriate point of reference for judging earnings levels. Since the $q$ ratio relates the market value of the firm's securities to the replacement cost of its assets, reproduction cost would, in effect, be reintroduced through the ratio's denominator.

In contrast, environmentalists and other proponents of soft-path solutions to the energy problem argue that the electric-utility industry is no longer cost-competitive with new sources of supply, whether judged in terms of average or marginal costs. Amory Lovins believes that conservation, the retrofitting of power-using equipment, and new sources of energy are far cheaper options for meeting consumer needs. Furthermore, Lovins argues that adopting the remedial actions recommended by the industry will simply worsen its problems and place it at an even greater cost disadvantage.[23]

To complicate the picture further, a new debate has arisen over the role of deregulation in electricity. Reformists argue that the old perception of a vertically integrated electric-utility operation, all under rate-base regulation, should be abandoned. But again, there is no consensus on the proper direction to take. Some advocate the deregulation of generation, while others advocate the relaxation of restrictions on diversification so that utilities can move into nonregulated activities.

In the gas industry the situation is equally confusing. There has been a dramatic departure from a cost-based standard in fixing the field price of natural gas. Area rates have been replaced by a series of vintage prices for old, flowing gas sales, while certain new sales of high-cost gas are exempt from regulation. Incremental pricing has been introduced for industrial-boiler fuel sales, but the basis of the incremental price is not a cost standard (whether incremental or average), but rather the price of alternative fuels (primarily number six fuel oil). Finally, efforts to introduce marginal-cost pricing into the design of rates at the retail level appear to have been largely abandoned in favor of a continuation of rolled-in or average-cost pricing.

The development of new sources of gas has also been marked by departures from the Bonbright model. Since the incremental cost of gas from both coal-gasification projects and the Alaska natural gas transportation system will be substantially higher than the average cost of flowing gas, a number of devices have been developed which minimize the potential price disadvantage of these projects and shift a portion of the risk forward to the consumer. These include CWIP in the rate base, rolled-in pricing, all-events tariffs (which permit costs to be recovered from gas consumers in the event that new sales do not reach anticipated levels), and federal loan guarantees. The cumulative effect of these departures from rate-base regulation and cost-of-service pricing is to understate the economic cost of the project and give the wrong price signals to the consumer.

In telecommunications new technology has created new markets, new systems of supply, and new entrants. As a consequence, there is a growing belief that the communications industry is highly competitive and that traditional regulation is no longer relevant—except possibly at the local-exchange level. But even here, critics of regulation point to the possibility of bypassing the local loop to reach the final user, arguing that such circumvention places an effective ceiling on any attempt by telephone companies to set monopolistic-access charges.

### Adapting Economic Regulation to a New Setting

The rationale for price/earnings regulation must be premised largely on the existence of imperfect competition and conditions conducive to market failure. Accordingly, the future of the Bonbright cost-based model will depend on the nature and scope of emergent competitive pressures in the public-utility industries. It is important, therefore, to examine the anticipated pattern of competition in electricity, gas, and communications, for that pattern will be a major determinant of the future of economic regulation.

It is highly doubtful that foreseeable structural changes in electricity and gas will radically transform the high levels of market concentration prevailing in these industries. There will still be monopoly focal points at the transmission and distribution phases of electricity and gas supply that retain a significant potential for monopolistic pricing and entry foreclosure. Economies of scale continue to characterize extra-high-voltage power transmission and pipeline transmission, and the high-threshold investment required for the final-distribution function, when combined with technical limitations, will restrict the number of suppliers at the retail level. Furthermore, the number of cities with direct competition between electric utilities at the retail level (primarily between public and privately owned distribution systems) has declined over time, an occurrence which indicates a degree of instability in this form of rivalry. On balance, it would seem reasonable to assume that variants of the basic Bonbright model continue to remain applicable to most transmission and distribution operations.

With respect to bulk-power supply, the potential for competition does exist, but it is doubtful that competitive markets will emerge without conscious government intervention. At present, cogenerators and small producers can enter the market, but sales must be made to adjacent utilities in accordance with guidelines set forth by the Federal Energy Regulatory Commission (FERC). Similarly, there are large wholesale markets where utilities sell power to each other at a variety of prices depending on the length of the transaction. However, access to these markets is usually restricted to members of power pools, and if a utility wants to sell outside the pool, or if a utility wants to negotiate a sale with another party which requires wheeling arrangements with an intermediate utility, then complications and costs rise dramatically. Furthermore, small distribution systems and cogenerators are usually denied access to this type of bulk-power market because they cannot qualify for pool membership or because they lack adequate generating capacity. In short, there is no broadly accessible bulk-power market capable of bringing together a large number of buyers and sellers. Nor is this market likely to evolve as long as potentially high transaction costs and information costs create the classic conditions for market failure.

The deregulation of generation under these circumstances would not constitute a move toward a competitive market. Rather, it would only serve to constrain the residual effectiveness of rate-base regulation by permitting the generation phase of electricity supply to earn higher profits by raising the price of power purchased by the regulated transmission and distribution phases of the industry. Separate generating subsidiaries would have little to fear from competitive entrants unless these entrants had access to transmission and distribution facilities. But this would require the establishment of a common-carrier network, cost-based rates for wheeling, and an agent to perform the clearinghouse functions associated with power transfers, billings, and payments. Such steps are clearly beyond the sphere of conventional rate-base regulation.

In the wholesale gas markets, attempts to establish pipeline transmission rates under FERC Order 533 have been very limited in scope and are not intended to create a broad-based competitive market.[24] At the same time, proposals to establish a white market for gas transfers and exchanges have not come to fruition—apparently because of the absence of an integrated transmission network capable of bringing together a large number of prospective buyers and sellers. The obstacles to the creation of a competitive wholesale gas market would appear to be similar to those confronting the establishment of a competitive bulk-power market.

At the gas-producer level, cost-based regulation appears to have ended. However, it is far from clear that competitive markets have emerged. The persistence of favored-nation clauses and indefinite price escalators in gas-supply agreements between producers and pipelines reflects either a demand greater than supply or the market power of the producers. In either case, the effectiveness of rate-base regualtion at the retail level will be just as hampered as it was in the original 1954 Phillips case.[25]

To summarize, there appear to be large segments of the electric-and gas-utility industries where rate-base/rate-of-return regulation remains applicable. Monopoly focal points and inelastic demand functions create a potential for the exercise of economic power just as much today as they did fifty years ago. The new challenge for regulatory agencies will be to apply rate-base regulation in a fashion that does not foreclose the emergence of competition in wholesale markets. To the extent that cost-of-service standards curb cross-subsidization, price discrimination, and limit-entry pricing strategies, a positive step will have been taken in this direction. Whether commissions will be able to employ the variables of structure regulation (which include entry policy, interconnection, diversification, and predatory pricing controls) to actually promote competitive pressures remains to be seen.

The future role of price/earnings regulation in telecommunications is an intensely debated issue which again turns on one's perception of the pervasiveness of competition. To appraise the adequacy of competition, it is possible either to speculate on the future impact of new technology and the course of potential competition or to examine structural and behavioral changes in the industry since 1968 to 1969 when the Federal Communications Commission (FCC) began to move aggressively to open new markets to competition. Neither approach is completely satisfying. The former is highly conjectural, anecdotal, and prone to technological determinism. The latter is plagued by inadequate data and the implicit assumption that past and current patterns of structural change and corporate behavior will continue into the future. In spite of the shortcomings of the second approach, changes in market shares, corporate behavior (particularly of the dominant firm), and the persistence of institutional and structural barriers to competition will be examined.

Four major markets have been opened to competition by the removal of legal barriers to entry. Terminal-equipment markets were opened when the FCC removed restrictions on foreign attachments in the Carterfone decision (1968) and when the commission adopted a registration and certification program in 1975. The private-line market has been freed of legal barriers to entry for a longer period than any other. In the Above 890 case (1959), the commission opened the frequencies above 890 megacycles to competitive entry.[26] In 1969, MCI was authorized to provide private-line service in competition with the Bell system. A procompetitive policy in private-line service was further emphasized in the Specialized Carrier decision (1971).[27] Finally, the Execunet case (1977) upset the FCC's policy of distinguishing between monopoly and competitive services by, in effect, opening all interexchange markets to competition.[28]

The question arises whether the removal of legal barriers to entry will induce competitive pressures sufficient to act as a surrogate for economic regulation. Empirical studies indicate that changes in market shares can have a discernible impact on profits. The sequence is essentially as follows: new entry affects market shares, and changes in market shares, in turn, have a direct impact on the level of profits. William G. Shepherd has set forth criteria for assessing the effectiveness of entry as a constraint on profits.[29] To be successful, entry must: be substantial, depressing the market shares of the established firm in prime markets; be rapid; reduce the market share of the dominant firm to less than 50 percent; assure that the decline in market share of the dominant firm is permanent; and permit the new entrant to achieve sales levels equal to at least 25 percent of the market, thereby providing a basis for independent behavior. Historical experience in telecommunications indicates that substantial entry and a major shift in market shares will depress the profits of the dominant firm. For example, when the Bell system held a patent monopoly on telephone service, its return on investment was estimated at 46 percent. However, after the original Bell patents expired in 1893-1894, the independent telephone companies increased their share of the market to 49 percent in 1906, and Bell's return on investment dropped to 8 percent.

Market-share data for terminal equipment shows mixed result.[30] The sales of PBX equipment indicate that the share of the private branch exchange

(PBX) market held by manufacturers affiliated with telephone companies dropped from 93 percent in 1968 to 56 percent in 1979, while new U.S. entrants increased their share from 0.1 percent in 1968 to 36 percent in 1979. For key telephones, entry has been virtually ineffective. The share of the market held by manufacturers affiliated with telephone companies dropped from 98.3 percent in 1968 to 89.4 percent in 1979, but no other source of supply accounts for more than 6 percent of the market. The same results apply to dial-in-hand set telephones. In contrast, there are terminal-equipment markets where manufacturers affiliated with telephone companies had no sales in 1968 but increased their portion of the business significantly. Decorator phones and automatic dialers stand out as cases where telephone company affiliates increased their share from 0 percent in 1968 to 38 percent and 45 percent respectively in 1979.

The changes in the pattern of market shares for private-line service may be examined by comparing intercity revenues for private-line services in 1968 and 1979. In 1968, AT&T accounted for 81 percent of this market, the independent telephone companies for 5 percent, Western Union for 13 percent, and the specialized carriers for 1 percent. By 1979, AT&T's share had increased to 85 percent, the independents remained at 5 percent, Western Union declined to 6 percent, and the specialized carriers' share increased to 4 percent.

In the message-toll telephone market, MCI has made impressive gains in geographic coverage since the Execunet decision. MCI receives about 75 percent of its revenues from Execunet, which is primarily a voice service. It currently covers 180 major metropolitan areas, 4,000 towns and communities, and thirty-nine states plus the District of Columbia. Furthermore, approximately 80 to 85 percent of the MCI Execunet traffic does not use transmission lines leased from the Bell system except for access to the local exchange. Despite these changes, MCI still accounts for no more than 1 percent of total MTS traffic based on revenues.

Market-share data thus provides little support for the argument that there is a rapid and widespread shift toward less concentration. In the private-line market, Bell's share has actually increased, while in MTS it maintains a position of massive dominance. Only in segments of the terminal-equipment market, principally PBX sales, does entry appear to be on a scale sufficient to depress profits.

Another perspective on competition in telecommunications can be obtained from examining the strategies and behavior of AT&T as the dominant firm. The difficulty with this approach is that it is necessary to disentangle Bell's participation in the regulatory process as a part of its strategy to maintain market dominance from the behavior pattern that would prevail in the absence of regulation. This precludes a discussion of many of the familiar confrontations that took place over Telpak, the Hi-Lo tariff, and Dataphone Digital Service or the MCI antitrust case. However, there are four examples that indicate corporate behavior that reflects substantial monopoly power which is undiminished by potential entry or technological substitution. The first is the Litton suit against AT&T, where allegations were made that AT&T and International Business Machines (IBM) met to divide international and national markets for terminal equipment. The second is AT&T's emergent terminal-equipment migration strategy, which indicates that the carrier possesses a high degree of latitude in manipulating price to foreclose entry into the terminal-equipment market.[31] The third is the emergence of price leadership in selected markets. After the recent demise of the Telpak tariff, AT&T raised its private-line rates by 16.4 percent; other specialized carriers followed by raising their private-line rates. The fourth example is AT&T's success in promoting accelerated-cost recovery for plant and equipment. The Bell system has been successful in persuading the FCC to substitute equal-life-group for vintage-group depreciation, to shift to remaining life depreciation, and to represcribe the service-life estimates for many categories of plant. It has also been able to assure that embedded station-connection charges will be amortized while new station connections will be expensed. Stepped-up depreciation will, of course, constitute a major source of internal funds for investment in new technology. There is little doubt that speeding up the rate of plant turnover and depreciation requires captive markets in MTS and exchange service that can withstand the attendant price increases.

Finally, there are other barriers to competition. For example, MCI and other potential entrants must have access to the local exchange in order to offer message-toll voice service. Present technology does not permit the use of cable systems, direct-broadcast satellites, or cellular systems to provide an efficient switched message-toll voice service. There are also specific segments of individual communications markets which are not susceptible to diversion. The best illustration is the interstate residential-toll market for customers with monthly billings below fifteen dollars (apparently twenty-five dollars is the cutover point where Execunet becomes financially attractive). Yet this segment of the interstate toll market contributes one-half of all residential interstate MTS revenues.

The dominant firm also enjoys significant product and service differentiation advantages. AT&T offers nationwide coverage, while competitive MTS services are plagued by allegations of poor-quality service and are foreclosed from access to rotary-dial phones. Similarly, rivals have no substitute for Bell's ability to permit callers to bill to third numbers, nor are they able to offer anything comparable to nationwide in-WATS (800) service.

It is clear that the thesis that new technology has transformed telecommunications into a highly competitive industry cannot be supported by current information or by experience in the decade since the Carterfone and

MCI decisions. At best the prospects for significant competitive-market penetration in telecommunications are uneven, varying considerabley between different markets.

In an industry characterized by the coexistence of monopoly and competition, the continued application of economic regulation requires control of the level of earnings for services retaining monopolistic characteristics (local exchange and interexchange message-toll telephone); control of cross-subsidization between monopoly and competitive markets; assurance of nondiscriminatory access to monopolistic facilities for all competitors; and an ability to monitor areas of market failure which may result in inadequate service or inadequate network coverage.

The FCC struggled with the cross-subsidization problem for more than eighteen years. It rejected the Bonbright concept of avoidable cost in favor of a fully allocated cost standard. However, difficulties in applying the concept and AT&T's apparent reluctance to comply with the commission's reporting and costing standards led to the search for a structural solution to this problem.[32] In the Computer II decision, the FCC held that AT&T must provide augmented services (for example, data processing) through a separate subsidiary.[33] The proposed modification of the consent decree represents another step in the direction of a structural solution by requiring that AT&T, Bell Laboratories, and Western Electric be separated from the Bell operating companies. Under this solution, AT&T will provide all interexchange services (including intra-and interstate MTS), customer-premises equipment, and all augmented services, while the operating companies will be confined to local-exchange service.

Structural solutions may diminish some traditional regulatory issues when separations and settlements are phased out and license contract fees disappear, but a host of new problems will be created. For example, the creation of separate subsidiaries gives rise to questions about asset-transfer prices, the impact of diversification on the overall rate of return, the allocation of common plant and services, and the adequacy of monitoring devices to assure arms-length dealings between parent and subsidiary. The separation of Bell operating companies also raises questions about transfer prices, including reimbursement for research and development rights paid for by past assessments against local exchanges, and the problems of establishing a revenue requirement for the exchange function. There may also be a potential conflict between the FCC and state commissions in setting exchange-access charges—especially if state agencies seek to set such charges at levels sufficient to replace the contribution previously made by interstate MTS.

An attempt to apply cost-based rate making to monopolistic services in this new structural setting poses two general problems. The first is the continuing need to allocate the cost of service for the regulated segment of AT&T between monopolistic and competitive services. The second is the challenge to devise a conceptual framework for applying cost-of-service standards to the local exchange. Unfortunately, past reliance on value-of-service criteria and a statewide approach to revenue requirements (which aggregated exchange, intrastate toll, and settlements revenues) offers little assistance. For the future, regulators would appear to have three options: to refine and apply separations procedures to isolate local-exchange revenues and costs; to establish the direct costs of single-purpose or stand-alone systems for providing local-exchange, message-toll, and other services (such as data transmission), and then allocate joint costs on the basis of relative use or the benefits derived from joint development; and to assume that the initial cost is incurred to provide basic-exchange service and that incremental costs are incurred to handle successive upgradings required for message-toll, high-speed data transmission, and other services. At this point, each approach appears to have certain advantages and disadvantages, and some effort at application appears to be the next logical step. Structure regulation and price/earnings regulation may enjoy a complementary relationship, but substantial problems of implementation remain to be resolved.

### Equity, Fairness, and a Final Note

Bonbright's emphasis on cost-based rates has also been challenged in the growing debate over equity issues in energy and communications pricing. The proponents of distributive justice argue that it may have been possible to overlook fairness in favor of efficiency as long as real prices were falling, but when price increases for electricity and gas exceed those of the consumer-price index, then something must be done. The recommended solutions involve lifeline rates for the poor, average or rolled-in prices for the firm, vintage prices or end-use prices for special classes of consumers, and loan guarantees or assured cost-recovery programs for investors. In practice, each of these proposals involves an effort to shield a specific party or special-interest group from the impact of price increases. In some cases, the proposals also represent an effort by a speical-interest group to capture the economic rents associated with older, low-cost sources of supply, or an effort to raise the effective rate of return by shifting the risk of new investment to someone else.

There may be public-interest considerations that justify adoption of one or more of these solutions, but the danger is that regulators will respond to special-interest pressures on the basis of incomplete information. If the Bonbright cost-based model were taken as the starting point in making equity judgments, then the policymaker would be compelled to be specific about the reasons for overriding the criterion that prices cover costs plus a fair profit for assuming all of the risks of the investment. Adherence to this procedure would also lead to a clearer understanding of the ultimate in-cidence of the benefits and costs of equity-oriented decisions.

The Bonbright model might also be applied to advantage in assessing the impact of welfare programs. For example, the conventional wisdom would argue that welfare payments are preferable to lifeline rates as the appropriate method for assuring that the poor and elderly will be able to maintain a minimum level of electricity and gas consumption in the face of rising prices. However, a broadened application of the cost-of-service approach could contrast the adverse distributional impact of lifeline rates with the high administrative costs and funding vagaries of the fuel-assistance program. A final decision could then be made on the basis of minimum overall cost and reliability.

Any concluding comment on Bonbright's contribution to public-utility economics must not overlook an important difference between the thrust of his work and that of much of the current literature in the field. At a time when attention focuses on the sustainability of natural monopoly employing Ramsey prices, and an endless series of econometric studies testing simple propositions of rather dubious general applicability, it is refreshing to review again Bonbright's efforts to develop regulatory tools capable of coming to grips with real-world problems. The net-investment cost standard is an excellent example of an effort to provide a method for establishing an empirically verifiable rate base that can employ the uniform system of accounts as an effective instrument for social control. Bonbright also strove for simplicity and clarity—a fact readily demonstrated by comparing his *Principles* text (which could treat pricing without recourse to a single equation) with any of the recent literature on pricing.

Perhaps most important, Bonbright sought to give economic regulation a public-interest orientation. Regrettably, much of the current research has focused on the causes of regulatory failure without being able to establish a consensus on the reasons for such failure or clearcut guidelines for reform. Policymakers are given few alternatives to curb economic power—other than to rely on franchise bidding, potential entry, or the expedient of defining away such power by reclassifying markets as workably competitive. The greatest tribute that a new generation of economists could pay to Bonbright would be to redirect the thrust of their research along the lines which he felt to be so important.

**Notes**

1. James C. Bonbright, *Principles of Public Utility Rates* (New York: Columbia University Press, 1961): chap. XVI, 287-316.

2. Ibid., p. 4.

3. Ibid., p. 9.

4. Ibid., p. 67.

5. Ibid., p. 23.

6. Ibid., p. 87. Bonbright's resistance to reproduction cost, fair value and value-of-service reappears in most of his writings from 1927 to 1961. A detailed institutional critique appears in James C. Bonbright, *Valuation of Property* (New York: McGraw-Hill, 1937) 2:1078-1156.

7. Bonbright, *Principles of Public Utility Rates,* p. 103.

8. Ibid., p. 107.

9. Bonbright refers to IDC rather than allowance for funds used during construction (AFUDC). However, it is clear that his IDC rate would approximate AFUDC for long-term construction projects.

10. Bonbright, *Principles of Public Utility Rates,* pp. 221-222.

11. Ibid., p. 214.

12. Ibid., p. 99.

13. Ibid., p. 264.

14. Ibid., p. 275.

15. Ibid., p. 368.

16. Testimony of James C. Bonbright, FCC Docket No. 16258, Bell Exhibit 25, May 31, 1966. Some question might be raised about the difficulty of reconciling a current escapable or avoidable cost standard for a class of service with a net-investment sunk-cost standard for a rate base. However, a number of economists accept both an original-cost rate base and marginal cost pricing for cost allocations to user groups and rate design. A defense of both original cost and fully distributed cost is provided by William H. Melody, "Interservice Subsidy: Regulatory Standard and Applied Economics," in *Essays on Public Utility Pricing and Regulation,* ed. Harry M. Trebing (East Lansing: Michigan State University, 1971), pp. 167-210.

17. For a comprehensive discussion of the seven-way cost study, the AT&T burden test, and the FCC's method seven, see Walter G. Bolter, "The FCC's Selection of a 'Proper' Costing Standard after Fifteen Years—What Can We Learn from Docket 18128?" in *Assessing New Pricing Concepts in Public Utilities,* ed. Harry M. Trebing (East Lansing: Michigan State University, 1978), pp. 333-372. Also, for a recent discussion and update covering the FCC's Interim Cost Manual, see Report to the Congress of the United States by the Comptroller General, *Legislative and Regulatory Actions Needed to Deal with a Changing Domestic Telecommunications Industry* (Washington, D.C.: Government Printing Office, September 24, 1981).

18. James C. Bonbright and Gardner C. Means, *The Holding Company: Its Public Significance and Its Regulation* (New York: McGraw-Hill, 1932), pp. 195-198.

19. Ibid., p. 199.

20. For an examination of the growing disenchantment with the public-interest theory of regulation, as well as the shortcomings of the capture, coalition-building, and equity-stability theories of regulatory behavior, see Harry M. Trebing, Equity, Efficiency, and the Viability of Public Utility Regulation," in *Applications of Economic Principles in Public Utility Industries,* ed. W. Sichel and T.G. Gies (Ann Arbor: University of Michigan, 1981), pp. 17-52.

21. *T.F. Carter and Carter Electronics Corp. v. AT&T et al.,* FCC Docket No. 17073, Decision, June 26, 1968.

22. *Application of Microwave Communications Inc. for Construction Permits to Establish New Facilities in the Domestic Public Point-to-Point Microwave Radio Service at Chicago, Ill., St. Louis, Missouri, and Intermediate Points,* FCC Docket No. 16509, Decision, August 14, 1969.

23. See Amory B. Lovins, Letter to Honorable Donald T. Regan, Secretary of the Treasury, "How to Keep Electric Utilities Solvent," February 26, 1981.

24. Federal Power Commission, Order No. 533, Docket No. RM 75-25, 54 FPC, Mimeographed (1975), p. 28. Federal Energy Regulatory Commission, *Policy with Respect to Certification of Pipeline Transportation Agreements,* Docket No. RM 75-25, Order No. 2, (Washington, D.C.: February 1, 1978).

25. The original Phillips case showed that the Wisconsin commission could not effectively control retail rates for gas in the absence of Federal Power Commission control of field prices. The problem is aggravated at the present time because purchased gas may now constitute 60 percent of the delivered, retail price whereas it constituted approximately 10 percent in 1954.

26. *Allocation of Frequencies in Bands Above 890 Mc,* 27 FCC 359 (1959).

27. *Specialized Common Carrier Services,* 29 FCC 2d 870 (1971).

28. *MCI Telecommunications Corporation v. Federal Communications Commission,* U.S. Court of Appeals, District of Columbia, Federal Reporter 561 F. 2d 365 (D.C. cir. 1977).

29. William G. Shepherd, "General Conditions of Entry," in *Regulation and Entry,* Michael W. Klass and William G. Shepherd (East Lansing: Michigan State University, 1976), pp. 35-60.

30. The following discussion of competition in telecommunications is based on Harry M. Trebing, "A Critique of the 'New Competition' in Telecommunications as a Surrogate for Regulation" (Paper presented at a joint session sponsored by the Transportation and Public Utilities Group and the American Economic Association, December 28, 1981). Also, see *Telecommunications in Transition: The Status of Competition in the Telecommunications Industry* (Report by the Majority Staff of the Sub-

committee on Telecommunications, Consumer Protection and Finance of the House Committee on Energy and Commerce, 97th Cong., 1st Sess., November 3, 1981).

31. For a detailed examination of terminal-equipment migration strategy, see statement of Lee L. Selwyn, *Hearings on Competition and Deregulation in the Telecommunications Industry* (House of Representatives Subcommittee on Telecommunications, Consumer Protection and Finance, July 2, 1981).

32. David Chessler, "Information Requirements in a Competitive Environment" (Paper presented at Thirteenth Annual Conference of the Institute of Public Utilities, Williamsburg, Virginia, December 14 to 16, 1981).

33. *In the Matter of the Amendment of Section 64.702 of the Commission's Rules and Regulations (Second Computer Inquiry)*, FCC Docket No. 20828, May 2, 1980.

# Part II
# Background Essays

# 2

# The Changing Environment of Public-Utility Regulation: An Overview

*Charles F. Phillips, Jr.*

The economic, political, and social environment within which public-utility regulation takes place has changed dramatically in the last decade. For some sixty years—until about 1968—the tremendous expansion of the public-utility sector was accomplished in a favorable and supportive environment. Economic growth was unquestioned. Annual rates of inflation, as well as interest rates, were low. Electric utilities, for example, could plan, construct, and finance new plants in a relatively short period of time and without great difficulty. Six- to eight-year planning periods for new generating facilities were common. Capacity and reserves were adequate. Rates, due to the achievement of economies of scale and sales growth, were relatively constant or declining (tables 2-1 and 2-2). Many felt that these trends would continue. Thus, the 1964 National Power Survey projected that there would be "a reduction in the nationwide average price per kilowatt-hour from 1.7¢ today to about 1.2¢ in 1980."[1]

## The New Environment

Beginning in the mid- to late-1960s, a series of events, which altered the environment within which public utilities operate, impacted on the U.S. economy. The annual rate of inflation began to accelerate, affecting both operating and construction costs.[2] Interest rates started to rise, forcing the capital-intensive utilities to pay record-high costs for their new capital (table 2-3). The adequacy of capacity and reserves became matters of concern, as construction cutbacks occurred.[3] Inevitably, utility rates began to rise. Consumers started to organize and to intervene in rate cases in opposition to such increases—increases which began to occur almost annually and which involved larger and larger requests—and to urge new rate-design concepts (particularly lifeline rates for those having difficulty paying rising monthly utility bills). The media, after years of neglect, began to cover utility hearings, often giving them top coverage.[4]

For electric and gas utilities, fuel prices started to escalate; by the end of the 1970s, many had tripled. U.S. consumers became seriously concerned about the environment, as reflected in policy measures which forced

**Table 2-1**
**Index of Average Charge per Kilowatt-Hour, Residential Service**
**(Index, 1935 = 100)**

| Date | 250 Kilowatt-Hours | 500 Kilowatt-Hours |
|------|--------------------|--------------------|
| January 1, 1935 | 100.0 | 100.0 |
| January 1, 1940 | 82.9 | 76.2 |
| January 1, 1945 | 79.8 | 73.6 |
| January 1, 1950 | 78.4 | 72.9 |
| January 1, 1955 | 80.6 | 74.4 |
| January 1, 1960 | 83.7 | 76.5 |
| January 1, 1965 | 82.9 | 75.1 |
| January 1, 1970 | 84.3 | 75.8 |
| January 1, 1975 | 129.2 | 129.6 |
| January 1, 1980 | 171.6 | 198.6 |

Source: U.S. Department of Energy, *Typical Electric Bills*, 1980.

business enterprises to cover both private and social costs and to invest millions of dollars in nonrevenue-producing pollution-control equipment. Intervention by environmental groups became common. Summarizes Douglas Anderson:

> Coinciding with the awakened interest of consumers, a second new, and more ideologically motivated group of intervenors began showing up at commission hearings in the early seventies: the environmentalists. Groups such as the Sierra Club and the Environmental Defense Fund (EDF) identified the electric power industry as a major source of environmental degradation. The industry's pro-growth ethos and pricing policies were especially suspect. Where the industry's engineers looked and saw modern, technically efficient generating units, enviromentalists looked and saw foul air, scarred landscape, and polluted streams. They argued that utilities failed to "internalize" these social costs in their pricing structure and so encouraged their users to consume more electricity than was optimal. Moreover, because the price of electricity did not vary by time of use, they claimed that utilities built more power plants than were needed in order to meet their peak demands. Starting in 1973, the EDF and other groups began making appearances in rate cases in Wisconsin, Michigan, New York, and California to urge regulators to pay more attention to the environmental effects of the industry's building and pricing plans.[5]

The Northeast power failure in November 1965 indicated the electric-power industry's potential vulnerability to widespread interconnections, and subsequent brownouts stressed the need for adequate capacity.[6] Natural-gas reserves experienced a rapid decline in the late 1960s and early 1970s, leading to the widespread curtailment of service in the early 1970s and to an acute shortage during the winter of 1976-1977.[7] Conservation began to be promoted as the major long-run solution to the energy crisis.

**Table 2-2**
**Index of Telephone Rates, Bell System**
**(Index, 1960 = 100)**

| Year | Intrastate | Interstate |
|------|------------|------------|
| 1960 | 100.0 | 100.0 |
| 1965 | 98.2 | 95.8 |
| 1970 | 103.4 | 91.0 |
| 1975 | 136.4 | 99.5 |
| 1980 | 163.8 | 104.7 |

Source: American Telephone and Telegraph Company, Tariffs and Costs Department, 1981.

And the accident at Three Mile Island[8] raised again the issue of nuclear safety and cast doubt over the future of nuclear power.[9]

For telecommunications utilities, continuous technological change in the post-World War II period (for example, microwave transmission, transistors, silicon chips, communication satellites, digital computers) made it

**Table 2-3**
**Consumer-Price Index and Yields on Newly Issued Public-Utility Bonds,**
**1960-1981**

| Year | Annual Increase Consumer-Price Index in Percent | Moody's Yearly Averages in Percent | | | |
|------|------|------|------|------|------|
| | | Aaa | Aa | A | Baa |
| 1960 | 1.6 | 4.77 | 4.78 | 5.02 | 5.33 |
| 1961 | 1.0 | 4.51 | 4.59 | 4.73 | 5.10 |
| 1962 | 1.1 | 4.36 | 4.34 | 4.45 | 4.75 |
| 1963 | 1.2 | 4.31 | 4.35 | 4.41 | 4.64 |
| 1964 | 1.3 | 4.46 | 4.46 | 4.55 | 4.74 |
| 1965 | 1.7 | 4.57 | 4.62 | 4.70 | 4.95 |
| 1966 | 2.9 | 5.44 | 5.57 | 5.76 | 5.98 |
| 1967 | 2.9 | 5.85 | 5.98 | 6.18 | 6.28 |
| 1968 | 4.2 | 6.57 | 6.72 | 6.90 | 7.11 |
| 1969 | 5.4 | 7.75 | 7.88 | 8.07 | 8.54 |
| 1970 | 5.9 | 8.61 | 8.63 | 9.19 | 9.68 |
| 1971 | 4.3 | 7.50 | 7.68 | 7.93 | 8.32 |
| 1972 | 3.3 | 7.31 | 7.45 | 7.60 | 7.85 |
| 1973 | 6.2 | 7.81 | 7.80 | 8.05 | 8.25 |
| 1974 | 11.0 | 9.02 | 9.04 | 9.75 | 9.16 |
| 1975 | 9.1 | 9.11 | 9.46 | 10.25 | 11.39 |
| 1976 | 5.8 | 8.43 | 8.60 | 8.96 | 9.57 |
| 1977 | 6.5 | 8.18 | 8.30 | 8.48 | 8.92 |
| 1978 | 7.7 | 8.93 | 9.23 | 9.21 | 9.66 |
| 1979 | 11.3 | 9.86 | 10.48 | 10.74 | 11.12 |
| 1980 | 13.5 | 12.55 | 13.08 | 13.41 | 14.26 |
| 1981 | | 15.90 | 15.92 | 16.35 | 17.20 |

Source: *Economic Report of the President,* January 1981; *Federal Reserve Bulletin,* April 1981; *Moody's Public Utility Manual,* 1981; *Moody's Bond Survey.*

possible for the industry to meet the demand for new types of communications services.[10] These same technological innovations, however, also have made possible new options for supplying telecommunications services. Stated differently, new technology, new markets, and new potential suppliers have all but rendered obsolete the traditional natural-monopoly concept (except perhaps only on a temporary basis for local-exchange service), thereby confronting policymakers with a series of issues affecting the very structure of the domestic telecommunications industry.[11]

These issues have been and are being debated at length in at least three forums: first, before the Federal Communications Commission, as new suppliers have sought entry. In a series of decisions, especially the *Carterfone* decision in 1968[12] and the Microwave Communications, Inc. decision in 1969,[13] the commission has adopted a procompetitive policy with respect to customer-premises equipment and augmented services. But the implementation of that policy raises a number of complex problems.[14] The second forum is before the Congress, as both the House and Senate struggle to rewrite the Communications Act of 1934. The third forum is in the courts. The Department of Justice filed an antitrust suit against the Bell system in 1974.[15] This suit appears to have been settled with the announcement of a consent decree early in 1982. Full implementation of the consent decree (if approved by the court and if left unaltered by Congress) may take as long as two years. In addition, some twenty-nine private antitrust suits have been filed against the Bell system by actual and potential entrants.[16]

**Some Implications**

As a consequence of these events, the decade of the 1970s was one of strain, change, and experimentation for the entire public-utility sector.[17] Many utilities and regulatory commissions were ill equipped to deal with the new environment. From the point of view of the utilities, their marketing departments had effectively promoted the use of energy and communications for over two decades. Indeed, the promotional practices of electric and gas utilities provided some regulatory nightmares in the late 1950s and early 1960s.[18] Conservation; competition; inverted, flat, and lifeline rates; and inflation all conflicted with this mission. It was almost impossible to obtain accurate load and financial projections from electric utilities.

Further, the electric-power industry was not even in charge of its technological destiny; for decades, it had relied upon its equipment manufacturers for technological advances, and, equally important, technological advances had slowed considerably.[19] The former Federal Power Commission's wellhead price regulation held natural-gas prices well below the competitive level, thereby discouraging exploration and development (and contributing to the natural-gas shortage).[20] In addition to these events, the telecommunications industry went through a decade of uncertainty and confusion, as the FCC and Congress debated the industry's future structure and the industry tried to anticipate policy changes.

From the point of view of the regulatory commissions, annual appropriations were too small (particularly at the state level) to permit adequate staffs, both in terms of numbers and of composition.[21] The regulatory process was oriented toward the past (for example, past or historic test years) and for rate reductions; some state commissioners were only part-time. Regulatory lag became a serious problem just at a time when public utilities found it essential to request larger and larger annual-rate increases. Substantial rate relief occurred. Table 2-4 shows annual-rate increases for electric and gas utilities, exclusive of the fuel-adjustment clauses. Fuel-adjustment clauses added $11.0 billion to consumers' electric and gas bills in 1977, approximately 80 percent of the total increase of $13.4 billion for that year.[22] Yet, despite this rate relief, the utility sector was in a precarious financial situation by 1974 (table 2-5), and another group began to organize and to intervene in rate cases—utility shareholders. For example:

Market prices fell significantly below book values, making it impossible to sell new common stock without dilution. In many cases, debt ratios started to rise in order to avoid dilution. At the same time, the utility's return on common equity was falling (averaging 10.5 percent for Moody's twenty-four utilities in 1974), while industrial earnings on common equity were rising (to an average of 14.7 percent for Standard & Poor's 400 industrials in 1974).

Not only were earnings falling but for electric utilities an increasing percentage of their annual earnings per share was comprised of allowance for funds used during construction (AFUDC) (35.9 percent in 1974; a percentage that was to increase in subsequent years to 56 percent in 1980), a paper (that is, noncash) item. Many utilities did not have cash earnings equal to their dividend payments.

As coverage ratios declined, bonds were downgraded. Several electric utilities were unable to issue new long-term debt since they were below the required indenture coverages. Even when they were able to issue new debt, the combination of high-interest rates and downgradings resulted in significant increases in the embedded cost of debt.

Nor has the situation improved very much since 1974. Moody's twenty-four utilities, for example, are still selling significantly below book value and AFUDC continues to represent a major portion of their annual earnings per share. Several important consequences follow:

1. Utilities, as well as their investors and customers, learned some lessons from these events. Marketing departments (in many electric firms) were abolished; planning departments were created. The planning period, moreover, more than doubled, especially for new electric-generating facilities—and construction costs skyrocketed.[23] Investors found that utility earnings could fluctuate both upward and downward, and that annual dividend increases were no longer guaranteed. (Indeed, dividends were no longer a certainty, as Con Edison's stockholders learned in April 1974.)[24] Customers found that even though rates were increasing, service interruptions could and did occur. Natural-gas companies began to invest time and money in alternative gas sources; electric and gas utilities began to study diversification moves into nonregulated activities.[25] Telephone utilities began to reorganize to confront the new competitive challenges.[26]

2. Annual appropriations and staffs of the traditional regulatory commisions were enlarged. Part-time commissions became full-time. Increased consumer pressures resulted in a trend toward elected, rather than appointed, commissioners. New duties were assigned to the commissions by state and federal legislatures or in some cases were simply assumed. Hearings became lengthy, expensive battles, even though many attempts were made to shorten the regulatory process.[27] In an effort to augment the economic- and technical-research capabilities available to state commissions, the National Regulatory Research Institute was established in 1977.[28]

**Table 2-4**
**Index of Electric- and Gas-Utility Annual-Rate Increases, 1965-1980**

| Year | Electric in Millions of Dollars | Gas in Millions of Dollars |
|------|---------------------------------|----------------------------|
| 1965 | .0      | 6.3     |
| 1966 | 33.4    | 8.6     |
| 1967 | .7      | 2.8     |
| 1968 | 20.7    | 43.3    |
| 1969 | 145.1   | 137.7   |
| 1970 | 430.6   | 229.6   |
| 1971 | 802.7   | 204.3   |
| 1972 | 827.1   | 130.3   |
| 1973 | 1,150.8 | 491.3   |
| 1974 | 2,337.7 | 401.1   |
| 1975 | 3,168.7 | 917.5   |
| 1976 | 2,385.9 | 503.1   |
| 1977 | 2,636.8 | 692.8   |
| 1978 | 2,362.7 | 993.6   |
| 1979 | 4,567.0 | 2,043.9 |
| 1980 | 5,667.4 | 1,500.3 |

Source: Data supplied by Ebasco Business Consulting Company.

Note: All figures exclude automatic fuel-adjustment clauses.

**Table 2-5**
**Selected Financial Data, 1965-1980**

| Year | Return on Average Equity in Percent | | Market Prices[a] | | Market/Book Ratios | | Pretax Interest Coverage | Allowance for Funds Used during Construction (AFUDC) as a Percentage of Earnings per Share |
|------|------|------|------|------|------|------|------|------|
| | Moody's Twenty-Four Utilities | Standard and Poor's 400 Industrials | Moody's Twenty-Four Utilities | Standard and Poor's 400 Industrials | Moody's Twenty-Four Utilities | Standard and Poor's 400 Industrials | Moody's Twenty-Four Utilities[b] | Moody's Twenty-Four Utilities |
| 1965 | 11.9 | 13.1 | 100.0 | 100.0 | 2.35 | 2.23 | 5.29 | 4.6 |
| 1966 | 12.2 | 13.2 | 87.9 | 97.4 | 2.00 | 2.04 | 5.10 | 5.4 |
| 1967 | 12.5 | 12.0 | 87.0 | 106.1 | 1.90 | 2.13 | 4.66 | 7.8 |
| 1968 | 11.8 | 12.6 | 84.0 | 115.0 | 1.74 | 2.19 | 4.25 | 10.2 |
| 1969 | 11.7 | 12.0 | 80.8 | 114.6 | 1.60 | 2.10 | 3.73 | 13.9 |
| 1970 | 11.1 | 10.4 | 67.5 | 97.7 | 1.27 | 1.75 | 2.98 | 21.5 |
| 1971 | 11.0 | 11.1 | 71.9 | 115.9 | 1.29 | 2.01 | 2.86 | 26.3 |
| 1972 | 11.3 | 12.0 | 68.5 | 130.3 | 1.17 | 2.14 | 2.96 | 30.3 |
| 1973 | 10.6 | 14.7 | 60.8 | 128.8 | 1.00 | 1.99 | 2.79 | 31.9 |
| 1974 | 10.5 | 14.7 | 41.2 | 99.4 | .67 | 1.42 | 2.51 | 35.9 |
| 1975 | 10.4 | 12.4 | 43.8 | 103.3 | .69 | 1.39 | 2.53 | 34.2 |
| 1976 | 10.7 | 14.5 | 51.3 | 122.3 | .79 | 1.55 | 2.75 | 31.5 |
| 1977 | 11.1 | 14.6 | 57.7 | 116.0 | .87 | 1.37 | 2.89 | 29.4 |
| 1978 | 10.8 | 15.3 | 54.3 | 113.6 | .80 | 1.24 | 2.94 | 37.4 |
| 1979 | 11.1 | 17.3 | 51.5 | 122.8 | .75 | 1.22 | 2.57 | 46.8 |
| 1980 | 10.9 | 15.6 | 47.3 | 143.9 | .67 | 1.30 | 2.39 | 56.0 |

Source: *Moody's Public Utility Manual*, 1981; *Standard & Poor's Current Statistics.*
[a] 1965 = 100.
[b] Including AFUDC.

Some important reorganizations occurred: the Atomic Energy Commission was abolished in 1974, and two new federal agencies were created—the Nuclear Regulatory Commission and the Energy Research and Development Administration. (The latter agency was consolidated into the Department of Energy in 1977.) The Federal Energy Regulatory Commission—an independent regulatory agency within the Department of Energy—replaced the Federal Power Commission in 1977. The Texas Public Utility Commission was created in 1975.[29]

3. New organizations outside of the traditional regulatory commissions were created at all levels of government to deal with many of the new public concerns—air and water control or pollution boards, consumer-protection agencies or divisions, and energy departments at the state level.[30] The Environmental Protection Agency (1970), the Occupational Safety and Health Administration (1973), the Consumer Product Safety Commission (1972), the Mine Safety and Health Administration (1973), and the Department of Energy (1977), among others, were created at the federal level.

Whatever their merits, many of these new agencies have added a new complexity to the regulatory process. For an electric utility contemplating a nuclear plant, it is not uncommon for the company to confront as many as twenty state and federal agencies for necessary licenses and permits, to say nothing about the possibility of subsequent court action initiated by environmental groups. Further, the multiplicity of agencies raises the important question: who is really in charge—a state's energy department or a state's regulatory agency?

4. State-federal jurisdictional problems have intensified. In 1978 Congress extended federal control to intrastate natural-gas prices, despite strong opposition from gas-producing states. However, stiff state opposition defeated an attempt to establish mandatory federal standards for the regulation of electric- and gas-retail rates. Instead, state commissions were required to consider and adopt, if appropriate, the specified standards.[31] The Federal Communications Commission's procompetitive policy with respect to intercity private-line markets and markets for terminal equipment has been opposed by a majority of the state commissions who fear that the removal of separations support for basic-exchange service will result in a significant increase in local-exchange rates.[32] In Texas two major electric utilities have restricted their transmission of electric power to intrastate commerce so as to avoid federal jurisdiction.[33]

5. The issues brought before the regulatory commissions, in particular, have shifted in emphasis. The most significant shift has been from a utility's total-revenue requirements to its rate design. Prior to the 1970s, utility-rate structures were developed by the companies themselves and especially by their engineers. The theoretical basis for the resulting structures was too often difficult to discern, other than an obvious emphasis on promoting

usage. Today, perhaps as much as one-half or more of a typical rate case is devoted to rate design, an emphasis heightened by enactment of the Public Utility Regulatory Policies Act of 1978 and by the introduction of competition in the telecommunications industry. The relevant issues include embedded versus incremental costs, peak-load pricing, lifeline rates, and so forth.

Nor was the shift to rate design the only important one. The proper regulatory treatment of construction work in progress (CWIP) and of deferred taxes (phantom taxes) are two obvious examples. So too are advertising expenditures and the efficiency of management. (Management audits were the rage of the 1970s!) Faced with growing financial problems, the determination of a fair rate of return received major emphasis. Inevitably, the regulatory agencies found themselves involved in areas once considered managements' prerogative—capacity expansion and financing, to cite but two illustrations. This raised once again the vital, but often neglected, question: how far should the regulatory commissions go in substituting their judgment for that of management?[34]

6. Congress and three federal commissions (that is, the Civil Aeronautics Board, the Federal Communications Commission, and the Interstate Commerce Commission) began to reevaluate public policy toward the public-utility sector. Specifically, should the public-utility sector continue to be subjected to detailed regulation or should competition be encouraged?[35] To date Congress has substantially deregulated the transportation utilities and the wellhead price of natural gas (at least by 1985); the FCC has established a policy favoring competition for some telecommunications services and in the equipment and related hardware market; a bill to deregulate most of the oil-pipeline industry has been introduced into Congress; and widespread discussions are underway about the desirability of deregulating the generation of electricity.[36] Whatever its advantages, it must be noted that the partial deregulation of an industry adds new compexities to regulation.

## Conclusions

It is not the purpose of this chapter to analyze the trends pointed out already. The purpose of this chapter is to suggest that the new environment of public-utility regulation is permanent and that the real challenge of the 1980s is adaptation for both regulators and the regulated.

It its earlier days, regulation was conceived to be essentially a negative or a restrictive force to limit the monpoly power of certain industries. Today it is widely believed that regulation—if it is to be effective—must be more than a protector. Inflation, consumerism, environmentalism, energy conservation, competition, and so forth are now the key issues and provide the environment within which regulation must take place. Within that environment more and more complex economic, social, and technical issues are being raised.

Perhaps the most crucial element with respect to adapation is state regulation. Deregulation has taken place at the federal level (in particular), but retail-utility rates are still subject to state jurisdiction. As Howard Perry has put it, with respect to the electric-power industry:

> It is worth remembering that state regulation is a venerable institution, dating back to the turn of the century. For six decades, the task of state regulators was essentially one of distributing among ratepayers the benefits of the progressively higher efficiencies achieved by utility managers. Not bad work, if you can get it. But you can't any more. What we are now witnessing in state regulation—and the rapid turnover among commissioners is the most visible symptom of this—is painful adaptation to an environment that was once comfortable, and has now become hostile. The regulatory process has become highly adversarial, as well as analytically demanding.[37]

State regulation will require highly trained and motivated personnel and great imagination to handle the tasks confronting public-utility regulation in the 1980s. New procedures and long-term planning are required, despite the fact that existing economic, political, and social pressures make it difficult to avoid lengthy, formal proceedings and short-run expediency. In some instances state regulation may have to be replaced by regional regulation. The challenge of the changing environment is all too obvious.

**Notes**

1. Federal Power Commission, *National Power Survey* (Washington, D.C.: U.S. Government Printing Office, 1964), vol. 1, p. 277.

2. "From 1972 to 1975 the cost per kilowatt of new nuclear capacity rose 80 percent while the cost of new coal-fired power plants doubled." Douglas D. Anderson, "State Regulation of Electric Utilities," in *The Politics of Regulation*, ed. James Q. Wilson, (New York: Basic Books, 1980), p. 22.

3. According to S. David Freeman:

> Much of the trimming back in construction programs to date has been efficient and cost-effective. The stress on conservation is long overdue and it certainly saves money for both the consumer and the utility. But the pendulum is now swinging too far the other way. Cancellations are now beginning to occur simply because utilties can't raise the money, even for plants

for which there will be an economical market. And utilities are not ordering the electric power plants the nation needs for the 1990s.

(Quoted in 108 *Public Utilities Fortnightly* 108 [November 19, 1981]), p. 12. Reprinted with permission.

4. The utilities also became the subject of movies and novels. Among the best are Burton Wohl, *The China Syndrome* (New York: Bantam, 1978) and Arthur Hailey, *Overload* (New York: Doubleday & Co., 1979).

5. From "State Regulation of Electric Utilities," Douglas. D. Anderson, in *The Politics of Regulation*, ed. James Q. Wilson, p. 24. Copyright © 1980 by Basic Books, Inc. All quotes by permission of Basic Books, Inc., Publishers, New York.

6. See, for example, *Northeast Power Failure*, A Report to the President by the Federal Power Commission (Washington, D.C.: U.S. Government Printing Office, 1965); and *Prevention of Power Failures*, vol. 1, Report of the Commission (Washington, D.C.: U.S. Government Printing Offfice, 1967).

7. In 1976 interstate pipelines were able to deliver only about three-quarters of the amount of gas they agreed to deliver under long-term contracts. See Federal Power Commission, *Gas Curtailment Report No. 22438: Requirements, Curtailments and Deliveries of Interstate Pipeline Companies*, (Washington, D.C.: U.S. Government Printing Office, 1977).

8. See, for example, Daniel Martin, *Three Mile Island: Prologue or Epilogue?* (Cambridge, Mass.: Ballinger Publishing Co., 1980).

9. According to Robert W. Scherer:

If the federal government seems a bit ambivalent about wanting the nation's electric utilities to use coal, it is even more circumspect about advocating nuclear energy. As a result, development of nuclear energy is under a virtual moratorium in the United States, despite the fact that its growth is accelerating in other industrial countries. No nuclear reactors have been ordered in the United States during the past two years, and about 70 nuclear projects have been delayed in each of those two years. Sixteen projects were canceled last year and six the year before. There are two reasons for this retreat. One is the deteriorating financial condition of electric utilities in America. The other is the rising cost and uncertainty of building a nuclear plant and getting it licensed in light of increasing regulatory requirements, especially in the wake of the unfortunate incident at Three Mile Island.

(Quoted in 108 *Public Utilities Fortnightly* 108 [November 19, 1981]), p. 12. Reprinted with permission.

10. See, for example, Kurt Borchardt, *Structure and Performance of the U.S. Communications Industry* (Boston: Graduate School of Business Administration, Harvard University, 1970).

11. See, for example, John R. Meyer, et al., *The Economics of Competition in the Telecommunications Industry* (Cambridge, Mass.: Oelgeschlager, Gunn & Hain, Publishers, 1980); and Gerald W. Brock, *The Telecommunications Industry: The Dynamics of Market Structure* (Cambridge, Mass: Harvard University Press, 1981).

12. *In re Use of Carterfone Device*, 13 FCC 2d 420 (1968), *reconsideration denied*, 14 FCC 2d 571 (1968).

13. In re Applications of Microwave Communications, Inc., 18 FCC 2d 953 (1969).

14. See, for example, *Re Second Computer Inquiry*, 35 PUR 4th 143 (FCC, 1980), and subsequent modifications to this final decision.

15. See Donald I. Baker, "Competition, Communications and Change," *Antitrust and Trade Regulation Reporter*, no. 698 (January 28, 1975):D1-D6.

16. In one of the largest of these private suits (as of this writing), a jury awarded MCI $1.8 billion in triple damages. The case is on appeal. See *Northeast Telephone Co.* v. *American Telephone and Telegraph Co., Western Electric Co., Inc., and the Southern New England Telephone Co.*, 1980-1981 TRADE CASES Par. 63,593, *reversed and remanded*, 1981-1 TRADE CASES Par. 64,027.

17. See, for example, Paul L. Joskow, "Inflation and Environmental Concern: Structural Change in the Process of Utility Price Regulation," 17 *Journal of Law & Economics* (October 1974): 291-327; Paul W. MacAvoy, "The Present Condition of Regulated Enterprise" (Working Paper no. 5, Series C, School of Organization and Management, Yale University, October 1978); and L.H. Knapp, "Earthquakes and Aftershocks: The Regulatory Management Landscape of the 1980's, 107 *Public Utilities Fortnightly* (January 1, 1981), pp. 11-16.

18. See, for example, Irwin M. Stelzer and Bruce C. Netschert, "Hot War in the Energy Industry," *Harvard Business Review* 45 (November-December 1967): 14-26, 190-192.

19. See Edward Berlin et al., *Perspectives on Power* (Cambridge, Mass.: Ballinger Publishing Co., 1974), pp. 1-11. As early as 1965, the industry sought to regain some control over its technological future by establishing the Electric Research Council to enable all segments of the industry—investor-owned and public—to sponsor research on an industry-wide basis.

20. See Stephen G. Breyer and Paul W. MacAvoy, *Energy Regulation by the Federal Power Commission* (Washington, D.C.: The Brookings Institution, 1974), chap. 3.

21. See Charles F. Phillips, Jr., "The Effectiveness of State Commission Regulation," in A Critique of Administrative Regulations of Public Utilities, eds. Warren J. Samuels and Harry M. Trebing, (East Lansing: MSU Public Utilities Papers, 1972), pp. 71-89.

22. *Electric and Gas Utility Rate and Fuel Adjustment Clause Increases, 1977* Committee Print, Senate, 95th Cong., 2d sess., Subcommittee on Intergovernmental Relations and Subcommittee on Energy, Nuclear Proliferation and Federal Services (Washington, D.C.: U.S. Government Printing Office, 1978), p. 7. The magnitude of rate increases is apparent when it is noted that electric and gas rates increased $6 billion in the twenty-six year period 1948 through 1973, compared with an increase of $48.3 billion in the four-year period 1974 through 1977. Ibid.

23. The examples are countless but to cite just one: Rochester Gas & Electric Corporation began construction of a nuclear generating facility in 1974, with an estimated completion date of 1977. "Its cost, which was estimated at $382 million, has ballooned to $3.7 billion, and the plant isn't expected to be completed before 1986." *The Wall Street Journal*, November 27, 1981, p. 31.

24. Consolidated Edison Company of New York was hard hit by the 1973 oil embargo, since the utility was producing 75 percent of its electricity by burning foreign oil. According to Anderson:

> Con Ed was immediately affected by the embargo. . . . A black market for oil developed with Con Ed buying oil on the high seas at $23 to $24 per barrel—up from $4 to $5 per barrel earlier. . . . Even through the New York Public Service Commission authorized a temporary increase of something like $75 million in February, 1974, in April the company was on the brink of bankruptcy because it couldn't raise working capital. . . . Banks were refusing to loan, and people weren't buying its bonds. When the commission refused to allow the company to use working capital to pay dividends, the company had to pass on its dividends in April. The stock stopped trading for a while. . . . It was the first time in eighty-nine years that the giant utility had failed to pay quarterly dividends on its common stock. . . . The shock of Con Ed's actions reverberated throughout the industry. The common stock of Boston Edison fell from over $25 on April 22 to about $15 on May 14. Duke Power's stock dropped over 12 percent.

("State Regulation," pp. 22-23).

25. During the 1960s several electric utilities diversified into coal mining in an attempt to secure assured and cheap sources of fuel. The more recent diversification move is into unrelated lines of business: Gulf States Utilities Company into oil exploration; American Natural Resources Company into trucking; and Pacific Power & Light Company into telephone communications. See "A High-Risk Era for the Utilities," *Business Week*, February 23, 1981, pp. 76-86. Warned one editorial: "Inevitably the attempts of the power companies to get their capital out of the utility industry brings to mind the sad history of the Penn Central and the collapse of what once called itself 'the standard railroad of the world'." Ibid., p. 162. See *Utility Diversification Study* (Arlington, Va.: Public Utilities Reports, 1981); and

"Utilities Buck the Trend to Diversify," *Business Week*, December 14, 1981, pp. 132-133.

26. See, for example, "Behind AT&T's Change at the Top," *Business Week*, November 6, 1978, pp. 114-126.

27. "A typical retail rate case for a medium to large utility costs about $300,000 to $500,000 in out-of-pocket costs and probably double that amount when company fixed expenses such as staff salaries are included." Michael Schmidt, *Automatic Adjustment Clauses: Theory and Application* (East Lansing: MSU Public Utilities Studies, 1980), p. 9. Also see "Legal Expenses and Utility Ratemaking," 102 *Public Utilities Fortnightly* 58 (October 26, 1978).

28. See David C. Sweet, "Meeting the Research Needs of State Regulators," 102 *Public Utilities Fortnightly* (August 17, 1978):11-15; and Douglas N. Jones, "Three Years in the Life of the National Regulatory Research Institute," 107 *Public Utilities Fortnightly* (January 15, 1981), pp. 13-16.

29. See Jack Hopper, "A Legislative History of the Texas Public Utility Regulatory Act of 1975," 28 *Baylor Law Review* (Fall 1976), pp. 777-822.

30. As Stelzer has noted: "Consumer advocacy is big business today." Between 1977 and 1979, for example, nearly $6 million was awarded by the Department of Energy "to state consumer offices to assist them in their role as consumer advocates. . . . There are approximately 170 nongovernmental Public Interest Research Groups nationwide. The Consumer Federation of America, a Washington-based lobby group, currently represents 200 so-called 'grass-roots' organizations." Irwin M. Stelzer, "A Policy Guide for Utility Executives: 'Know When to Hold'em; Know When to Fold'em'," 106 *Public Utilities Fortnightly* 106 (October 9, 1980):62-66. Also see "Reimbursing Intervenors for Attorney's Fees," *Public Utilities Fortnightly* 42 (February 28, 1980): 42-45. Reprinted with permission.

31. Public Utility Regulatory Policies Act of 1978 (PURPA), (P.L. 95-617). See, for example, *State of Mississippi* v. *Federal Energy Regulatory Commission* Civil Action No. J79-0212(C) (1981), where a federal judge held unconstitutional certain provisions of PURPA. The act, declared Judge Cox, "usurps and dispells the intrastate jurisdiction and activity of the Mississippi Public Service Commission. . . . The sovereign state of Mississippi is not a robot, or lackey which may be shuttled back and forth to suit the whim and caprice of the federal government, but was and is the prime benefactor of the power and authority designated by the Constitution and allocated as desired by this instrument as the supreme law of the land." The decision has been appealed. Also see Jay B. Kennedy, "DOE Mandates: Taking Power Away from the States," *Public Utilities Fortnightly* 106 (November 6, 1980):11-14.

32. See, for example, Edward P. Larkin, "Separations and Settlements in the Telephone Industry" (Washington, D.C.: National Association of Regulatory Utility Commissioners, 1979).

33. See *West Texas Utilities Co.* v. *Texas Electric Service Co.* 1979-2 TRADE CASES Par. 62,851 (N.D. Tex., 1979).

34. See "Managerial and Regulatory Functions Distinguished," *Public Utilities Fornightly* 74 (July 2, 1964):67-70. "Management—Utility and Commission Power," *Public Utilities Fortnightly* 79 (March 2, 1967):57-59; Charles F. Phillips, Jr., "The Thin Red Line," 57 *Bell Telephone Magazine* 10 (Summer 1978):10-13; and Richard B. McGlynn, "The Regulator as Manager," mimeographed (Paper presented at the Third Annual Utility Regulatory Conference, Washington, D.C., October 7, 1980).

35. See, for example, Donald L. Martin and Warren F. Schwartz, eds., *Deregulating American Industry: Legal and Economic Problems* (Lexington, Mass.: Lexington Books, D.C. Heath, 1977).

36. See, for example, Tom Alexander, "The Surge to Deregulate Electricity," *Fortune*, July 13, 1981, pp. 98-105.

37. Howard Perry, "The New Federalism, Free Market Economics, and Utility Regulation," in *An Economic Medley—From Economic Analysis to Economic Justice*, ed. Charles F. Phillips, Jr. (Lexington, Va.: Washington and Lee University, forthcoming).

# 3 Is Public-Utility Regulation beyond *Hope*?

*Roger Sherman*

From the slender coverage given public-utility regulation in recent law journals one might think the long U.S. experiment in public control of private monopoly had ended successfully, the right of states to prescribe prices (as affirmed in *Munn* v. *Illinois*)[1] having found effective operational form between *Smyth* v. *Ames* and *Hope Natural Gas Co.*[2] But the daily paper refutes that conclusion. Public-utility rate hearings are more frequent and intricate than ever, and almost everyone who pays a utility bill is concerned about regulation. Although legal issues are settled, so that law journals are quiet on the subject, the basis for their settlement has made economic issues very complicated. Economic regulation is by no means simple, but the genuine issues are fewer and more basic than debates in modern rate cases would suggest.

Clarifying economic questions about rate-of-return regulation is the main purpose here. This chapter begins with a brief background of the *Hope* decision, which provides the framework for contemporary rate-of-return regulation and points out operational shortcomings that prevent sound application of its rate-of-return guidelines. Undesirable effects of rate-of-return regulation for economic efficiency are discussed in the section on efficiency consequences of *Hope*. Some avenues for reform are reviewed in the section describing sources of regulation, and conclusions are summarized at the end of the chapter.

First, however, the title question will be answered in the negative: public-utility regulation has not passed beyond the framework of the *Hope* decision. The other question intimated in the title, whether the task of regulation literally is beyond hope, will also be answered, though with more hesitation, in the negative. As answers to these questions unfold, it should become clear that efficient public-utility regulation will remain beyond hope until it moves beyond *Hope*. Although the *Hope* decision provided a practical compromise that narrowed debate on allowed profit for nearly four

I am grateful to Leonard Herk for research assistance and to the National Science Foundation for financial support through Grant SES-7914081. A visit at Berlin's International Institute of Management in the summer of 1980 led to many improvements. I benefited also from comments made in seminars at AT&T Longlines Division, Auburn University, the University of Connecticut, Duke University, the University of Georgia, the College of the Holy Cross, and Rutgers University.

41

decades, it remains nevertheless an unsatisfactory basis for the economic regulation of public-utilities today. This chapter will show why it is inherently unsatisfactory for achieving economic aims of regulation and will discuss alternative schemes for specifying prices while eliciting efficient performance.

## The Sources and the Soundness of *Hope*

The shortcomings of the *Hope* decision can be seen and understood best if its achievement is first appreciated. A brief review of the question it was intended to settle follows: what profit should investors receive? That question was first perceived largely as a matter of fairness. Yet it was unanswerable as debated because fairness would require some basis for investor expectation which the very existence of legal debate denied. That is why the instrumental value of the *Hope* decision lay in its endorsement of one answer to the profit question. It does not necessarily mean that this answer was sound. Indeed, there are inconsistencies in the *Hope* procedure that still complicate its application. What is more, as this chapter will emphasize, from an economic-efficiency standpoint the question of profit for investors should not have been addressed so directly. Doing so entirely ignored the role of profit as efficiency incentive within a business organization.

### *The Sources of* Hope

The institutions for the regulation of monopoly were built during the past century of spectacular economic expansion and change. The groundwork for this was laid after the Civil War, when a steady decline in price level made farmers feel they were suffering unfairly (along with small merchants and investors in railroad stocks) and brought the great midwestern farm belt to life politically. Although the Supreme Court acquiesced after the Illinois legislature regulated prices for grist mills by saying "[f]or protection against abuses by legislatures the people must resort to the polls, not to the courts,"[3] subsequent decisions drew the courts back into regulation.[4] But regardless where regulatory power was lodged, the substantive question being pursued would remain the same: how much profit should be allowed a publicly regulated firm?[5] Whether it was an appropriate economic question to pose or not, it was the question the *Hope* case was to answer.

By the time of the *Hope* case the task of regulating prices had been delegated to regulatory commissions in state after state, and as they wrestled with the question of what profits to allow the public utilities they regulated, these commissions were guided by judicial review. Court guidance grew out of extreme cases, however, involving confiscation of investors' property on the one hand and unreasonable burdens for rate payers on the other. These cases did not immediately reveal the underlying economic process any more than the rules of a game can be quickly inferred by consulting the *Guiness Book of Records*. Principles were set out mainly as boundaries that left much scope for commission discretion. Some of the principles might even be inconsistent, especially when there were changes in the economic conditions on which they had been based. That is one reason early decisions created conflicts for the *Hope* decision to resolve.

The grounds on which the allowed-profit question was settled in *Hope* go back to the late nineteenth century, when a generally declining price level made it all the more puzzling. Falling prices raised the issue whether profit should be allowed on the amount investors originally invested in assets years earlier or on the lower, current-asset value that resulted after the price level fell. Basing profit on original investment seemed fair, and the actual outlay had the added advantage of being precisely known. But using the current value appeared to reflect more faithfully the developing competitive-market circumstances, and relying on it would mimic the market system on which the rest of the economy turned.[6] This issue of asset valuation was important in *Smyth* v. *Ames*.[7] This dispute arose out of Nebraska's effort not merely to regulate railroad rates but, as the court concluded, to set rates on intrastate traffic sometimes below costs. In defense of its 1893 rate-setting statute the state of Nebraska could argue that investors had made poor investments because their values fell with the general price level and that investors rather than the public should suffer as a result. The court apparently was prepared to use almost any basis for valuing assets, even the low current value urged by Nebraska, because no matter how returns were calculated, the court found them inadequate under the disputed rates. The court held that fair value of property used by a corporation for the convenience of the public should be the basis for rates, and that fair value would consider, inter alia, "the original cost of construction, the amount and market value of its bonds and stocks, the present as compared with the original cost of construction."[8] These three possible bases rest on very different principles of valuation. Mixing them carelessly can cause serious implementation problems. Other potential inconsistencies in *Smyth* v. *Ames* need not be discussed here for they have already been well analyzed.[9]

The price level finally began to rise after 1898[10] when the court's previous willingness to entertain present estimates of the value of property was seized upon by the utilities because such values were growing larger, and their use as a basis for profit might benefit rather than harm investors. Whether current value should be used as a basis for rates and how to measure current value—as physical-replacement cost or as the market value of bonds and stocks—was still unclear. On this valuation point the confusion under *Smyth* v. *Ames* is well illustrated by three important Supreme Court decisions rendered in 1923, when the price level was twice as high as it had been in 1898.[11] The first of these three decisions, the *Southwestern Bell Telephone Co.* case,[12] ruled that a return had been set too low because the current-reproduction cost had not been used for valuing assets. A dissent written by Justice Brandeis (although he concurred in the judgment for reversal) called instead for original cost, meaning accounting-book value as a basis of valuation. The second and third cases, *Bluefield Water Works and Improvement Co.*[13] and *Georgia Railway*,[14] were both handed down on the same day three weeks later. In *Bluefield* reproduction cost was supported but in *Georgia Railway* a commission's use of original cost was endorsed for rate-base valuation.

Ambiguity in the *Smyth* v. *Ames* fair-value guideline was criticized by Justice Brandeis in his opinion (joined by Justice Holmes) in the *Southwestern Bell Telephone Co.* case. Brandeis saw the investor contributing to the enterprise a sum of capital which was well defined and did not go into costs of later improvements and current-market values of bonds and stocks or the many other notions of asset value that litigants pursued under *Smyth* v. *Ames*. And an explicit return on that capital also was demonstrably acceptable to the investors. Besides being well defined, these historical investment values and rates of return avoided the extreme variations in allowed profit that could follow if current estimates were used for valuing the rate base.[15]

Although the *Bluefield Case* was settled on quite a different basis from that urged by Brandeis, it also sought consistency between valuing assets and allowing a rate of return. *Bluefield* valued assets at current-reproduction cost and focused on comparable risk[16] as a basis for setting a current rate of return. Rather than merely listing possible factors to consider, as in *Smyth* v. *Ames*, the court in *Bluefield* accepted a risk mechanism that presumably determined current returns in unregulated competitive markets and might therefore provide the logic needed for setting returns on current-valued assets in regulated markets. Of course this basis for allowing profit that mirrored the market process differed sharply from the Brandeis proposal with its historical terms. But by tying rate-of-return and rate-base valuation together each method now offered the coherence that had been missing before. Indeed, the two views are polar-extreme ways of dealing with price-level change, the historical Brandeis proposal favoring consumers (investors) when the price level increases (decreases) unexpectedly since returns need not rise accordingly. By the same token the current-valuation proposal is better for investors (consumers) when the price level increases (decreases) more than anticipated.

The *Georgia* decision is noteworthy because in upholding the original-cost basis for asset valuation it seems so blatantly contradictory to *South-*

*western Bell* and *Bluefield*. But in *Georgia* the court did not find rates confiscatory as it had in the other two cases.[17] Rates might have been judged confiscatory in *Southwestern Bell* and *Bluefield* whether the rate base was determined by using original or reproduction cost, and in those cases some valuation beyond original cost was urged to set things right, whereas in *Georgia* the court found rates based on original cost could allow an adequate payment to investors. In stating the majority opinion Justice Brandeis specifically noted the commission had considered reproduction cost and that it had correctly held that reproduction cost did not have to be used for valuing the rate base. The question of the proper way to value assets thus remained open.

Under the 1938 Natural Gas Act, efforts by the Federal Power Commission (now the Federal Energy Regulatory Commission, FERC) to determine reasonable rates for natural gas transmitted across states lines led to more exacting treatment of economic issues and finally to the decision that has guided rate-of-return regulation since 1944. The *Hope Natural Gas*[18] decision ended confusion from *Smyth* v. *Ames* over whether to value assets at their going-concern fair-market value, which would give a large role to the market value of stocks. Because of its ultimately circular dependence on the allowable rate of return, the going-concern market value was sensibly rejected in *Hope*, and an external cost basis for asset value was recommended. *Hope* did not specify a uniquely correct basis for valuing assets or calculating allowed profit, but it deemed one method acceptable. That method was a compromise between two external bases for asset valuation: the current reproduction-cost benchmark of the *Bluefield* decision and the well-defined, historical benchmark set out in the dissent of Justice Brandeis in *Southwestern Bell*.[19] *Hope* followed the Brandeis position with respect to debt capital, accepting original-historical cost as reasonable for valuing the debt portion of the asset rate base and allowing the historically agreed upon interest rate as its rate of return. But *Hope* followed the *Bluefield* decision with respect to equity capital by allowing any reasonable basis for valuing that portion of the asset-rate base as long as it was external to, and thus not dependent on, the commission's decision. The rate of return to equity "should be commensurate with returns on investments in other enterprises having corresponding risks,"[20] and "should be sufficient to assure confidence in the financial integrity of the enterprise, so as to maintain its credit and to attract capital."[21] These two *Hope* guidelines for equity returns are well known as the comparable-earnings and capital-attraction standards. After separately determining one historical return for debt and one current return for equity, the two could be weighted together by the respective debt and equity portions of the capital structure of the firm into an overall rate of return on all assets, thus yielding an implied level of profit for the firm.[22]

The effect of *Hope* is difficult to trace precisely, in part because it encouraged regulatory authorities in all the states to follow their own procedures.[23] But in one way or another every regulatory commission follows the general scheme advised in *Hope*; it defines an asset rate base for each firm under its jurisdiction and then rules on the maximum rate of return the firm may earn on those assets. In valuing the asset rate base most commissions today use original-historical cost, recorded as accounting-book value, although others use variations which involve estimates of the current replacement or reproduction cost of assets,[24] a practice that also can comply with the guidelines articulated in *Hope*. Some commissions include facilities under construction as part of the asset rate base while others create an allowance for construction funds that will warrant higher revenues once the facilities are operational.[25] When it comes to allowing a rate of return on those assets commissions follow different practices also, although the embedded interest rate on debt is typically accepted as the allowed return on debt capital. Difficulties in determining the rate of return to allow on equity capital have caused it to receive the most attention, and because large capital needs in electricity and other regulated industries make capital cost very significant in total cost, it has become the major issue in many rate hearings.

Thus regulatory commission practice under the *Hope* guidelines largely separates the determination of a firm's allowed rate of return into two problems: the determination of an allowed rate of return on debt using historical facts; and the determination of an allowed rate of return on equity based on current conditions. Each return is then applied only to that portion of total assets financed by each respective source of capital, debt and equity. The result is a compromise between two alternative ways of dealing with changes in the general price level: the historical basis put forward by Brandeis in his opinion in *Southwestern Bell*; and the current basis set out in *Bluefield*.

### The Soundness of Hope

In undertaking a criticism of regulation under *Hope*, treating operational weaknesses here before analyzing economic-efficiency consequences, one should not be unmindful of the fact that other goals were sought through the *Hope* decision beyond those of economc efficiency and operational effectiveness. Indeed, since at any one time consumers might argue for one of the two valuation principles adopted in *Hope*, current and historical, while investors would favor the other—their positions shifting with changes in the direction of the price-level trend—the *Hope* compromise obviously balanced effects on the incomes of those groups. It also avoided large fluctuations in equity returns that would arise from allowing a current-market return on all assets while a constant, historical-interest rate was actually being paid on the debt portion of capital.[26] Applying a separate return to debt and equity portions of the asset-rate base as the *Hope* guidelines suggested would prevent any such spillover of return fluctuations from debt to equity. In seeking to balance effects on income and to moderate fluctuations in equity returns, however, the court did not ensure that an operational mechanism would result. It also did not analyze consequences for economic efficiency, although a goal of efficiency was implicit in the comparable-earnings guideline. Shortcomings of either kind could undermine the *Hope* objectives.

For operational soundness the *Hope* guidelines require some basis for estimating a return to equity capital based on current conditions. Yet the *Hope* framework complicates this task enormously and may even prevent it from being carried out. First, the hybrid mixture of current and historical valuation principles *Hope* prescribes for debt and equity does not match that affecting unregulated firms, which are valued on a current basis so that no true benchmark exists in the unregulated firms that could reveal comparable earnings for regulated firms. Second, observing returns of other unregulated firms will not reveal true investor judgments reliably because they can be affected by regulators' actions. To sketch these points will require brief discussion of the role stocks and bonds play in unregulated corporations, but that will also be useful in the following sections.

Bonds exist because the less daring among potential investors are willing to invest only if they have to bear very little risk; the bond is a safe low-risk investment vehicle which tempts these more timid souls to join the ranks of regular investors; bonds promise first priority to payments out of earnings and first claim to assets too in the event of failure. Of course a side effect of making such an offer to bondholders is that the risk in common stock shares will increase. From this one might expect that the better any one firm can tailor its mixture of bonds and stocks to meet the preferences of potential investors, the more effectively it can raise capital and hence the lower its overall cost of capital will be. In small ways this expectation is sound, particularly when disequilibrium situations can be uncovered by the firm or when stocks and bonds are subject to different tax treatments. But it is now known that with the capital market in equilibrium under simple assumptions (admittedly limiting assumptions, such as the absence of taxes), it would be wrong; the particular mixture of debt and equity instruments any one firm issues can be shown to have no effect on the value of that firm. Over twenty years ago this claim by Franco Modigliani and Merton Miller threw financial theorists and practioners into an uproar, sparking a controversy that has since been settled on a theoretical level but still simmers over the interpretation of empirical results.[27] The Modigliani-Miller conclusion can be sketched thus: if we lived in a no-tax world in which it cost nothing beyond the prices involved to make transactions and neither firms nor individuals would ever fail, and if the level expected on average for a firm's earnings before interest payments and the probability distribution of such earnings were known based entirely on its commercial prospects, then the expected level and probability distribution of a firm's earnings alone would determine its value, and nothing the firm did by way of adjusting its capital structure could affect that value.

The logic behind this Modigliani and Miller claim depends on having no bankruptcy so firms and individuals can borrow currently at the same rate of interest.[28] Then if the firm had no debt its shareholders could borrow money at the going interest rate to finance some of their share purchases and thereby be in the same financial position as if the firm actually had issued debt. Or if the firm already had a large amount of debt in its capital structure, any shareholder who preferred less could lend money at interest in order to reach a position as creditor and shareholder the same as if the firm had less debt in its capital structure. By substituting debt capital for equity, or vice versa, the firm then cannot change its value. If it did investors would immediately want to trade (arbitrage) between personal debt and corporate debt, and their action would eliminate the change in value. Even though the debt of unregulated firms may be issued with a promise to pay interest in nominal terms that can differ from current-interest rates later, the market nevertheless evaluates debt values at current rates and the arbitrage will take place in current terms. The reason current terms are controlling is that equilibrium outcomes in unregulated competitive markets are determined by new entrants whose opportunity costs are based on current-interest rates and current-profit rates. Lower (or higher) historical-interest rates are an advantage (or a disadvantage) to shareholders of already existing firms, but because it motivates entry decisions the current-interest rate influences the return to shareholders who also borrow or lend at the current rate in adjusting their portfolios.

Under *Hope* guidelines there is of course no role for new entry, and only the return to the equity portion of capital is to be based on current conditions. The historical cost of debt and the importance of debt in the capital structure of the regulated firm might therefore affect the overall allowed rate of return. Current debt cannot always be interchanged with the historical debt that influences allowed return because current- and historical-interest rates may differ. Then since current rates do not influence returns as they do in unregulated markets, no arbitrage process can offset the effect of capital structure on allowed rate of return in regulated firms. And the capital-market valuation mechanism cannot be counted on to operate in the same way for regulated firms as the Modigliani and Miller theory describes for unregulated firms. Even though profits taxes, transaction costs, and the possibility of bankruptcy may alter the Modigliani-Miller valuation process, the fact remains that regulation according to *Hope* guidelines may interfere in a basic way with the underlying valuation process. Thus basing regulated firms' returns on unregulated firms' returns may be inappropriate.[29]

Rather than new entrants' opportunity cost of debt, which influences returns in unregulated industries, *Hope* guidelines let the historical-interest rate on bonds influence a regulated firm's allowed rate of return and, ultimately, its output price. Under this procedure shareholders no longer gain or lose by offsetting risks borne by bondholders, and it is possible that consumers will instead bear risks of price-level or interest-rate change. Moreover, where regulators tie returns to the original cost of assets, shareholders as well as bondholders may experience nominal returns in the face on any unanticipated price-level change, because original-cost valuation of a rate base tends to fix returns to equity in original-period dollars. Just such nominal returns for equity have been observed in regulated firms during recent periods with high rates of inflations.[30] In essence the *Hope* guidelines for setting a return to equity capital can destroy the financial comparability between regulated and unregulated firms on which the guidelines supposedly rest.

Now it is conceivable that investors' valuations reflecting comparable risks can be observed from the shares of other regulated firms or from a regulated firm's own shares. But stringent conditions are required for obtaining investors' judgments about regulated firms independently of regulators' actions, and the conditions are not apt to be satisfied. In particular, the regulatory process itself requires time to reach decisions. Sudden cost increases in fuel and other inputs prompt rate requests, but the delays between requests and regulatory actions can be so great that more problems, calling perhaps for more rate requests, may arise before the first request is settled. Such delays in adjustment interfere with the valuation process, and because of the way the *Hope* guidelines mix historical-accounting measures with current measures, there is no clear way to undo the consequences. Willard Carleton has demonstrated[31] that without prompt response to changed conditions, market values will be affected such that the ordinary market-valuation process is irreparably distorted. This means that by observing other regulated firms it is very hard, if not impossible, to apply properly the comparable earnings standard, because observed capital costs for regulated firms will reflect effects of regulation rather than investor judgments alone.[32]

It also is seldom possible to observe a regulated firm's own equity cost as a basis for determining comparable earnings, although some proposals for this will be noted in the following section. A major difficulty arises when a public utility is regulated by more than one commission, a common situation because the service areas of most utilities do not stop at state boundaries. The utility has only one cost of equity capital, but its profitability and thus its cost of capital will be affected by decisions of, say, two regulatory commissions. Neither commission can easily trace the consequence of its own rulings or observe investors' judgments independently of regulatory effects because other regulators also influence the firm's profitability. Related problems arise in the regulation of only a portion of a firm's activities. Market returns for the firm will then reflect investors' judgments about activities beyond those being regulated, a situation that will confound the determination of capital cost for the regulated activity.

That *Hope* guidelines lack a sound basis for estimating the very rate of return they sanction is important beyond the obvious practical difficulty it causes. That practical difficulty gives regulators much discretion when almost any decision they reach will be feasible because the monopoly public utility they regulate would usually be able to earn far more than they allow. In the worst cases this discretion opens the way for corruption. Even in the best cases it makes investors wonder not merely about inherent business risk, the risk of the business itself, but rather about what regulators will decide. Then the firm's return on equity capital possesses uncertainties introduced by the regulatory process itself.

But even if rate-of-return regulation according to the comparable earnings standard could somehow be employed perfectly and continuously, it might fail for lack of incentive. Then all possible gains would essentially have to be given up, and the firm's incentive to operate efficiently would be completely sapped; there would be no profit reward for efficiency, no incentive that would elicit extra effort. In part because of delays between price changes, all incentive is not eliminated in regulated firms. But the incentive that remains in firms regulated according to *Hope* guidelines do not serve the efficiency goal particularly well.

## Efficiency Consequences of *Hope*

The attempt to establish a firm's profit by administrative-judicial process, which was begun in the late nineteenth century and facilitated by the *Hope* decision, not only distorts risk bearing in the firm but also fails to control monopolistic reliance on price discrimination and biases the firm's choice among productive inputs. Each of these properties causes an economic inefficiency and will be discussed, beginning with the Harvey Averch and Leland Johnson input bias which favors capital use. The second problem, price discrimination, is less well known and may cause the levels of a public utility's outputs to be inefficiently chosen. And finally the distortion in risk bearing disrupts the incentive of investors to oversee the performance of the firm's management.

*Input Inefficiency*

Although this chapter will question the strength of its profit motivation later, suppose for now that the monopoly firm whose rate of return on assets is limited according to *Hope* guidelines faithfully pursues profit for its shareholders. Then in choosing inputs to produce any particular level of output its incentives will be distorted. For if the regulated firm is allowed to earn a rate of return greater than the competitive cost of capital but below the monopoly return, it will want to expand its capital beyond the monopoly level. This incentive by itself is desirable since it will lead to more output. But in hiring inputs other than capital, the regulated firm remains monopolistic. It even becomes schizophrenic in deciding capital use differently from the use of other inputs, and it succumbs to what is now well known as the Averch-Johnson effect: to produce any given output, it uses more capital relative to other inputs than is most efficient.[33]

The simplest way to view the incentive for capital use of the rate-of-return regulated firm is to realize that whereas an unregulated firm has one main aim, the rate-of-return regulated firm has two. The unregulated monopolist seeks to earn high profit; the rate-of-return regulated monopolist seeks not only to earn high profit but also to be allowed to keep it. And since the regulated monopolist's profit is limited to some fraction of its assets, the amount of profit it is allowed to earn can be increased as more assets are employed. Imposing rate-of-return regulation on the monopolist may therefore bring greater output as its asset base in expanded from the original monopoly position, but such regulation also invites the use of more capital than is efficient when judged in relation to other inputs. Indeed, at the extreme where the equity rate of return almost satisfies the comparable-earnings standard, there can be more inefficiency at the margin through distortion of input choice than social gain from a lower price.[34]

One situation brings out the potential perversity of incentives in the rate-of-return regulated firm especially well. Suppose that as regulation is introduced a single-product monopolist is forced away from its unregulated monopoly position and soon would have to enter an inelastic portion of its demand curve, because as price falls and output expands quantity responds less to any given percentage change in price. The regulated firm would want to avoid an inelastic region of its demand curve just as an unregulated monopolist would.[35] As it expands output where demand is inelastic, its total revenue declines while its total cost increases. The regulated monopoly has a simple way to avoid reducing its profit by expanding output; it merely wastes capital (if it can get away with it), and thereby raises the amount of profit it is allowed to earn. Regulatory commissions try to prevent such capital waste, of course, but the incentive to waste can come directly from rate-of-return regulation.

Rate-of-return regulation can even invite conspiracy between regulated firms and their suppliers to set high-capital-equipment prices. After electrical-equipment producers were convicted of price fixing in 1962, Fred Westfield demonstrated convincingly "that it can be in the interest of a regulated private power generating company to pay a higher rather than a lower price for the plant and equipment it purchases."[36] Increased equipment costs could be passed through to the consumer in the form of higher prices and at the same time could increase the amount of profit the company was allowed to earn by increasing its asset-rate base; under rate-of-return regulation, the capital side of the firm is essentially subject to cost-plus regulation.

The general problem here is that under the procedures endorsed in *Hope*, a firm's allowed profit depends on one of the inputs in the firm's control, capital. By strategically adjusting that input while anticipating the regulatory authority's behavior, the firm can improve its allowed profit.[37] And it need not always use excessive capital. If the allowed rate of return is set below the cost of capital as recent regulation has sometimes done, the firm may use less capital than would be efficient relative to other inputs.

Nevertheless, empirical tests based on years of normal operating conditions (after the Great Electrical Equipment Conspiracy but before the Arab oil embargo) have indicated there was a bias toward capital inputs.[38] These studies, all of which have used data from the electric-utility industry, have tested a strong form of the Averch-Johnson hypothesis by focusing on new base-load electric plants to see whether any bias toward capital could be detected within them. A weaker hypothesis would allow for capital biases in the mixture of different kinds of plants, or even in the utilization of capacity, but because more precise methods can be applied there, the best studies have sought a bias only within particular plants. The finding of a bias in studies so narrowly confined is strong evidence that rate-of-return regulation reduces input efficiency.

### Output Inefficiency

When a monopoly produces only one product for which demand is everywhere elastic, and if the profit motive is still assumed, rate-of-return regulation can push the monopoly almost to an ideal price and output solution. The only problem comes from input inefficiency, the Averch-Johnson bias toward capital just discussed. However, when a regulated firm sells more than one product—and examination of their price structures will show that all public utilities really sell more than one product—there is a question whether it will choose efficient relative prices, that is, whether its mixture of outputs will be chosen efficiently. In choosing prices the multiproduct public utility regulated according to *Hope* guidelines actually will rely on demand elasticities just as an unregulated monopoly would, and rate-of-return regulation does nothing to thwart this monopolistic behavior. Rate-of-return regulation introduces an Averch-Johnson capital bias through rate structures and causes the firm to favor with lower rates those products that will contribute most to the rate base. Thus two factors influence the firm's mixture of outputs—demand elasticities in a monopolistic way plus a bias toward capital-intensive products—and these two factors distort the outputs of the firm away from an efficient combination.

Figure 3-1 represents simplified costs and demand conditions for a single-product monopoly and illustrates the reasonably efficient solution rate-of-return regulation can achieve when demand is elastic. Demand for the product is *DD* while marginal cost (*MC*) is constant and equal to average cost (*AC*) at all output levels (*Q*). The marginal (and average) capital need is constant at *k* units of capital per unit of output, and there is no Averch and Johnson input bias. Then if the allowed rate of return is to be no more than *s* and the true cost of capital is lower, at *r*, allowed profit will be equal to *Qk (s – r)*, which is represented as rectangle *OQ\*BA* in figure 3-1. The firm attempting to maximize profit but regulated by rate-of-return constraint will earn just this profit, shown also as area *P\*EFG*, by choosing price *P\** and selling output *Q\**. Figure 3-1 also can be used to illus-

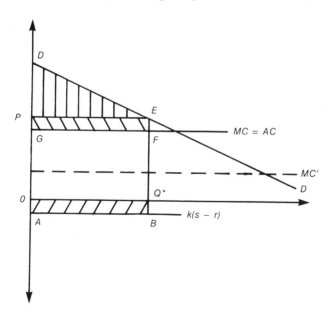

**Figure 3-1.** Demand and Cost Conditions for a Single-Product (*Q*) Monopolist

trate a solution that will maximize welfare while allowing a rate of return on capital of at least $s$. Suppose welfare to be the sum of consumer surplus (the vertically lined difference between what consumers were willing to pay as represented by the demand curve and what they have to pay as price) and producer surplus (the slanting lined difference between what the producer receives and the cost of inputs), the latter under these cost conditions simply being profit. While still allowing a return of $s$, the greatest possible value for this welfare sum will be achieved at the price $P^*$ and quantity $Q^*$, as experimentation with any other prices will quickly reveal. When more than one product is produced by the firm, however, this identity of welfare and regulated monopoly solutions can no longer be expected.

Figure 3-2 shows demands and costs for two goods, $Q_1$ in panel $a$ and $Q_2$ in panel $b$. These demands and costs are assumed independent of one another and consumption of neither good affects other activities importantly. So that the effect of capital alone on prices can be seen, demands for the two goods are assumed to be similar but costs differ; the capital required to produce a unit of the first product, $k_1$, is greater than the capital, $k_2$, required to produce one unit of the second product. The (constant) marginal cost is also higher for the first product. These differences make the allowed profit increase more with output of the first product, as comparison of allowed profits in the lower sections of the two panels will show. The firm regulated only by an overall constraint on total profit can be expected to take full advantage of this effect on allowed profit of producing $Q_1$. It does so in figure 3-2 by choosing a large $Q_1^*$, even causing a loss from the first product, and by using the handsome profit allowance thereby created to justify high profit earned on $Q_2$ at the price $P_2^*$.

Because it brings a profit benefit, the allowed profit from producing any good can be viewed implicitly by the firm as a reduction in that good's marginal cost. Where the allowed profit is large this reduction in marginal cost also will be large. In figure 3-2 implicit marginal costs are represented as $MC_1'$ and $MC_2'$, with $MC_1'$ at a greater reduction from $MC_1$ than $MC_2'$ is from $MC_2$ because the allowed profit on $Q_1$ is greater. In terms of thus adjusted marginal costs, the firm maximizes profit as shown in figure 3-2, essentially by subsidizing $Q_1$ and making high profit on $Q_2$.

A special form of this bias can be seen in the failure of regulated firms to offer lower prices during off-peak periods, at least until pressured recently by state and federal agencies and forced to suffer returns below their capital costs. In the simplest cases only peak-demand users press upon available capacity and call for its expansion, so for efficiency they should be the ones to pay for it, whereas at off-peak times capacity is abundant relative to demand so consumers do not have to be turned away by a high price. Utilities allowed rate of return above their capital costs lack incentive to employ this very sound pricing principle, however. They would rather lower the price

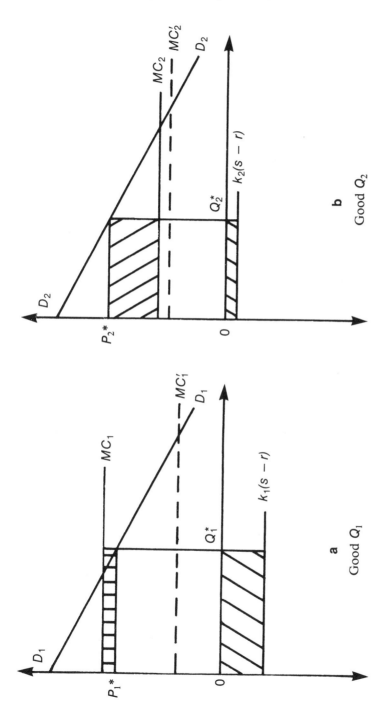

**Figure 3-2.** Similar Demands and Different Costs for Two Independent Goods, $Q_1$ and $Q_2$

for capital-intensive peak demand in order to justify more capital assets and charge a high price at off-peak times to realize profit that greater capital will justify.[40] Imagine that $k_1(s-r)$ for the regulated firm's good $Q_1$ depicted in the first panel of figure 3-2 is large because marginal usage requires capital expansion, whereas $k_2(s-r)$ is zero because good $Q_2$ is at the off-peak time when service can be expanded without more capacity. Then the regulated firm's peak price for $Q_1$ might even be lower than shown, and the off-peak price even higher. Probably because the practice of rate-of-return regulation is widespread here, the United States lags far behind other countries in the use of peak-load pricing.[41] This perverse reluctance to lower off-peak prices is not something to be blamed on any unduly selfish utility president, though; it is directly motivated by rate-of-return regulation.

Now assume the two products have the same marginal-cost and marginal-capital requirements but different demand elasticities. In figure 3-3, $MC_1 = MC_2$ and $k_1 = k_2$, but the demand for $Q_1$ is less elastic than the demand for $Q_2$. The lower shaded areas of both panels indicate that one unit of each product adds the same amount to allowed profit because production conditions are assumed the same for both products. More profit can be earned from less elastic demand $D_1D_1$ than from $D_2D_2$, however, and the regulated firm will take advantage of that fact. The firm sets a very profitable price $P_1^*$ on $Q_1$ and uses the output of $Q_2$ mainly to generate allowed profit in order that profit from $Q_1$ can be retained. Indeed, in the figure 3-3 example a loss is sustained on $Q_2$ in order that more profit from the sale of $Q_1$ can be retained. By again representing a marginal cost adjusted for allowed profit, in this case the same for both products at $MC_1' = MC_2'$, the firm's solution prices can be seen as profit-maximizing ones where marginal revenue equals implict marginal cost given the rate-of-return constraint.

One knows immediately that solutions reached in figure 3-2 and figure 3-3 cannot maximize welfare because in each case one price is below marginal cost. A price below marginal cost might conceivably add to welfare when some external benefit can be claimed or when one such subsidized product stands in a strong complementary relationship to another.[42] Here such interrelations have been ruled out by assumption. Without any such justification a price below marginal cost causes inefficiency by attracting to the industry resources that would be valued more by consumers in other uses (at least their marginal costs); in addition a financial loss results from pricing one product below marginal cost, which requires that the price of the other product be even farther above its marginal cost, causing a greater welfare loss there.

These examples thus show that a rate-of-return regulated firm can adopt nonoptimal price structures, either because of differences in capital intensities of the two goods (and the argument easily extends to a greater number) or because of differences in the price elasticities of their demands.

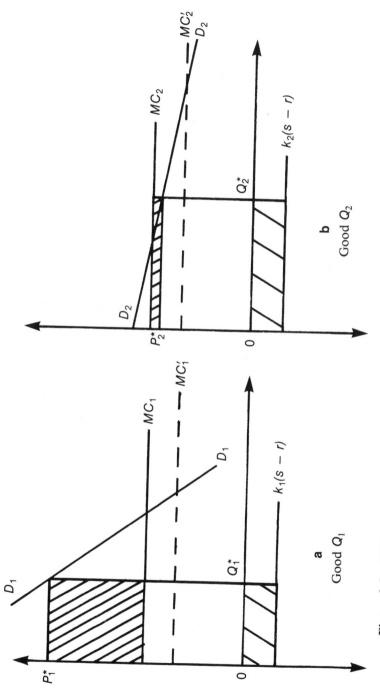

**Figure 3-3.** Different Demands and Same Costs for Two Independent Goods, $Q_1$ and $Q_2$

Once again inefficiency can be traced to the firm's controlling something, in this case its output mix, which it can use strategically to influence its profit. The output mix can affect allowed profit through the capital intensities required for the various outputs and can affect actual profit through their demand elasticities. This failure of *Hope* regulation to supply efficiency incentives will be discussed further in the next section of this chapter.

### Residual Risk Bearing and Oversight Incentives

In choosing a way to decide what profit investors are to receive, a regulatory agency inevitably is deciding, inter alia, how the risks of the enterprise will be borne. So it is appropriate to look explicitly at the risk-bearing consequences of alternative rules.[43] If an original return is applied to an original-cost rate base for instance, as Brandeis urged and as debt is handled according to *Hope*, the return will be well defined but will not necessarily reflect current economic conditions. Table 3-1 indicates the differences that might be expected under original rather than current returns and asset values in the face of three hypothetical events. As noted earlier an increase in the rate of inflation beyond what was anticipated by bondholders in the nominal returns they agreed to will bring a lower than current payment to the bondholders.[44] Relative to basing profit on a current return and rate base, the original or historical basis would then benefit consumers through a lower-profit allowance and hence lower rates. On the other hand, adhering to the original, nominal returns despite a decline in demand or despite management bungling will tend to help investors, because either of these developments would ordinarily lower profit under current competitive-market circumstances. What these examples illustrate is that once a binding agreement has been reached with investors they no longer occupy a residual claimant's position, and events which ordinarily affect profit will instead affect consumers through the rates they pay.

Since adherence to an originally agreed upon rate of return and rate base can cause consumers to bear business risks, one might think that using

### Table 3-1
### Effect of Original Return on Original-Rate Base Relative to Current Return on Current-Rate Base

| Event | Who Gains | Who Loses |
|-------|-----------|-----------|
| Unanticipated inflation | Consumer | Investor |
| Decline in demand | Investor | Consumer |
| Management failure | Investor | Consumer |

the current return and current reproduction-value rate base would avoid it. But even though choosing a current return gives a regulatory agency the opportunity to reward good performance and punish bad, complete business risk still is not apt to be borne by investors as it is in competitive markets. The reason is that a regulatory authority cannot distinguish the efficiency of management performance as would a competitive market, where alternative suppliers, including new entrants, set an unambiguous efficiency standard and impose harsh penalties on those who fail to meet it. Surely no such standard exists now in regulated markets where allowable profit is determined by regulatory commissions. If costs rise due to management failings or if excess capacity results from its bad planning, the regulatory commission may not detect the true causes. And if the commission is unable to make such judgments reliably and set appropriately low current returns when management is at fault, consumers will bear the consequences or the risks. For example, if a regulatory commission accepts the firm's estimate of circumstances as reasonable and merely adds on a current rate of return to determine rates then obviously the consumer is bearing risks of management performance that should ordinarily fall to the investor.

Attempts by regulatory commissions to evaluate management tend to probe the prudence rather than the effectiveness of decisions and to examine procedural rather than substantive achievements. Somewhat like the use of original-cost valuation and original returns, the prudence of a decision is judged on circumstances at the taking of a decision rather than on its results. Of course prudent decisions may turn out inappropriate later on—like buying a large car before the price of oil quadrupled—and it is possible to rationalize such actions. Decisions that failed to anticipate such developments would seldom be ruled imprudent by any jurist. Many prudent decisions would fail the market test, however, as the owner of any gas guzzler knows today. Relying as they do on actual events, markets provide a far more ruthless test of economic performance than an ex post weighing of prudence. Naturally, the manager who is held to a prudence test will lean toward what will later be defensible as prudent, rather than taking risks to improve efficiency.

Whether original or current-asset values or returns are used to estimate allowed profit, there is considerable scope for discretion by a regulatory commission in deciding what rates to allow, owing partly to the operational difficulty that was noted earlier in this chapter supra of measuring equity-capital cost as a basis for allowed return. Commission discretion can be a source of uncertainty since, for their returns, investors may depend more on how the discretion is exercised than on the underlying risks of the business. That is why major Wall Street advisory services seem to spend as much time evaluating commissions as they do analyzing the circumstances of individual public utilities. They systematically consider not only the rate of return a commission tends to allow, but such other factors as the time taken to process rate cases, how construction work in process and other accounting matters are handled, whether automatic input-price adjustment clauses are allowed, and whether the basis for a decision is a recently completed test year or a hypothetical future period in which anticipated input-price changes are taken into account.[45] The ratings given commissions correlate well with bond ratings and stock values of the utilities they regulate, and the ratings also have been explained empirically by political variables (for example, elected commissions tend to have less favorable ratings than appointed commissions) and competence measures (for example, higher salaries tend to be earned at commissions with more favorable ratings).[46] Thus regulatory commissions have scope to create different environments for the firms they regulate, and apparently they use it.

This possibility that the regulatory commission may influence a firm's market value is itself an important matter. It is seldom possible to observe the cost of capital for a regulated firm independently of the commission's actions. The reason is that investors' expectations about commission behavior will influence firms' values. In unregulated competitive firms, where equilibrium is forced by new entrants' actions at current-capital costs, shares have values growing out of their residual claim on earnings. In regulated industries, on the other hand, a great reserve of monopoly power stands between the shareholder and a genuine residual claimant's position. Since the commission essentially decides how much of that monopoly power will go unused, the reserve-monopoly power gives the commission great discretion, and investors naturally form expectations about how it will be used. It is not surprising then that ordinary-valuation mechanisms for unregulated firms may not function in the same way for regulated firms.

What is wanted here is regulation that will yield market values consistent with investors expectations about underlying economic conditions, without the intrusion of separate and unrelated effects from the regulatory process. Robert J. Gelhaus and Gary D. Wilson sought such consistency through their recommendation that commissions estimate a firm's cost of equity capital from the earnings-price ratio for its common stock.[47] Allowing a higher return on the physical-capital rate base will so enhance market value that the earnings-price ratio will tend to fall, while lowering the allowed return will raise the earnings-price ratio so that use of the earnings-price ratio as basis for allowed return should converge on some proper, consistent result. Unfortunately, the earnings-price ratio is so much affected by the allowed return that it is not a simple matter to observe one as basis for the other. The Federal Power Commission (now the Federal Energy Regulatory Commission) proposed (but did not adopt) a similar policy of using the dividend-price ratio plus an observed growth rate of dividends to estimate equity-capital cost rather than the earnings-price ratio.[48] Here again observed returns in a firm cannot be used currently as basis for allowing the returns because they depend so heavily on them.

The difficulty of observing a firm's equity return to use as basis for its allowed return is one reason to question how effectively valuation theories for unregulated firms can be applied to regulated firms. Consider, for example, whether financial leverage will affect returns to equity in regulated firms exactly as the Modigliani and Miller theory would predict.[49] There is little reason for the capital market to enforce the Modigliani and Miller result in the regulated firm because the firm's reserve-monopoly position can insulate share values from effects of leverage changes. And even if the market did reflect such effects the regulatory commission might not be able to act on them to adjust allowed returns accordingly.

If valuation does not follow the Modigliani and Miller theory, or if it does but the commission cannot trace the effect of leverage on equity value to determine allowed return, then by controlling its capital structure the firm may improve its profit. This is yet another case where the firm controls something—in this case its capital structure—which can influence its profit. An example in which greater equity will raise profit has been demonstrated,[50] and the general form of this effect of capital structure on price has also been described.[51] While the problem is more serious when a current return is being estimated, it may also exist to some degree when original returns are maintained for both debt and equity if valuation does not follow the Modigliani and Miller theory.

Deciding what role to give the original basis for estimating asset values or returns, as opposed to the current basis with all its difficulties in estimating the cost of equity capital and judging prudence in performance, can depend partly on one's view of the skill and effectiveness of a regulatory commission. Pessimism about achieving human perfection in the regulatory mechanism may favor the narrower original basis, which gives less discretion to the commission. All parties would simply be required to make binding advance contracts, either with a risk of unanticipated price-level change being created in the process or with some price-level adjustment formula, some indexing scheme, being used to reduce it.[52] And consumers would knowingly bear risks, even risks of management lapses which they might then try to guard against through oversight effort. On the other hand, confidence that the regulatory mechanism can mirror a market process favors reliance on current-asset values and current rates of return, with management evaluation attempted and with more room for political factors and commission competence to affect results. The latter also should be more costly in regulatory effort, because it represents a more ambitious regulatory goal, and without the possibility of genuine new entry into the market it is almost impossible to achieve completely. Moreover, for technologies like nuclear power, which requires capital-intensive facilities that take a long time to build, a case might reasonably be made for placing a greater share of risk on consumers to lower capital cost by maintaining originally agreed upon returns.[53] Perhaps a word should be added here about the incentives of regulators. Not all regulatory commissioners are skillful enough or motivated enough to reach ambitious regulatory goals. And so shareholders of public utilities, consumers, and others affected by regulation can have their fortunes change as regulators change. These effects of the quality of appointments to regulatory posts are seldom stressed but they certainly matter, due largely to the range of possible actions now available to a regulatory commission.

Returning to risk bearing in the firm, it is wrong to think the risks that shareholders are protected from merely vanish; those risks are shifted to consumers.[54] The shift in risk changes incentive and motivation. Consider again the possibility that a regulated firm's management errs, say, by overestimating demand. If the firm were operating in an unregulated competitive market, capacity built in excess of actual demand could precipitate a price war in which consumers would benefit from temporarily low prices but shareholders would suffer. Through their boards of directors these shareholders might sack their overly optimistic managements. Similar results would follow if the management of an unregulated firm failed to control its costs, except then the consumers would see no benefit while the shareholders suffered. In a rate-of-return regulated firm, on the other hand, if demand falls below the level anticipated or if management errors increase costs, the firm almost certainly will ask its regulator to approve higher prices in order that its allowed rate of return be preserved. Because only the most extreme mismanagement is apt to be found imprudent, a rate increase may be awarded, thus shifting the consequences of poor management to consumers. The important point is not merely that a shareholder's burden is placed on consumers through regulation according to *Hope* guidelines, but that as a consequence the shareholder's incentive to see the firm operated efficiently is weakened.

### Sources of *Hope*

Three problems of economic efficiency have been identified in public-utility regulation according to *Hope*: the input determining allowed profit and capital is an object of choice for the utility, so that choice may be biased; outputs may be inefficiently chosen because monopolistic motives remain in the utility to influence rate structure; and setting allowed profit by *Hope* methods interferes with the residual role of profit and distorts risk bearing and oversight functions of investors. Behind each of these problems is the same general cause: allowed profit depends on something the firm can influence, and the exercise of that influence brings inefficiency. After briefly examining alternative proposals, the discussion will again consider these problems to see if they can be avoided.

Four major alternative proposals would use markets in different ways than does current regulation under *Hope* guidelines. First and most complete in its reliance on markets is the alternative of no regulation at all. Even one firm alone in a market will be subject to competitive pressure from potential entrants if entry and exit are easy in a case, for example, where there is no sunk cost. Wherever this pressure from new-market entry can serve to discipline firms, it should give results superior to administrative procedures following *Hope* guidelines. And deregulation is now proceeding in the case of the airline industry, which offers an example where any one market can be entered or departed easily.[55]

In many industries sunk costs are so important that free entry will not reliably exert pressure on existing firms, and for such cases a bidding solution has been proposed.[56] If economies of scale or scope are so great relative to the size of the market that a few firms could achieve lower cost than many firms, competition may not work effectively. Indeed, one firm may be the optimal number for achieving lowest cost, and for its efficiency advantage in this circumstance a community may authorize one supplier to serve its citizens exclusively. Yet when protected from entry, that monopoly firm almost certainly would exploit its market position. To serve the twin purposes of choosing which firm will be awarded the monopoly and of controlling its market power, firms would be required to bid for the position of monopoly supplier. Bidding would be in the form of prices for outputs, prices which would have to be maintained by the winning firm over a well-defined contract period. Since the firm could keep any profit earned under the prices set by its winning contract, a clear efficiency incentive would result. Unfortunately, there are serious weaknesses in this second alternative to rate-of-return regulation.[57] It is not easy to compare bids and thereby to define a winner when there are many outputs to consider, especially if prices are scheduled to change with time over the contract period. And if a winner defaults in any of a large number of possible ways, the public has only limited remedies. The winner also will ordinarily have advantages over other bidders when the contract is to be reconsidered at a later time.

A third proposal would influence incentives by controlling the dynamic setting in which regulated firms make choices, while retaining the *Hope* principles for calculating allowed profits. This proposal simply formalizes and makes predictable the present delay in effecting price changes through the regulatory process, a delay called regulatory lag, by maintaining prices for a specified period during which the firm could keep (suffer) gains (losses) from efficiency improvements (declines).[58] Klevorick and also Vijay S. Bawa and David S. Sibley[59] have shown in detail how incentives in the dynamic setting of firms subject to regulatory lag serve to reduce the worst Averch and Johnson effects. There is still a bias toward capital when the allowed return exceeds the cost of capital, but the bias gets smaller as the allowed return approaches the cost of capital. Moreover, Ingo Vogelsang and Jörg Finsinger[60] have demonstrated that if the levels of the firm's outputs on which allowed profit is calculated are not in the firm's control, as would be partly true when allowed revenue is calculated from some prior period's output levels, the firm can be induced to choose socially desirable relative prices. The firm whose allowed profit at chosen prices must be calculated at preset quantities will not work with marginal revenue, as a monopolist does when its prices determine its outputs. Indeed, if it is required to meet allowed profit by applying proposed prices to preset quantities the firm approaches second-best, or Ramsey, prices.[61] The Vogelsang and Finsinger proposal thus opens up possibilities for overcoming the monopolistic pricing tendencies of utilities regulated according to *Hope* guidelines.

Relying on output prices that are set in advance and maintained over a time interval may cause gains and losses not only from improvements or declines in efficiency, but also from changes in the prices of inputs, prices which are beyond the firm's control. To prevent changes in input prices from seriously affecting the firm's profit while its output prices are predetermined, suitable adjustments in output prices may automatically be made. But even when they are well designed such price adjustment schemes may be perversely exploited by the firm.[62] The firm may use more of the inputs that are included in the automatic-adjustment scheme in order to gain protection from a generally rising-price level, for example, or the firm may raise input quality if that is not controlled to get more productivity as well as higher-output prices. And the firm may not try as hard to find lower prices for inputs when higher prices can be passed quickly to consumers through automatic price-adjustment clauses. Of course whenever output prices are preset, and the firm is free to keep gains from providing services at those prices, there is also the possibility the firm may earn more profit by lowering output quality.

Some of these problems over the specified time interval can be avoided if, instead of adhering to a predetermined price structure, prices are systematically tied to some target that is based on industry costs, a fourth alternative to present practice under *Hope*. Using industry data prevents any one firm from influencing its prices through its own inefficient choices of inputs, outputs, or capital structure, because its own choices no longer influence its prices. A target based on industry data also permits simple adjustment in output prices when input prices change without the perverse consequences of automatic-adjustment formulas, because the industry benchmark responds to input-price changes. A target for price setting based on industry costs was used on any given air-travel route by the Civil Aeronautics Board (CAB) before deregulation. Experience there demonstrated that such a target could be constructed, although it also revealed problems with competition in nonprice dimensions when prices were set too high and new entry was forbidden.[63]

This set of alternative proposals may not be very encouraging when studied singly, since each is not always applicable or it has apparent drawbacks. The properties of the different arrangements might be combined in a variety of ways, however, to improve public-utility regulation. For example, suppose that a target cost from industry-cost data can be predicted in one electric-utility firm as a basis for its prices. The industry-cost data would have to be adjusted skillfully to make a target reasonably suited to a particular firm's circumstances, but suppose that would be possible. Then an appropriate level of capital input would be implicit in a target based on the firm's outputs. The firm's own capital choice would no longer influence its profit allowance so the Averch and Johnson bias could be avoided.[64] And, as already noted, using industry cost can automatically change output prices in response to input-price changes without automatic-adjustment formulas and the perverse responses they elicit. Allowed profit also can be calculated from an output mixture that is fixed and unaffected by currently chosen prices by using, for example, outputs from past history. Then the Vogelsang and Finsinger method creates an incentive in the firm to choose an efficient set of relative prices.

Recent high inflation has caused greater use of a future-test period in rate cases, which in light of the Vogelsang and Finsinger analysis has the drawback that outputs may reflect currently chosen prices. The future-test period is used because it allows costs to reflect anticipated input-price increases that will occur with high inflation. With a target revenue based on industry-cost data, the inflation problem would be less serious because current prices continuously could affect the industry-cost target, making the future-test period unnecessary for easing the impact of inflation. Thus using an industry-cost target could make a past-test period, and the Vogelsang and Finsinger efficient-pricing incentives more feasible. It is true that a past-test period will not eliminate all control by the firm over output. The firm might anticipate the effect current outputs will have when in the future they become past outputs on which allowed profit will be calculated. But altering outputs for such future advantage will require a sacrifice in profit currently, and if the time period between formal reviews is long enough, the current profit opportunity should dominate.

When combined with control over the dynamics of firms' choices, an industy-cost target thus could improve efficiency incentives markedly, because the firm could then improve its profit primarily by improving its efficiency rather than distorting input, output, capital structure, or other choices.[65] Greater efficiency in pricing would also make regulated firms such as electric utilities more comparable to an industry standard. As utilities attempted to achieve better utilization of capacity through efficient-peak and off-peak pricing, their demand patterns would become less distinctive. Problems of comparability between individual conditions and industry patterns would still exist. Solving them is a task all state regulatory authorities could reasonably share collectively. Thus the undertaking could be significant and the chance of success promising.

**Conclusion**

The regulation of privately owned U.S. public utilities has had great difficulty escaping circular reasoning, which in one way or another causes regulatory policy to be determined by regulatory policy. The 1898 *Smyth v. Ames* decision assigned to assets a fair value on which a rate of return was to be allowed. But its reasoning was circular because that fair value of assets actually would depend on the rate of return yet to be determined. To avoid circularity the *Hope* decision in 1944 would reckon assets by any well-defined standard that was independent of the firm's market value, like original-accounting cost or replacement cost, and it shifted attention to setting the rate of return. For the debt portion of capital *Hope* suggested relying on historical-interest rates as capital costs, while for equity it advanced guidelines intended to determine current-capital cost. These debt and equity costs were then weighted together by their associated asset values to obtain an overall return for the firm. Unfortunately these *Hope* procedures for separately treating debt and equity interfere with the market-valuation process for equity and can prevent observation of its true cost. Even if they could be successfully implemented, the *Hope* guidelines ignore their effects on incentives for efficiency in the regulated firm, which their use tends to weaken and distort. These consequences raise serious problems for the already substantial and still growing regulated sector of the U.S. economy.

Many of the problems of rate-of-return regulation have already been identified, and some remedies have been proposed. But none attacks the greatest weakness in rate-of-return regulation, the fact that it jumps directly to the question of what profit to allow owners of a firm rather than specifying a procedure that would relate profit allowances to enterprise performance. When added to the firm's own operating cost to determine revenue requirements, present profit allowances can shift risk bearing to consumers and at the same time remove from shareholders the incentive to pursue efficiency. In addition to weakening the incentive for efficiency, present rate-of-return regulation also distorts it by inviting the use of more capital than is efficient relative to other inputs and by allowing the firm to use demand elasticities in choosing relative prices much as an unregulated monopoly would. Thus, alternative arrangements have been offered for determining capital cost as a basis for allowing profit. But the better defined these arrangements are, the less likely they will reflect current-opportunity cost so necessary to efficient-resource allocation. Assigning franchises by a bidding process, or using regulatory lag, are far from perfect ways to create efficiency incentives.

Many attractive incentives can be created for any public utility if a target can be prepared from industry data as a basis for setting its output prices. For one electric utility, data from 100 others nationally might be used, for example, or from a smaller number of comparable regional utilities. Knowledge about major determinants of cost for that group could be applied to the one utility's mixture of past outputs and other particular circumstances to determine a target revenue. The target revenue would include a target profit based on industry experience. Such a target revenue would be used, rather than the firm's own cost and profit allowance, in establishing its revenue requirement and thus its output prices. As a consequence of this procedure the bias toward capital in electric utilities can be eliminated, as can the regulated firm's incentive to discriminate in price excessively. Probably more important, under this procedure shareholders can suffer more than consumers from poor performance so their incentive to oversee management, which withers under *Hope* guidelines, will be restored. Admittedly, there are many ways to construct the target, and variations can lead to different ways of sharing economic risks and different efficiency incentives.

The existence of feasible improvements to *Hope* regulation suggests embarking on a time of experimentation in which regulatory commissions attempt to move beyond the framework of *Hope* to overcome its major shortcomings.[66] Introducing efficiency incentives can enhance profit, especially for the firms that are first regulated under them, so that except for the incompetent performance of some managers, there is no reason for anyone to lose. Experiments need not bring more chaos to regulation either. Indeed, their main purpose should be to specify and define the regulatory process better, to end the now almost mystical pretense that some market process is being followed.

The goal is to reduce vagueness and ambiguity while giving attention to efficiency incentives and risk bearing. The lessons from alternative arrangements can foster more exact resolution of equity issues that have claimed so much attention already. But because in the past attention was focused almost entirely on what should be the result of a process—profit for shareholders—rather than on the process itself, this century of regulation has yielded remarkably little experience in designing efficiency incentives. If there is to be any hope beyond *Hope* one cannot continue to ignore them.

**Notes**

1. *Munn* v. *Illinois*, 94 U.S. 113 (1877).

2. *Smyth* v. *Ames*, 169 U.S. 466 (1898), and *Federal Power Commission* v. *Hope Natural Gas Co.*, 320 U.S. 591 (1944).

3. *Munn* v. *Illinois*, 94 U.S. 134 (1877).

4. See especially *Chicago* v. *Minnesota*, 134 U.S. 419 (1889), where the court reserved power to declare illegal a rate fixed by state legislature or commission, and *Reagan* v. *Farmers' Loan and Trust Co.*, 154 U.S. 362 (1893), where it exercised such power.

5. Allowed profit was added to a firm's actual operating costs with depreciation and taxes to determine the total revenue that rates, once fixed, would be allowed to generate. The way low rates would then benefit consumers or high rates would benefit investors was articulated in *Covington and Lexington Tpk. Rd. Co.* v. *Sandford*, 164 U.S. 578 (1896).

6. A classic analysis of this asset-valuation issue is available in James C. Bonbright, *Valuation of Property*, 2 vols. (New York: McGraw-Hill, 1937).

7. *Smyth* v. *Ames*, 169 U.S. 466 (1898).

8. Ibid., pp. 546-547.

9. See, for example, John Bauer, *Effective Regulation of Public Utilities* (New York: Macmillan Co., 1925), pp. 68-76, and James C. Bonbright, *Principles of Public Utility Rates* (New York: Columbia University Press, 1961), pp. 136-171.

10. From 1898 to 1907 was also a time when commissions were formed in many states to regulate public utilities. For a history that emphasizes the utilities' role in this development see Douglas D. Anderson, "State Regulation of Electric Utilities," in *The Politics of Regulation*, ed. James Q. Wilson (New York: Basic Books, 1980), pp. 3-41. See also Douglas D. Anderson, *Regulatory Politics and Electric Utilities* (Boston: Auburn House, 1981).

11. For price-level data over the period see George F. Warren and Frank A. Pearson, *Prices* (New York: John Wiley and Sons, 1933).

12. *Southwestern Bell Telephone Company* v. *Public Service Commission of Missouri*, 262 U.S. 276 (1923).

13. *Bluefield Waterworks and Improvement Company* v. *West Virginia Public Service Commission*, 262 U.S. 679 (1923).

14. *Georgia Railway and Power Company* v. *Railway Commission of Georgia*, 262 U.S. 625 (1923).

15. For an analysis of Justice Brandeis' proposal see Roger Sherman, "Ex Ante Rates of Return for Regulated Utilities," *Land Economics* 53 (1977):172-184.

16. Comparative risk had been introduced in 1909 in *Willcox* v. *Consolidated Gas Company*, 212 U.S. 19 (1909), the first important case after

*Smyth* v. *Ames*. A commission had found no constitutional basis for allowing a return greater than the rate of interest, but the court said compensation for risk was appropriate beyond the rate of interest.

17. Bauer, *Effective Regulation of Public Utilities,* pp. 97-103.

18. *Federal Power Commission* v. *Hope Natural Gas Company,* 320 U.S. 591 (1944).

19. For a review of these influences on the *Hope* decision, see Harold Leventhal, "Vitality of the Comparable Earnings Standard for Regulation of Utilities in a Growth Economy," *Yale Law Journal* 74 (1965):989-1018.

20. *Federal Power Commission* v. *Hope Natural Gas Company* 320 U.S., p. 603. Besides applying this earnings guideline to equity rather than to all of the firm's assets, *Hope* did not specify the comparison to earnings of firms in the same region of the country as the *Bluefield* decision did.

21. *Ibid.,* p. 603.

22. Such a division of the firm's assets by source of capital had been suggested in Bauer, *Effective Regulation of Public Utilities,* p. 260.

23. Of course *Hope* helped spawn this variety in practice by emphasizing end results. A record of the creation of many state-regulatory commissions is available in George J. Stigler and Clair Friedland, "What Can Regulators Regulate?: The Case of Electricity," *Journal of Law and Economics* 5 (1962):1-16. For a review of major, early regulatory decisions see Robert H. Montgomery, "Judicial Fair Return and the Price Level," *Southwestern Social Science Quarterly* 12 (1931):221-253, and Harold Leventhal, "Vitality of the Comparable Earnings Standard for Regulation of Utilities in a Growth Economy," pp. 989-1018. A description and criticism of monopoly regulation is available in Richard Posner, "Natural Monopoly and Its Regulation," *Stanford Law Review* 21 (1969):548-643. More recent practice is described in Howard E. Thompson and Lionel W. Thatcher, "Required Rate of Return for Equity Capital under Conditions of Growth and Consideration of Regulatory Lag," *Land Economics* 49 (1973):148-162.

24. For brief descriptions of practices by states see H. Craig Petersen, "The Effect of Regulation on Production Costs and Output Prices in the Private Electric Utility Industry," Memo 151 (Stanford, Calif.: Stanford University Center for Research in Economic Growth, September 1975).

25. Lawrence S. Pomerantz and James E. Suelflow, *Allowance for Funds Used During Construction: Theory and Application* (East Lansing, Mich.: Michigan State University Press, 1977).

26. If the current return on all assets fluctuates, while the return paid to debt is constant, great fluctuations may occur in the residual falling to equity in unregulated firms. For all fluctuations, whether from changes in price level or in interest rate or other cause, must be absorbed entirely by equity capital when the payment to debt is fixed.

27. Franco Modigliani and Merton H. Miller, "The Cost of Capital, Corporation Finance, and the Theory of Investment," *American Economic Review* 48 (1958):261-297. There are many possible ways that changes in policies can affect bondholders relative to shareholders. For analysis of these relations see Michael Jensen and William H. Meckling, "Theory of the Firm: Managerial Behavior, Agency Costs and Ownership Structure," *Journal of Financial Economics* 3 (1976):305-360. On the empirical controversy see Franco Modigliani and Merton H. Miller, "Some Estimates of the Cost of Capital to the Electrical Utility Industry, 1954-57," *American Economic Review* 56 (1966):331-366; Eugene F. Brigham and Myron J. Gordon, "Leverage, Dividend Policy and the Cost of Capital," *Journal of Finance* 23 (1968):85-103; and Robert C. Higgins, "Growth, Dividend Policy and Capital Costs in the Electric Utility Industry," *Journal of Finance* 29 (1974):1189-1201.

28. Bankruptcy is analyzed in Joseph E. Stiglitz, "A Re-Examination of the Modigliani-Miller Theorem," *American Economic Review* 59 (1969):784-793.

29. The consequences of relaxing strong assumptions are shown in William J. Baumol and Burton G. Malkiel, "The Firm's Optimal Debt Equity Combination and the Cost of Capital," *Quarterly Journal of Economics* 81 (1967):547-578.

30. Michael Keran has found empirically that with respect to dividend yields equity shares in regulated firms behave very much like bonds when the rate of inflation is high. This result can be traced to the reliance of most regulatory commissions on the orginal-cost valuation of assets, which effectively makes stockholder returns more like nominal returns. See Michael Keran, "Inflation, Regulation, and Utility Stock Prices," *Bell Journal of Economics* 7 (1976):268-274.

31. Willard T. Carleton, "Rate of Return, Rate Base and Regulatory Lag under Conditions of Changing Capital Costs," *Land Economics* 50 (1974):145-151.

32. Immediate adjustment in rates to maintain an allowed rate of return is possible, but it leaves consumers as risk bearers while treating shareholders essentially as bondholders. For an experiment with this policy see "Cost of Service Index for the Public Service Company of New Mexico" (Santa Fe, New Mexico: New Mexico Public Service Commission Decision and Order in Case No. 1196 April 22, 1975).

33. For the classic analysis see Harvey Averch and Leland L. Johnson, "Behavior of the Firm Under Regulatory Constraint," *American Economic Review* 52 (1962):1052-1069. For elaboration of the split personality that comes to firm's input decisions see Roger Sherman, "The Rate-of-Return Regulated Public Utility Firm is Schizophrenic," *Applied Economics* 4 (1972):23-32. More general dynamic formulations of the commission's

review process tend to moderate the bias toward capital, and to imply efficient outcomes if the allowed return exactly equals the cost of capital. In particular, see Vijay S. Bawa and David S. Sibley, "Dynamic Behavior of a Firm Subject to Stochastic Regulatory Review," *International Economic Review* 21 (1980):627-642, and Alvin K. Klevorick, "The Behavior of a Firm Subject to Stochastic Regulatory Review," *Bell Journal of Economics* 2 (1971):122-153. But there is still a bias if the allowed return is above the cost of capital, and accommodating more realism by considering stochastic demand seems to make the potential bias even greater. On the latter point see Michael A. Crew and Paul R. Kleindorfer, *Public Utility Economics* (New York: Macmillan, 1979), pp. 140-143.

34. This trade-off between the gain from expanded output and the loss from input inefficiency is treated in William S. Comanor, "Should Natural Monopolies Be Regulated," *Stanford Law Review* 22 (1970):510-518; Eytan Sheshinski, "Welfare Aspects of a Regulatory Constraint: Note," *American Economic Review* (1971):175-178; and Roger Sherman, *The Economics of Industry* (Boston: Little, Brown, 1974), p. 390.

35. When demand is inelastic a cut in price of say 5 percent will bring an increase in quantity of less than 5 percent, so the marginal effect is to lower total revenue; that is, marginal revenue is negative. Since marginal cost is always positive, a profit-maximizing firm trying to have marginal cost equal marginal revenue will want to operate where marginal revenue is positive and hence not where demand is inelastic.

36. Fred M. Westfield, "Regulation and Conspiracy," *American Economic Review* 55 (1965):424-443.

37. The general form of this incentive problem in rate-of-return regulation is described by David P. Baron and Robert A. Taggart, Jr., "Regulatory Pricing Procedures and Economic Incentives," in *Issues in Public Utility Pricing and Regulation,* ed. Michael A. Crew (Lexington, Mass.: D.C. Heath and Co. 1980), pp. 27-49. Broader dynamic considerations which again may weaken the bias toward capital are discussed in Paul L. Joskow, "Inflation and Environmental Concern: Structural Changes in the Process of Public Utility Price Regulation," *Journal of Law and Economics* 17 (1974):291-328.

38. Empirical evidence supporting a bias toward capital intensity is presented in Robert M. Spann, "Rate of Return Regulation and Efficiency in Production: An Efficiency Test of the Averch-Johnson Thesis," *Bell Journal of Economics* 5 (1974):38-52; Léon Courville, "Regulation and Efficiency in the Electric Utility Industry," *Bell Journal of Economics* 5 (1974):53-74; and H. Craig Petersen, "An Empirical Test of Regulatory Effects," *Bell Journal of Economics* 6 (1975):111-126. Some empirical tests have failed to confirm the Averch-Johnson bias. See W.J. Boyles, "An empirical Examination of the Averch-Johnson Effect," *Economic Inquiry* 14

(1976):25-35, although this study is marred by its reliance on data from years of the great electrical conspiracy that was revealed in 1962; and David R. Graham, "A Test of the Averch-Johnson Model of Regulation Using Electric Utility Data," (Ph.D. diss., University of California at Los Angeles, 1976). For a review of all previous evidence and a well constructed test that confirms the Averch-Johnson hypothesis see Frederick W. Jones, *Input Biases Under Rate of Return Regulation* (New York: Garland, forthcoming).

39. An early demonstration of the peak and off-peak pricing problem was provided by Stanislaw H. Wellisz, "Regulation of Natural Gas Pipeline Companies: An Economic Analysis," *Journal of Political Economy* 55 (1963):30-43. See also Elizabeth E. Bailey, "Peak-Load Pricing Under Regulatory Constraint," *Journal of Political Economy* (1972):662-679.

40. Demand elasticities at peak and off-peak times conceivably can offset this tendency. See Elizabeth E. Bailey and Lawrence J. White, "Reversals in Peak and Off-Peak Prices," *Bell Journal of Economics* 5 (1974):75-92. The existence of diverse technology, such as base-load, intermediate, and peaking plants in electricity also can complicate the simple case treated in the text. See John T. Wenders, "Peak-Load Pricing in the Electric Utility Industry," *Bell Journal of Economics* 7 (1976):232-241. Rate-of-return regulation nevertheless does not induce peak-load pricing where it would be efficient. A similar case can be made for the effect of rate-of-return regulation on multipart rate structures; see Roger Sherman and Michael Visscher, "Rate-of-Return Regulation and Two-Part Tariffs," *Quarterly Journal of Economics* 97 (1982): forthcoming. For the case of the multiproduct firm see Roger Sherman, "Pricing Inefficiency under Profit Regulation," *Southern Economic Journal* 48(1981):475-489.

41. For examples of peak-load pricing in Europe see Bridger M. Mitchell, Willard G. Manning, Jr., and Jan Paul Acton, *Peak-Load Pricing: European Lessons for U.S. Energy Policy* (Cambridge, Mass.: Ballinger, 1978).

42. See, for example, Herbert Mohring, "The Peak Load Problem with Increasing Returns and Pricing Constraints," *American Economic Review* 60 (1970):693-705.

43. The effective payout and growth rate over time will differ under the two valuation schemes, original or current, but the effective rate of return actually can be made the same. See Myron J. Gordon, "Comparison of Historical Cost and General Price Level Adjusted Cost Rate Base Regulation," *Journal of Finance* 32 (1977):1501-1512.

44. Note that some anticipated rate of inflation is assumed by a bondholder in originally accepting a fixed rate of interest on principal. To the extent they receive the return expected, including enough to offset the rate of inflation plus the risk of not knowing what that rate will be, bondholders

come out about as they would with current returns and current-(reproduction-cost) asset values. On the other hand, if bondholders guess wrongly about inflation they may gain or lose. Although binding early commitments thus force bondholders and consumers to bear the risk of whether the rate of price-level change will differ from what they anticipated, there is one important difference in their positions: the bondholder can insist on being compensated for bearing the risk of price-level change, so consumers ultimately will pay for that risk-bearing function. This risk of price-level change can be reduced by any of a variety of indexing schemes applied to new investments. To adopt such an adjustment after a period of inflation for originially nominal instruments would bring a windfall gain to investors. And with an indexing scheme in force to cut price-level risk, consumers will bear business risks because well-defined financial obligations to bondholders and to shareholders must be met out of the rates they pay.

45. For an example of such an evaluation with a rating of each commission on a scale of one to five see "Utility Research: Recent Regulatory Decisions and Trends" (New York: Securities Research Division of Merrill, Lynch, Pierce, Fenner and Smith, Inc., November 1980). A more general description of these evaluations is available in Peter Navarro, "Electric Utility Regulation and National Energy Policy," *Regulation* 5 (1981):20-27.

46. Peter Navarro, "Public Utility Commission Regulation: Performance, Determinants, and Energy Policy Impacts" (Cambridge, Mass.: Discussion Paper E-80-05, Harvard University Energy and Environmental Policy Center, October 1980).

47. Robert J. Gelhaus and Gary D. Wilson, "An Earnings-Price Approach to Fair Rate of Return in Regulated Industries," *Stanford Law Review* 58 (1968):287-317.

48. "Just and Reasonable Rate of Return on Equity for Natural Gas Pipeline Companies and Public Utilities," (Washington, D.C.: FPC Docket No. RM 77-1, Federal Power Commission Notice of Proposed Statement of Policy, October 15, 1976).

49. See Modigliani and Miller, "The Cost of Capital, Corporation Finance, and the Theory of Investment."

50. Roger Sherman, "Financial Aspects of Rate-of-Return Regulation," *Southern Economic Journal* 44 (1977):240-248.

51. Robert A. Taggart, Jr. "Rate-of-Return Regulation and Utility Capital Structure Decisions," *Journal of Finance* 36 (1981):383-391.

52. See note forty-four. The Accounting Principles Board endorsed in 1969 an accounting practice that would adjust historical cost for general price-level changes, and some fair-value regulatory jurisdictions use such a method for adjusting asset values; see "Accounting for Inflation" (New York: Accounting Principles Board, American Institute of Certified Public Accountants, June 1969. See also the Institute's "Financial Reporting in

Units of General Purchasing Power," December 31, 1974, Exposure Draft. Under this method each asset was given a current value based on the ratio of the current-year price-index value at the time the asset was originally purchased. Problems which arise in accounting for changes due to inflation are treated in Sidney Davidson and Roman L. Weil, "Inflation Accounting for Utilities," *Financial Analysts Journal* 31 (1975):30-34, 62. A review of ways to account for costs during inflation is available in J.A. Kay, "Inflation Accounting—A Review Article," *Economic Journal* 87 (1977): 300-311. After adjusting to make rates of return and rate bases comparable, Petersen found that where the rate base is valued according to fair value the allowed rate of return tends to be higher. See H. Craig Pertersen, "The Effect of 'Fair Value' Rate Base Valuation in Electric Utility Regulation," *Journal of Finance* 31 (1976):1487-1490. See also Walter J. Primeaux, Jr., "Rate Base Methods and Realized Rates of Return," *Economic Inquiry* 16 (1978):237-248.

53. A general argument for having a large population bear risks in order to reduce the burden borne by any one is set out in Kenneth J. Arrow and Robert C. Lind, "Uncertainty and the Evaluation of Public Investment Decisions," *American Economic Review* 60 (1970):364-378.

54. We should note also that since the rates they pay may be above or below current-opportunity costs at any one time, consumers are misled by such rates and will seek less or more of the electricity, natural gas, or other regulated service than prices based on true current-opportunity costs would warrant.

55. John C. Panzar, "Regulation, Deregulation, and Economic Efficiency: The Case of the CAB," *American Economic Review* 70 (1980):311-315, and William J. Baumol and Robert D. Willig, "Fixed Costs, Sunk Costs, Entry Barriers, and Sustainability of Monopoly," *Quarterly Journal of Economics* 96 (1981):405-431.

56. See Harold Demsetz, "Why Regulate Utilities?" *Journal of Law and Economics* 11 (1968):55-65. The original proposal goes back more than a century to Edwin Chadwick, "Results of Different Principles of Legislation and Administration in Europe: of Competition for the Field, as Compared with the Competition Within the Field of Service," *Journal of the Royal Statistical Society* 22 (1859):381-420.

57. See Oliver E. Williamson, "Franchise Bidding for Natural Monopolies—In General and with Respect to CATV," *Bell Journal of Economics* 7 (1976):73-104; Victor Goldberg, "Regulation and Administered Contracts," *Bell Journal of Economics* 7 (1976):426-448; and Walter Schulz, "Conditions for Franchise Bidding in the West German Electricity Sector," in *Regulated Industries and Public Enterprise,* ed. Kleindorfer and Bridger M. Mitchell, (Lexington, Mass.: D.C. Heath and Company, 1980), pp. 57-69.

58. William J. Baumol, "Reasonable Rules for Rate Regulation: Plausible Policies for an Imperfect World," in *The Crisis of the Regulatory Commissions,* ed. Paul W. MacAvoy (New York: W.W. Norton, 1970), pp. 187-206.

59. Klevorick, "Behavior of a Firm Subject to Stochastic Regulatory Review," and Bawa and Sibley, "Dynamic Behavior of a Firm Subject to Stochastic Regulatory Review."

60. Ingo Vogelsang and Jörg Finsinger, "A Regulatory Adjustment Process for Optimal Pricing by Multiproduct Monopoly Firms," *Bell Journal of Economics* 10 (1979):157-171. See also David Sappington, "Strategic Firm Behavior under a Dynamic Regulatory Adjustment Process," *Bell Journal of Economics* 11 (1980):360-372.

61. Ramsey prices differ from marginal cost but only to meet a necessary budget constraint, and in a way that minimizes welfare loss caused by not pricing at marginal cost. For a review of literature defining Ramsey prices see William J. Baumol and David F. Bradford, "Optimal Departures from Marginal Cost Prices," *American Economic Review* 60 (1970):265-283. An illustration showing how the firm might be made to approach Ramsey prices is provided in Roger Sherman, "Hope Against Hope," in Michael Crew, ed. *Issues in Public-Utility Pricing and Regulation,* chapter 2.

62. Frank A. Scott, Jr., "An Economic Analysis of Fuel Adjustment Clauses" (Ph.D. diss., University of Virginia, 1979); Michael Schmidt, *Automatic Adjustment Clauses: Theory and Application* (East Lansing, Mich,: Michigan State University Press, 1981); and David P. Baron and Raymond De Bondt, "Fuel Adjustment Mechanisms and Economic Efficiency," *Journal of Industrial Economics* 27 (1979):24-41.

63. George Douglas and James C. Miller, III, *Economic Regulation of Domestic Air Transport: Theory and Policy* (Washington, D.C.: Brookings, 1974).

64. Sherman, "Hope Against *Hope,*" pp. 15-17.

65. Indeed, target revenue would combine the efficiency advantage of unchanging (and therefore out of the firm's control) output prices with the responsiveness of adjustment clauses, yet not require the trade-off between those efficiency and responsiveness goals as described in Richard Schmalensee, *The Control of Natural Monopolies* (Lexington, Mass.: D.C. Heath and Co., 1979), pp. 101-137.

66. Several states, notably Florida, Massachusetts, Michigan, New Mexico, Utah, and Wisconsin have recently adopted new procedures in an experimental way that should yield valuable information about alternative arrangements.

# 4 Electric-Utility Pricing Issues: Old and New

*Robert G. Uhler*

Pricing electricity has been a fascinating puzzle since the days of Thomas A. Edison. The wizard of Menlo Park, for example, considered selling light rather than electric energy but settled for cents per kilowatt-hour. He also thought that it might make good business sense to price electricity in a way that encouraged daytime usage—Edison had earlier captured the lion's share of the nighttime-illumination market in cities. Since then equally ingenious ideas about pricing have popped up like mushrooms in fertile soil as the ubiquitous kilowatt-hour has become one of the all-time success stories in consumer marketing. Pricing a service that now produces annual revenues in excess of $100 billion is still fascinating but is no trivial undertaking because of long-unresolved costing and rate-making issues.

For decades this marvelous service brought new wonders into the marketplace—light bulbs, air conditioners, television, and home computers. Moreover, as if the electric-utility industry's engineers had invented a perpetual-motion machine, the cost of electricity fell and so did its price. Finally, electric-utility marketing experts were eager and able to unleash the genie of economies of scale. They designed electric rates with declining blocks, demanded forgiveness provisions, and other sophisticated pricing wrinkles to spread the use of electricity. The industry was successful—sales doubled each decade.

Not only were families in rural areas connected to the magic of a turbine generator, but the whole society was electrified—literally and figuratively. With a kilowatt-hour sometimes selling for mills not cents, the use of electricity crept into almost every nook and cranny of economic activity—from production to consumption and all points in between.

During this golden era Edison's legacy produced an enormous amount of consumer satisfaction relative to price—usage spread even further. Nevertheless, most ratepayers were oblivious to the grubby details of electricity pricing; not so the crafty engineers who could see beyond Ohm's law. As early as the turn of the century, many of the pricing issues of the 1980s had been spelled out by electric-industry entrepreneurs such as Henry L. Doherty.[1] Other experts, perhaps less colorful than Doherty, such as John Hopkinson and Arthur Wright, set forth the technical intricacies of rates.

In the 1920s utility-cost analysis emerged as it is known today. Back in the roaring twenties, the rate engineers of the electric-utility industry were busy grinding out articles about allocating capacity costs, gauging peak responsibility, and sharing diversity benefits.[2] By 1927, however, one rate expert was compelled to point out the fallacies and limitations of the existing methods of allocating fixed costs. He went on to describe his own way of determining the "true cost of service to each consumer."[3] That particular costing expert no more solved the joint-cost problem than his predecessors or successors.

After World War II the industry surged ahead—hooking up its 40 millionth customer and selling more than one-quarter trillion kilowatt-hours in a year. In almost every home, store, and factory, a glass-enclosed meter spun relentlessly on, silently measuring energy used. Edison's wildest dreams were surpassed—a virtually uninterrupted flow of service was being sold to almost everyone around the clock. Costs fell and so did prices.

By the 1950s utilities began to purchase tabulators and later computers for billing and bookkeeping. With these office machines, rate managers and accountants learned to arrange a utility's costs in infinite patterns of increasing complexity. The two-pound cost-of-service study based on accounting costs emerged as the empirical, often impressive, and sometimes opaque basis for rate design.

These cost studies, actually elaborate arithmetic-computer runs, converted the cost-allocation ideas of the rate experts of the mid-1920s into the rate hearing exhibits of the 1960s. The ability to manipulate enormous amounts of data quickly and accurately obscured an important point: the basic logic of costing for rate making had not changed much in some thirty-five years. The wondrous calculating machines, however, allowed rate managers to try different costing approaches and to compare the end results on a consistent basis. Within the traditional conventions of embedded costs, creative costing for rate making was possible. Nevertheless, the joint-cost allocation debates continued. (Some utilities eventually "solved" the problem by programming their computers to do the cost-of-service study five different ways—one for each allocation method.)

In the early 1960s Professor James C. Bonbright reviewed the industry's formidable costing and pricing issues. He wrote that the "nightmare of utility cost analysis" is the apportionment of joint costs.[4] Bonbright recognized that this particular problem involved the allocation of capacity-related costs both to customer classes and to time periods—both seasonal and diurnal. Thus, some twenty years ago, he anticipated various key issues about time-differentiated costing and time-of-day pricing.

An academician as well as a consultant to utilities, Bonbright pointed out that traditional accounting cost-based methods might fail to distinguish between mere cost apportionment and actual-cost causality.[5] He cautioned that some fully distributed cost studies were based on a "compromise formula of apportionment that depends not on principles of cost imputation but rather on types of apportionment [of joint costs] which tend to justify whatever rate structure is advocated for noncost reasons."[6]

Bonbright also explained—in the early 1960s—that demand-related costs "are usually derived from book values of plant and equipment that reflect sunk costs in dollars of original investment" and that these costs cannot "be said to vary, except in a very indirect way, with present and future increases in plant capacity."[7] He noted that there were two ways of dealing with the costing problem. Bonbright argued that the really important cost analyses were not those which attempt to apportion total capital and operating costs among the different classes or units of service. Instead, he urged that cost analyses disclose differential, incremental, marginal, or escapable costs. Bonbright said that such costs ordinarily are not derivable from total costs and cannot be added together to equal that total. Thus, Bonbright anticipated both the marginal-cost study and the revenue-reconciliation problem of electric rates based on marginal costs.

Bonbright wrote that "a thorough reexamination of the whole philosophy of modern public utility cost analysis has been long overdue."[8] He made this observation at a time when the electric-utility industry was approaching its apogee. Costs were still falling, growth seemed unlimited, and consumers were happy. Investors were satisfied, and utility managers were enjoying the boom. Nevertheless, Bonbright observed that if this were Great Britain, a government commission would be appointed to make such a study of costing and rate making. It is hardly surprising that a rigorous self-appraisal of the industry's pricing issues was not launched in those heady times.

In the 1960s state regulators presided over rate decreases—cutting up the pie to see which group of customers got the biggest reduction. Declining-block rates were in vogue as growth in usage precipitated still lower costs and rates—growth in demand was good for everyone. Or so it seemed, as all-electric, gold-medallion homes sprung up in suburbia. Annual sales passed the trillion kilowatt-hours level in 1966.

Like most U.S. institutions, the electric industry took its lumps in the late 1960s and then almost suffered a mortal wound in the early 1970s. At first gradually, and then with a rush after the oil embargo, the industry's costs began to mount—in real terms as well as in nominal terms. Customers grew restive in direct proportion to the increase in their monthly bills. Growth in the demand for electricity actually stopped for a year in 1974, yet incredibly, monthly bills continued to rise. Outrage replaced concern, as rate payers grappled with double-digit inflation, shrinking paychecks, and soaring energy costs.

The regulators' happy days were over. Utility financial executives crumpled—investors choked, and the glory days of the electric-utility industry ended when Consolidated Edison failed to pay a dividend. The Organization of the Petroleum Exporting Countries (OPEC) and inflation were too much for state regulators to swallow. The industry's financial juices were sucked dry; bond ratings tumbled, market-to-book ratios dropped below one, and interest coverage slid downhill. Electric-utility rate managers were perplexed, hardly enjoying their emerging prominence in the corporate hierarchy.

In this era of calamity, Bonbright's ideas of rate reform, particularly marginal costing and time differentiation, found new champions. One of them, Alfred E. Kahn of Cornell University, produced a timely and definitive economic textbook on marginal-cost pricing.[9] His book included a careful and detailed argument for marginal-cost pricing. Then, metamorphosed into the chairman of the New York Public Services Commission, Kahn conducted a postgraduate seminar on modern-day utility pricing. The lawyers called this the New York generic hearings, although it seemed more like an examination of doctoral candidates in economics. After the hearings, Kahn wrote his decision and tersely explained why marginal costs were always relevant for electricity pricing and absolutely necessary in the 1970s.[10] Gone were the annotated academic asides, stripped away were the tortuous theoretical arguments.

A year earlier one of Kahn's students—Irwin M. Stelzer, had led a hardy band of economists across the Hudson River and into the heartland. There in Wisconsin in the now famous *Madison Gas & Electric Company* case, Stelzer et al. set out the conceptual framework for what was then called LRIC—long-run incremental costs—what Bonbright had argued for and Kahn had written about—had finally materialized in a utility-rate case.[11]

Later this group reiterated its marginalist views in New York (at the generic hearings noted above), California, North Carolina, and a dozen other states. The industry's reaction to the marginalists was mixed. LRIC was translated by some rate engineers as "Let's Run Irwin's Coming!" Other rate managers were somewhat more open minded.

In 1974 some thirteen years after Bonbright had called for a government commission to examine pricing issues, the National Association of Regulatory Utility Commissioners passed Resolution No. 9. This started the Electric Utility Rate Design Study—a nationwide investigation of electric-utility costing and rate-making issues. That study eventually produced over 100 reports on rate design and direct-load controls—what came to be known as load management.[12]

While the study was in process, the industry also was engaged in the great rate debate in hearings and symposia all over the United States and Canada (the costing issues were also debated in England, France, and elsewhere). On the one hand hundreds of people were trying to weigh the merits of Bonbright's suggestion to analyze differential, incremental, marginal, or escapable costs. On the other hand even more people were trying to pump new life into fully distributed costs by time-differentiating accounting costs—a task that would challenge Sisyphus.

Not to be outdone by state regulators and local utility-rate experts, the federal government weighed in belatedly with its National Energy Act. The new law included provisions which Mississippi regulators later branded as unconstitutional. The offending law—the Public Utility Regulatory Policies Act of 1978 (PURPA)—was not the national exercise envisioned by Bonbright (perhaps the Rate Design study came close). Instead, PURPA forced each state to consider such issues as marginal-cost pricing, time-of-day rates, and below-cost lifeline rates.

Part of the state regulators' aversion to PURPA was directed at the federal camel as the beast poked its nose into the tent of state regulation. Until 1978 utility pricing at the retail level had been the sacrosanct turf of state government. Another part of the commissioners' reluctance to embrace the rate-making standards of PURPA was a fear of upsetting the delicate balance among rates of various customer classes and within classes that had been constructed over the glory years. But that balance was already threatened by the huge cost increases of the 1970s. Rate increases were tough enough for regulators to justify to consumers—changing the rules of costing and rate design were seen as running the risk of adding insult to injury.

Thus, Bonbright's wisdom—not heeded in the 1960s because those times were too good—was transformed and catalogued remorselessly in PURPA in the 1970s because times were so bad. Yet there was no denying a set of ideas whose time had finally come. In brief, utility managers and state regulators could no longer ignore the link between changes in output and changes in costs as well as the time-varying nature of costs. Bonbright's criticism and foresight had finally and broadly surfaced.

Moreover, support for rate reform widened. Utility executives, pummeled by inflation, recognized that inappropriate costing and rate making had contributed to their woes. Environmentalists saw the repeal of declining-block rates as proconservation. And consumer advocates quickly noted the possibility of using marginal costing as a means of attaining their ends. Economists, of course, saw marginal-cost pricing as the means of balancing efficiency, conservation, and consumer sovereignty.

Today, annual sales exceed 2 trillion kilowatt-hours. And most utilities pay close attention to marginal costs not only for rate making but also for evaluating conservation programs and setting rates for cogeneration (the term avoided costs had been added to Bonbright's other synonyms for marginal costs). Moreover, many state regulators have found ways to move toward marginal costs and time-of-day rates as ways of improving electric-utility pricing without destroying the industry or its customers in the process.

The issue for the 1980s is not to debate the merits of marginal-cost pricing or time-of-day rates—ideas articulated by Bonbright two decades ago and clearly understood by the industry experts of today. The issue for the 1980s is to reaffirm Bonbright's three primary criteria for sound rate making—revenue adequacy, optimal use of service, and fairness—and doggedly pursue marginal-cost pricing as a means to achieve those time-honored ends.

## Notes

1. Henry L. Doherty, "Equitable Uniform and Competitive Rates," in *Proceedings of National Electric Light Association* (May 1900), pp. 291-321.

2. See, for example, W.J. Greene, "Determining Demand Charge," *Electrical World* 86 (November 7, 1925):947; H.A. Snow, "Sharing Benefits of Diversity in Loads," *Electrical World* 87 (February 20, 1926):403-404; A.S. Knight, "Peak Responsibility as a Basis for Allocating Fixed Costs," *Electrical World* 87 (February 20, 1926):495-496; W.J. Greene, "Allocating Capacity Costs," *Electrical World* 87 (May 29, 1926):1190-1193; H.W. Hills, "Demand Costs and Their Allocation," *Electrical World* 89 (January 22, 1927):198-203; H.W. Hills, "Proposed Allocation of Demand Costs," *Electrical World* 89 (January 22, 1927):249-252; and W.J. Greene, "Excess Peak Responsibility versus Demand in Cost Studies," *Electrical World* 90 (July 23, 1927):165-167.

3. H.W. Hills, "Demand Costs and Their Allocation," pp. 198-203.

4. James C. Bonbright, *Principles of Public Utility Rates* (New York: Columbia University Press, 1969), pp. 350-351.

5. Ibid., p. 367.

6. Ibid.

7. Ibid.

8. Ibid.

9. Alfred E. Kahn, *The Economics of Regulation: Principles and Institutions*, vol. 1 (New York: John Wiley & Sons, Inc., 1970).

10. State of New York Public Service Commission, *Opinion and Order Determining Relevance of Marginal Costs to Electric Rate Structures*, Opinion No. 76-15, August 10, 1976.

11. Wisconsin Public Service Commission, Decision in Docket No. 2-U-7423, August 8, 1974.

12. See the various publications of the Electric Utility Rate Design Study, Electric Power Research Institute.

# Part III
# Trends and Issues in the Structure and Functions of Regulatory Agencies

# 5 Regulation in the Southeast

## Introduction

### John B. Legler

From the perspective of the consumer probably no state agency, not even the state legislature, affects their pocketbook as much as their state public-service commission. From the perspective of the utility companies, regulatory risk, although discretely played down, is of equal importance as business and financial risks. For the commissioners themselves, regulation is a no-win situation. In the current environment of inflation, high cost of money, and consumerism, theirs is a tough job with little prospect of pleasing many.

It is apparent that no two commissions are alike. The structure, staffing, and policies of commissions are of vital concern to us all. Thus, trends and issues concerning the structure and functions of public-service commissions are topics worthy of discussion. What follows are edited versions of discussions on structure, staffing, and policies made by three commissioners from different states. These commissioners, Leigh Hammond of North Carolina, John Marks of Florida, and Ford Spinks of Georgia represent three states with notable differences in the structure of their respective commissions. The commissioners themselves represent both elected and appointed office holders.

## Comments

### Leigh H. Hammond, Commissioner

The earlier history of regulation in North Carolina shows that its regulatory commission evolved in much the same manner as most states. Initially the railroad commission was created and then, over time, the state assumed many other different responsibilities, such as banking, insurance, and the whole spectrum of utility operations.

In the early part of this century, some of those functions began to be assumed by other agencies and other commissions such as the Banking Commission or the Insurance Commission. The North Carolina commissions then concentrated primarily on the transportation utilities, such as intrastate railroad, intrastate trucking, the electric utilities, and the telephone and natural-gas distribution companies. The commission regulates some 500 or 600 small-water and sewer companies ranging from 15 customers up to 600. When developers go outside city limits and develop a housing complex that is not on either county or city utilities, they often set up a private water-sewer utility. If this utility expands beyond ten customers, then it comes under the regulation of the commission. The commission also regulates two water-transportation companies on the coast. Boat owners who take tourists from the mainland to some of the outer banks and leave them off are regulated by the commission. If they just take them out, let them look at the outer banks, then bring them back, the commission does not regulate them. Obviously the commission handles a wide spectrum of activities.

## The Commissioners

In the early history of the commission there was only one commissioner. As the workload expanded, two associate commissioners were appointed. The two associate commissioners came into town periodically to help the other. In the early forties, they expanded to five fulltime commissioners, which is how it remained until the 1970s. Until that time there was not a great deal of controversy. In fact, many of the citizens probably did not even know that the commission existed. They dealt primarily with transportation issues; occasionally they would lower electric rates during that period when rates were decreasing.

Then, in the early 1970s, which brought the Arab oil embargo, things fell apart rapidly. There was a backlog of cases; before one case could be determined, another case would come in. Not only did consumers get angry in public hearings, they got so angry they went to the legislature. The legislators realized some changes had to be made.

Regulatory lag was rampant. In 1975 the legislature expanded the commission from five to seven members and changed the process of appointing the commissioners. Previously the governor would appoint whomever he wished. Now the governor nominates the person and the House and Senate have separate hearings by their utilities committee on the individual. Once these committees approve the nomination, the House and Senate come together in joint session to confirm the nominee. This provides a little more involvement by the legislature, and the public can also participate in these confirmation hearings.

Also in 1975, the legislature imposed some strict standards on the time limitations to get through a rate case once it was submitted. There is a six-month deadline from the effective date of the rate increase. The company also has to give a thirty-day notice before they come in for a rate case. Once they file a rate case with an effective date of, say, April 1, then six months from that effective date a decision must be completed, all investigation completed, hearings completed, and an order issued. Otherwise, the rates go into effect under bond. If the six-month deadline is not met, there is another nine-month deadline. If the case is not finished by this time, then the commission gives up its involvement, and the rates become permanent. There is a proviso that rates put into effect under bond cannot be higher than a 20 percent increase on any customer class. So there is a ceiling, but a 20 percent rate increase is high.

*Commission Staff*

There was still concern by the public regarding how well they were represented in the commissions proceedings. Between 1975 and 1977 when there was an expanded commission and more strict deadlines on getting out the cases, there was much study of what could be done to improve the representation of the general public before the commission. Previously, the attorney general's office had that responsibility. It had a very small staff. The commission had a staff of accountants, lawyers, economists, and engineers who could file testimony in rate cases, yet there was always the feeling that the commission staff was not really free to truly represent the public point of view. They had to take a judicial role almost like the commissioners, although some of the companies felt that they were advocates. But still, there was the question of how strongly they could represent the public and still have essentially the same concerns as the commissioners in weighing all sides, and of how they could be sure the company was viable, while at the same time trying to keep rates down.

Some companies were concerned that the commission's staff had an undue advantage because they had the last say with the commissioners. The staff actually sat right in the office in the decision-making conferences, and they could come back and reinforce the positions they had taken in the case. The company didn't have that privilege, so this exparte communication issue was a valid one.

In 1977 the legislature took essentially half of the commission staff and set it apart as an independent, autonomous public staff of the commission. An executive director, who is nominated and confirmed in the same manner as commission members, was placed in charge of the staff. The commission has no authority over the public staff, although they are housed in the same building. They are an independent agency and serve as an advocate for the using and consuming public in all the rate cases. They have economists, engineers, and accountants who file testimony in the interest of the public.

That system has worked well. Thus far there has been no abuse of this opportunity by an executive director who wants to make a political name for himself, which certainly is possible. They can take, if they so choose, some very harsh positions and get the headlines. Then the commission has to mediate the different points of view and come out with a reasonable decision. Generally, the public staff has taken a fairly responsible position. There are always some instances open to question, but most critical in importance is that the executive director has not taken totally unreasonable positions. They probably will not in the future, by virtue of the process of nomination and confirmation. If it does happen, then this type of public-staff operation would be very difficult, and it would be very difficult for the commissioners. If somebody in every instance says companies should not get a raise and that in fact they should be cut, that makes it very difficult for the commission in an inflationary environment.

*Types of Cases Heard*

An important part of this structure is that the commissioners essentially hear all cases. There was a law that, up until this year, said that if any utility came in and asked for more than $100,000 increase in revenue, either a single commissioner, a panel of three, or the full commission had to hear the case. There aren't too many utilities that are coming in and asking only $100,000 increase in revenue—only small-water and sewer companies and similar operations. Hearing examiners hear these smaller cases and come with a recommended order. There is a time limit during which any party can take exception to the recommended order. If they do take exception, they come before the full commission and have oral arguments. Then the full commission either affirms that order or changes it.

By virtue of that provision on revenue requirement, legislation was sought this year to increase that level to $300,000. This will take off some additional burden yet will still dictate that the commission, either as a full commission or a panel of three, hear all major cases involving natural gas, electric, and telephone. Occasionally, some truck or railroad issue would also come before the commission. So this is the sort of division of responsibility or work load between the commissioners and hearing examiners.

In other states some of the commissioners don't have to sit in on hearings at all. If they so choose, they can, but an examiner or administrative-law judge runs the hearing, and they sit mainly for their own enlightenment. In North Carolina one of the commissioners chairs the hearing and runs the whole proceeding.

*Issues that Face the Commission*

Looking at recent issues that have come before the commission, there have been many hearings and debates on the issues of load management, that is, how to moderate the increase in demand for electricity. North Carolina, like many other states, has had experiments, and many of those have ended with mixed and uncertain results. It isn't certain whether time-of-day pricing and direct-load-control procedures are cost effective. As the cost of fuels and the cost of building new plants continue to escalate, the commission will have to get serious about load management and rate-design procedures to be sure the customer is really paying what its costing to provide that power at the time the customer wants it. That issue has got to be kept before the commission.

By looking at some of the small utilities, which essentially purchase all of their power, such as the co-ops, one can see the impact of demand charges that are put on them when they are taking that electricity at peak time—there is a great incentive for load management. They search and use direct-load-control procedures, perhaps more than time-of-day pricing, but they use those procedures effectively and cut their costs of electricity by keeping that peak demand from jumping up so much.

The commission has data from some of the small utilities in New England with 100,000 customers, and they have water-control devices on essentially half of their water heaters. They have programs to install efficient water heaters and charge five or six dollars a month to the customer. They are installing 500 or 600 of those a month on a small system. If that's effective there, then a utility that has a million customers and is having to build nuclear plants and coal plants to meet that peak demand, and if there is an effective rate system to really trace those costs, then it would be desirable to be more vigorous and aggressive in doing the same types of load-management procedures that those other small companies are doing.

The commission in recent years, by virtue of increased cost construction, has gotten more serious about looking at where the commission is going and what will be the future demand for electricity. Load-forecasting procedures have become a more important aspect of commission work in North Carolina and of other commissions. During the legislative change in 1975 and 1977, the state passed a law that says the commission itself must make an independent load forecast of the future demands for electricity.

Previously, the companies would come in and say "this is what we project our demand to be, we are going to build these plants to meet that demand," and the commission reviewed it in a hearing procedure. That was all right as long as one accepted the idea of extending-the-straight-line-another-notch-up-each-year process at 8 percent or 10 percent growth, which was normal for a long period of time. However, when all the elements of the oil embargo and other factors started infringing upon the cost of electricity and therefore on the demand, the commission needed better estimation techniques. According to the legislature, it needed independent evaluations of future demand. Each year the commission does an independent forecast of what the future demand for electricity is going to be over the next fifteen years or so. Then hearings are held where the companies present their estimates, the public staff comes with their projections, and then the commission reaches a judgment from all these projections.

The legislature also passed a rather permissive law that says the commission could engage in a management audit of the major electric, telephone, and natural-gas companies every five years. That has been done in a number of instances, and it is about time to face the decision of whether the commission is going to do these again on some of the major utilities. The real value of these audits is questionable. There has never been a management-audit report that said things were bad or even marginally bad. So one asks these consultants about this, and they say that the advantage to the thing is that in the commission's interaction with the company it pointed out many of these things and many got corrected in the process of the management audit. That happens, but the commission's reservations about management audits is not limited to utility companies. How much does a management audit of a private firm really help? It is not just that they do not come across critically for utilities. They do not really get down to the nub of things in management audits in general.

Another big issue is the financial condition of the industry, especially electric utilities. Regulatory lag is an issue, inadequate rate of return on equity is an issue. All of those issues are very much up front. There are many proposals for improving the financial condition of the industry. No one seriously questions the need for this.

Talk about deregulation is happening in the telephone industry and in trucking. I am generally supportive of deregulation because I am an economist and believe in the beneficial things that can happen with a free market. But there is no need to rush pell mell into deregulation because there was a rationale for regulation originally and that rationale still exists. I may have become too deeply involved, yet all the issues of deregulation need to be examined. Deregulate where it is clearly beneficial, but where an exclusive franchise exists, some regulation must be kept to protect the customers.

There have been discussions about deregulation of electric-generating facilities. There has not been a great deal of thought given to what the impact of that would be and how it would really work. It is easy to say the state should deregulate the generation of electric energy. It is a different matter to say how it would work in a real setting. If it is opened up, who would enter the business? In a free market, there must be entry and exit. Is anyone chomping at the bit to build a multibillion-dollar nuclear-generating plant? People have not really gotten down to what is involved and the ultimate impact of the issue. The issue calls on the regulatory community, the academic community, and the utility companies to start digging in on this. Some information should be gotten out on what would be involved, how it might work, and whether deregulation would be beneficial.

Another catchword for solving the financial condition in the industry is diversification. Some utilities have gotten into energy sources such as coal and uranium mining as well as things that are not closely related to the utility function. Recently there has been debate about getting into the insulation business or the solar business. No responsible regulator wants the regulated portion of the business to gain any unfair advantage by virtue of any diversification efforts. By the same token, the diversified operation, that is, the nonutility function, should not gain an advantage by coming in under the umbrella of the regulated business. Those things should be kept separate.

Looking to the future, the commission is going to have to begin taking a more in-depth look at the actual performance of the utility systems. It needs to look both at the system and the plant level of operations, at the availability of the units within a system to produce power, at their scheduled and nonscheduled outage, their forced outages, how they are performing, and make some in-depth evaluations of how those systems are functioning and whether they are functioning as they should.

One could discuss many of the issues such as deregulation and diversification for any particular type of utility for which all of those things apply. One could go down the list of telephone, natural gas, truck, water, and sewer and talk about some aspect of those major issues that are before commissions at this time. It is important that the commission deal effectively with these things because of the impact that regulation of utilities and provision of utility services has on the general public.

A judge on the appeals court was introduced to one of the state interns in order to acquaint the intern with some of the processes of the court. The judge commented about the important role that a utility commission plays in the life of the citizens. He said that except for the general assembly of North Carolina, the utilities commission has a greater impact on the life of the citizens in North Carolina than any other state agency; and it turns out the commission may actually impact a little more in billions of dollars than the legislature passes in taxes. This is just an illustration of how serious these problems are. It takes a joint effort and takes essentially firm regulation but not unreasonable regulation. One has to recognize how all the parts fit together, the impact on the citizens, the impact on the company, and how one mediates all of these to come out with a firm regulatory process.

**John B. Legler:** When you went to the appointment system it apparently is a serious confirmation hearing situation. What kinds of people are now on the commission, and what kind of expertise do they bring that might improve the regulatory process?

**Commissioner Hammond:** The present governor made a commitment in his campaign to restructure the commission. The changes were an important plank of his campaign and flowed from that commitment. But after he was elected, he had several positions to fill. I was the first person he talked to. I was an economist on the faculty of North Carolina State University and was assistant vice-chancellor for extension and public service when the governor called me. He said, "I want an economist on the commission and you are the first one I thought about and I want you to consider taking the appointment."

The only reason this happened is that he and I were in graduate school together. He had gotten a masters in economics while I was getting my doctorate. He then went to law school instead of getting his Ph.D. and ultimately got into politics. He called me and that started the chain of circumstances. As things progressed, I decided why not. I needed a challenge here in late life but it has turned out to be something of an aggravation!

When the governor was about to announce my nomination he said, "I'm going to nominate another one and do it at the same press conference. You are going to be pleased with whom I name." That person was Bob Koger, who was head of the engineering staff on the commission. Koger also has a master's in economics from North Carolina State University. He is an engineer with a background similar to mine. Next, the governor appointed a Ph.D. in physics and that individual ultimately left the commission and went over as the public-staff director. Then, he appointed a female lawyer from the Raleigh area. Next, he appointed counsel from the commission staff who had been there fourteen years, and, finally, he appointed a black businessman who had been a member of the North Carolina Senate. I think you can see the governor lived up to his promise to appoint qualified people to the commission.

## Comments

### John R. Marks III, Commissioner

Several comments will appear to be similar to those given by Commissioner Hammond of North Carolina and will point out the contrasts and the similarities between the Florida commission and the North Carolina commission.

The Florida commission's genesis was very similar to that of the North Carolina commission. It began as a result of the populist movement prior to the turn of the century. One facet of that movement was directed at regulating the railroad industry, and initially the commission was called the Florida Railroad Commission. The name was later changed to the Florida Railroad and Public Utilities Commission and then to the Florida Public Utilities Commission. Not until the mid-1960s was the name changed to the Public Service Commission (PSC). At its inception the commission only regulated the railroad industry. Then about 1911 the commission was delegated the responsibility of regulating the telephone industry. As history indicates the commission began regulating trucking and bus transportation in the early 1920s, the electric industry about 1952, and the water and sewer utilities around 1970.

*Commission Jurisdiction*

Jurisdiction over the utilities in Florida is fairly direct and simple. The commission regulates only the investor-owned utilities for rates and services. That would include the major electric, gas, telephone, and water and sewer companies. Florida is probably the only state in the nation with a scheme that requires it to regulate only those water and sewer companies from those counties that indicate that they want the commission to regulate them. It takes an affirmative vote of the County Commission in the individual county to establish this regulation jurisdiction. Such regulation must remain in effect for at least four years at which time the County Commission, through another affirmative vote, can opt to revert to the county regulation of the water and sewer utilities in that county. So far, not many, if any, have chosen to do that.

There are certain matters in which the commission regulates all of the utilities in Florida, including the electric co-ops and the city- or municipally owned utilities. Those are matters of rate structure, conservation, and territorial disputes.

In transportation the comission is quite unique because it deregulated the entire trucking and bus industry last year. As far as I can determine, Florida is the first state to do so. New Jersey has deregulated a portion of their trucking or transportation industry, and Arizona has followed suit, but as of July 1980, the commission no longer has any jurisdiction over the transportation industry with the exception of railroads. Furthermore, it would appear that in light of the Staggers Act relating to railroads, the commission may let the federal government regulate that particular industry in its entirety. The Staggers Act requires the federal government to become much more involved in the regulation of the railroad industry. The Florida commission is leaning in the direction that if it cannot do what it considers to be a thorough job in the intrastate regulation of railroads, the commission will let the federal government preempt the area.

In the electric industry there are six major companies, the largest of which is Florida Power and Light (FP&L) with which the commission is in the middle of a rate case. Florida Power and Light's request at this time is almost a half-billion dollars; $476 million to be exact. FP&L is the fifth largest electric utility in the nation, and it continues to grow as Florida continues to grow. As a result of growth, one can ask whether Florida is really prospering or rapidly approaching the point of suffering. As I look at the electric-utility industry, and for that matter, the entire utility industry in Florida, I tend to think they are beginning to suffer. By 1990 Florida will be the fourth largest state in the nation behind New York, California, and Texas. That has some frightening implications, and the commission is trying desperately to deal with that reality.

In the telephone industry the commission regulates some nineteen telephone companies, the largest of which is Southern Bell with almost half the state's customers. There are not many investor-owned gas utilities in Florida. Peoples Gas is the largest of approximately ten gas utilities within regulatory jurisdiction.

The water and sewer industry, with the limited jurisdiction discussed previously, requires the commission to regulate over 700 utilities. However, that will increase because the commission obtained jurisdiction over four additional counties recently. The total only includes about half of the state's counties.

*The Commissioners*

The commission up until the 1978 legislative session was a statewide elective body of three members. By an overwhelming majority of one vote in the state senate, the commission was changed to a five member body appointed by the governor. It was a very controversial issue and still is. Only with the help and urging of the then governor, Ruebin Askew, did the measure pass. Governor Askew made two appointments prior to the expiration of his term. One of those appointments was a former state budget director, Joe Cresse, and the other was an individual with an engineering background from the aerospace industry who had local political experience, Jerry Gunter. The newly elected governor, Bob Graham, later reappointed Commissioners Billy Mayo and Robert Mann. The governor then probably made his most controversial appointment because he had an opportunity to reappoint now Senator Paula Hawkins, but decided to appoint me. I, therefore, have the dubious distinction of replacing Ms. Hawkins on the commission. Hindsight might tend to indicate that the governor's decision may have been a blessing in disguise . . . certainly for Ms. Hawkins.

There are minimum statutory qualifications for appointment. Commissioners should have backgrounds either in accounting, engineering, economics, finance, law, or public affairs. Florida's appointment process appears to be just the reverse of that in North Carolina. Apparently, the governor of North Carolina nominates and the legislature confirms. In Florida there is a nominating council comprised of three members appointed by the president of the senate, three appointed by the Speaker of the House and those six appoint three more, for a total of nine members. It is the PSC nominating council's responsibility to proffer at least three names to the governor for possible appointment to any one vacancy. The governor's appointments must then be confirmed by the senate. To provide for continuity the terms are staggered. The present commission (Commissioners Katie Nichols and Susan Leisner have replaced Commissioners Mann and Mayo) is composed of individuals with accounting, engineering, finance, public affairs, and legal backgrounds. The appointment process thus far appears to have worked well.

## The Commission Staff

The commission has a staff of over 300 employees, headquartered in the capitol, Tallahassee, with other offices located in Miami, Tampa, and Orlando, major metropolitan centers. A number of offices throughout the state were closed as a result of deregulation of transportation.

The commission has an executive director and two deputy executive directors. The deputy executive director for administration is primarily responsible for the internal affairs and day to day operations of the commission. The deputy executive director for technical is responsible for the technical aspects of the commission's operations, that is, the regulatory functions. Under the deputy director for technical, the commission is basically organized into various departments along industry lines. They are electric and gas, communications, water and sewer, research and management studies, and accounting and financial analysis.

On the same organizational level as the executive director is the general counsel who handles the legal aspects of the commission's responsibilities. There are two departments located within the office of the general counsel; one is the legal department and is primarily concerned with the rate-making responsibilities, that is, the presentation of evidence by the commission's staff in our rate-making function. The other department within the general counsel's office is the advisory staff, responsible for advising the commission and handling legislative matters. The advisory staff is also responsible for initiating and pursuing rule making.

*The Public Counsel*

Jack Shreve is the public counsel in the state of Florida. His responsibility is to represent the people of the state of Florida in all matters before the commission. He is totally and completely independent from the commission. It has been mentioned that the public counsel has the opportunity to take advantage of the office politically. This is not the case in Florida. Participation by the public counsel has tended to cut down on the number of intervenors and increased scrutiny in rate cases, both of which are desirable.

*The Hearing Process*

The commission's hearing process is somewhat similar to that as mentioned by Commissioner Hammond of North Carolina. It sits in panels or as a full commission, or it can refer cases to a hearing examiner. The hearing examiners were at one time a part of the commission's staff but now have been transferred to a separate agency, the Division of Administrative Hearings in the Department of Administration. The commission does refer a number of cases (primarily water and sewer) to the division of the hearing examiners.

Hearing procedures have changed significantly in the state of Florida except for the major rate case. For minor or small rate cases generally involving the water and sewer industry, the commission provides for staff assistance and indexing. In those assisted cases the staff proposes action that they believe the commission should take. That proposed agency action can be modified by the commission, and if accepted by all the parties it becomes final commission action. Otherwise, it is assigned to a hearing examiner for a full evidentiary hearing on the disputed issues.

*Major Issues*

The major issues in Florida are probably the same as in other states. The state has embarked on a fairly ambitious conservation program. It will require a lot of work by the commission and by the entire electric and gas industry. The utilities appear to realize this and the initiative has been received very well. In telecommunications the big issue in Florida right now is local measured service (LMS), a matter to be addressed in the coming Bell case. There is tremendous opposition in south Florida. But that opposition is almost nonexistent in other parts of the state. It is more of a complacement attitude. It has not been determined specifically why this is the case, but it is certainly something to contend with.

Conservation is important, but the biggest impact on regulation over the next ten years will come in telecommunications. By the year 2000 it may be possible to communicate with another person at any point on earth via a personal wrist radio. The consumer really does not understand the impact of the changes occurring in this industry. When federally mandated deregulation and other changes imposed by the federal government take effect, there is going to be a lot more action and reaction from consumers.

Another matter related to the electric industry is the fuel-adjustment charge. Florida's fuel-adjustment charge was revised about a year ago to include a generating-plant efficiency factor. This is a new and innovative approach to calculating the fuel-adjustment charge. The problem with all fuel-adjustment charges is that nobody but regulators and those closely associated with the utility industry understands it. That presents a tremendous problem with the public. Some even ask why they should pay for any fuel.

The financial condition of the utility industry is also a big problem. Florida Power and Light sold some bonds in May for 15.25 percent. With those kinds of cost one can readily see why the financing of the electric-utility industry is a serious problem. It is certainly an issue that the commission is going to look at very seriously.

## Comments

### Ford B. Spinks, Commissioner

The history of the Georgia Commission is similar in many ways to the Florida and North Carolina Commissions. It was born as the Railroad Commission of Georgia in 1897. Telephones, electrics, gas, and streetcars were added in 1907. In 1922, the name changed from the Railroad Commission of Georgia to the Public Service Commission (PSC). In 1929, motor carriers were added and in 1960 radio telephones were added.

Something that badly needs to be regulated in Georgia is cable television. An effort was made to bring this industry under some type of regulation, but it failed. Perhaps the Public Service Commission should not regulate this industry, but it does need regulating by someone. What regulation exists is by city officials, which means there is no regulation. There is no state agency that has the authority to regulate this industry. Telecommunications being what it is and what it is going to be in the future, this industry will be of great importance. It ranks in importance with the telephones and electrics.

As with some of the other states, the commission does not regulate water, sewage, or things like that. Nor does it regulate municipally owned gas or electric systems, except where their service area goes outside their jurisdiction—their city limits, county limits, or whatever their jurisdiction is. Of course the commission does not regulate the Electric Membership Cooperatives (EMCs). What needs to be regulated in order to regulate the utilities, especially the electrics, is oil, coal, transportation, or labor. These are the things that are killing—killing the companies and killing the commission when it has to make decisions on those big, bad rate cases.

I came to the commission ten years ago as a junior member. After serving ten years, I am now one slot away from being the senior member, and heaven knows, I sure hope I don't ever make it. It was said earlier that there are no two commissioners alike, and I said under my breath "amen." In Georgia there are five commissioners. They have staggered terms—two elected in one election year, two the next, then one. The term of office is six years. The commissioners are all very different.

Ten years ago the public service commission was a little known part of state government. There were sixty state employees. Now it is up to 120 employees. When the commission asks for more, it gets them by ones, twos, and threes. The help comes slow—slower than it should in relation to the responsibilities.

When I came on the commission, oil was $3.85 per barrel, now it is $37 to $40; coal was $6.00 a ton, now its $37 to $40 a ton. The public was completely unaware of the public service commission and its functions in these early days of cheap energy. However, in these changing times the public has become very much aware of the commission. They now know who to call and curse about their light bills and telephone bills. One reason they were not aware of it in the past was that they really did not need to be. In Georgia from 1935 to 1969 there were sixteen rate reductions. The commission was not totally responsible for this happy state of affairs; it was just that the power companies were doing an excellent job, and the times were right for that kind of thing to happen. But when I came on the commission, the situation reversed.

The first case that faced me on the commission was a rate case by Georgia Power Company. They have not been out of sight or out of mind since. Groups are coming out of the woodwork to get involved in the rate cases. The commission is the target for everyone. Of course the public thinks the only problems the commission is interested in solving are the problems of the utilities. It is interested in solving those problems, but it is also interested in looking after the public. The news media has not told the story properly. They haven't informed the public as to the true duties and responsibilities of the commission, not just Georgia's commission, but all of the other commissions in the state and in the United States. Just as more responsible public-service commissioners are needed, so do we need a more responsible press.

Today there are eight companies that are before the commission with rate increases. The total requests of those eight companies amounts to more than $600 million plus an additional $700 million in financing. The commission has never faced a problem of this magnitude before. In the early days of the commission the number of people who came to participate in the hearings was practically none. Now, in the major cases, the room is filled. Many times there is a night session and sometimes a Saturday session in order to give the people an opportunity to be heard. But how can you tell the public that their input is useless. They are not going to add anything to the rate case that is going to be substantive—nothing that will help you make the decision that has to be made. They are going to tell you, "I don't want my light bill to go up," or "I don't want my telephone bill to go up." I already know that, they did not have to drive miles to tell me. But what evidence can they offer to help me decide whether it should only go up 40¢ instead of 80¢? They just do not have that information. So, it is an exercise in futility. However, it is the job of the commission to listen, and listen it does.

One of the big interests now besides how many dollars are going to be awarded is who is going to pay these dollars, in other words, rate design. It has gotten to the point where people realize that the price has to go up. However, they want these increases to effect someone else, not them. A very important part of future battles with special-interest groups and those who participate in the rate hearings will be on the subject of rate design.

Commissioner Marks says that he has twenty lawyers in Florida. That boggles my mind. I can't imagine a commission having 300 employees and 20 lawyers. The Georgia Public Service Commission doesn't even have one lawyer on its staff. The attorney general has assigned two people on a part-time basis to assist, and they do an excellent job, but the Georgia commission has no lawyer that it can claim as its own.

I believe that 85 percent to 90 percent of the commissions in the United States are now appointed, the remaining 10 percent to 15 percent are elected. The Georgia legislature is now in the process of trying to design a new constitution. One of the things that they are considering in this new constitution is whether or not the legislature should appoint the commissioners. There is a lot of support upstairs for this. Of course there are also a lot of people who are opposed to an appointed commission. They say that it's taking something away from the people by instituting an appointment process instead of an electoral process. But I, for one, do not think there will be a commission that Georgia will be proud of until it is an appointed commission. There are too many issues that the elected commissioners can use as political footballs in order to get their names in the paper and further their own political career at the public's expense.

Serving on the Public Service Commission is a difficult job. When you cannot make anyone happy on any issue that comes up, when the only way you know you have done your job correctly is for everyone to go away unhappy and mad, that is a bad situation—and this is the situation that many commissioners find themselves in.

# 6

# Utility Regulation Revisited

*Alfred E. Kahn*

I know that you who are embroiled on a daily basis with the frustrations and pressures of public utility regulation will find this hard to believe, but it is with a feeling of relief, even delight, that I return after four years to the scene of my earlier tribulations. I am grateful for this opportunity to take my first look at what you have been doing during these four years, and what the world has been doing to you. I apologize in advance for the necessarily impressionistic nature of my remarks; I hope, however, that the observations of someone who has been off to other wars will be of interest to you, as well as serve as an agenda for future thinking on my part.

## Deteriorating Earnings

The first and most dramatic problem is the deterioration in the financial condition of the utility companies. Moody's twenty-four electric utilities showed returns on equity (see table 6-1) of 11 percent in both 1979 and 1980—in striking contrast to the 17.3 percent earned by Standard and Poor's 400 industrials in the former year, and an estimated 15.6 percent in the latter. It is not surprising, therefore, that the market-to-book ratio (see table 6-2) for the electrics averaged only 0.75 and 0.66, respectively, in 1979 and 1980, while the corresponding figures for the industrials were 1.23 and 1.32. Over the last twenty years until 1973, the returns on equity of the electrics and the industrials were really very close (see figure 6-1). For the rest of the decade there is a gap—averaging four points. The gap between the respective market-to-book ratios opens up somewhat earlier in the late 1960s (see figure 6-2). The ratios then dropped quite dramatically for both the industrials and the electrics, reflecting the dramatic spurts in interest rates, but the electrics fell further, and the gap is now disturbingly large.

This deteriorated performance of the electrics was in important measure an inescapable result of the sudden slowing down in the rate of growth of demand and the consequent emergence of an unanticipatedly large margin

This chapter is a revised version of a paper presented on June 15, 1981, at the Annual Symposium of the New England Conference of Public Utility Commissioners. It was financed in part by a grant from the New England Telephone Co.

**Table 6-1**
**Return on Average Equity, 1960-1980**

| Year | American Telephone and Telegraph | | Moody's Twenty-Four Electric Utilities | | Standard and Poor's 400 Industrials | | Return on Average Equity in Percent | | |
| | Earnings Per Share in Dollars (1) | Average Book Value Per Share^a in Dollars (2) | Earnings Per Share in Dollars (3) | Average Book Value Per Share^a in Dollars (4) | Earnings Per Share in Dollars (5) | Average Book Value Per Share^a in Dollars (6) | American Telephone and Telegraph [(1)÷(2)]×100 (7) | Moody's Twenty-Four Electric Utilities [(3)÷(4)]×100 (8) | Standard and Poor's 400 Industrials [(5)÷(6)]×100 (9) |
|---|---|---|---|---|---|---|---|---|---|
| 1960 | 2.72 | 28.23 | 4.12 | 39.52 | 3.40 | 33.00 | 9.64 | 10.43 | 10.30 |
| 1961 | 2.72 | 29.65 | 4.33 | 41.22 | 3.37 | 34.30 | 9.17 | 10.50 | 9.83 |
| 1962 | 2.86 | 31.22 | 4.73 | 43.28 | 3.83 | 35.61 | 9.16 | 10.93 | 10.76 |
| 1963 | 3.03 | 32.54 | 4.99 | 45.36 | 4.24 | 37.27 | 9.31 | 11.00 | 11.38 |
| 1964 | 3.21 | 34.51 | 5.41 | 47.66 | 4.85 | 39.20 | 9.30 | 11.35 | 12.37 |
| 1965 | 3.41 | 36.44 | 5.92 | 49.84 | 5.50 | 41.86 | 9.36 | 11.88 | 13.14 |
| 1966 | 3.69 | 37.88 | 6.30 | 51.47 | 5.87 | 44.54 | 9.74 | 12.24 | 13.18 |
| 1967 | 3.79 | 39.44 | 6.67 | 53.56 | 5.62 | 46.68 | 9.61 | 12.45 | 12.04 |
| 1968 | 3.75 | 40.84 | 6.67 | 56.41 | 6.16 | 49.00 | 9.18 | 11.82 | 12.57 |
| 1969 | 4.00 | 42.07 | 6.92 | 59.24 | 6.13 | 50.96 | 9.51 | 11.68 | 12.03 |
| 1970 | 3.99 | 43.54 | 6.89 | 62.32 | 5.41 | 52.18 | 9.16 | 11.06 | 10.37 |
| 1971 | 3.91 | 44.94 | 7.14 | 65.23 | 5.97 | 53.96 | 8.70 | 10.95 | 11.06 |
| 1972 | 4.34 | 46.44 | 7.73 | 68.39 | 6.83 | 56.81 | 9.35 | 11.30 | 12.02 |
| 1973 | 4.98 | 48.32 | 7.55 | 71.04 | 8.89 | 60.59 | 10.31 | 10.63 | 14.67 |
| 1974 | 5.27 | 50.40 | 7.63 | 72.45 | 9.61 | 65.32 | 10.46 | 10.53 | 14.71 |
| 1975 | 5.13 | 52.12 | 7.77 | 74.52 | 8.58 | 69.32 | 9.84 | 10.43 | 12.38 |
| 1976 | 6.05 | 53.97 | 8.15 | 76.37 | 10.69 | 73.55 | 11.21 | 10.67 | 14.53 |
| 1977 | 6.97 | 56.43 | 8.64 | 77.88 | 11.54 | 79.24 | 12.35 | 11.09 | 14.56 |
| 1978 | 7.74 | 59.22 | 8.59 | 79.46 | 13.08 | 85.78 | 13.07 | 10.81 | 15.25 |
| 1979 | 8.04 | 62.05 | 8.95 | 80.86 | 16.29 | 94.02 | 12.96 | 11.07 | 17.33 |
| 1980 | 8.19 | 64.47 | 8.98 | 82.72 | 16.11 | 103.40 | 12.70 | 10.86 | 15.58 |

Source: Columns (1) and (2): The Value Line Data Base 1-2.
Columns (3) and (4): *Moody's Public Utility Manual*, 1981.
Columns (5) and (6): Standard and Poor's *Analysts Handbook*, 1981 and Monthly Supplement, February 1982.
^a Average of beginning-year and end-of-year book value per share.

**Table 6-2**
**Price to Book Ratio, 1960-1980**

| Year | American Telephone and Telegraph | | Moody's Twenty-Four Electric Utilities | | Standard and Poor's 400 Industrials | | Price to Book Ratio | | |
| | Average Price[a] in Dollars | Average Book Value[b] Per Share in Dollars | Average Price[a] in Dollars | Average Book Value[b] Per Share in Dollars | Average Price[a] in Dollars | Average Book Value[b] Per Share in Dollars | American Telephone and Telegraph | Moody's Twenty-Four Electric Utilities | Standard and Poor's 400 Industrials |
| | (1) | (2) | (3) | (4) | (5) | (6) | $(1) \div (2)$ | $(3) \div (4)$ | $(5) \div (6)$ |
| | | | | | | | (7) | (8) | (9) |
|---|---|---|---|---|---|---|---|---|---|
| 1960 | 47.10 | 28.23 | 69.82 | 39.52 | 60.18 | 33.00 | 1.67 | 1.77 | 1.82 |
| 1961 | 60.80 | 29.65 | 90.55 | 41.22 | 68.78 | 34.30 | 2.05 | 2.20 | 2.01 |
| 1962 | 58.55 | 31.22 | 91.50 | 43.28 | 65.01 | 35.61 | 1.88 | 2.11 | 1.83 |
| 1963 | 63.95 | 32.54 | 102.79 | 45.36 | 72.36 | 37.27 | 1.97 | 2.27 | 1.94 |
| 1964 | 70.20 | 34.51 | 108.76 | 47.66 | 85.52 | 39.20 | 2.03 | 2.28 | 2.18 |
| 1965 | 65.30 | 36.44 | 117.08 | 49.84 | 92.49 | 41.86 | 1.79 | 2.35 | 2.21 |
| 1966 | 56.65 | 37.88 | 102.90 | 51.47 | 89.24 | 44.54 | 1.50 | 2.00 | 2.00 |
| 1967 | 56.30 | 39.44 | 101.87 | 53.56 | 95.73 | 46.68 | 1.43 | 1.90 | 2.05 |
| 1968 | 53.20 | 40.84 | 98.37 | 56.41 | 106.54 | 49.00 | 1.30 | 1.74 | 2.17 |
| 1969 | 53.30 | 42.07 | 94.55 | 59.24 | 107.00 | 50.96 | 1.27 | 1.60 | 2.10 |
| 1970 | 47.15 | 43.54 | 79.06 | 62.32 | 89.22 | 52.18 | 1.08 | 1.27 | 1.71 |
| 1971 | 47.35 | 44.94 | 84.16 | 65.23 | 107.60 | 53.96 | 1.05 | 1.29 | 1.99 |
| 1972 | 47.30 | 46.44 | 80.20 | 68.39 | 122.57 | 56.81 | 1.02 | 1.17 | 2.16 |
| 1973 | 50.20 | 48.32 | 71.21 | 71.04 | 118.96 | 60.59 | 1.04 | 1.00 | 1.96 |
| 1974 | 46.30 | 50.40 | 48.26 | 72.45 | 90.59 | 65.32 | 0.92 | 0.67 | 1.39 |
| 1975 | 48.40 | 52.12 | 51.25 | 74.52 | 92.56 | 69.32 | 0.93 | 0.69 | 1.34 |
| 1976 | 57.85 | 53.97 | 60.10 | 76.37 | 111.26 | 73.55 | 1.07 | 0.79 | 1.51 |
| 1977 | 62.00 | 56.43 | 67.55 | 77.88 | 109.40 | 79.24 | 1.10 | 0.87 | 1.38 |
| 1978 | 60.75 | 59.22 | 63.54 | 79.46 | 107.12 | 85.78 | 1.03 | 0.80 | 1.25 |
| 1979 | 58.20 | 62.05 | 60.28 | 80.86 | 115.78 | 94.02 | 0.94 | 0.75 | 1.23 |
| 1980 | 50.55 | 64.47 | 54.80 | 82.72 | 136.02 | 103.40 | 0.78 | 0.66 | 1.32 |

Source: Columns (1) and (2): *The Value Investment Survey*, February 4, 1977, and January 29, 1982, and The Value Line Data Base-2.
Columns (3) and (4): *Moody's Public Utility Manual*, 1981.
Columns (5) and (6): Standard and Poor's *Analysts Handbook*, 1981 and Monthly Supplement, February 1982.

[a] Average of high and low price for the year.
[b] Average of beginning-year and end-of-year book value per share.
[c] Average of twelve monthly closing prices.

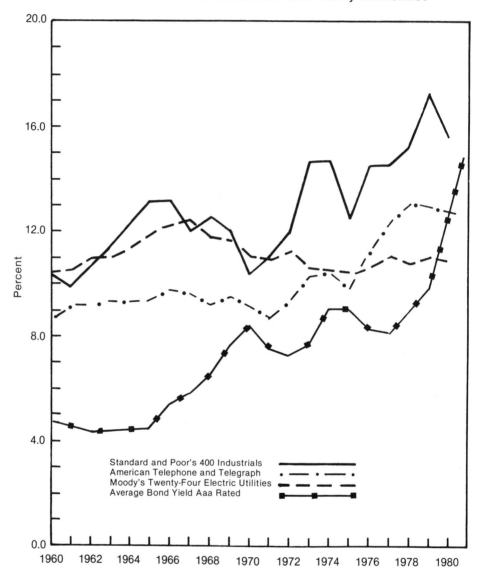

**Figure 6-1**. Return on Average Equity and Average Bond Yields, 1960-1981

of reserve capacity in many places. There is no escaping the inference that it represents also a profound failure of the institution of regulation itself.

As we contemplate the long lead times required to build additional base-load generating capacity; the real possibility of power shortages in parts of the country by the end of this decade; the apparently clear economic desir-

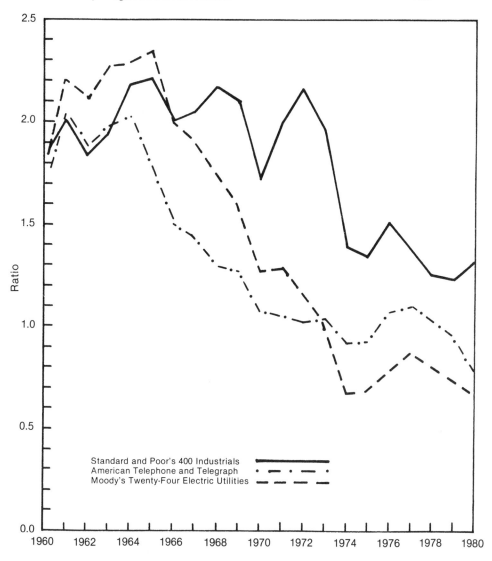

**Figure 6-2.** Price to Book Ratio, 1960-1980

ability of conversions from oil to coal running up against the dilemma of companies earning 11 percent on equity in the face of long-term borrowing costs in excess of 15 percent, and thus facing the necessity, if they are to raise the necessary capital, of massively diluting stockholders' equity or running up against prohibitively low interest-coverage ratios; and the perverse incentives created by the combination of automatic fuel-adjustment clauses, enabling them to recover the costs of oil, no matter how high, and a lack of prospect of recovering the requisite capital costs of conversions from oil, it is impossible to avoid the necessity for drastic changes in the way this industry is governed.

In the circumstances, it is hardly surprising that it seems to be impossible to have a discussion about the condition of electric utilities today without someone raising the question of possible deregulation. There is undoubtedly a good deal of intellectual faddism in this suggestion: just because deregulation may have been exactly the right thing to do for the airlines and motors carriers does not mean it makes equal sense for the electric utilities, where feasibility of broadly effective competition is by no means so obvious. It also undoubtedly reflects a great deal of wishful thinking: electric companies that have more or less willingly accepted regulation in the past as a necessary price to pay for franchised monopoly are understandably wondering whether they have such a good deal after all.

The critical question is whether there is the possibility in this industry of providing the required protection of the consumer by some other device— for example, competition—sufficiently effective to justify releasing the industry from the excessively tight regulatory grasp in which it now finds itself.

Although the telephone companies are by no means in the same dire straits as the electrics, what has happened to them in the last few years is in some ways more troubling. According to tables 6-1 and 6-2, and figure 6-1 and 6-2, the return on equity of the Bell system has risen since the middle 1970s from the 10.5 percent to the 12.5 to 13 percent range; but that remains several points below the earnings of the industrials; and when one compares those figures with the increase in the average yield on triple-A bonds, from 8.2 percent in 1977 to an astounding 15.9 percent in 1981 (see table 6-3), it is hardly surprising that American Telephone and Telegraph's (AT&T's) average market-to-book ratio plummeted from around 1.1 to 0.8 in 1980.

There is no suggestion in the financial record to date that the telephone companies as a group are anywhere nearly as close as the electrics to being unable to raise the capital they will need in the years ahead. But the needs are enormous—to meet the constantly growing demands for service, to modernize antiquated plants, and to embody in investments the benefits of rapidly developing communications technology with its accompanying opportunities for diminishing real costs and for expanding the range of available services. The financial prospects of the local operating companies have been additionally complicated by the subjection of their various operations to accentuated competition, their prospective loss of part of the subsidy from interstate operations, and in the case of the Bell companies, even more by the prospective severance of their financial connections with AT&T and their future confinement to the local telephone business under the terms of

**Table 6-3**
**Moody's Average Yield on Newly Issued Aaa Public-Utility Bonds, 1960-1981**

| Year | Average Bond Yield Aaa Rated in Percent |
|------|------------------------------------------|
| 1960 | 4.77 |
| 1961 | 4.51 |
| 1962 | 4.36 |
| 1963 | 4.31 |
| 1964 | 4.46 |
| 1965 | 4.57 |
| 1966 | 5.44 |
| 1967 | 5.85 |
| 1968 | 6.57 |
| 1969 | 7.75 |
| 1970 | 8.52 |
| 1971 | 7.58 |
| 1972 | 7.34 |
| 1973 | 7.76 |
| 1974 | 9.16 |
| 1975 | 9.13 |
| 1976 | 8.33 |
| 1977 | 8.17 |
| 1978 | 8.96 |
| 1979 | 9.86 |
| 1980 | 12.55 |
| 1981 | 15.90 |

Source: *Moody's Public Utility Manual,* 1981; *Moody's Bond Survey,* various issues.

the proposed consent settlement of the AT&T antitrust case. The cloud is still on the horizon; but it is nevertheless clearly visible, and it must be confronted.

A market-to-book ratio of around 80, a return on equity lower than the cost of triple-A debt, and recent borrowing costs for Bell companies of more than 15 percent are not to be ignored. Nor can the company ignore the continuing large disparities among the rates of return the Bell companies are able to earn in their several jurisdictions: the 12.7 percent on equity for the entire system in 1980 masks a spread between 8.75 percent in California and 14.2 percent in Indiana. There is a similar spread among the states represented at this conference: according to the company, one can derive the following returns on equity on intrastate jurisdictional business alone in 1980: 7.9 percent for Rhode Island; 11.0 percent for New Hampshire; 9.0 percent for Vermont; 7.0 percent for Maine; and 13.6 percent for Masachusetts.

There will be a number of explanations for the discrepancies these numbers reflect between the returns on equity that was allowed the company in its last rate case and these achieved returns, most of them absurdly low on their face—net contributions from interstate separations, disallowances of various expenses and rate-base items, differences between the company's and regulator's assignment of revenue requirements between intra- and interstate jurisdictions, and failures of rate awards fully to anticipate increases in cost in a time of rapid inflation.

At the same time, some of these discrepancies call into question the integrity of the regulatory process. If individual states—and some much more than others—consistently refuse to have their rate payers pay for costs that the company feels it necessary to continue to incur; if they disclaim responsibility for a larger volume of common costs than the joint boards and the Federal Communications Commission have agreed are properly charged to interstate service, regulation is reduced to an attempt by each participating party to shift to the others costs that they must in the long run bear jointly, a beggar-my-neighbor game that must ultimately be thoroughly discredited.

The attempt by individual states, independently and on their own initiative, to shift revenue responsibility to interstate usage is troublesome for two reasons. The first is the one already suggested: the individual parts must somehow, with reasonable consistency, add up to the whole. If fifty-one individual jurisdictions go their own way, each explicitly or implicitly trying to shift a disproportionate share of the aggregate burden to the others, there is no way in which the regulated enterprise can have the honest opportunity to which it is legally and economically entitled.

The second reason is that an excessive part of the burden of total revenue requirements has been shifted to interstate usage. The consequence, which is to hold those rates at least 40 percent above incremental costs, is the single most flagrant distortion of our national pricing of communications services, the single greatest source of inefficiency. Furthermore, it does not even have the justification of being necessary to hold down the cost of truly basic service, but instead wastefully subsidizes unlimited calling with the effect of inflating total costs and pushing the entire rate level higher than it would otherwise go.

**Dangers to the Public**

From the standpoint of the public, the danger of depressed public-utility company earnings is of course that it will result ultimately in a deterioration in the quality of service. One of the few ways in which an electric company can respond is by deferring maintenance of generation, transmission, and distribution facilities—for example, pole inspections, switch maintenance, and tree trimming.

National Economic Research Associates (NERA) have found some empirical evidence of this tendency. A comparison of the availability of coal-generating plants, after a lag, with earned rates of return showed that where returns were high, availability was high; where returns fell consistently below what would generally be considered adequate rates, availability was low. This relationship held consistently across the country and in each year measured.

Even more ominous in the long run is the relationship between inadequate earnings and planned reliability. Some companies find themselves with earnings so far below allowed levels that they are consciously designing their systems with reserve margins that are uneconomically low by any reasonable measure—from the standpoint of their customers.[1]

Bell system officials earnestly deny that they are influenced in making their investment decisions—including the apportioning of incremental capital among the various jurisdictions—by a failure to earn the cost of equity capital, either in the aggregate or in individual states. They assert that in testing proposed investments for economic feasibility, they consider only the cost of capital, not the returns actually achieved. If the system were to react to niggardly treatment differentially among the states, or even across the board, they observe, it could prove self-defeating in the long run, leading to a cumulative spiral of low-rate awards, deteriorating quality, even lower awards in an atmosphere of recrimination, and so on.

While this kind of investment behavior might strike the economist or the economic consultant as irrational, it is not necessarily irrational for a company that expects to be in business for a long period of time. It may not be merely good public relations for the Bell officials to express the expectation that in the long run they will receive fair treatment, as they evidently have over the major portion of their history; it may well be in their interest to do so.

Since what people say they do, or even believe they do, sometimes differs from what they actually do, other NERA studies analyzed the relationship between service quality and adequacy of earnings in five New England states over a ten-year period ending in 1979. Although their early results are far from conclusive, they do suggest that inadequate earnings may have led to deterioration of service quality.

In any event it is questionable whether Bell can continue such a policy indefinitely, even if they try. AT&T reviews the proposed construction budgets of the operating companies, which are made up of projects that their engineers believe meet the proper economic test—namely, that the promised returns will recover the cost of capital—and cuts them back, company by company, on the basis of what it sees as the availability of funds, including what it feels it can reasonably raise in the capital markets and—necessarily—on the basis of the respective merits of the proposed investments. It denies that it is influenced in determining the cuts for each jurisdiction by their respective achieved returns: what would one expect them to say? However, how long can it continue to behave in this fashion?

The vice-chairman of Continental Telephone Corporation last year openly raised the question of whether the industry could afford to continue to provide the highest quality of service in the light of its immense financial requirements, its increasing cost of capital, and its exposure to competition from companies with lower service standards.[2]

The Bell system's managers are going to have to confront the same question, if they have not already done so, and whether they now say so or not. In June of 1981, the company announced plans to offer 16.5 million-plus shares of common stock to raise about a billion dollars while selling at about 86 percent of book value.[3] Sooner or later, managements and stockholders, faced with the need to finance growth and service improvements by selling stock at less than book value, will inevitably engage in searching re-examinations of the need for the dilution-producing expenditures and may decide that deterioration of service quality is, after all, not such a terrible thing—at least compared to still more dilution. The progressive reduction of once sacrosanct reliability standards in the electric industry came only after years of industry claims that its standards would be maintained at all costs.

The question that regulators must sooner or later ask themselves—and especially regulators in states that have consistently provided lower actually realized returns than the average—is whether they are really not asking for poorer quality and less variety of service than their neighbors. Some of them may quite consciously be counting on other states to make a dispro-portionate contribution to the revenue requirements of the entire system; such a policy may have been possible so long as the economy was compara-tively stable or any tendencies it had to inflation of costs were offset in the telephone industry by above-average technological progress. The question is whether they can continue in the present circumstances to count upon sub-sidization by their neighbors.

If they cannot and will sooner or later find themselves confronted with increased frequency of busy circuits, or slower responses to calls for repair service on weekends, it seems time for state regulators to start asking them-selves whether they should be making such choices for all their subscribers as a group, or whether they cannot be ingenious enough to find ways of leaving the choice to the individual customers. It is desirable to offer con-sumers the widest possible range of price/quality choices, whenever the of-ferings can in fact be varied. One of the reasons airline deregulation was vigorously pursued was to free both the incumbent carriers and eager new entrants to offer travelers just such variety in convenience of scheduling, density of seating, availability of reservations at the last moment, even exposure to bumping, all at fare differentials (including negative fares for people volunteering to give up their seats on overbooked flights) corresponding to the differentials in cost of providing those various services.

Public-utility regulators are, of course, far from unaware of these possibilities and of the strong case that can be made for them in terms of the interest of consumers—interruptible rates, special rates for subscribers willing to have their use subject to utility-load management, rates varying by season and time of day, and so on.

**Expanding Customer Choice**

Wherever the individual consumer can be given the opportunity to choose among as refined a set of kinds and qualities of service as it is economic to offer, at prices reflecting their respective costs, social welfare will be improved; and offering such choices—rather than starving the utility company—is the way in which a state can best express its solicitude for impecunious customers. This is the essence of the case for usage-sensitive pricing and what the phone companies now call measured service. From the standpoint of the telephone companies, a progressively finer differentiation of rates per call, per minute of calling, per mile, by time of day, and the unbundling of services such as directory assistance—all as distinguished from a flat monthly charge for unlimited local service over wider and wider areas— has the virtue of making revenues rise more nearly automatically with increases in costs. From the standpoint of consumers, however, these differentials have enormous attractions:

> Offering them a variety of choices, so that each can pick the price/ quality/quantity combination that best meets individual needs;

> Offering people who want to economize an opportunity to see the results in their own bills of their reducing equivalently the cost that they impose on the system;

> Holding down the inflation of cost and therefore the burden on all ratepayers by subjecting all takings of service that impose additional costs on the system to a price that reflects those costs.

According to New England Telephone there are still some jurisdictions that are unwilling to permit them to introduce directory-assistance charging. Surely regulators cannot still be sensitive to the ignorant or demagogic criticism that in so doing they would be letting the companies charge subscribers for something they previously got for nothing. Surely they are aware that subscribers as a group pay for those costs whether they are charged or not.

In New York state the public service commission introduced directory-assistance charging outside the context of a general rate case, so that it was able to combine the charges with the offer of rebates to customers who would make only a few such calls per month. Within a month the number of directory assistance calls was reduced 40 to 45 percent, and 85 percent of the rate payers in the state were able to receive something like a twenty-million-dollar rate reduction on an annual basis.

These are lessons regulators were learning in the first half of the 1970s. What lends them enormously increased urgency at the turn of the 1980s are two changes: first, the squeeze of inflation on the telephone companies on the one side, and the intensification of the competition to which they are being subjected on the other. According to the same vice-chairman of Continental Telephone, the average load on the Direct Distance Dialing (DDD) network today ranges between 15 and 20 percent, whereas the average load of the specialized common carriers is above 60 percent; and during the peak busy hour the DDD network load is between 60 and 65 percent, and that of the specialized common carriers over 95 percent.[4] This means a palpable difference in quality of service at correspondingly differing prices.

This is all to the good in terms of giving customers an economic choice—provided they are aware of the differences in quality. But it is certainly not to the good if the telephone companies themselves are prevented from offering a similar variety—or are expected instead to definitely provide service of a uniform, higher quality at rates that systematically deny them an opportunity to earn their costs of capital.

### Problems of the Transition to Full Competition in Terminal Equipment

There is one striking respect in which the New York commission has moved forward. The state level and the Federal Communications Commission were both moving to open the terminal-equipment market to competitive entry, but the commission was still being forced to cope at the national level with the various Home Telephone and Consumer Communications Reform Acts, the clear intention of which was to preclude competition. I was strongly opposed to those Bell bills.[5] Since then there has not only been Computer II—not to mention Execunet—but also very considerable progress in Congress to amend the 1934 Communications Act in the direction of mandating freer and fuller competition and in the proposed antitrust consent settlement.

But this approaching resolution of the competition issue is clearly raising the most complex set of problems, the solutions to which are still not in sight. The fundamental problem that all these recent initiatives have tried to solve is one of devising structural arrangements or rearrangements to ensure that the competition between the regulated common carriers on the one side and the unregulated companies on the other will be tolerably fair, and not be distorted by the participation in it of companies a major part of whose present operations are and will continue to be regulated monopolies. Such provisions include the requirement that the common carriers act through the medium of companies separated from their monopoly operations in order to preclude the possibility of their competition being subsidized by revenues from those operations; the imposition of requirements of arms-length dealing between the separated, competitive subsidiaries and the monopoly carriers; and/or the requirement that access to the monopoly services be available to all competitors on equal terms. Although the way in which this task is accomplished will have profound implications for state regulators the problems are too broad to be treated in this chapter. The one thing that is certain is that they make it more urgent than ever that regulators permit the telephone companies to bring their rate structures into much closer alignment with costs than in the past.

Among the problems with which regulators will be forced to grapple is the way in which the pricing of terminal equipment is to be regulated in the period of transition to the ultimate structural resolution and, once that resolution is reached, the terms on which the pertinent assets of the regulated carriers are to be transferred to the competitive entity (AT&T itself under the consent settlement). On the matter of pricing, regulatory commissions are properly concerned that terminal-equipment revenues not be so low as to impose a burden on basic service: the commissions are aware of a series of decisions in New York state, beginning in 1975, requiring the New York Telephone Company to raise these rates, which were found to be insufficient to cover revenue requirements.

In doing so the commissions inevitably find themselves not just protecting customers of the monopoly services, but also affecting the terms of competition in terminal-equipment markets. In its latest decision of this kind, the New York commission is uncomfortable playing the role of competitive handicapper—forcing New York Telephone to raise its toll-exchange (TE) charges well above revenue requirements in part at least to protect competitors. It was right to feel uneasy; the commission was among the first in the country to open this market to competition; and that is fundamentally incompatible with regulators telling management how they must price.

Experience with the Civil Aeronautics Board (CAB) and with such agencies as the Interstate Commerce Commission (ICC) makes one very suspicious of the use of regulatory authority to raise prices, once it is assured that the competitive rates are not a burden on captive, monopoly customers. Public-utility commissions are very poor agencies for protecting the goals of the antitrust laws; the sooner they get out of that business the better.

As for the terms on which existing equipment is to be transferred, under the proposed antitrust consent settlement, from the Bell operating companies to AT&T, one is dealing with scores of billions of dollars. The terms of their transfer can have a substantial effect on the revenue requirements and rates for the residual monopoly services. Whether it is likely to have a critical effect on the character of the ensuing competition between AT&T and the unregulated companies is much more questionable.

These interrelated subjects—the pricing of terminal equipment in the transition and the terms of its transfer—are too complex to treat adequately in this chapter.[6] Nevertheless, the most important thing from the point of view of the public interest is to get over the transition to competition as quickly as possible. There are no structural arrangements that will guarantee its perfection. Pragmatic compromises will have to be accepted.

Total separation of the Bell system's competitive from its monopoly operations—if one could unequivocally identify which is which—would erect the strongest protections against unfair competition, but it would also undoubtedly entail some sacrifice of the economic benefits that flow from the close integration that now exists between AT&T's research, development, manufacturing, and service, which embraces the entire field of communications.[7] Conversely, there is no way of denying even a fully separated, competitive AT&T (paradoxically Baby Bell has turned out to be the Ma!) the technological and marketing advantages that flow from its previous association with the operating companies. The most important task is to get the competitive and the regulated monopolistic operation separated as fully as possible, that is, to the extent this can be done without major sacrifices of efficiencies of common operations.

Moreover, although billions of dollars are at stake in the proper evaluation of assets to be transferred, it is easy to exaggerate their importance so far as the feasibility of competition is concerned. The competitive success or failure of AT&T over any significant period of time will depend far less on whether the assets it takes over from the operating companies are over- or undervalued on its books than on how well it is able to meet the challenge of competition in its future offerings on a current basis. Both it and its competitors will stand or fall preponderantly on their ability, by virtue of their efficiency and innovation, to provide customers with superior offerings at low cost.

### Conclusions

The financial condition of the utility companies—most obviously in the case of the electrics, but also of the telephone companies—casts serious doubt on the integrity of regulation and threatens serious deterioration in the quality of service.

The proper course for regulators, concerned—as they should be—about the burden of rising rates on consumers, is not to starve the utility companies but to force them to offer their subscribers the widest feasible choice of price/quality options—which means making rates and rate structures as finely cost differentiated as possible.

The potential benefits to the public of competition in communications (and in electricity, to the extent it can be achieved) far outweigh the probable imperfections in the structural protections and financial settlements that have to be made to get it going. The main job is to get it going.

**Notes**

1. This should not be surprising. The kind of behavior predicted by Averch and Johnson when earnings exceed the cost of capital will indeed be reversed when the opposite condition prevails.

2. Robert E. La Blanc, "The Telephone Industry Facing the 80s with Business and Capital Competition" (Paper delivered at the 1980 Annual Meeting, American Bar Association Honolulu, Hawaii, August 4, 1980).

3. *The New York Times*, June 11, 1981, p. D4.

4. La Blanc, "The Telephone Industry," p. 12.

5. See Alfred E. Kahn, Testimony before the House Subcommittee on Communications, Committee on Interstate and Foreign Commerce, on the *Consumer Communications Reform Act of 1976*, HR 12323, Sept. 30, 1976; and before the U.S. Senate Subcommittee on Communications, Committee on Commerce, on *The Communications Act of 1934 Revisited*, March 21, 1977.

6. See Alfred E. Kahn, "The Pricing of Telephone Terminal Equipment in the Transition to Competition" (Draft paper, 1981).

7. Recent commentary on the proposed resolution of the Department of Justice's antitrust suit against AT&T poignantly illustrates this dilemma. In general it seems recognized that freeing AT&T, Western Electric and Bell labs to enter whatever competitive markets they choose to enter is highly desirable, and that separating them entirely from the more or less naturally monopolistic provision of local-exchange service goes far to eliminate the danger of unfair competition arising out of combining competitive and monopolistic operations. On the other hand, one would be hard put to claim that AT&T has no monopoly power in message-toll service, which it would retain along with the other, more competitive interexchange communications services, leaving unresolved the definition and control of cross-subsidization. And the most worrisome aspect of the settlement, is what it does to the operating companies, which it would—in the interest of fair competition—confine strictly to the provision of regulated local exchange service, and separate from Western Electric and Bell labs.

# 7 Challenges for Electric Utilities and Regulatory Commissions

*J. Robert Malko*
and *Gregory B. Enholm*

During the 1970s, the cost of providing electricity rose substantially because of general inflation, rising fuel costs, increases in system peak demand, and difficulties in raising financial capital.[1] This increased cost has, in turn, resulted in ever-increasing bills for utility customers of all classes. In response to these rising costs and bills, utilities, regulators, and electricity rate payers have focused increased attention on issues of electric-utility regulation.

Electricity consumers, accustomed to declining electricity rates, are frustrated by rapidly increasing rates and are demanding action from legislators, regulators, and utilities. Even with rapidly increasing rates, electric utilities find that they cannot earn the rate of return allowed by their regulators. Regulators encounter difficulties developing appropriate policies that balance the diverse componponents of the public interest. Since options are available to reduce electricity rate increases in the short run, regulators must consider how their decisions will affect electricity customers in the long run. The impacts of regulatory actions on electric utilities, especially regarding their financial condition, need serious attention.

This chapter addresses current regulatory issues of concern to electric-utility management, investors, and rate payers.[2] The primary purpose is to provide a framework to conceptualize potential solutions to the financial problems facing the electric-utility industry during the 1980s. The chapter is organized as follows: financial problems are presented, and potential solutions are discussed. These solutions include regulatory reforms, modifications of current utility operations, and diversification. In the summary, the need for strategic planning by utilities and regulatory commissions to analyze and resolve issues is discussed.

## Electric-Utility Financial Problems

According to a nationally known utility financial analyst, Charles A. Benore, "the financial status of energy utilities and the related ability to

The views expressed herein are those of the authors and do not necessarily represent the views of the Public Service Commission of Wisconsin.

raise capital varies substantially between the natural gas and electric power industries."[3] As indicated by table 7-1, the relative market value and performance during the period between 1970 and 1980 of a sample of electric-power companies has been below natural-gas distribution companies and substantially below natural-gas pipeline companies. According to information from Moody's index for the period, 1970 to 1980, and presented in table 7-2, the return on equity for a sample of electric-power companies has remained at approximately 11 percent, but the return on equity for natural-gas distribution and pipeline companies has increased from approximately 12.5 percent to about 13 percent and 15 percent, respectively.

Financial analysts foresee investor-owned electric utilities facing serious financial problems in the 1980s such as low earned rates of return, low market-to-book-values, and low coverage ratios.[4] Some reasons given by the analysts for these financial difficulties include: increased capital cost of generating plant per kilowatt; increased inflation causing general utility costs to rise rapidly; rising fuel prices; small or no growth in kilowatt-hour sales; large nonrevenue-producing investment to meet regulatory and environmental requirements; and electric-utility securities remaining less attractive to investors as compared to the past.[5]

Three interrelated potential solutions to these financial problems exist. The two primary players are regulatory commissions and utilities. Regulators could act to reform the regulatory process in order to increase the likelihood that electric utilities will earn their allowed rate of return. This potential solution, however, requires the regulators to take actions to which the utilities will respond. Utility management and regulators can act

**Table 7-1**
**Relative Market Performance**

| Year | Industrials | Gas Pipelines | Gas Distributors | Electrics |
|------|-------------|---------------|------------------|-----------|
| 1970 | 100.0 | 100.0 | 100.0 | 100.0 |
| 1971 | 120.6 | 108.6 | 107.6 | 109.3 |
| 1972 | 137.4 | 118.2 | 107.6 | 103.4 |
| 1973 | 133.3 | 110.6 | 101.7 | 91.9 |
| 1974 | 101.5 | 90.5 | 81.6 | 67.3 |
| 1975 | 103.7 | 100.9 | 97.1 | 67.9 |
| 1976 | 124.7 | 121.3 | 118.8 | 79.6 |
| 1977 | 122.6 | 137.9 | 140.5 | 87.5 |
| 1978 | 120.0 | 132.5 | 129.4 | 82.4 |
| 1979 | 129.8 | 161.5 | 143.8 | 75.7 |
| 1980 | 150.2 | 217.7 | 175.1 | 68.8 |

Source: *Standard and Poor's Analysts Handbook,* (New York: 1981), pp. 1, 82-84. Reprinted with permission.

Note: Average annual nominal prices used in calculations.

**Table 7-2**
**Average Return on Equity**

| Year | Twenty-Four Electrics in Percent | Nine Gas Distributors in Percent | Nine Gas Pipelines (Transmission) in Percent |
|---|---|---|---|
| 1970 | 10.8 | 12.8 | 12.3 |
| 1971 | 10.8 | 12.3 | 13.6 |
| 1972 | 11.0 | 12.6 | 12.7 |
| 1973 | 10.5 | 11.5 | 13.2 |
| 1974 | 10.4 | 11.9 | 15.2 |
| 1975 | 10.3 | 11.5 | 14.7 |
| 1976 | 10.6 | 12.6 | 15.6 |
| 1977 | 11.0 | 13.6 | 15.9 |
| 1978 | 10.7 | 15.2 | 15.5 |
| 1979 | 11.0 | 14.2 | 17.7 |
| 1980 | 10.7 | 13.2 | 14.7 |

Source: *Moody's Public Utility Manual,* Vol. 1 (New York: 1981), pp. a14, a18. Reprinted with permission.

together to modify current utility operations in order to alleviate the financial problems. Such actions include the implementation of load management and cogeneration in order to reduce the need for costly additions to capacity. Utility management can choose to diversify and pursue new lines of business in the hope of increasing overall earnings. Here, regulators must respond to utility initiatives.

Investors will react to actions taken to implement the three potential solutions. Successful attempts to solve the financial problems will spur investor interest and increase the attractiveness of electric-utility securities. These three potential solutions are depicted in figure 7-1. This diagram provides a conceptual framework to consider the potential solutions.

**Regulatory Reform**

The inability of many electric utilities to earn their allowed rate of return, the relatively low market-to-book ratios of electric-utility stock, and relative financial problems have prompted serious consideration of reforming the regulatory process.[6] The National Association of Regulatory Utility Commissioners (NARUC) passed resolutions during August 1981 to establish two special committees or task forces to study and prepare reports concerning the financial health of the electric-utility industry and utility diversification.[7]

There are several reasons why regulators must consider reforming the regulatory process. There is a need to address utility financial difficulties; a need to shorten regulatory procedure and reduce litigation; and a need to improve incentives for managerial efficiency. In addition, it is becoming increasingly apparent that the regulatory institutional framework developed

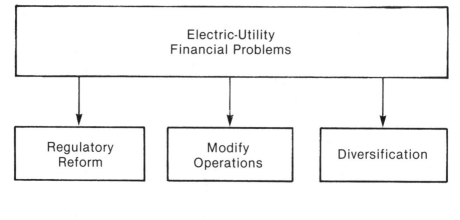

**Figure 7-1.** Three Potential Solutions

in the first half of the twentieth century may need significant modification.

There is general agreement that the regulator's job is becoming much more demanding. It is not unusual for an electric utility to have two or more rate cases pending at one time.[8] Many participants in regulatory proceedings have stated that there is too much litigation and not enough negotiation.[9] The time has come to critically reexamine regulatory lag, historic test years, universal service requirements, inflexible rate structures, and embedded-cost calculations which may now contribute to the inability of electric utilities to earn their allowed rate of return.

According to Charles A. Benore, the principal financial problem faced by electric utilities is "the lack of adequate rate relief to cover the costs of providing electric power service including capital cost."[10] However, Dennis Bakke of Carnegie-Mellon University argues that rate increases for electric utilities would be as useful to their financial health as sticker-price increases would be for Chrysler corporation.[11]

Federal and state regulatory commissions must initiate regulatory reforms. In order to address the financial problems faced by electric utilities during the 1980s, the following issues relating to modifying or reforming the regulatory process should be carefully examined by commissioners and their staffs:

1. *What standard of financial health should regulators use?* The candidates include market-to-book-value ratios of one or greater; attaining allowed return on equity; maintaining an AA-bond rating; and maintaining an acceptable times-interest-coverage ratio.
2. *Should construction work in progress (CWIP) be included in the rate base?* Traditionally, most commissions have excluded CWIP from the rate base. A major concern is that including CWIP will encourage excessive construction programs. CWIP is not used or useful in delivering current service to ratepayers. Allowing a return on CWIP would increase utility earnings.
3. *Should a future test year be adopted?* Using historic costs results in cost projections which are too low during inflationary times. However, historic costs can be specifically determined while future costs must be predicted with an unknown likelihood for error.
4. *If historic test years are retained, should an attrition factor be used to compensate for inflation?* Attrition factors may be easier to understand and compute than using cost projections. Attrition factors will increase the likelihood that the utility will earn its allowed rate of return.
5. *Should utility rates be indexed?* This action could virtually guarantee that a utility will earn its allowed return. However, the choice of an index is crucial and likely to be controversial. Ratepayers may react to overall indexing as they did to the fuel-adjustment clause (or fool-adjustment clause as called by some observers). Limited indexing of rates is permitted to the public service company of New Mexico by its regulators.
6. *Could rate proceedings be shortened by separating noncontroversial issues from controversial issues?* One major complaint about the regulatory process is its length and the amount of litigation. The Wisconsin public service commission is experimenting with a two part (noncontroversial/controversial) approach to rate cases.
7. *Should the U.S. Congress authorize the Federal Energy Regulatory Commission (FERC) to prescribe voluntary guidelines or standards for state regulatory commissions in order to achieve the objectives of providing for both adequate rates of return based on current money costs and adjustments to ensure that actual earnings do not fall below these rates?* The formulation and implementation of these guidelines could be controversial. The Mississippi commission has challenged the constitutionality of the Public Utility Regulatory Policies Act of 1978 (PURPA).
8. *Would regionalizing electric-utility regulation improve the quality of regulation and subsequently the financial health of the electric-power*

*industry?* There are questions as to how regional regulatory commissions would function and be funded. State commissions would be hesitant to give up their regulatory authority.

Regulatory reform must be initiated by regulators. Utilities, law firms, consultants, public counsels, citizens' groups, financial firms, and intervenors all have an interest in the regulatory process, but they can only make recommendations to regulators. Regulators should not be embedded in outmoded procedures merely out of respect for tradition.

## Modifying Current Operations

Utility managements are continuously readjusting utility policies to adapt to changing economic conditions. Regulatory commissions also can modify utility policies. Many modifications are the result of a joint regulatory/ utility assessment of major challenges to the industry. Two challenging modifications now being explored and implemented by electric utilities and commissions are load management and cogeneration.[12]

Since the conclusion of an important and forward-looking *Madison Gas & Electric Company* (Wisconsin) case in August 1974, several state regulatory commissions, utilities, and intervenors have been seriously analyzing the desirability and feasibility of implementing time-of-day (TOD) rates and direct-load controls for electricity.[13] Some state regulatory commissions have directed electric utilities to implement TOD tariffs and direct mechanical load-control programs.[14] In addition, each state regulatory commission must consider and make a determination by November 1, 1981, concerning the electricity rate-making standard of TOD rates in order to comply with the Public Utility Regulatory Policies Act of 1978.[15] Load management of electricity usage is defined to include direct (mechanical) controls on end-use equipment and time-differentiated (by day and season) rates. Load management generally has the following objectives: reduce growth in peak demand, thereby reducing the need for capacity expansion and shift a portion of load from inefficient peaking units to more efficient base-load plants, thereby obtaining some savings through reduced use of gas and oil fuels.

Six issues concerning the selection and implementation of load-management alternatives follow:

1. *Under what conditions can intrautility (load-shape modifications) data be transferred on an intrautility basis (within a utility) and on an interutility basis (among utilities)?* The issue of transferability of elasticity information has important implications for rate making, forecasting, and estimating benefits associated with load management.[16]

2. *Under what conditions can load-research information be transferred on an intrautility basis and on an interutility basis?* The issue of transferability of load-research information has important implications for costs of implementing a workable load-research program, rate-making, forecasting, and estimating benefits associated with load management alternatives.

3. *Should regulatory commissions provide special financial incentives for utilities that assume the risks and uncertainties associated with implementing a load-management program?* This issue has significant implications concerning the speed and level of implementation of load-management programs.

4. *How can both accounting costs and marginal costs be effectively used, in combination, for designing time-of-use rates in order to meet pricing objectives?* This issue has implications for reducing the polarization of attitudes on accounting costs and marginal costs.[17]

5. *Are time-of-day rates and direct-load controls substitutes, complements, or both?* This issue has implications concerning the planning and implementation of a comprehensive load-management program.

6. *Should residential time-of-day rates be mandatory or voluntary?* This issue relates to considerations and uncertainties associated with cost-effectiveness analysis and selecting and ranking of pricing objectives.

Cogeneration of electricity has been described as a way to both conserve energy resources and increase energy production.[18] Waste heat from industrial processes can be used to run turbines that can supply electricity to a utility's grid or reduce the need to draw on the utility's power. The Federal Energy Regulatory Commission (FERC) estimates that one-fourth of the energy used to raise steam for industrial use would be wasted if not used for cogeneration.[19] Cogeneration, however, has not been used extensively because of regulatory barriers and lack of interest by utilities.[20]

PURPA has provisions which encourage cogeneration by requiring that utilities pay the full avoided cost for all electricity supplied by a cogenerator. Also, utilities must not charge unreasonable rates for standby and maintenance power which would otherwise limit the incentives for cogeneration. Qualified cogenerators are not considered to be public utilities, a status which frees them from many regulations. Many questions need to be answered as to how to price cogenerated electricity appropriately. Various issues follow:[21]

1. *On what basis should the rate paid for cogenerated electricity be calculated?* A rate in excess of the least-cost alternative actually available to the utility would cause an increase in utility costs which would be passed on to its customers. Interestingly, a rate below this

least-cost alternative would also increase utility costs assuming that more cogenerated electricity would be available if a higher rate is paid (least cost is, unfortunately, not easily defined).

2.  *What costs should be included to determine a least-cost alternative?* The utility's avoided generating costs can be calculated without much difficulty. However, cogenerated electricity supplied at peak usage avoids capacity expansion if no excess capacity exists. FERC rules require that cogenerated electricity rates include an avoided-capacity cost component.

3.  *How should avoided-capacity costs be calculated?* Two choices are embedded cost and replacement cost. The price could vary substantially depending on whether embedded cost of capital or the market cost of capital is used.

4.  *While cogenerated electricity replaces costly incremental utility-generated electricity at peak hours, its value to the utility at off-peak hours is much less. How can this be accounted for?* Clearly, to reflect more accurately avoided costs, the rate paid for congenerated electricity must vary by time-of-day. A rate appropriate for peak hours would be too high off-peak. A rate based on off-peak costs but used at peak times would not provide as much incentive as a rate based on on-peak costs.

5.  *What guidelines should regulators provide to utilities for pricing maintenance and standby power for cogenerators?* Maintenance activities can be scheduled to the mutual convenience of the utility and the cogenerator. Maintenance power rates should reflect this. Standby power rates must account for each individual cogenerator's outage probability in the context of all cogenerated electricity available to the utility. The utility must make reasonable estimates of reserves needed to cover expected outages and charge accordingly.

6.  *Should cogenerated electricity rates vary by cogenerator?* Small cogenerators may object to receiving a different rate than that received by large cogenerators. The decision may depend on the consideration given to reliability. However, if the utility avoids adding capacity because of the availability of cogenerated electricity, this apportioning the savings among the cogenerators will be complicated if their electricity production exceeds the utility's needs.

7.  *How frequently should cogenerated electricity rates be reviewed?* Commissions could set rates in each utility's rate case or have specific hearings semiannually or annually.

8.  *If cogenerated power is wheeled to another utility, how should the wheeling charges be apportioned?* Generally, wheeling costs are paid by the originator.

9.  *When cogenerators are both supplying electricity to a utility and drawing electricity from a utility, how should the payment be calculated?* Using simultaneous or net buy-sell can result in substantially different payments.

10. *Should PURPA be revised to include a requirement that each state regulatory commission set a target for cogeneration as a percentage of total power production?* Such mandatory encouragement could result in distortions in electricity supply. The impact such a requirement would have on the price paid for cogenerated electricity is uncertain.

Both load management and cogeneration, as modifications of current utility operations, can reduce the need for costly capacity expansion. When a utility can delay or eliminate capacity expansion during times of high-interest rates and rising kilowatt-hour costs from new capacity, overall utility costs will not rise as much as they would with the expansion. This activity increases the likelihood that the utility will earn the return allowed by its regulators.

## Diversification

The inability of electric utilities to earn their allowed rate of return has prompted serious consideration of the option of business diversification by extending utility operations into areas related, and not related, to energy production.[22] For the purposes of this chapter, diversification is defined as the initiation of any line of business apart from the traditional functions of the utility. For electric utilities, these traditional functions are the generation, transmission, and distribution of electricity.

According to David Arthur and Andrew Harris of the Corporate Planning Division, Portland General Electric Company, "electric utility diversification has entered a second era. The first era was characterized by a limited number of 'accidental' diversification ventures."[23] Concerning the second era of diversification activities for electric utilities, Arthur and Harris state that the current financial problems have "encouraged electric utility executives to consider other business (diversification)."[24] According to Terry A. Ferrar, vice-president of economics at the Edison Electric Institute, "a prudent diversification venture may simultaneously improve financial health, while increasing the supply of alternative products that society values more than electric service."[25]

There are economic and financial reasons for believing that diversification may help energy utilities. A National Association of Regulatory Utility Commissioners (NARUC) committee, chaired by Joseph Swidler, analyzed possible reasons for diversification in some depth.[26] This committee's report, submitted in 1972, outlined several ways in which a diversification effort could help a utility. Among the report's observations were that successful diversification could improve the risk profile of a utility, favorably affect growth of revenues and profits, and tap synergistic effects.

NARUC decided to reexamine the issue of utility diversification by forming a new committee in late 1981. Stanley York, chairman of the Wisconsin public service commission, was appointed to chair the committee of eight state regulators. The committee plans to issue a report by summer 1982.

An electric utility investigating the possibility of diversification must first consider the legal and organizational implications of diversification. Next, the economic aspects must be given careful consideration. The response of regulators must also be gauged. Finally, the potential impacts on other firms and markets should be analyzed. As mentioned previously, each of these present questions need answers:[27]

1. *How will utility diversification be affected by federal and state laws, particularly the anti-trust laws?* These could pose legal barriers to diversification.

2. *If the legal issues can be resolved, can the utility adapt its organizational structure to manage efficiently a diversified operation?* Utilities have operated as monopolies subject to government regulation. In many diversified ventures the utility will be competing against non-monopoly business.

3. *Even if the utility management believes that their organization can handle diversified operations, are those operations desirable from an economic standpoint?* Diversification could have a negative effect on the utility's stock price and bond rating. Diversification could affect the basic energy-production activities of the utility.

4. *How will regulators view diversification?* Regulatory commissions are in a position to either block diversification or encourage it. However, they could also let the utilities decide for themselves. Utilities will be concerned about how involved regulators will be in decision making in diversified operations. Regulators must balance their legislative mandate to regulate utilities against the utilities need for freedom to act in diversification. Regulators may react negatively if they discover that the rate of return in a diversified operation exceeds that allowed in energy production by a substantial margin.[28] Policies followed by regulators should reflect the public interest.

5. *Does the form of business organization chosen affect diversification?* Utilities can set up diversified ventures in three forms: internal utility operations; wholly owned subsidiaries; and utility holding-company subsidiaries. The choice will affect the feasible extent of diversification, the possibilities for external financing and acquisition, as well as the degree of regulatory control over diversification.

6. *How will a utility's decision to diversify affect other firms and markets?* If an electric utility attempts to internalize operations, such as waste disposal and coal transportation, which is currently contracts out, the utility will displace similar activities by nonutility firms. Similar problems arise if a utility actively promotes conservation ac-

tivities by its customers. These activities raise questions concerning fair competition, particularly if overhead expenses charged to ratepayers subsidize these activities. Such subsidization could be challenged by competitors as illegal. However, utilities could diversify into areas where no market exists presently.

Diversification could yield higher profits for utilities, lower rates for customers, reduced need for capacity expansion, and reduced fuel usage and pollution through conservation efforts promoted by diversified utilities. Increasing attention is being devoted to diversification by utilities as well as financial analysts[29] and consultants[30] as a potential solution to the financial problems faced by electric utilities. However, diversification involves risk both for the stockholder and the ratepayer and can take many years to develop successfully.[31]

**Conclusions**

The decade of the 1980s presents serious challenges to electric utilities and regulatory commissions. In the past, when steady growth accompanied by declining costs and rates appeared to be a permanent phenomenon, it was possible to view and solve problems in isolation. Groups or departments within utilities were able to work separately without significant consideration of how their efforts affected the problems of the other groups. Now an integrated, team approach is needed to assure that actions taken by one group within a utility are compatible with the actions of other groups.

Staffs of utilities and commissions must have an understanding of the major issues and challenges facing electric utilities. An integrated conceptual framework, such as the one presented in figure 7-1, is useful to increase understanding. However, to guide the utilities and commissions on a path into the uncertain future, both should develop strategic-planning capabilities.

While an electric utility has engaged in planning since its formation, this planning has been from a monopolistic, serve-all-takers perspective. Implementing substantial modifications in current operations requires much more sophisticated planning activities within an overall strategic framework. This would be particularly important if utility management chooses to diversity operations.

Regulatory commissions have not needed to plan their activities extensively. Until the 1970s, commissions spent much of their time approving rate reductions and noncontroversial utility-plant expansion. However, since 1970, the regulator's work had become increasingly complicated, indicating a need to develop a regulatory strategic-planning capability.

Regulatory reform should be undertaken in a logically consistent framework developed with consideration of the future prospects for regulation. Both utilities and commissions face serious challenges and uncertainties. The costs of developing a forward-looking strategic-planning capability are relatively small, and the savings from avoiding serious errors could be substantial.

The financial survival of electric utilities will be the critical issue facing the industry in the 1980s. After two decades of prosperous financial health in the 1950s and 1960s, the industry began to encounter serious financial problems in the 1970s. Increasing regulatory attention must be directed to the financial problems of electric utilities, or regulators will find that adequate service at reasonable rates to utility customers will be jeopardized.

**Notes**

1. For a discussion concerning increasing electricity costs, see J. Robert Malko and Robert G. Uhler, "The Rate Design Study: Helping Evaluate Load Management," *Public Utilities Fortnightly*, 103 (October 11, 1979), pp. 11-17.

2. This is based on two earlier papers: J. Robert Malko and Gregory B. Enholm, "Regulation and Electric Utilities: Some Current Issues" (Paper presented at the Ninth Annual National Utilities Conference sponsored by Planmetrics/Energy Management Associates, Chicago, May 1981). J. Robert Malko, Gregory B. Enholm, and Theodore M. Jaditz, "Energy Utility Diversification, Holding Companies, and Regulation". (Paper prepared for the Wisconsin public service commission in September 1981 and presented at the Fourth Annual Public Utilities Conference sponsored by New Mexico State University, El Paso, Texas, October 1981).

3. For a discussion of these reasons see Charles A. Benore, "Energy Utilities—A Financial Status Report" (Report presented at the California Public Utilities Commission Symposium, Energy Utilities: The Next 10 Years, (March 27, 1981), pp. 2-3.

4. For a discussion of financial issues at the federal regulatory level see Informal Task Force to the Energy Transition Team, "Recommendations For Restoration of Financial Health To The U.S. Electric Power Industry" (NARUC, Washington, D.C.: January 30, 1981).

5. Benore, "Energy Utilities—A Financial Status Report," p. 2.

6. For a discussion of this issue within the overall context of electric-utility financial viability, see Malko and Enholm, "Regulation and Electric Utilities: Some Current Issues."

7. Resolutions were passed by the NARUC Executive Committee at the summer meetings in San Diego, California, August 1981, to establish

the following two special committees or task forces: Ad Hoc Committee on the Financial Health of the Electric Utility Industry, and Ad Hoc Committee on Utility Diversification.

8. During 1981 Wisconsin Electric Power Company had three rate cases pending before the Wisconsin public service commission.

9. Statement of Brian Lederer, People's Counsel of the District of Columbia Hearings before the National Association of Regulatory Utility Commissioners, Ad Hoc Committee on Financial Health of the Electiric Utility Industry, October 15, 1981, official report forthcoming.

10. Benore, "Energy Utilities—A Financial Status Report," p. 2.

11. Quoted in testimony of Richard E. Morgan, Research Coordinator of the Utility Project of the Environmental Action Foundation, before the National Association of Regulatory Utility Commissioners Ad Hoc Committee on the Financial Health of the Electric Utility Industry, Washington, D.C.: October 15, 1981.

12. Malko and Enholm, "Regulation and Electric Utilities: Some Current Issues."

13. *Madison Gas and Electric Company*, (Wis. 1974) Docket No. 2-U-7423. For an analysis of the major issues in this case, see Richard D. Cudahy and J. Robert Malko, "Electric Peak-Load Pricing: Madison Gas and Beyond," *Wisconsin Law Review*, (1976), pp. 47-73.

14. For information on regulatory and utilities activities concerning load management see Elrick and Lavidge, Inc., San Francisco, Calif., "1979 Survey: State and Federal Regulatory Commissions: Electric Utility Rate Design and Load Management Activities" (Palo Alto, Calif.: Electric Utility Rate Design Study, Report no. 80, Electric Power Research Institute (EPRI), June 1979).

15. For a detailed discussion of rate-making standards and related issues in PURPA, see "Reference Manual and Procedures for Implementing PURPA" (Palo Alto, Calif.: Electric Utility Rate Design Study, Report no. 82, EPRI, March 1979). For additional information concerning implementation activities, see J. Robert Malko, Dennis J. Ray, and Nancy L. Hassig, "Time-of-Day Pricing of Electricity Activities in Some Midwestern States," *Journal of Business Administration* 12, no. 2 (Spring 1981): 143-170.

16. For additional information see Ahmad Faruqui and J. Robert Malko, "Time-of-Use Rates and the Modification of Electric Utility Load Shapes," *Challenges for Public Utility Regulation in the 1980s*, ed. Harry M. Trebing (East Lansing: Michigan State University Public Utilities Papers, 1981), pp. 617-634.

17. For an analysis of another major modification of utility policies see J. Robert Malko, Darrell Smith, and Robert G. Uhler *Costing for Rate-making*, Topic Paper no. 2 (Palo Alto, Calif.: Electric Utility Rate Design Study, Report no. 85, EPRI, August 1981), chapters 1-2.

18. Argonne National Laboratory issues a regular report, *District Heating/Cogeneration Bulletin*, which provides timely information on cogeneration developments.

19. See Federal Energy Regulatory Commission (FERC) "Rulemakings on Cogeneration and Small Power Production," June 1980, and U.S. Department of Energy, *Guidelines for Developing State Cogeneration Policies*, Washington, D.C.: April 1979.

20. A concise summary of these is provided in Thomas R. Casten and Harold E. Ross, "Cogeneration and Its Regulation," *Public Utilities Fort-nightly* 107 (March 26, 1981): 1-14.

21. Most commissions are holding hearings on cogeneration issues. See Robert M. Spann, "Testimony before the South Carolina Public Service Commission. Docket 80-251-E," January 1981, and Idaho Public Utilities Commission, "Cogeneration and Small Power Production. Case P-300-12. Order 15746," June 1980.

22. For a comprehensive primer on this subject see Malko, Enholm, and Jaditz, "Energy Utility Diversification, Holding Companies, and Regulation."

23. David L. Arthur and Andrew B. Harris, "Diversification In The Electric Utility Industry," mimeograph. (Corporate Planning Division, Portland General Electric Company, January 1981), p. 5.

24. Ibid., p. 6.

25. Terry A. Ferrar, "Planning For Business Diversification" (Paper presented at Edison Electric Institute Finance Committee Annual Meeting, New York City, May 22, 1981), p. 10.

26. National Association of Regulatory Utility Commissioners (NARUC), "Report of the Ad Hoc Committee on Nonutility Investments", in *Proceedings Eighty-Fourth Annual Convention*, Washington, D.C.: 1972.

27. Wisconsin Gas Company (Milwaukee) is an example of a firm which has taken each of these steps while Wisconsin Power and Light Company (Madison) has just begun consideration of the legal and organizational aspects.

28. This issue has reached the courts. A commission ruled that a utility's coal subsidiary was overcharging the utility for coal and reduced the allowed coal expense. The utility has appealed. (*Montana-Dakota Utilities* v. *Montana Public Service Commission*, 1980.)

29. According to Salomon Brothers, "diversification does not appear to be a viable option for most electric utilities" although it is "the latest 'hot issue' for electric utilities seeking new ways to boost lackluster earnings." Jennifer Proga, "Electric Utility Diversification: Sound and Fury" (New York: Salomon Brothers, Inc., Stock Research Industry Analysis, November 27, 1981).

30. See Richard J. Metzler, "A Consultant's View of Utility Diversification" (Los Angeles: Theodore Barry and Associates, September 1981). Metzler concludes "diversification is, in our opinion, not only a viable strategy but perhaps even a necessary strategy for utilities in the future."

31. See "A High-Risk Era for Utilities," *Business Week*, February 23, 1981, pp. 76-86.

# 8
# On Information and the Regulation of Public Utilities

*Jim J. Tozzi* and
*Edward H. Clarke*

Privately owned public utilities are perhaps the most heavily and often badly regulated sector in the U.S. economy. Against the current backdrop of regulation affecting utilities, this chapter looks at recent efforts to contain and control federal regulation while improving state regulation and private initiative. The inquiry considers:

The implications of recent efforts to improve the social efficiency of regulation through new analysis and oversight procedures at the federal level.

The provision and dissemination of better information that will make it possible for states to regulate in more socially efficient ways.

Improved decision rules that can strengthen private initiative and competition in the provision of public-utility services.

## Federal Regulation: Improved Analysis and Oversight Procedures

On February 17, 1981, President Reagan signed an executive order on federal regulation.[1] Executive Order 12291 differs from previous orders in two significant ways. The order requires that executive agencies:

Establish regulations that will achieve the greatest net social benefit to the extent permitted by law. For major regulations agencies must prepare a regulatory impact analysis of the benefit and costs of the regulation and important alternatives.

Submit all regulations to the Office of Management and Budget for review, for a minimum of ten days (for nonmajor regulations) and up to sixty days prior to final promulgation of a major regulation.

This chapter should not be interpreted as reflecting the official views of the Office of Management and Budget or any other government agency.

A major regulation is defined as one that could have an impact of at least $100 million or a substantial impact on particular sectors or geographic areas.

Despite much criticism, benefit-cost analysis can bring about improvements in federal regulatory performance. However, the social efficiency norms underlying benefit-cost analysis are often in direct conflict with decision-making rules and criteria used by legislators, regulators, and the courts. The problem of conflict between social-efficiency norms and the decision rules used by these bodies is illustrated by the following case study.

### The Revised New Source Performance Standard (NSPS) for Electric Utilities

The process by which this major regulation evolved has become a classic case study in the ills of recent federal regulatory policy. Its evolution between 1970 and 1979 is the subject of a recent book by Bruce Ackerman and William Hassler at the Yale law school.[2] The book provides a penetrating study of how perhaps the biggest and most costly multibillion-dollar regulation in recent regulatory history was promulgated, the net effect of which is likely to be emissions increases in those areas in which the threat to human health is most severe.

The NSPS issue—involving requirements for the installation of scrubbers on new coal-fired boilers—illustrates the dominance of distributive considerations over those of social efficiency between the cradle and maturation of a major regulation. According to Ackerman and Hassler, the experience also demonstrates the myth of majority rule in its legislative evolution. In this instance, the Clean Air Act's NSPS requirement bore little resemblance to a high-level pursuit of environmental-policy objectives in the political arena guided by formal majoritarian decision rules. Much more important in explaining the actual outcome were the informal decision rules employed by congressional staffs and regulatory agencies constrained by considerations of distributive politics and prescriptive, means-oriented legislative mandates.

Ackerman and Hassler also point to the departures from social-efficiency norms that can arise when regulators are precluded from looking broadly at cost-minimizing policies at all stages of the production process. Environmental clean-up costs can obviously be imposed at different stages of this process—for example, to coal mining, oil refining, electric-power generation, or auto manufacturing. The wide range of policy choices about where to impose clean-up costs can motivate the formation of strategic coalitions—among, say, coal producers and environmental groups in the case or NSPS—which result in imposing costs on other production stages (that is, electric-power generation) while increasing society's total clean-up burden.

To avoid such results in the future, better ways of understanding the distribution of benefits and costs as well as how to motivate alternative, more social efficient policies are needed. The NSPS experience illustrates the fact that even extensive analysis involving multimillion dollar modeling by Department of Energy (DOE) and Environmental Protection Agency (EPA) over several years could not remedy the kinds of problems that grew out of the politics of section three of the Clean Air Act. Of course EPA could have done a benefit-cost analysis of the scrubbing option, but it was argued by high-level EPA staff that since it was EPA's goal to require scrubbers in the first place, such analysis would have been counterproductive.

Although EPA has recently taken steps to remedy some of the problems with the revised NSPS, probably only an action by Congress to change section three of the Clean Air Act will permit EPA to deal with the more fundamental problems. Much credit for such a beneficial result will be owed to Ackerman and Hassler for a broad and penetrating analysis of institutional behavior and performance that demonstrated how narrow distributive considerations can often dominate the high-level pursuit of social efficiency.

That kind of analysis is admittedly rare in the formulation of a single major regulation since few such regulations exhibit the magnitude of impacts and choice of alternatives that characterized the NSPS experience. However, their analytical approach deserves far more attention in the analysis of complicated interactions among regulations and their cumulative effects, particularly in areas involving the environment, energy, and the economy.

## Cumulative Effects of Regulations Affecting Public Utilities

The executive order takes an important step in this direction by encouraging Office of Management and Budget (OMB) and the agencies to look beyond individual regulations toward their cumulative impact on the national economy. OMB is authorized to make an annual compilation of the costs (and benefits) of regulation for purposes of a regulatory budget.[3] In turn, agencies are now undertaking to better analyze the cumulative impacts of regulation on particular sectors of the economy.

For example, OMB recently requested that the Energy Information Agency undertake a study of the cumulative impacts of energy and environmental regulations affecting the public-utilities sector.[4] One motivation for the study had been the 1980 Report of the Council on Environmental Quality, which had shown a threefold increase in estimated incremental expenditures (those resulting from federal requirements) of public utilities for air-pollution control—from $2.8 billion in 1978 to $8.4 billion in 1979. Though in part the increase reflected a new procedure for measuring incremental expenditures, EPA had been placing a growing share of the national pollution-control cost burden on the utilities sector. It is important to understand better the possible impact of these compliance burdens in relation to other regulatory policies and conditions affecting the industry.

The results of the cumulative-impact study are not surprising, simply showing that when allowance is made for shifts in utility and consumer behavior, the likely impacts of increased environmental compliance costs are significant but not as great as might be normally expected. The reason is that under normal demand and supply conditions the cumulative effects and regulation can be subadditive. That is, the cost impacts of individual regulations taken together may not be as great when allowance is made for substitution between one input and another—for example, between high-sulphur and low-sulphur coal. However, the real effects of environmental regulations tend to be heavily dependent on the degree to which existing energy regulations would allow for substitution. Also, the cumulative impacts, particularly on electricity prices, could be much more significant—that is, superadditive—under a set of unfavorable energy-supply scenarios. Regulatory constraints on substitutions would also enhance the tendency for the cumulative impact to be greater than might be naively assumed.

Studies of this kind serve an important public-awareness function that can bring about profound changes in regulatory policy. For example, an earlier study by the Energy Information Agency (EIA) had demonstrated rather conclusively that a number of individual federal subsidy and regulatory programs aimed at single objectives relating to energy conservation or increasing supply had the cumulative effect of offsetting each other. Indeed, the EIA study estimated that the cumulative effect of these programs would result in no positive impact in terms of the relevant objectives—reduced foreign imports and domestic consumption or enhanced domestic-supply availability.[5] This kind of information has led to dismantlement of a large part of the unwieldly federal-energy-regulatory apparatus not mandated by law.

Many remaining energy programs and regulations, however, continue to be legally mandated. In particular the Energy Act of 1978 and other statutory authorities have created several dozen subsidy programs, involving nonresearch expenditures of approximately $3.7 billion in fiscal year 1982 that discriminate in favor of particular firms and industries. These are combined with numerous energy programs and regulations that discriminate against individual firms and industries.

More recently the Department of Energy has been evaluating these programs and regulations from the standpoint of their contribution to an effective supply-side economic policy. The department is looking in particular at the social-efficiency objectives of those programs—apart from distributive and other political considerations—from the standpoint of who possesses or has access to the relevant information. It is logical to argue that, judged by these criteria, many remaining programs would be found lacking simply because the government has access to less information than the private sector. The capacity of the federal bureaucracy to absorb information must be less than the combined capacity, for example, of millions of investors and investing institutions.[6]

Inefficient and discriminatory energy programs and regulations are, of course, only one piece of a much larger mosaic of federal and state regulations affecting the energy sector. Dissatisfaction with the federal energy program and regulations, however, is leading to a broader look at the actual as opposed to the intended effects of other federal regulations and programs, including their interaction with state regulation of public utilities.

### Federal and State Regulation: Improved Information

Before turning to these issues of federal/state regulatory interaction, a key aspect of OMB's implementation of the new executive order has been built around the disclosure of information, particularly economic data and analysis. That disclosure alone can be a powerful tool for the reform of federal regulation. As instanced earlier, the recognition that energy regulation really generated no significant benefits, just a lot of costs, led to significant reforms in the very early days of the new administration.

The emphasis on information disclosure is also an outgrowth of new statutory oversight authorities, created by Congress in the Paperwork Reduction Act (PRA) of 1980.[7] In addition to the review requirements of the executive order—where OMB reviews all nonmajor regulations within ten days—it is necessary to review almost all requests for information that the federal government makes to more than nine nonfederal entities. These information requests include the submission of data to the federal government as well as the maintenance of records for review by the federal government.

The new responsibilities given to OMB in the PRA are significantly greater than those assigned to OMB in the 1942 Federal Reports Act, the precursor to the PRA. The new act, for example, restores OMB oversight of information requirements of independent regulatory agencies. Therefore, OMB is now reviewing information requirements associated with NRC licensing procedures in addition to those of the Energy Department and FERC.

The act also created, within OMB, a new Office of Information and Regulatory Affairs which exercises day-to-day responsibility for information management as well as implementation of E.O. 12291. The informational role of the office is not merely one of managing information within the government but rather one that is tied closely to the management of regulatory affairs that affect those outside the federal establishment. As a result, the use of information is being sought as an alternative to command and control regulation to bring about more efficient approaches to regulation. An example is an attempt to deal with the most significant emerging environmental regulation issue of the 1980s—protection of groundwater supplies. One alternative to a national-groundwater-regulatory program is to strengthen the states' role, in part through more effective provision of information.

**Example: Using Information to Achieve More Efficient Regulation**

The groundwater problem is probably unsurpassed in its complexity form both an informational and regulatory standpoint. Attempts to deal with the information problem are being made by broadly interpreting the social-efficiency role in matters affecting budgetary policy, information collection activities, and regulatory burdens on the private sector. To do so, one must begin by thinking carefully about the suitability of existing state and federal arrangements for various regulatory and informational functions.

To illustrate, the OMB begins with the view that proximity of decision-making centers to groundwater problems improves the ability of regulatory bodies to obtain accurate and unbiased information. It appears, for example, that grass-roots information—about constituent preferences or aquifer uses—is most efficiently collected at the state level. At the conclusion of this section, some novel techniques will be presented for eliciting accurate preference information at the state level that may be superior to traditional ways of trying to measure benefits at the federal level.[8]

For other kinds of more generic information, the federal government may do a better job of collecting and disseminating information. For example, it may be able to collect and codify certain data more efficiently than the states and may have a strong edge in the collection and analysis of research data on groundwater-contamination problems.

Efficient information provision is also essential to efficient groundwater regulation that requires differentiation among aquifer uses. This also requires recognition of the administrative costs of regulation and a sensitivity to the hierarchical distortions of information that can result from federal, in lieu of state, regulation. Consequently, in the exercise of its budget and information oversight responsibilities, OMB must ensure that it does not reduce the opportunity for regulatory differentiation so as to lead to a socially inefficient level of regulation and industrial compliance costs.

The collection of information on groundwater problems as well as the development and implementation of regulatory programs often takes place within an often controversial and emotional political climate that can lead to a costly adoption of uniform standards. More specifically, there is danger in the groundwater area of repeating the history of the 1970s in air and water regulation—that is, pressures for regulation that require all groundwater to be maintained at a uniform quality level. Such pressures, surprisingly enough, often come from state officials and are usually supported by well-meaning attempts at the federal level to achieve greater consistency in federal regulations affecting groundwater.

Efforts to develop an effective federal/state groundwater protection strategy are illustrative of broader opportunities for relying on information as a means of reducing federal dominance in the regulatory arena. This kind of strategy, of course, can have mixed blessings for those who must comply with regulations. On the one hand, nonuniform state regulation can achieve reduced industrial-compliance burdens while improving social efficiency. On the other hand, the proliferation of differing state requirements can create uncertainty and confusion in the regulated community.

In the last several years, for example, there has been a remarkable shift from federal dominance to state initiative in the management of nuclear and hazardous wastes. Between 1976 and 1980, forty-one states passed laws banning, requiring state approval for, or regulating radioactive-waste transportation or disposal within their borders. This has been accompanied by a strong activist role by states in the regulation of hazardous wastes, particularly those activities affecting transportation and disposal of these wastes under the Resource Conservation and Recovery Act. The proliferation of different state requirements affecting interstate transporters has recently led the admininstration to consider the imposition of a uniform national-manifest system for the transport of hazardous wastes. In those cases where information on the movement of hazardous wastes must be collected, the federal government may be the most effective provider of the information.

These examples also illustrate a blurring of the traditionally dominant federal role in the environmental area, accompanied by federal intrusions into an economic regulatory role that had been primarily reserved for the states. In some respects the intrusions outside the purview of energy regulation were not widely foreseen. There is little doubt, however, that the strong new source bias of most environmental regulations in the 1970s has dominated the role of state public-utility commissions in regulating entry.

In other cases, federal preemption has been more direct. With the passage of the Public Utility Regulatory Policy Act (PURPA) in 1978, the federal government became rather significantly involved in the rate-setting process of the state utility commissions. In addition to encouraging more efficient rate structures, PURPA also exempted small nonconventional power producers from state regulation while requiring that utilities purchase power from the new producers at a price equal to what it would have cost to provide it themselves.

At times the pressures for preemption seem to reflect the inexorable tendency toward increasing the span of regulatory control so as to enhance the effectiveness of federal regulation. In this case the growth of federal energy, environmental, and social controls has fueled pressures for federal interventions in the economic regulatory arena, traditionally the preserve of state regulatory bodies. The costs and burden of federal regulation may, of course, be only one of many contributors to the problem faced by public utilities in obtaining adequate rates of return. On the other hand, one can be sympathetic with the frustations of utility executives who have complained about the imposition of large and increasing compliance costs which cannot be adequately reflected in utility-rate structures as a result of delays in state public-utility rate proceedings.

Such problems might be addressed, however, not by illinformed federal interventions but rather by strategies that link improved information to improved decision rules in the regulatory arena. Decision rules means both the formal decision rules used by majoritarian legislatures and the informal rules used by regulators. This also includes competitive decision rules that guide behavior in the private marketplace.

The importance of decision rules in improving institutional performance at both the federal and state levels is clear. As instanced by the NSPS experience, federal agencies can be required to produce voluminous amounts of information and analysis that may, at times, have little or no relevance to decisions guided by distributional, in lieu of social-efficiency, considerations.

One means of dealing with the problem is to broaden the effective participation of those outside the Washington arena who are affected by decisions now made largely within that arena. Such a process would involve provision of more information about the cumulative effects of federal policies as well as the use by Federal decision makers of preference information revealed by those outside the federal establishment.

Going back to the problem of passthrough of regulatory costs, a simple thought experiment will illustrate such a process. What if the heads of twenty federal regulatory agencies had to justify each year the cumulative costs of their regulations before public-utility commissions in each of the fifty states? These costs would be determined on a nationwide basis by a federal agency. The federal regulatory agencies would then justify these costs in formal rate proceedings where they also bore the burden of proof for justifying rate increases reflecting the passthrough of compliance costs. Clearly there would be an end to the alleged regulatory blank check on the national income (including electricity price increases) and to many federal regulations as well.

The thought experiment is intended to illustrate simply the possibility of changes in decision rules that fundamentally alter the nature of regulatory decisions outside the cozy confines of the Washington establishment. The Washington debate over regulatory reform is, in some respects, symptomatic of that problem. The effort has been aimed largely at changing the burden of proof within the Washington arena.

Currently there are numerous variants of congressional, presidential, and judicial veto of regulations advanced by a wide variety of regulatory reformers and interest groups. Some seemingly frivolous proposals would add a different wrinkle to the veto game. For example, the suggestion has been made to think about a governors' veto where no one is quite sure where to put the apostrophe. However, serious proposals to change the focus of decision making in many areas formerly dominated by the federal government could give state and local elected officials the opportunity to make the important trade-offs involving environment, energy, and the economy. And these changes could lead to more rational and efficient regulation of the public-utilities industry.

The discussion now will turn to the possibility of improved decision rules that differ from a simple panoply of veto mechanisms in that these decision rules are aimed at providing more than just simple checks and balances over the growth of federal regulation. In this context, the introduction of decision rules of a rather nontraditional kind is aimed at obtaining more accurate and unbiased preference information in a decentralized economy.

### Example: Using Nontraditional Decision Rules to Obtain Accurate Preference Information

The nontraditional decision rules achieve the revelation of accurate information by giving any person in a social-decision process a basic choice. The person is given the choice of accepting a decision that would be made without his participation or changing the decision to what he wants upon payment of an amount of money equal to the net cost to all other persons of doing what he wants done instead of what would otherwise be done.

The motivation to reveal accurate preference information, which has been called demand revelation, results from the imposition of a penalty calculated separately for each individual that represents the social costs of each individual's choices.[9] In choosing between two social alternatives the level of expected benefits or costs related by any individual may affect aggregate net benefits such that one social alternative is chosen over another. Without a particular individual's evaluation, a second alternative might have been preferred as indicated by the aggregate reports of the other individuals. The penalty imposed on any individual is equivalent to the losses incurred by others because of the inclusion of the individual's report and the resultant choice of the first alternative. The imposition of a penalty of this kind ensures that each individual will receive a lower level of actual net benefits if he misrepresents his expected benefits and costs. To preserve an incentive structure that avoids strategic behavior, however, the aggregate of the penalties collected cannot be returned to the individuals involved in the reporting procedures.

It has been observed that such a penalty structure is conceptually similar to an auction, where the highest bidder pays not the amount of his bid but rather the second highest bid. This, too, would motivate bidders to reveal an accurate willingness-to-pay for the desired object.

The scientific bodies of the federal government, such as the National Science Foundation, have begun sponsoring research on these nontraditional mechanisms and the OMB has begun thinking about their use in a variety of policy contexts. For example, OMB is exploring their use in more accurately determining state needs for hazardous waste clean-up and groundwater protection. The existing super-fund of $1.6 billion may be rapidly exhausted by clean-up requirements associated with 115 priority sites and many more that may be identified as a result of current efforts to detect and measure groundwater contamination.

More specifically, the government is examining alternative mechanisms for allocating super-fund appropriations that might be different from the current arrangement requiring the federal government to fund 90 percent of the clean-up cost of the site while the state makes up 10 percent of the remaining cost from general fund revenues. By certain interpretations of the law states are now prohibited from raising these dollars from those who are taxed for this purpose in the super-fund legislation. Dissatisfaction with the federal preemption provisions of the existing super-fund has fueled broader interest in the effectiveness of the current allocative mechanism as compared with some alternative mechanism.

One proposal under study would establish a variable matching arrangement—called the limited fund mechanism—that would base the allocation of super-fund dollars on the revealed willingness-to-pay of state recipients.[10] In contrast to the current fixed (ninety-ten) matching arrangement, state recipients would pay a share based upon the revealed preferences of potential recipients in other states whose projects cannot be funded during any given year. The process could lead to the accurate and unbiased expression of a state's willingness-to-pay for funding of a clean-up project financed by super-fund. Such an approach might also better motivate states to find ways to determine preferences for clean-up and avoid some of the problems encountered in the attempt to apply traditional benefit-cost analysis to this area. It is common knowledge that the analyses conducted by federal agencies are frequently incomplete reflections of actual benefits and costs and rarely reflect subjective preferences or entrepreneurial opportunities foregone. The approaches OMB is studying would relate federal decisions more directly to the real opportunity costs, including subjective preferences expressed by decision makers who are closer to the problem conditions and the preferences of individuals.

The benefit information could not only improve the allocation of public funds but also regulatory decisions in the hazardous waste clean-up area. In particular, federal and state enforcement authorities would be better positioned to equate the scale of private clean-up efforts with those that reflect willingness-to-pay for publicly financed clean-up efforts.

In the water pollution area, this willingness-to-pay criterion has guided regulatory efforts for controlling conventional pollutants since the 1977 amendments to the Clean Water Act. For hazardous wastes it may also serve as an appropriate criterion for the level of private clean-up activity.

Thus far this chapter has dealt largely with issues of devolution between the federal government and the states, predominantly in the area of environmental regulation. The concluding section, will examine some of the more traditional issues of public-utility economics and will look in particular at some of the implications of the nontraditional decision rules.

## Traditional Issues of Public-Utility Economics: Improved Decisions through Nontraditional Decision Rules

State public-utility regulation lies somewhere in the middle of a social-control continuum ranging from nationalizing public utilities to completely privatizing them. The federal government has traditionally had little direct interest in this area except to consider ways of putting the federal house in order and, more recently, to consider alternatives to preemption of state economic regulation.

In the view of some, federal regulation has already wrought a subtle kind of socialization in the economics of this sector. However, explicit policies going in the direction of nationalization are, for good reason, rarely discussed. In fact there is rather good data on the relative performance of federal entities in the production of hydroelectric power that suggest such policies would be very poor ones. A 1979 General Accounting Office (GAO) study, for example, showed that if federal government hydroelectric plants were as efficient as comparable plants in the private sector, the annual savings would be more than $10 million. The cost of producing electricity in about fifty private electric-power plants was $2.72 per kilowatt-hour compared with $3.29 per kilowatt-hour in the approximately one hundred government plants that GAO studied.[11]

Similar comparisons are also often made of purely private unregulated, as opposed to publicly regulated utilities. A recent article "Two Utilities Are Better Than One," pointed to the comparative studies of Walter J. Primeaux at the University of Illinois who suggests that the cost-reducing effects of competition substantially outweigh economies-of-scale effects for small and medium-size firms up to an annual power output of 222 million kilowatt-hours. It also appears that even for large firms economies of scale have been substantially reduced because of technological changes and the cost conditions affecting generating capacity.[12]

In addition to these changes in technology and cost conditions, one needs also to take account of recent changes in economic theory. The natural-monopoly theory, which justified public-utility regulation because of economies of scale dates back to the mid-1800s writings of John Stuart Mill and Edwin Chadwick. It is closely related to public-goods theory which had been also used to justify so much of recent governmental activity over the last twenty-five years. However, the latter theory has been undergoing substantial revision in recent years and will be reflected in changing theories about how to deal with natural-monopoly problems.

In his 1958 formulation of the public-goods problem Paul Samuelson described the natural-monopoly problem as "analytically almost exactly like my model of public expenditure" and the problem of obtaining information in the case of indivisibilities and increasing returns arises for "the same game-theoretic reasons that compel rational men to hide their desires for public goods;" the problems presented by "almost all deviations from constant returns to scale and almost all externalities must inevitably involve some of the same analytic properties and dilemmas of my polar (public goods) case."[13]

The existence of demand-revealing solutions to the free-rider or public-goods problem thus naturally leads one to consider demand-revealing, natural-monopoly solutions to problems of indivisibilities that lie at the heart of the marginal-cost-pricing problem of public-utility economics. Indeed, the problem in theory is solved by a multipart tariff that recovers costs associated with increasing returns or indivisibilities in ways that would avoid the incentive for consumers to misrepresent their preferences for the provision of what amounts to a quasi-public good.

The solution to the marginal-cost-pricing problem has recently been carried further into the real-world problems of information provision. As with public goods, individual consumers of public-utility services may have little or no knowledge of preferences that they would otherwise misrepresent. In the real world, in fact, suppliers may be able to more efficiently obtain and provide the relevant information. For example, General Motors (GM) or Toyota may know more about consumer demand for automobiles than consumers would be able to provide themselves. The situation may be the same for producers and consumers of electricity.

Indeed, recent developments linking demand revelation to a solution to the natural-monopoly problem show the conditions under which a discriminating monopolist will provide the socially optimum level of information. A demand-revealing, natural-monopoly solution could achieve these conditions and thus motivate suppliers to achieve a socially efficient level of services along with an efficient set of discriminatory prices that reflect marginal cost. The firms are also motivated to gather the relevant information about consumer preferences that would be used in making decisions about pricing.[14]

The new theory is an expansion of a previous theory of franchise monopoly in public-utility economics that dates back to Edwin Chadwick's notions about "competition for the field" as compared with "competition within the field of service."[15] That theory has shown how franchise-bidding schemes might result in monopoly provision of the optimum quantity at the lowest per unit price. Where the service is provided at decreasing cost, as in the case of public utilities, one can avoid certain traditional ex post monopoly problems through an ex ante bidding process involving a potential large number of franchises, one of which will become the supplier through competition for the field.

During the last decade, critics of the original franchise-bidding approach had observed that although it prevents the winning firm from obtaining a monopoly return, it gives no assurance that the output will be priced efficiently on marginal-cost terms. More fundamentally, the original approach ignored problems of how the relevant information about consumer valuations is to be obtained so as to determine both the optimum output and marginal-cost prices. Finally, it ignored the issue of how potentially complex contingent contracts are to be determined and enforced in a world of uncertainty, complex product-quality dimensions, and changing tastes and technologies.

The possible key to operationalizing the franchise monopoly approach, not only for public utilities but for public goods generally, is through a natural-monopoly approach that relies in part on nontraditional decision rules. Such an approach would permit potential competition to discipline the performance of an existing supplier because consumer groups can select a more efficient alternative supplier in a rather straightforward and unambiguous way. A crucial element in the process is the way in which the motivation to price at marginal cost also provides an incentive for the provision of a socially efficient amount of information.[16] Such an approach does require some regulation—for example, to prevent collusion between providers and consumer groups and to provide rules for determining exchanges of assets between an existing provider and a new entrant. However, the regulatory apparatus bears little resemblance to traditional economic regulation of public utilities.

It is, of course, possible that recent solutions to the natural-monopoly problem, while interesting from the standpoint of public goods or public-utility pricing theory, may have less relevance than once thought to the practical economics of public utilities. In fact, the new approach was developed for its possible applicability to the provision of a broad range of public goods other than utility services, which are more clearly subject to indivisibilities and increasing returns to scale.

In the case of public utilities and absent natural-monopoly conditions of supply, simple deregulation could be a preferred alternative, at least when compared with the results of existing state public-utility rate-of-return regulation. In sum, it is possible that the best immediately practical decision rule for achieving both socially efficient results and the effective provision of information may in some cases be through simple competition. However, if deregulation is a socially desired remedy, recent experience with federal interventions in state economic regulation indicates that there are problems in getting from here to there.

Although all the lessons that will be learned from our recent experience with PURPA have yet to be learned, one basic conclusion is already clear. Just as the federal government has been a poor producer of hydroelectric power, the federal establishment can be a poor producer of competition as well as the means of regulating it. Society may need decision rules other than those presently used in Washington, D.C., for producing competitive decision rules that are workable and adequate for the needs of public utilities and the consumers they serve.

A small city in Texas has found a rather simple decision rule for, at a minimum, protecting competition. In Lubbock, Texas, two utilities—Lubbock Power and Light and Southwestern Public Service Company—each provide services at very low rates. The city charter states that any change in the competition between these two companies must be approved by three-fourths of the registered voters.

## Notes

1. *Federal Regulation*, Executive Order 1229], 46 FR 13193-98 February 17, 1981.

2. Bruce Ackerman and William Hassler, *Clean Coal and Dirty Air* (New Haven: Yale University Press, 1981).

3. Jim J. Tozzi and Gail B. Coad, *"Constraining Regulatory Costs: A Budgetary Perspective"* (Paper presented to the Society of Government Economists, Allied Social Science Association Meetings, Washington, D.C., December 1981).

4. Energy Information Agency, "Cumulative Impacts of Regulation, Illustrative Examples for the Public Utilities Sector," DOE/EIA/AR-0286, May 1981.

5. Energy Information Agency, "Energy Demand/Energy Markets," DOE/EIA-0201/16, July 1980.

6. Department of Energy, Office of Planning and Analysis, "The Role of DOE Programs and Regulations in Supply Side Economic Policy," DOE-PE-0037, September 1981.

7. Paperwork Reduction Act of 1980, P.L. 96-511, December 11, 1980.

8. David E. Goetze, "The Efficiency of Federal, State and Nontraditional Arrangements: The Case of Groundwater Regulation," *Resources for the Future Working Paper*, December 1980.

9. Edward Clarke, *Demand Revelation and the Provision of Public Goods* (Cambridge, Mass.: Ballinger Publishing Co., 1980).

10. Edward Clarke and David Goetze, "Regulation and Subsidy of Hazardous Waste Disposal" (forthcoming).

11. U.S. General Accounting Office, "Increased Productivity Can Lead to Lower Costs at Federal Hydroelectric Plants" (Report by the Comptroller General of the United States: FGMSD-79-15 May 29, 1979).

12. Jan Bellemy, "Two Utilities Are Better Than One," *Reason Magazine*, 13, no. 6 (October 1981):23-30.

13. Paul A. Samuelson, "Aspects of Public Expenditure Theories," *The Review of Economics and Statistics* 40 (November 1958):332-338.

14. Clarke, *Demand Revelation* chap. 5.

15. Harold Demsetz, "Why Regulate Utilities?" *Journal of Law and Economics*, April, 1968; Edwin Chadwick, "Results of Different Principles of Legislation and Administration in Europe; of Competition for the Field as Compared with Competition within the Field of Service," 22 *Journal Royal Statistical Society* 1 (1859):381-420.

16. Clarke, *Demand Revelation*, chap. 5.

**Part IV
Contributions to the
Principles of Rate Making**

# 9 Price Structures in Electricity

*William G. Shepherd*

There seems little doubt that marginal-cost pricing is correct and desirable up to the limit set by metering costs. The question today is how much has its use developed and what have the effects been?

Despite the signs of action not much has yet been done. The effects so far have also been slight, but that can be blamed partly on special conditions, including electric overcapacity and general recessions. The case for universal time-of-use pricing has been made, both on theoretical and practical grounds. As capacity is more fully used in coming years, there will be much larger yields from marginal-cost pricing. In presenting these points the issues will be reviewed as they were before 1968, the changes since then, the pricing actions, and then their probable effects. Throughout, I write as a long-time advocate of rational electricity pricing who is learning to distinguish between words and actions, and between actions and effects.

## The Experts and Issues before 1970

Before 1970 U.S. utilities lived in so favorable a world that marginal-cost pricing could be neglected. At least six unusual conditions existed. Scale economies were being realized, especially in generating and transmission electricity. The cost of capital (particularly as reflected in interest rates) was relatively low. Fuel prices were stable and low with little concern about future supplies. Sites for generating power were not scarce. Amenity and safety were of little public concern. Nuclear power was seen as a rich future source of energy, not as a threat to security. Therefore official approval of new plants was easy and quick.

Accordingly the long-run marginal cost of peak-load power seemed to be low, and so the early promotional rate design lived on. Declining-block and two-part tariffs were meant to promote use, and they certainly did. Once connected, a customer was given marginal incentives to use more power virtually at any and all times. The all-electric home—with low rates particularly for uses (winter heating and summer air conditioning) which were likely to occur precisely during the system peak—was only the most striking among the many rate features which ignored true costs.

I am grateful to Harry Trebing and to a number of regulatory and company officials for discussions about the issues in this chapter.

151

One can understand why costs were neglected: in the euphoric pre-1970 world marginal costs at peak did appear to be low. But this was largely an illusion created by excess capacity. By the 1960s reserve margins were about 25 percent above peak loads, generous by any standard. How had such large reserves come to be considered acceptable? Partly there was the Averch-Johnson rate-base effect that enlarged the volume of capital which the constrained profit-maximizing firm would choose to install. Partly, too, there was the shared regulators' and utilities' intense aversion to any and all service breakdowns. They, and users, came to regard large-capacity reserves as necessary. And that extra capacity automatically made it appear that short-run marginal cost—as well as some vague measures of long-run marginal cost—was low. The whole circular system of promotional rates and excess capacity therefore pulled itself ahead by feeding on its own biases.

The error was not so much the failure to foresee how the cost levels would change sharply after 1968. Rather the failure was in denying even the correct conceptual basis. To pre-1968 utilities and most regulators, marginal-cost pricing was not only unfamiliar but actually disloyal to the growth ethic and even vaguely socialist. After all it had only been tried in publicly owned systems such as in France, Britain, and other European places. If instead there had been an understanding of cost guidelines for pricing, the devastating post-1968 crisis in the power industry could probably have been smoothly accommodated.

There was plenty of advance notice by distinguished analysts. W. Arthur Lewis (1948) laid the basis of marginal cost, and then Hendrik Houthakker (1951), Ian Little (1953), James Bonbright (1961), and William Vickrey (1955) developed much of the needed theory. At the French Electricite de France (EDF) Marcel Boiteaux applied the ideas in practice, and James R. Nelson (1964) brought the message to the United States. Then in Britain Ronald Meek (1963) and Ralph Turvey (1968) took up the issue in the early and middle 1960s.

Yet by 1966 my own survey of U.S. electric rates found less than 10 percent of utilities with any significant marginal-cost pricing feature. Most of those cases were off-peak discounts to limited groups of users, rather than high prices aimed specifically at peak loads. Even in these few cases the rest of the utilities' rates had a strong antimarginalist structure.

In short, Houthakker, Vickrey, Bonbright, and Nelson had provided the concepts, and European practice gave plenty of practical guidance. But U.S. firms and regulators were firmly set in the opposite direction.

## Events since 1968

It took a seismic reversal of basic conditions to jar the old complacency. Every one of the six favorable conditions was altered. Scale economies reached their limit in generation. The cost of capital rose strongly and then, since 1978, dramatically. Fuel prices multiplied. Sites for generation units grew much scarcer. Nuclear hazards and pollution costs became major hindrances to electricity growth. And the approval of many new plants became slow, contentious, and unpredictable.

Suddenly from 1968 to 1978 there was a need to conserve capacity rather than enlarge it. It became clear that marginal costs at peak-load times were indeed much higher than in off-peak periods. The brownouts in New York and elsewhere made that plain enough for everyone to see, and reserve margins slipped below 10 percent of normal peak load in large areas. Marginal-cost pricing's virtues were quickly seen in some quarters as a way to ease the pressure. The post-1973 oil price rise elevated the issue to one of energy independence from foreign controls, and so such federal agencies as the Federal Energy Administration (FEA) set up sections to promote peak-load pricing. There was funding for some fourteen rate-design experiments in various states. The Wisconsin commission, with advice from Leonard Weiss and then leadership by Charles Cicchetti, adopted major new structures from 1974 to 1977.

In short, peak-load pricing became a la mode, an easy way out of severe problems. The Public Utility Regulatory Policies Act (PURPA) of 1978 embodied this optimism in requiring state commissions to consider marginal-cost pricing. But it was a weak approach without force or clear standards. And it set in motion a costly process of studying. A form of fifty-state multiplier took hold in which the same ideas were to be articulated over and over state by state. The more progressive commissions were already involved. The other commissions could hire the studies and then let the matter rest if they wished.

PURPA has therefore enlarged the income of economic-consulting firms. Earlier the FEA and Electric Power Research Institute (EPRI) rate-design studies had drawn many academic economists into profitable research work. (Indeed, I have found a startling number of my theorist and econometric colleagues around the country to be benefiting since 1970 from the ideas that I and others pursued in the lonely 1960s.) By 1978 it seemed that nearly everyone had become an expert on marginal-cost pricing. If nothing else has occurred, at least the profession has been drawn to the subject and has studied its possibilities as never before.

Yet this research momentum has run up against strong resistance from three sources. One is the caution of the firms, which have been enduring a series of pressures and—to put it mildly—are not eager to rush into major tariff revisions which raise prices during the main business hours. Only a pressing need to share peak-load capacity requirements during 1968 to 1976 has impelled them to experiment. Such changes naturally put the utilities under intense pressure from customers who face the higher rates. Therefore the commission cannot just order the new rates. It must persuade the utility firm and its major customers that rate reform is not only logical but not a threat to them. When I advised the Massachusetts regulators on rate reform in 1976-1979, they recognized this need for persuasion, and they were energetic and successful at it.

The second source of resistance is the complexity of measuring marginal costs. There are at least several internally consistent alternative methods that give varying results. Each has its advocates among academics, consultants, regulators, and customer groups who hope to gain from it. A determined advocate can even turn the debate into a fog of technical points and uncertainties. Indeed in some states the proceedings have become stalled in fine points which the commissions are unable or unwilling to resolve.

Yet such an impasse is quite unnecessary. The reasonable approach is to lay out simple concepts of marginal costs, adopt preliminary rates, and then make one or two later adjustments as needed. Elasticities are inherently uncertain, and so some iteration is bound to be necessary. This sensible approach has been applied with conspicuous success by the Wisconsin commission under Charles Cicchetti. The opposite kind of approach seeks to define an exact comprehensive solution on the first try. Such perfectionism breeds endless doctrinal debates, and it is favored by purists and by parties who do not want any rate reform at all.

A third complication has been the campaign for lifeline rates. In many states it has diverted attention and support from the more basic need to fit rates to cost structures. It has also generated large fees for consultants arguing in state after state that lifeline rates are an illogical and loose method.

Yet lifeline rates have not interfered frontally with marginal-cost pricing. And they have been installed in many states with little apparent harm. Indeed they illustrate the basic resiliency of electric pricing. As long as the main structure of rates is sound, imperfect lesser modifications cause little harm.

The fourth source of resistance has probably been the most important: the relative drop in demand for electricity. It has been caused mainly by demand elasticity, as electric prices have risen sharply after 1973. Also there have been the recessions of 1974, 1980, and 1981. Utilities have found themselves with excess reserve capacity much as in the 1960s. Why, they reason, should we set radically higher rates to cut peak-load demand? Or in more correct analytical terms, peak-load electricity does not have high marginal costs in the present situation. It is illustrated simply in figure 9-1. Rate restructuring for high peak-load prices is not needed, at least temporarily.

This is a powerful truth, which ambivalent firms and regulators have been quick to apply as a reason for holding back on marginal-cost pricing.

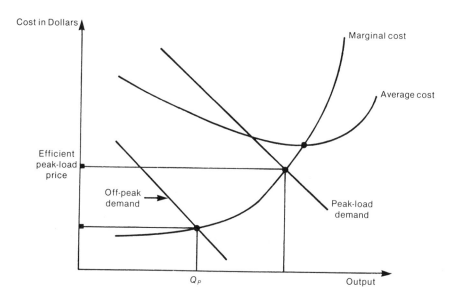

**Figure 9-1.** When Capacity Is Idle the Peak-Load Price Is Not High

Consequently the drive for rate reform has slowed in the last several years. This pause is half appropriate in the shortrun. But for the other half—the cutting of off-peak prices down to low marginal costs—there is as much need as ever. And in the longer run in the later 1980s, when demand growth again brings peak-load demand up to capacity, there probably will be an especial need for peak-load pricing. The excess capacity during the 1976 to 1982 interval will be remembered fondly, perhaps with wishes that the time had been used to establish the framework for peak-load pricing.

Load management has also experienced a boom and then a pause. Attempting to restrain peak usage by direct controls is the alter ego of peak-load pricing. Its technology has advanced from the mere shutting off of interruptible service such as to residential water heaters and certain industrial users. Now the techniques are more advanced at costs which make them more widely applicable. Equally important, customer knowledge and acceptance are broader, and so load management can now be more effective. It can deal even more decisively than pricing can with certain problems, such as needle peaks and other inelastic demands which strain capacity. Since it is exclusively peak-load oriented, it too has lost impetus during the last several years. But it too will probably be needed in several years when capacity once again comes under strain.

**Probable Effects**

The main actions in the U.S. so far are

1. Experimental rate demonstration programs in fourteen states, including various residential customers on a mandatory or voluntary basis.
2. Actual system-wide rates in several states, applied mainly to larger industrial customers on a mandatory basis.

Before assessing these actions, one must consider the larger surrounding changes. First the level of all electric prices has risen sharply. The resulting drop in electricity growth has reflected a substantial price elasticity higher than most observers had expected. The response is continuing to grow as conservation develops further. Yet even the medium-run elasticity is significant. That suggests that peak-load demand would be at least as elastic if load can be shifted to off-peak times as well as directly cut back. Peak-load pricing will undoubtedly reduce peak demands in the United States. The main question is whether the peak-load responses have been sharp in the short-run periods covered by the pricing experiments.

Second, there has been one sizable reform in price structure: the elimination of most antimarginalist declining-block tariffs. Also, many firms have moved their demand charges onto a coincident peak basis. It has occurred quietly, almost by consensus, with little study of its effects. The effects have surely been important, but they can only be guessed at in the absence of thorough analysis. The peak-load pricing experiments merely add to these underlying reforms. The effects of peak-load pricing, when they eventually develop, may be smaller than those of the more basic changes.

*Rate Demonstrations*

These projects have had mixed results in part because their methods have varied. The price structures have ranged from differentials as low as 1.67 to 1.0 to as high as 22.8 to 1.0 between peak and base prices. The peak periods, the lengths of the experiments, and the customers' basis (compensated or not, voluntary or mandatory) have also varied. Further, the methods for calculating elasticities have involved differences that are still intensely debated. Tables 9-1 and 9-2 indicate the diversity of conditions.

Accordingly, the reported results have varied as tables 9-3, 9-4, and 9-5 indicate. Both the elasticities and the actual load reductions have been estimated. Despite the variety among results there has clearly been a reduction in load, even during these brief periods of adjustment. The changes fit

**Table 9-1**
**Major Study Characteristics, by Project**

| Project | Customer Participation | | Experimental Period | Number of Experimental Rates | Sample Size | | Percentage of Service Area Residential Customers in | |
|---|---|---|---|---|---|---|---|---|
| | Mandatory | Payments | | | Control | Experimental | Sampled Population | Effective Population |
| Arizona | No | Yes | May 1976 to October 1976 | 28 | 0 | 140 | 55 | 19 |
| Connecticut | No | Yes | October 1975 to October 1976 | 1 | 200 | 200 | 63 | 29 |
| North Carolina (BREMC)[b] | Yes | No | October 1977 to October 1978 | 1 | 98 | 102 | 100 | 87 |
| Ohio | No | No | June 1976 to November 1977 | 1 | 60 | 100 | 58 | 12 |
| Rhode Island | Yes | Yes | November 1977 to December 1978 | 1 | 130 | 170 | 100 | 60 |
| Wisconsin | Yes | No | May 1977 to May 1980 | 10[a] | 92 | 506 | 44 | 43 |

Source: Miedema and White, 1980, table 4-1, p. 38.

[a]Not including a three-part rate applied in the experiment.

[b]Blue Ridge Electric Membership Corporation, hereinafter referred to as North Carolina (BREMC).

**Table 9-2**
**Summary of Time-of-Use Electricity Rates, by Project**

| Project | Number of Rates | Season | Combined Length of Weekday Rating Period | | | Length of Weekend Rating Period | | | Range of Weekday Peak to Base Price Ratios | Weekday Price Differential in Cents per Kilowatt-Hour Peak Minus Base Price |
|---|---|---|---|---|---|---|---|---|---|---|
| | | | P | I | B | P | I | B | | |
| Arizona | 16 | Summer | 3 | 10[a] | 11 | 3 | 10[a] | 11 | 2.75 to 12.0 | 7.0 to 13.0 |
| | 6 | Summer | 5 | 8[a] | 11 | 3 | 8[a] | 11 | 3.0 to 6.0 | 5.0 to 10.0 |
| | 6 | Summer | 8 | 5 | 11 | 8 | 5 | 11 | 1.67 to 6.0 | 3.0 to 7.0 |
| Connecticut | 1 | Summer | 4[a] | 9[a] | 11 | 13 | — | 11 | 16.0 | 15.0 |
| | | Winter | 4[a] | 9[a] | 11 | 13 | — | 11 | 16.0 | 15.0 |
| North Carolina (BREMC) | 1 | Summer | 8[a] | — | 16 | 8[a] | — | 16 | 2.1 | 1.26 |
| | | Winter | 8[a] | 8[a] | 8 | 8[a] | 8[a] | 8 | 3.8 | 3.39 |
| Ohio | 1 | Summer | 6 | — | 18 | — | — | 24 | 22.8 | 8.7 |
| | | Fall | 6 | — | 18 | — | — | 24 | 7.8 | 2.7 |
| | | Winter | 6 | — | 18 | — | — | 24 | 22.8 | 8.7 |
| | | Spring | 6 | — | 18 | — | — | 24 | 7.8 | 2.7 |
| Wisconsin[b] | 3 | Summer | 6[a] | — | 18 | — | — | 24 | 2 to 8 | 3.10 to 11.08 |
| | | Winter | 6[a] | — | 18 | — | — | 24 | 2 to 8 | 2.64 to 9.32 |
| | 3 | Summer | 9[a] | — | 15 | — | — | 24 | 2 to 8 | 2.86 to 8.55 |
| | | Winter | 9[a] | — | 15 | — | — | 24 | 2 to 8 | 2.45 to 8.31 |
| | 3 | Summer | 12 | — | 12 | — | — | 24 | 2 to 7.6 | 2.62 to 6.61 |
| | | Winter | 12 | — | 12 | — | — | 24 | 2 to 6.9 | 2.31 to 5.88 |
| | | Summer | — | — | 24 | — | — | 24 | N/A | 0 |
| | | Winter | — | — | 24 | — | — | 24 | N/A | 0 |
| Rhode Island[c] | 1 | Summer | 9 | 4 | 11 | — | — | 24 | 1.8 | 1.53 |
| | | Winter | 13 | — | 11 | — | — | 24 | 1.8 | 1.53 |

Source: Miedema and White, 1980, table 4-2, p. 39.

[a] Total of two nonadjacent periods.

[b] Three-part ratre not included.

[c] A demand charge for generation facilities was applied during peak hours to the average of the four highest fifteen-minute demands in the billing cycle. In addition, a demand charge for distribution facilities was applied to the average of the four highest fifteen-minute contiguous demands during all hours of any day in the billing cycle.

**Table 9-3**
**Ranges of Uncompensated Partial Own-Price Elasticities of Residential Electricity Demand, by Time-of-Day**

| | Connecticut[a] | Arizona[b] | | Wisconsin[c] | |
|---|---|---|---|---|---|
| | Narrow Peak (four hr) | Narrow Peak (three hr) | Broad Peak (five to eight hr) | Narrow Peak (six hr) | Broad Peak (nine to twelve hr) |
| Peak Period | | -1.454<br>-0.412 LL | (-1.362, -1.428) RTI | (-0.412, -0.655)<br>-0.806 | (-0.475, -0.844) CC<br>(-0.812, -0.826) AT |
| Summer | | | (-0.169, -0.483) AH<br>(-0.723, -0.780) AT | | |
| Winter | (-0.455, -0.657) | -0.679 | | | |
| Midpeak period | | -1.547<br>-0.261 LL | (-1.479, -1.723) RTI | | |
| Summer | | -0.479 | (-0.378, -0.474) AH<br>(-0.309, -0.527) AT | | |
| Winter | (-0.240, -0.497) | | | | |
| Offpeak period | | -1.640<br>-0.461 LL | (-1.516, -2.034) RTI | (-0.514, -0.769)<br>-0.094 | (-0.300, -0.636) CC<br>(-0.210, -0.239) AT |
| Summer | | | (-1.88, -0.362) AH<br>(-0.570, -0.643) AT | | |
| Winter | (-0.294, -0.360) | -0.409 | | | |

Source: Reprinted in Malko and Faruqui, 1980, table 9-1, p. 156.

Source: D.J. Aigner and D.J. Poirier, Electricity Demand and Consumption by Time-of-Use: A Survey (Palo Alto, Calif.: Electric Power Research Institute, 1980), table 4-2, p. 44.

[a]From Lawrence and Braithwait (1977), table 6, pp. 1-167. Ranges for Connecticut are constructed over results of the months of November 1975 and January 1976 and over subperiods of the day (two of which were designated peak; three, midpeak; one, offpeak.

[b]The entry noted "AT" is from Atkinson (1977), tables 8 and 9, pp. 33 and 34, respectively. Since he pools the data over months, the ranges are constructed for the broad-peak period only. Aigner and Hausman (AH) attempt to correct for truncation bias in their results. They use the one summer month of August. Moreover, since length of the peak period is an independent variable in their model, a single elasticity is reported, although separate elasticities for individual pricing periods could have been calculated. The ranges are constructed by contrasting with their results without truncation accounted for. See table 2, p. 16; table 4, p. 21. Lau and Lillard (1978) (LL) work only with households that faced the narrow-peak period, over the period from May to October 1976. They pool the data over months. Results reported appear in table 3, p. 27. The Research Triangle Institute 1978 (RTI) uses data aggregated over the period from July to September 1976.

[c]The first entries are from Caves-Christensen (1978), tables 6 and 7, pp. 25 and 26, respectively, and are marked "CC." Ranges were constructed over the results for the months of July and August 1977, over alternative definitions of the peak period (in the case of "broad peak"), and over alternative TOD rate differentials from 2:1 to 8:1.

The second entries, marked "AT," are from Atkinson, table 11, p. 39. Since he pools the data over the two available months and over prices, the ranges constructed are for the broad-peak period only.

**Table 9-4**
**Kilowatt-Hour Usage Reductions, by Time-of-Use Customers in Selected Summer Months as Percentage of Control Group Usage**

| Project | Average Day | | | | Peak Day | | | | Peak Hour | Month[a] |
|---|---|---|---|---|---|---|---|---|---|---|
| | Peak | Intermediate | Base | Total | Peak | Intermediate | Base | Total | | |
| Arizona | 7.3[b] | 1.3 | — 3.4 | 1.3 | 39.0[b] | 22.7[b] | 3.5 | 19.1[b] | 39.0[b] | July 1976 |
| Connecticut | 30.9[b] | 16.8[b] | 0.2 | 12.6[b] | 39.7[b] | — | −12.6 | 4.4 | 40.2[b] | June 1976 |
| Ohio | 38.0[b] | — | − 5.9 | 3.9 | 7.6 | 11.7 | −19.6 | 0.8 | − 8.0 | August 1976 |
| Rhode Island | 10.2 | 1.2 | −11.0 | − 2.4 | | | | | | June 1978 |
| Wisconsin | | | | | | | | | | |
| six-hour peak | 25.6[b] | — | 5.3 | 10.2[b] | 28.0[b] | — | 10.2[b] | 14.3 | | |
| nine-hours peak | 22.9[b] | — | 10.9[b] | 15.3[b] | 22.9[b] | — | 7.7 | 12.9 | 21.9 | |
| twelve-hour peak | 20.7[b] | — | 10.4[b] | 15.5[b] | 21.3[b] | — | 9.2 | 14.5 | 19.6 | |

Source: Miedema and White, 1980, table 4-4, p. 42.

Note: The North Carolina (BREMC) project is omitted because system demand is lowest in summer.

[a] Most are for actual peak months, days, and hours. Only August and September 1976 system load data were available for Ohio.

[b] Only estimates that were different from zero by a statistically significant margin (10 percent level) are denoted. Dashes indicate that associated estimates were undefined; and blanks, that they could not be estimated due to data constraints.

**Table 9-5**
**Kilowatt-Hour Usage Reductions, by Time-of-Use Customers in Selected Winter Months as Percentage of Control Group Usage**

| Project | Average Day | | | | Peak Day | | | | | Month[a] |
|---|---|---|---|---|---|---|---|---|---|---|
| | Peak | Intermediate | Base | Total | Peak | Intermediate | Base | Total | Peak Hour | |
| Connecticut | 18.7[b] | 1.8 | − 18.5[b] | − 3.7 | 14.4 | − 0.1 | − 23.1[b] | − 6.4 | 12.0 | January 1976 |
| Ohio | 21.2 | — | − 11.6 | − 5.8 | | | | | | January 1977 |
| North Carolina | 2.1 | − 2.6 | − 4.0 | − 1.7 | 0.0 | − 6.4 | − 7.1 | − 4.2 | − 0.1 | February 1978 |
| (BREMC) Rhode Island | 11.7 | — | 0.6 | 5.5 | 23.5 | — | 10.0 | 18.7 | 26.1 | February 1978 |
| Wisconsin | | | | | | | | | | December to February 1978 |
| six-hour peak | 15.2[b] | — | − 0.3 | 7.5 | 21.7[b] | — | 2.5 | 3.8 | 23.8[b] | |
| nine-hour peak | 8.1 | — | − 4.1 | 1.2 | 15.7 | — | 4.7 | 9.3 | 20.7[b] | |
| twelve-hour peak | 8.4 | — | − 1.6 | 3.5 | 12.0 | — | 4.8 | 8.0 | 21.6[b] | |

Source: Miedema and White, 1980, table 4-5, p. 43.

Note: The Arizona project is omitted because the study covered only summer months.

[a]Most are for actual peak months, days, and hours. Only August and September 1976 system-load data were available for Ohio.

[b]Only estimates that were different from zero by a statistically significant margin (10 percent level) are denoted. Dashes indicate that associated estimates were undefined; and blanks, that they could not be estimated due to data constraints.

the predictions: sharper price differentials usually give larger changes. So far the shifts are smaller than comparable European experience would suggest. Moreover they may be mingled with the two basic shifts (in price levels and declining-block rates) that have been also occurring in parallel.


*Industrial Rates*


By 1981 over 60 utilities (among 170 total) had time-of-use rates for larger customers. The resulting changes in loads have been as outlined in table 9-6, where comparison with twenty years of French and British experience are also given. Jan Paul Acton and Bridger M. Mitchell (1980, 1981) regard the United States responses as being comparable to the European patterns once sufficient time has elapsed to permit full adjustments. They also offer the projections in table 9-7 as estimates of the next gains to the United States from applying peak-load pricing if responses are as extensive as in Europe. Such cost savings of $1.6 to $4.1 billion annually would be significant. It is not clear if their calculations allow for existing overcapacity, but the results accord with what Houthakker, Vickrey, Nelson, and others have long predicted.

With such gains in prospect, the case for marginal-cost pricing seems to be established. Yet there are two reservations. One is that the gains are small in some states where load factors are already high. These include the states where antimarginalist features have been eliminated as well as middle-belt states with moderate peaks in both summer and winter.

A second reservation arises from the social effects of load shifting. Much peak-load cutting by companies involves the shifting of operations to off-peak periods, particularly by expanding night-shift work. Such work imposes various personal costs by disrupting the normal family routines. These extra costs can be compensated in the long run by higher wages. Those wage increments would then offset some of the gains from lower electricity costs. But the wage rises do not fully offset the personal burdens borne by the workers when the demand for labor has a significant degree of elasticity. Figure 9-2 illustrates the outcome. It is likely that the long-run demand for labor usually has significant elasticity, often rising above a value of 1.0.

Therefore peak-load pricing incurs higher costs and lower net benefits than the narrow calculations indicate. The size of these offsetting costs is unknown in the absence of research. I know of no research yet on the subject. Yet the costs are likely to be significant.

Equity also belongs in an appraisal of rate reform's effects. Even if no efficiency gains occurred, marginal-cost pricing would still yield important

**Table 9-6**
**Summary of Estimated Reductions in Peak-Period Load**

| Utility | Estimating Method | Type of Data | Percent Reductions in | | |
|---|---|---|---|---|---|
| | | | System Load (Kilowatts) | Time-of-Use (Kilowatts) | Load (Kilowatt-Hour) |
| *Long-term change* | | | | | |
| Electricite de France (EdF) | Evolution of load curve | System load | 14 | | |
| Electricite de France (EdF) | Individual-customer load shapes | Subscribed demand | | 12-14 | |
| Central Electricity Generating Board (CEGB) | Evolution of load curve | System load | 13 | | |
| Electricite de France/ United States | Individual-customer load shapes | Manufacturing customers | | 14-25 | 14-25 |
| *Intermediate-term change* | | | | | |
| Electricite de France | Trends in hourly load | System load | 5 | | |
| Central Electricity Generating Board (CEGB) | Individual-customer load shapes | Load-management customers | | 40[b] | |
| *Short-term change* | | | | | |
| Pacific Gas & Electric (PG&E) | Evolution of load curve | Time-of-use class | | 1.3-2.0 | |
| Southern California Edison (SCE) | Evolution of load curve | Time-of-use class | | 0.6-1.6 | 0.7-1.2 |
| San Diego Gas & Electric (SDG&E) | Evolution of load curve | Time-of-use class | | 3.5[b] | 5-6 |
| Wisconsin Power & Light (WP&L) | Customer survey | Reported scheduling and equipment changes | | | |
| Wisconsin Power & Light | Evolution of load curve | Time-of-Use class | | 10 | 9,,7 |

Source: Acton and Mitchell, 1981. Copyright © 1981 The RAND Corporation. Reprinted with permission.

[a] Response to load management warnings above normal time-of-use response.
[b] Reductions in demand coincident with system peak.

**Table 9-7**

**Projected National Effects of Peak-Load Pricing for U.S. Manufacturing Industries at 1980 Values**

| Type of Effect | Extent |
|---|---|
| Reduction in peak-period electricity consumption | 30.0 billion kilowatt-hours |
| Reduction in maximum electricity demand | 19.8 million kilowatts |
| Proportion of peak demand in manufacturing industry | 25 percent |
| Proportion of U.S. noncoincident peak demands | 5.3 percent |
| Annual cost savings | |
| Reduction in short-run fuel costs (fuel and operating costs) | 0.5-2.1 billion dollars |
| Reduction in long-run costs (fuel, operating and capital costs) | 1.6-4.1 billion dollars |
| Construction of peak generating units | |
| Reduction in 200 megawatt (MW) units | 99 units |
| One-time saving in capital expenditure | 4.0 billion dollars |

Source: Acton and Mitchell, 1981. Copyright © 1981 The Rand Corporation. Reprinted with permission.

gains in equity. At present peak users are often heavily subsidized by other users by up to 70 or 80 percent of the cost of peak supply. Much of the peak-load use is by businesses and other groups who are not needy. Off-peak users pay prices well above their costs of supply. Many of them are residential customers with relatively low incomes. To that extent, correct time-of-use rates will improve distributional equity.

The weight of experience in Europe and the United States suggests that the optimal extent of time-of-use pricing will be approximately as follows. It will be mandatory for all larger customers down into the middle ranges of residential customers. The precise location of that margin will depend on the cost of metering compared to the extent of load fluctuations; the margin will differ somewhat among electric systems. There will usually be three daily periods, weekend periods, and—usually—separate winter, summer, and fall-spring periods.

The peak-off-peak differentials will vary from system to system over a wide range. The utility will devote extensive effort to explaining the rates and persuading users to adjust to them. There will also be load management mainly directed at larger users.

In short, virtually all systems would have the basic rate structure, but the rates and load management will apply mainly to larger customers. The approach would fit closely the patterns common in western Europe. The effects on loads are also likely to be similar. There is no surprise in this. The only surprise has been the slowness of action and the continuing doubts that there will be significant benefits.

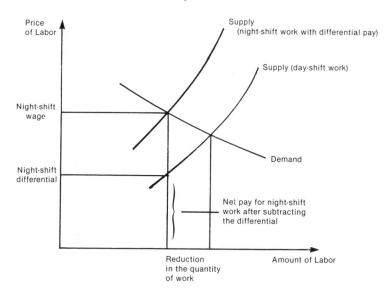

**Figure 9-2.** Added Costs of Time-of-Use Pricing

Taken altogether the reforms toward cost-based rates have been far greater than seemed attainable in the 1960s. Yet they are far less than is ultimately needed. The rate-demonstration studies and actual industrial rates have shown significant demand elasticities. But these were foreshadowed by the response to rising average electricity prices. Those responses have also been mingled with the passing of the most antimarginalist features of declining-block and two-part tariffs. And a further complication has been the recessions and excess electric capacity, which temporarily have abated the need for peak-load pricing.

Therefore the rate restructuring has had slender results so far. Yet its eventual value seems firmly established, and within several years its net economic benefits may become very large. The current pause is a chance to make widespread shifts toward more rational pricing, not an excuse to wait and see. The conceptual basis for time-differentiated rates is valid for all electric systems, whether the net gains in each system will ultimately be large or small.

**References**

Acton, Jan Paul, and Mitchell, Bridger M. "Do Time-of-Use Rates Change Load Curves?" R-2588-DWP/EPRI. San Monica, Calif.: The RAND Corporation, May 1980.

Acton, Jan Paul, and Mitchell, Bridger M. "The Effect of Time-of-Use Rates: Facts vs. Opinions." R-2760-HF/FF/NSF. San Monica, Calif.: The RAND Corporation, April 1981.

Averch, Harvey, and Johnson, Leland L. "Behavior of the Firm Under Regulatory Constraint." *American Economic Review*, December 1962, pp. 1052-1069.

Barnes, Roberta; Gillingham, Robert; and Hagemann, Robert. "The Short-Run Residential Demand for Electricity." *Review of Economics and Statistics*, (November 1981), pp. 541-552.

Bonbright, James C. *Principles of Public Utility Rates*. New York: Columbia University Press, 1961.

Faruqui, Ahmad, and Malko, J. Robert. "Time-of-Use Rates and the Modification of Electric Utility Load Shapes." In *Challenges for Public Utility Regulation in the 1980s*, edited by Harry M. Trebing. East Lansing: Graduate School of Business Administration, Michigan State University, 1981, pp. 617-634.

Houthakker, Hendrik S. "Electricity Tariffs in Theory and Practice." *Economic Journal*, (March 1951), pp. 1-25.

Kahn, Alfred E. *The Economics of Regulation*, 2 vols. New York: Wiley, 1971.

Lescoeur, B. and Francony, M. "Marginal Cost Pricing: Updating the French Electricity Tariffs to Reflect Changes in the Characteristics of the Supply-Demand System." Draft paper, the 13th Annual Conference-Institute of Public Utilities, December 14 to 16, 1981, Williamsburg, Virginia.

Lewis, W. Arthur. *Overhead Costs*. London: Allen & Unwin, 1948.

Little, I.M.D. *The Price of Fuel*. Oxford: Clarendon Press, 1953.

Malko, J. Robert, and Faruqui, Ahmad. "Implementing Time-of-Day Pricing of Electricity: Some Current Challenges and Activities." In *Issues in Public Utility Pricing and Regulation*, edited by Michael A. Crew. Lexington, Mass.: D.C. Heath and Company, 1980.

Malko, J. Robert; Ray, Dennis J.; and Hassing, Nancy L. "Time-of-Day Pricing of Electricity: Activities in Some Midwestern States." In *Journal of Business Administration*, University of British Columbia, 12 (Spring 1981):143-170.

Meek, Ronald L. "The Bulk Supply Tariff for Electricity." *Oxford Economic Papers* (July 1963), pp. 107-123.

———. "An Application of Marginal Cost Pricing: The "Green Tariff" in Theory and Practice." Parts 1 and 2. *Journal of Industrial Economics* (July, November 1963):217-236 and 45-63.

Miedema, Allen K., and White, S.B. *Time-of-Use Electricity Price Effects: Summary I*. Washington, D.C.: Office of Utility Systems, U.S. Department of Energy, June 1980, pp. 1-79.

Mitchell, Bridger M.; Manning, Willard G.; and Acton, Jan Paul. *Peak-Load Pricing: European Lessons for U.S. Energy Policy*. Cambridge, Mass.: Ballinger, 1978.

Nelson, James R., ed. *Marginal-Cost Pricing in Practice*. Englewood Cliffs, N.J.: Prentice-Hall, 1964.

Shepherd, William G. "Marginal-Cost Pricing in American Utilities." *Southern Economic Journal* (July 1966):58-70.

Shepherd, William G., and Wilcox, Clair. *Public Policies Toward Business*. Homewood, Ill.: Irwin, 1979.

Steiner, Peter O. "Peak Load Pricing Revisited." In *Essays on Public Utility Pricing and Regulation*, edited by Harry M. Trebing. East Lansing: Graduate School of Business Administration, Michigan State University, 1971.

Taylor, Lester. "The Demand for Electricity: A Survey." *Bell Journal of Economics* (Spring 1975):74-110.

Turvey, Ralph. *Optimal Pricing and Investment in Electricity Supply*. London: Allen & Unwin, 1968.

Vickrey, William S. "Some Implications of Marginal Cost Pricing for Public Utilities." *American Economic Review*, (May 1955):605-620.

Weiss, Leonard W., and Klass, Michael W., eds. *Case Studies in Regulation: Revolution and Reform*. Boston: Little Brown, 1981.

Wilder, Ronald, and Willenborg, J. "Residential Demand for Electricity: A Consumer Panel Approach." *Southern Economic Journal* (October 1975):212-217.

# 10 Marginal-Cost Pricing: Theory and Practice

*Ronald P. Wilder*

These are exciting times for students of public-utility pricing. Deregulation in some industries has led to a renewed interest in pricing principles; a good example is the case of the airlines. In other industries changes in federal and state regulation have transformed utility rate schedules in a direction which conforms more closely to economic concepts of marginal-cost pricing. For example, some state regulatory commissions are beginning to introduce time-of-day pricing and seasonal-pricing rate schedules for electric utilities. Examples of a renewed interest in marginal-cost pricing may also be found in the telecommunication industry, with a movement by the Federal Communications Commission (FCC) to establish a clear correspondence between prices and cost.

Changes in the economic environment in which utilities operate have also led to significant changes in public-utility pricing practices. During the 1960s and early 1970s, most electric-utility rate schedules incorporated a declining-block rate design. This rate schedule was typically justified on the grounds that electric utilities were producing subject to decreasing long-run incremental cost during that period because of economies of scale, technological change, and relatively stable input prices. (Of course decreasing-block rate schedules also may have reflected value-of-service pricing concepts.) Since the energy crisis of 1973 to 1974, an increasing number of electric utilities have been urged by their regulatory commissions to move to flat or inverted rate schedules. Although the movement away from decreasing-block rates was in the beginning motivated by regulatory interest in conservation, it appears to be true also that electric-utility operations are no longer subject to increasing returns to scale.[1]

It is interesting to note the extent to which public-utility pricing practices have come to correspond more closely to the marginal-cost principles which have long been advocated by Bonbright and others. This trend appears to be related both to the gradual acceptance of the marginalist concepts by practitioners and to the change in economic conditions.

## Theory of Marginal-Cost Pricing

The theoretical justification for marginal-cost pricing is derived from a fundamental concept in welfare economics. Marginal cost is a measure of the opportunity cost of resources used to produce an additional unit of output. Since price is a measure of what consumers are willing to give up to obtain another unit of input, consumer welfare will increase by expanding output in any situation in which price exceeds marginal cost. Consumer welfare will increase in this instance because the production of another unit will cost less in opportunity-cost terms than consumers are willing to give up. This condition will continue to hold until price equals marginal cost. Conversely, if marginal cost exceeds price, consumer welfare would increase by reducing output for similar reasons.

Because most public utilities are monopolists or near monopolists, the correspondence between price and marginal cost may not be insured by competitive forces. To some extent, therefore, the correspondence of price and marginal cost depends directly upon the actions of regulators. Regulators are frequently confronted with nontrivial problems related to how best to apply marginal-cost principles.

One of the first issues that a regulatory commission must face if it chooses to apply marginal-cost concepts is the issue of short-run versus long-run marginal cost. The abstract conclusion from economic theory appears to be the following, as presented by Alfred Kahn: "The economic ideal would be to set all public utility rates at short-run marginal cost . . . and these must cover all sacrifices, present or future and external as well as internal to the company, for which production is at the margin causally responsible."[2] As Kahn also points out, however, that pricing prescription is based on static theory and may not be optimal and practical in a dynamic world. Among the reasons which prevent the correct application of short-run marginal-cost pricing in practice are the following:[3]

1. The calculation of marginal cost may be impossible or prohibitively expensive.
2. Short-run marginal cost may be changed so frequently that pricing changes would be infeasible.
3. Pricing based on short-run marginal cost may not cover fixed cost.
4. The prevalence of common costs leads to difficulty in calculating marginal costs for individual product lines.

As a result of these and other considerations, long-run marginal cost may be the more practical standard for marginal-cost pricing. Pricing at long-run marginal cost would also ensure that the price level is high enough to compensate firms for new investments required to meet an increasing demand.

A traditional means of enabling utilities both to charge relatively low marginal rates to some users and to cover their total cost is to allow price discrimination. It is at this point that value-of-service and cost-of-service pricing are related. The economic theory of optimal departures from marginal-cost pricing suggests that such departures be inversely proportional to the elasticity of demand.[4] Residential versus industrial pricing for both electricity and telephone service are examples of pricing practices which incorporate both cost-of-service and value-of-service (elasticity of demand) concepts.

Peak-load pricing is an important element in the marginal-cost pricing literature. The demand for many services, especially services of the public-utility type, is variable according to the time of day and season of the year. With these sorts of fluctuation in demand existing capacity can be best allocated by charging higher prices during the peak period relative to the off-peak period. In effect the peak-period customers would be paying prices which include fixed cost while off-peak customers would be paying only short-run marginal cost. There have been many interesting applications of peak-load pricing concepts in public-utilities industries recently.

**Marginal-Cost Pricing in Practice**

Although economists have been talking about marginal-cost pricing for electric utilities for nearly half a century, regulatory practice has incorporated marginal-cost pricing only relatively recently. Interestingly, marginal-cost pricing concepts were applied much earlier in France and England than in the United States. Economists at Electricite de France developed the famous *tarif vert* which applied to industrial customers in the mid-1950s. The British also adopted marginal-cost pricing during the 1950s and 1960s.[5] The first explicit application of marginal-cost pricing in an electric-utility rate case in the United States was in Wisconsin in 1974.[6] By 1977 most state commissions had moved in the direction of rates based on marginal-cost concepts. A survey done by Irwin Stelzer in November 1977 found that the majority of states had implemented seasonal rate differentials and about half the states had time-of-day rates for large industrial and commercial customers.[7]

In 1978 the Carter administration's National Energy Act included the Public Utility Regulatory Policies Act. PURPA established a series of standards relating to marginal-cost pricing. By requiring that the commissions consider the applicability of a number of marginal-cost pricing concepts, this act created an upsurge of interest and a flurry of activity, especially among consulting economists. Among other things, PURPA requires commissions to consider lifeline rates, time-of-use rates, and procedures for collecting cost-of-service data based on incremental-cost concepts. These provisions have been to some degree controversial, but the details of the controversy are beyond the scope of this chapter.[8]

The general trend in electric-utility rate structures since the 1970s has been in the direction of making rates more closely related to cost of service. Declining-block rates have given way to flat- or inverted-block rate schedules. Demand charges for large industrial customers have come to be based upon the time of the system peak rather than the users' peak regardless of time.

For illustrations, consider the two electric-utility rate schedules shown in table 10-1 and 10-2 which were filed by a major southeastern utility in 1981. The conventional rate schedule shown in table 10-1 features a basic facilities charge of $7.00 per month plus an inverted-block rate schedule with the first 800 kilowatt-hours per month of electricity at $.052 per kilowatt-hour and the excess over 800 kilowatt-hours per month at $.058 per kilowatt-hour in the summer and $.046 per kilowatt-hour in the winter months. (The electric utility in question is a summer-peaking utility.) This conventional rate schedule features an inverted block in the summer months when the peak occurs and the declining-block rate in the winter months for the purpose of promoting the use of electricity in space heating. It would appear to represent a blend of value-of-service and cost-of-service pricing principles.

The time-of-use rate schedule shown in table 10-2 features a higher basic-facility charge than the conventional rate in recognition of the higher metering costs. There is a three-part tariff, with an on-peak demand charge in addition to the basic-facility charge and an energy charge which is lower than the energy charge of the conventional rate structure. The demand charge is greater during the summer months than during the winter months, and both summer and winter rate schedules feature higher on-peak energy charges relative to off-peak. The on-peak energy charge is higher in summer months than in winter months.

**Table 10-1**

**Rates Proposed by a Southeastern U.S. Electric Utility for Residential Service in 1981: Conventional Rate Schedule**

|  | Rate Per Month | |
|---|---|---|
|  | Summer Billing Months June to September | Winter Billing Months October to May |
| Basic facilities charge in dollars | 7 | 7 |
| Plus energy charge in dollars First 800 kilowatt-hours | .05222 per kilowatt-hour | .05222 per kilowatt-hour |
| Excess over 800 kilowatt-hours | .05817 per kilowatt-hour | .04581 per kilowatt-hour |

Source: South Carolina Electric & Gas, Rate Request to South Carolina Public Service Commission, Docket No. 81-72-E, 1981.

**Table 10-2**
**Rates Proposed by a Southeastern U.S. Electric Utility for Residential**
**Service in 1981: Time-of-Use Rate Schedule**

---

*Rate Per Month*

---

Summer months, June to September

Basic facilities charge in dollars
    10.65
On-peak kilowatt demand charge in dollars
    3.60 per kilowatt for all on-peak billing demand
Kilowatt-hour energy charge in dollars
    .03769 per kilowatt-hour for all on-peak kilowatt-hour
    .02939 per kilowatt-hour for all off-peak kilowatt-hour

Winter months, October to May

Basic facilities charge in dollars
    10.65
On-peak kilowatt demand charge in dollars
    2.60 per kilowatt for all on-peak billing demand
Kilowatt-hour energy charge in dollars
    .03308 per kilowatt-hour for all on-peak kilowatt-hour
    .02939 per kilowatt-hour for all off-peak kilowatt-hour

---

Source: South Carolina Electric & Gas, Rate Request to South Carolina Public Service Commission, Docket No. 81-72-E, 1981.

This rate structure appears to reflect a combination of short-run and long-run marginal-cost concepts. Perhaps the main departure of this schedule from the peak-load pricing scheme found in most textbook treatments is the demand charge for peak demand in both the peak season and nonpeak season.

**Telecommunications**

In the 1960s at the urging of the FCC, the Bell system instituted off-peak long-distance rates. After encountering some problems with shifting peak, Bell settled on a rate structure with high rates during the day before five P.M., medium-level rates between five and eleven P.M. and the lowest rates during the late nighttime and early morning hours. Although this rate structure was not based explicitly on marginal-cost considerations, it does appear to have had the effect of increasing system-load factor.[9]

Traditionally local-telephone service was priced on a flat monthly rate basis. This pricing method has the disadvantage of being insensititve to both the time of use and the intensity of use. In effect, the marginal cost per telephone call is zero. In recognition of this problem, many state commissions have been moving in the direction of instituting message-unit rates in which there is a flat monthly charge which includes some allowed number of calls per month with an incremental charge per call beyond the message-unit allowance. In some jurisdictions the message-unit charge is variable with the time of day, but as yet this is the exception rather than the rule.[10]

By the early 1980s the majority of states were offering message-rate service both to business and residential users.[11] However, in most states the message-rate service was optional rather than mandatory. As long as consumers have a choice between flat-rate and message-rate service, the high-intensity users would be expected to select flat-rate service and the low-intensity users would opt for message-rate service. This behavior could still potentially lead to resource misallocation due to a pricing system which does not discourage use at peak periods.

Many other pricing innovations have taken place in the pricing of local-telephone service. In some jurisdictions message units are timed, while in other areas they are untimed. There is a general trend toward the unbundling of station rates to three elements: access line, inside wire, and equipment. In areas in which total unbundling has occurred, the customer need only pay the telephone company for the access line and can provide his own inside wiring and equipment.

Examples of the array of pricing schemes available in 1980 to telephone customers in the New York metropolitan exchange (New York state is a relatively progressive regulatory jurisdiction) are shown in tables 10-3 and 10-4. While residential customers had a choice between flat-rate and message-rate (timed or untimed) schedules, business service was available only on a timed message-rate basis.

As can be seen in table 10-4, the message-unit charges varied considerably between peak and off-peak periods, reflecting the marginal-cost pricing principle that peak users should be responsible for capacity costs. The illustrated schedule is not fully consistent with marginalist principles, however, since some residential calls may be made during peak periods at zero marginal costs by those households which select the flat rate.

The large recent increases in energy prices and relative increases in transportation costs have led to the substitution of communications for transportation. This trend will likely continue in the future, especially with the spread of computer technology to small business and the household. The increased demand placed on the telephone network by these structural changes will continue to exert pressure for innovative pricing methods. At the same time, further conversion to electronic switching systems will make pricing flexibility in telecommunications more feasible.

**Conclusions**

The last decade has brought a large number of substantial changes in the pricing of electricity and telephone service. Most of these changes have been

**Table 10-3**
**Examples of Telephone Rate Schedules for Local Service for the New York Metropolitan Exchange in 1980 in Dollars**

|  | *Business* | *Residence* |
|---|---|---|
| Flat rate | Not offered | 10.11 (access only) |
| Message rate <br> Basic | 9.70 (access only) | 6.04 (access only) |
| Message unit <br> allowance | 4.00[a] | 4.00[b] |

Source: The National Association of Regulatory Utility Commissioners (NARUC), 1980.
[a]Timed message-unit basis only.
[b]Available with timed or untimed message unit basis. With timed basis, basic charge is $1.03 less.

in the direction of a closer correspondence between actual utility-pricing practice and marginal-cost pricing concepts. It is interesting to speculate regarding the degree to which these pricing changes have been brought about by regulatory coercion or voluntary pricing changes on the part of the regulated firms.

With respect to electric utilities, conditions in the 1960s were such that utilities sought to grow rapidly and had no real fear of overcapacity. In fact Averch-Johnson considerations along with decreasing long-run marginal cost may have led electric utilities to consciously over expand. (The empirical evidence on this issue is mixed.) With the advent of increasing marginal costs and capital scarcity in the 1970s and early 1980s, electric utilities tended to be much more conscious of avoiding overcapacity. As a result, they have been interested in rate structures which encouraged more efficient utilitization of plant in recent years.

**Table 10-4**
**Message-Unit Charges for New York Metropolitan Exchange in 1980**

| | *Timed Message Units* | | *Untimed* |
|---|---|---|---|
| *Time of Day* | *First* <br> *Five Minutes* <br> *in Cents* | *Each* <br> *Additional Minute* <br> *in Cents* | *Message Units* <br> *Per Call* <br> *in Cents* |
| 8 A.M.-9 P.M. <br> Weekdays | 7.6 | 1.1 | 8.2 |
| 9 P.M.-11 P.M. <br> Weekdays | 5.0 | 0.7 | 5.3 |
| 8 A.M.-11 P.M. <br> Weekdays and holidays | 5.0 | 0.7 | 5.3 |
| 11 P.M.-8 A.M. <br> Daily | 3.0 | 0.2 | 3.3 |

Source: The National Association of Regulatory Utility Commissioners (NARUC), 1980.

With respect to telephone utilities, similar considerations apply. Although initially reluctant to institute marginal-cost based rates, telephone utilities, because of financial market conditions in recent years, have been more willing to initiate or at least go along with marginal-cost pricing methods. In conclusion, recent history suggests that the move to marginal-cost pricing has been a result both of the gradual acceptance by regulators of the marginal-cost principles long advocated by economists and of the changing economic conditions faced by the regulated utilities.

**Notes**

1. David Huettner and John Landon, "Electric Utilities: Scale Economies and Diseconomies," *Southern Economic Journal* (April 1978), pp. 883-912.

2. Alfred E. Kahn, *The Economics of Regulation: Principles and Institutions* (New York: John Wiley, 1970) 1:75.

3. Ibid., pp. 83-84.

4. This and other points related to this paper are discussed in Leonard W. Weiss, "State Regulation of Public Utilities and Marginal-cost Pricing," in *Case Studies in Regulation*, ed. Leonard W. Weiss and Michael W. Klass (Boston: Little, Brown, 1981) chapter 9, pp. 262-291.

5. Ibid., p. 275.

6. Ibid., p. 275.

7. Ibid., p. 278.

8. For a discussion of problems in implementing PUPRPA see Gregory Crespi, "Marginal Cost-of-Service Studies: Some Practical Difficulties," *Public Utilities Fortnightly* 106 (December 4, 1980):19-23; and Warren J. Samuels, "Problems of Marginal Cost Pricing in Public Utilities," *Public Utilities Fortnightly* 105 (January 31, 1980):21-24.

9. Weiss, "State Regulation," p. 288.

10. For a recent discussion of telephone tariffs see John R. Meyer et al., *The Economics of Competition in the Telecommunications Industry* (Cambridge, Mass.: Oelgeschlager, Gunn and Hain, 1980), chap. 3.

11. National Association of Regulatory Utility Commissioners (NARUC), *Exchange Service Telephone Rates in Effect June 30, 1980* (Washington: NARUC, 1980).

# 11 Minimum and Maximum Pricing Principles for Residual Regulation

*William J. Baumol*

Recent moves toward abolition of regulation of prices in a number of industries bring with them some concern about the desirability of complete elimination of all constraints upon the price-setting process. Though many of the industries involved are actually or potentially highly competitive, none of them can by any stretch of the imagination be said to approximate a state of atomless perfect competition. As a result at least some of the prices which can be expected to emerge from their markets, if unimpeded by government interference, may well not exhibit the optimality properties described by our theoretical models of perfect competition. Is it not possible, then, in those markets in which there is little or no competition that some of the resulting prices will in some sense be too high or even too low? This suggests that one should consider the possibility of giving deregulated firms power to select their own prices but constraining that freedom by a floor and a ceiling in markets in which competition is extremely weak.

This is not to be misunderstood as raising doubts about the desirability of deregulation. I continue to be a strong supporter of deregulation of air, rail, and truck transportation, and there are no doubt other regulated economic activities that will serve the public far more effectively when their pricing decisions are freed from government control. More specifically, by examining reasonable criteria for the residual regulation of price floors or ceilings, this does not imply that the adoption of such constraints will serve the general welfare. There are very strong arguments which suggest that the heavy efficiency costs of the regulatory procedures needed to oversee any such residual rules may far outweigh their benefits. This is merely an inquiry as to whether there is any analytic basis for the formulation of such rules and, if so, to describe the nature of such rules. But as will be seen this chapter has not succeeded in attaining even this limited objective. While the rules to be discussed are fully defensible in terms of the underlying theory, most of them are clearly too complicated to be used as they stand. Reason-

I am extremely grateful to the National Science Foundation and the Sloan Foundation whose support greatly facilitated the preparation of this chapter. This chapter has been adapted with permission from an article that appeared in the *Eastern Economics Journal* 5 (January/April 1979):235-248.

able compromises and approximation procedures will be required to permit their employment in practice.

The rules which emerge from the discussion will not be entirely unfamiliar. They are certainly related to some of the results that emerge from the marginal analysis and the theory of optimal pricing. However, their primary basis will not be the usual one—the rules of efficiency in resource allocation. While it is unusual in economics, equity rather than efficiency will serve as the main foundation for those principles, though they do promote economic efficiency as well.

## Previous Discussions of Price-Floor Criteria

To begin, turning for guidance to earlier discussions of minimum and maximum pricing rules will prove useful. An unsophisticated but intelligent observer would naturally expect the bulk of these to be devoted to price ceilings designed to prevent the use of monopoly power to gouge consumers, for surely that is the immediate danger to the public welfare threatened by market power. It is therefore curious but not inexplicable that the vast preponderance of regulatory and antitrust pricing cases, and almost all of the pertinent discussions, have been devoted to limitation of price reductions rather than price increases.

There is a very simple explanation of this anomaly. A seller's high prices are likely to be harmful to his customers, but his low prices are apt to harm his competitors. The competitors (who themselves are often giants of industry) are in a far better position to organize an effective protest than are the consumers. Inscribing on their banners fairness in competition, prevention of predatory pricing, and other equally persuasive mottos, they have not only succeeded in making headway among regulators, they have even managed to provide an aura of respectability to their self-interested attempt to shield themselves from the rigors of competition. "It always is and must be the interest of the great body of the people to buy what they want of those who sell it cheapest," wrote Adam Smith. "The proposition is so very manifest, that it seems ridiculous to take any pains to prove it; nor could it ever have been called in question, had not the interested sophistry of merchants and manufacturers confounded the common sense of mankind" (1776, p. 461).

Two interrelated issues are cited by those who hold that floors upon the prices charged by firms with some degree of market power are needed. First, it is maintained that without such floors there is nothing to prevent one group of a seller's customers from benefiting at the expense of another. If the seller has market power he may be tempted to sell one of his products at a loss and make up for it by a suitable overcharge of other customer groups. This issue is usually referred to as cross subsidy of one product's customers by another. The second issue involves the relation between the seller and his competitors. The firm will wish to sell some of its products below cost if by this means potential entrants can be deterred from opening for business in that field or current competitors can be prevented from growing or even be forced to leave the market. A variety of pejorative terms are used to describe this sort of practice, predatory pricing or destructive pricing being adjoined to cross subsidy, though until recently no one seems to have attempted to offer a definition for either term. As one of our leading courts has remarked,

> The use of the term "predatory" to describe conduct violative of the anti-trust laws has left much to be desired. This court has noted, the term probably does not have a well-defined meaning in the context it was used, but it certainly bears a sinister connotation (U.S. Court of Appeals, 10th Circuit, 1977).

Implicit in discussions of concepts such as predatory pricing are somewhat elusive concepts like intent which in practice are not easy to measure or perhaps even to define. But many of the discussions seem to adopt or at least to flirt with the notion that a scarlet letter should be affixed to any price which lies below some floor regarded as the boundary of the region of cross subsidy. A price higher than that borderline is considered acceptable on that score, while a price below that floor stands condemned, at least in the absence of unusual exonerating circumstances.

Almost all commentators agree that in designing such a floor a critical role must be assigned to the cost of the product whose price is in question. The problem, however, is which cost datum should be assigned this determinant role and just how that cost figure should be used in the calculations process. Three basic approaches have been considered. They may be called the full-cost test, the marginal-cost pricing test and the test of net-incremental contribution. The meaning of the first two may seem self-evident, though this appearance is deceptive. The third is rather less familiar and will later be described somewhat more carefully.

## Full-Cost Price Floors

Full cost, alias fully allocated costs, alias fully distributed cost, is a concept closely associated with the more routine procedures of the accountants. The basic idea underlying its use as a standard for pricing is that a price below that cost level must condemn the supplier to a financial loss. In a single-product firm full cost is merely a synonym for average combined cost, that is, it is equal to the sum of total fixed and variable cost divided by output.

Since that cost figure is calculated so as to include a normal rate of return on capital, pricing in this way means that the firm should earn normal competitive profits on its investment, no more and no less.

Even in the single-product firm of the elementary textbook there are some flies in this ointment. For wishing does not always make things so. As early as 1900 Gustav Cassell pointed out that a rise in the price of a commodity in an attempt to get it up to the full cost of current output will reduce the quantity sold and that this in turn can lead to a rise in the full-cost figure itself. He tells a tale of a railroad whose average cost is a decreasing function of output and whose price initially is below full cost. Successive attempts to raise price to the full-cost level only lead to successive reductions in volume of traffic, each accompanied by such a rise in full cost that the supplier is saddled with greater and greater losses. Thus, he concludes, full-cost pricing is not the guarantee against loss that it seems to be.[1]

However, the really serious problems that beset full-cost pricing arise in a multiproduct firm, that is, in any firm one can expect actually to encounter in the real world. In any such firm some expenditures (the salaries of its officers, if nothing else) are inevitably expended on behalf of several of the company's products simultaneously with no identifiable portion of such expenditures being attributable to any one of the products.[2]

Now to calculate on a rational basis the average or full cost of any one product in such a firm, it is necessary to be able to do the impossible, to divide up the firm's total cost so that each of its products is assigned its appropriate share. But unattributable common costs are precisely what their name implies: they are simply unattributable to particular products on any sensible economic basis. At this point accounting conventions undertake to come to the rescue. Using admittedly arbitrary procedures for the apportionment, total-supplier costs are simply divided up among the firm's different products. These accounting rules are not uncontested, because there is so much to be gained or lost by the choice of apportionment criterion. If a railroad line carries three products—steel, feathers, and platinum—the steel shippers can be relied upon to fight against the use of weight as a basis for assigning cost responsibility. The feather shippers will combat the use of volume for that purpose, and the platinum shippers will fight tooth and nail against market value as the criterion of cost allocation.

Most economists have long been passionate in their rejection of the full-cost pricing criterion. There are many reasons for the strength of their feelings on this matter of which only three will be mentioned here: the arbitrariness of the criterion, the resource misallocation it is likely to produce, and its tendency to undermine the competitive process at the consumer's expense.

Of course, everyone recognizes that arbitrary decisions are sometimes unavoidable and that arbitrariness can occasionally be superior to complete indecision. Perhaps the most irritating practice of full costers in this regard is their propensity to adopt cosmetic procedures which give the allocation process a spurious appearance of rationality. Cost of common facilities are allegedly allocated on the basis of the relative use of those facilities by different products. But this veneer is easily stripped away. The preceding railroad example shows how different the results of the calculation can be depending on whether weight, volume, or market value is used as the criterion determining the relative use of the roadbed and tracks by the different goods transported along it. The appearance of reasonableness imparted by a relative use criterion only increases the danger of full-cost procedures because it lulls its advocates and even some uncommitted observers into overlooking the arbitrariness of the calculation and the very serious consequences which can result from the choice of allocation procedure.

The likelihood that full costing will produce a misallocation of resources follows at once from its arbitrariness. There is obviously not the slightest reason to expect that the prices emerging from a full-costing process will bear the slightest resemblance to those known to be necessary for efficiency in resource utilization. Whether one deals with the Hotelling rule (1938), or the Ramsey rule (1927), or any other optimality principle, it is clear that marginal rather than fully distributed cost is involved in the relevant test. Prices based on fully distributed costs will almost certainly be inconsistent with efficiency in resource use, and so they will be harmful to the general welfare. Some reservations which will emerge in the next section must be expressed about this argument. But no such doubts need be felt about the remaining argument against full costing and its substantial handicap upon efficiency which the discussion will point out.

In practice the role of fully distributed cost has been a burning regulatory issue because competitors of the firm under attack almost inevitably use it to claim that the prices of the products in direct competiton with their own are noncompensatory—that they are financed by cross subsidy. In this way fully distributed cost is normally used as a protectionist instrument preventing buyers from benefiting from price reductions which suppliers are willing to offer them.[3] Competitors battle for a high floor under the regulated firm's prices in order to make life easier for themselves. Since the rules of full costing are arbitrary, the results can always be skewed, deliberately or unconsciously, to maximize the competitive handicap imposed upon the regulated firm, and one can generally rely upon the complaining competitor to try to do so.[4] Regulators are regularly persuaded to bow to this position in the belief that unless such a full-cost floor is imposed to protect competitors they will be unable to survive. But thereby, in protecting inefficient competitors who could not otherwise fend for themselves, the regulators obviously succeed only too well in undermining the competitive process. Customers are forced to pay prices higher than they otherwise would, ostensibly in their own best interests! The extreme distaste shown by most economists for the full-cost arguments thus is not very difficult to explain.


## Marginal-Cost Criteria

The notion that price should be permitted to be set as low as marginal cost seems to follow in an obvious way from the principles of welfare economics. As every economist knows, optimality of resource allocation as achieved under pure competition requires the prices of all commodities to be set equal to their respective marginal costs. It would seem an easy inference that any rule which prevents prices from reaching marginal costs is an indefensible source of inefficiencies.

Economists have long flirted with this sort of argument, though the position most of them have ended up with is somewhat different. Their conclusion nevertheless remains altogether marginalist in logic.

Most recently the marginal-cost pricing criterion has been espoused with considerable influence upon the judicial process by two eminent lawyers, Phillip Areeda and Donald Turner. In a widely cited article (1975)—which deals, actually, with antitrust law rather than regulation—they took the position that no price which equals or exceeds short-run marginal cost should be considered predatory. Conversely they assert any price which falls below short-run marginal cost can be presumed to be predatory. They note, in addition, that in practice it will sometimes be difficult to estimate the value of short-run marginal cost and that in these circumstances average variable cost can be used as an acceptable proxy. Thus the Areeda-Turner criterion effectively approves of any price that can be shown to exceed either of these cost figures or both. This criterion in the past few years has been cited with approval by a growing number of courts.[5] The Areeda-Turner position is extremely attractive despite the questions this chapter will raise about their arguments. Among the reasons the rule is attractive is that the adoption of any such testable criterion is an enormous contribution to the general welfare; without it decision makers must act without knowing whether they will be running afoul of the law, and the resulting indecisions, delays, and needless litigation are enormously wasteful.[6] Moreover, in proposing the adoption of a test based on average variable cost, Areeda and Turner have done better than they thought. Rather than being only a poor cousin of marginal cost, average variable cost turns out to be a very reasonable criterion in its own right.[7]

One can complain that the Areeda-Turner discussion seems never to have explained clearly why it advocates the use of short-run rather than long-run marginal cost. In fact, the authors seem never to have defined precisely what they mean by the terms *short-run marginal cost*[8] *or average variable cost.* This chapter will later explain the nature of the ambiguity in the latter concept.

But the main fault one can find with the Areeda-Turner discussion of their position is the basis on which they choose to espouse it. They argue the desirability of marginal-cost pricing on the welfare-theoretic grounds already mentioned. Unfortunately, there are at least three critical weaknesses in this position. First, the second-best theorem reminds us that there is no necessary advantage to satisfaction of some Pareto-optimality conditions while others are being violated. If prices are above marginal costs in some sectors of the economy, it is not necessarily beneficial to bring prices into equality with marginal costs in the remainder. Indeed, one can easily see how a misallocation of resources will be produced in this way, with an excessive proportion of society's resources devoted to products whose demand has been stimulated by marginal cost prices and an undesirably low proportion of the community's resources consequently going to the remainder of the economy. Second, welfare economics says nothing about the desirability of setting prices temporarily equal to marginal cost and then reraising them above marginal cost after competitive pressures have declined. Yet such an intertemporal price pattern is perfectly compatible with the Areeda-Turner criterion. Third, whatever can be said on welfare grounds for the desirability of prices equal to marginal cost, there seems little particular allocative virtue to prices set at some unspecified level higher than marginal costs. Yet the Areeda-Turner criterion is impartial in its approval both of prices equal to and prices which exceed marginal costs.[9]

None of this is in any way meant to imply that the Areeda-Turner price floors are indefensible. The point simply is that while price floors, appropriately chosen, may help to promote efficiency, any price floor is simply too coarse an instrument to be able by itself to achieve optimality in resource allocation.

**Compensatory Pricing: Incremental Cost and Revenue**

Since the 1880s economists have been proposing, at least by implication, the use of incremental cost, a close relative of marginal cost, in the setting of price floors. Incremental cost may be defined as the addition to the firm's total cost by a specified change in the output of each of the firm's products. Thus, marginal cost is simply the limiting case of incremental cost as the change in question approaches zero. Obviously, a similar definition applies to revenues.

However, this chapter uses incremental cost and revenue in a more restricted manner, to refer to what has been described as the incremental cost (revenue) of an entire product. This is the difference in the total cost (revenue) of the supplier of some specified vector of outputs and the corresponding total cost (revenue) of its output if the one item whose price is in question were reduced to zero. This chapter will use two different incremental-cost (revenue) concepts which are best described symbolically.

Let $x =$ the quantity of some commodity $X$;

$y =$ the corresponding vector of outputs of all the firm's other products, $Y$;

$y + \Delta y =$ the vector of outputs of $Y$ which would be demanded if output of $X$ were reduced to zero as a result of complementarity or substitution;

$C(x,y) =$ the total cost function.

Then we may define:

Gross Incremental Cost of $X = C(x,y) - C(O,y)$ (11.1)

Net Incremental Cost of $X = C(x,y) - C(O,y + \Delta y)$. (11.2)

Gross and net incremental revenues are defined as the obvious analogues of (11.1) and (11.2). It is then proposed to test the adequacy of the price of product $X$ by checking whether it equals or exceeds the corresponding average incremental cost, that is, the incremental cost divided by output. Since the (gross) incremental revenue of $X$ at price $P_x$ is simply $P_x x$, if the price of $X$ equals or exceeds its (gross) incremental cost the total incremental revenue of $X$ must obviously exceed its incremental cost; that is, if

$$P_x \geq [C(x,y) - C(O,y)]/x$$ (11.3)

then

$$P_x x \geq C(x,y) - C(O,y).$$ (11.4)

This price is then said to be compensatory or to involve no cross subsidy on the grounds that under these circumstances the revenues contributed by purchasers of $X$ must at least cover the costs imposed upon the supplier in the course of serving them.

Indeed, particularly where the firm's profits are effectively constrained by some ceiling, as they are intended to be under rate-of-return regulation, there is more to the argument. A price of $X$ which satisfies this rule can be shown to be Pareto superior from the viewpoint of all affected customers to any higher prices which would cause the firm to lose all (or a substantial proportion of) the customers for product $X$. Thus, suppose the test criterion (11.4) is passed as a strict inequality. Then customers of $X$ must be making a net contribution to company profits. But if the prices, $P_y^*$, of goods in the vector $Y$ were otherwise enough to bring profits up to the ceiling, this revenue contribution of $X$ must put the company over the top. The firm must then reduce the prices of $Y$ to a level represented by the vector $P_y$ in order to comply with the ceiling. That is, let $P_y^*$ be a price which drives customers of $X$ from the market; then at any lower price, $P_x$, which satisfies (11.3) as an inequality and thus attracts the corresponding demand for $X$, consumers of $Y$ must also benefit as their prices are reduced from $P_y^*$ to $P_y$.

This argument goes back at least to the 1880s (Hadley, 1886, chapter 6; Alexander, 1887, pp. 2-5, 10-11; and Ackworth, 1891, chapter 3; see also Lewis, 1949, p. 20ff., for an excellent discussion). It is fundamentally valid, though at least in principle it does require some amendments as it stands. But before coming to these, several observations are in order.

First, this is not primarily an argument based on grounds of efficiency of resource allocation. Rather, it is founded first and foremost on considerations of distributive equity among different groups of the supplier's customers. The test is intended to assure that the customers of each product bear the costs imposed by them and do not shift any portion of these costs to buyers of other company products. In other words, by implication, each customer group then bears its contribution to total company costs. Moreover, since such prices pass a test of Pareto improvement it follows that the gains from such pricing policy are shared among the company's customers.

Second, while this discussion has emphasized the interpretation of the incremental-cost criterion as a test of fairness, its role as an inducement of efficiency must not be overlooked. For if price were to violate the rule it would exclude potential entrants who are more efficient producers of the product in question. For if $AC^m$ and $AC^e$ are, respectively, the unit incremental costs of the incumbent and the potential entrant, then the item should at least partly be supplied by the entrant if $AC^e < AC^m$. However, if the incumbent's price is $P^m < AC^e$, then this (cross-subsidized) price will obviously exclude the more efficient producers of the item.[10] Thus, the incremental-cost floor is a necessary condition for economic efficiency.

Third, we may note that the incremental-cost test is directly related to the second Areeda-Turner criterion—the comparison of price with average variable cost. For it is natural to define[11] average variable cost as the right side of expression (11.3), that is, as the amount per unit of $X$ by which the firm's total cost varies as a result of the decision to supply $x$ units of $X$. Then (11.3) or (11.4) become identical with the average-variable-cost test of Areeda and Turner. One can conclude that, far from being defensible only as some sort of approximation to the ideal marginal-cost criterion, there are strong grounds for advocating the average variable cost test as something with validity of its own. Note also that this view provides a foundation for the Areeda-Turner test quite different from the one they themselves offer, one which is considerably stronger than theirs.

Let the discussion turn next to the ways in which it has more recently been proposed to amend the incremental-cost criterion. Here two such modifications will be described. First, it has been proposed that the test require a comparison not between gross incremental cost and revenues but between their net counterparts. That is, from the revenue contributed by $X$ one should substract any revenues lost by other company products as the result of the availability of $X$, if the two goods happen to be substitutes. The reverse is proposed in the case where they are complements, and similar adjustments for cross-elasticity effects are suggested on the cost side. The argument for this position is self-evident. Product $X$ should be credited with all revenues it contributes directly or indirectly and debited with any indirect revenue losses it causes, and the same is true on the cost side. Along this line, it is easy to show that the Pareto-improvement argument is valid for the incremental-cost test only if net cost and revenue figures are used in carrying out the test. For suppose that the price of $X$ were to satisfy the gross criterion but fail the net test. Then a moment's thought confirms that the company's net profits will actually be reduced by the supply of product $X$ and so, under an overall profit ceiling, consumers of its remaining products, $Y$, may well be required to make up the deficiency.

The second amendment that has been proposed (see Faulhaber, 1975) is that compensatory pricing of product $X$ is not proved if only $P_x$ is shown to satisfy the criterion

$$\text{net incremental revenue} \geq \text{net incremental cost.} \qquad (11.5)$$

Rather, to show that their prices are compensatory it is held necessary to show that each and every product of the company, taken separately and in combination, also satisfies criterion (11.5). If the firm produces $X$, $Y$, and $Z$, each alone must satisfy (11.5); but in addition this must be shown for the four combinations: $(X, Y)$, $(X, Z)$, $(Y, Z)$ and $(X, Y, Z)$. The reason is, once more, made clearest by example. Suppose $X$ and $Y$ are the only two goods shipped along a particular railroad route which is constructed and maintained specifically for the purpose. Then the incremental track-construction cost of product $X$ by itself will be zero since that track, in any event, must be built if any $Y$ is to be transported along the route. Similarly, the incremental track-construction cost of $Y$ must also be zero. However, if the two products each were to contribute revenue just sufficient to pay for their own incremental costs nothing would be available for replacement of track, and accordingly it would make little sense to describe that set of rates as compensatory. On this view it follows that in order to pass an appropriate test of compensatory pricing, the incremental revenue of each product and every combination of products must contribute net-incremental revenues which equal or exceed the corresponding net-incremental costs, including the costs of any associated incremental capital and the normal rate of return on that incremental capital.

This definition will also prove relevant later when the discussion turns to an appropriate maximum-price criterion. The preceeding test must be passed by the totality of the firms' products, that is, in terms of this discussion's three-product example, it requires that the incremental revenue of all three company products, $X$, $Y$, and $Z$, together cover their total incremental cost. This last requirement implictly assures that the prices of the firm's products cover all of the company's costs including a normal return to its capital. If, in addition, these returns are constrained to be no higher than the normal yield of capital, this amounts to assurance that the firm's price vector yields revenues that just exactly cover its total costs and bring in what regulators sometimes call a fair rate of return.

It may even be maintained as a result, albeit somewhat perversely, that these prices correspond to a full allocation process. But, of course, it is only so in retrospect. No accountant has been asked to perform the voodoo rites involved in assigning the unassignable costs. Rather, the price-setting process, as constrained by the market, has yielded a set of prices which together cover total costs. If, as a matter of aesthetics, one then wishes to allocate company costs in proportion to the revenues yielded by those prices, it is possible to maintain that the result constitutes a full allocation of costs and that the prices are consistent with that full allocation. Anyone who derives pleasure from such an exercise should of course not be deprived of it.

This completes the discussion of appropriate criteria for price floors, should these be considered desirable either for regulated or deregulated industries. It must only be added that the last criterion, the compensatory-pricing test, seems to be the preferable criterion in terms of theory. In practice one must, of course, be prepared to compromise when such a test imposes unreasonable and unrealizable data and calculation requirements. Another consideration is the desirability of optimally imperfect decision criteria which balance off the cost and feasibility of a more demanding decision process against its benefits. Clearly, granted the desirability of any such criterion, one which is usable in practice will be preferable to one which is not. The main task then, is the design of reasonable approximations to the ideal criterion of compensatory pricing which do not impose impossible or even excessive demands upon those who want to use them.

**Toward a Reasonable Criterion for Price Ceilings**

Though common sense would seem to suggest that in the presence of market power, price ceiling are rather more to point than price floors, this chapter will have much less to say about the former than about the latter. In part, this is because so much less analysis seems to have been devoted to appropriate criteria for the setting of ceilings; in part it is a result of the inherent difficulty of the problem.

One way to get around its difficulties is simply to follow the dictates of Ramsey theory which requires each regulated price to be set at a level that maximizes consumers' and producers' surplus subject to a profit constraint. One might, for example, just require prices as an approximation, to obey the famous inverse-elasticity rule, under which the percentage deviation between price and marginal cost is inversely proportionate to the elasticity of the demand for the item in question.

In practice this solution will not do; first, because if applied only to a small subset of the economy's prices, it loses its welfare-theoretic standing. More important, the immediate objective of deregulation is to broaden management's range of freedom in making economic decisions, not to narrow it further, let alone extinguish it altogether. One is therefore led to seek a permissible range within which management can exercise its judgment in setting price but beyond which it will not be permitted to go in markets in which competition is ineffective. It can be argued that by permitting this degree of freedom and by making the bounds of the permissible range as specific and observable as possible, one contributes to the scope and incentives for the exercise of aggressive entrepreneurship.

What then can one propose as an appropriate upper bound upon price? The one criterion which seems to have been suggested rests upon Faulhaber's concept of stand-alone cost. The (average) stand-alone cost of a particular service is the minimum amount per unit it would cost to provide if it were offered by a single-product supplier. That is, it is the amount the customers would have to pay if they were, in effect, to secede from their implicit association with the buyers of the supplying firm's other products.

It is to be noted that a price equal to stand-alone cost does deprive the customer of any share in the economies of scope[12] derived from simultaneous production of the other items in the firm's product line. But like the price floors discussed, its justification rests primarily (but not exclusively) on an equity principle—the view that it is unfair to extract more from a customer group than it would cost that group to serve itself.

Here one must be careful to distinguish two interpretations of stand-alone cost which so far have implicitly been confused in this discussion. One way to measure stand-alone cost is in terms of what it would cost the current supplier to provide the product in question after divesting itself of all other items in its product line. The second interpretation is the cost of serving the customers if they were to form their own company in competition with the existing firm. An example will bring out the distinction. Suppose a railroad carries several different goods over a route through the only mountain pass between the origin and destination, so that any alternative route would be prohibitively expensive. Here the second stand-alone cost of one of the freight items, that of an (imaginary) rival carrier, is obviously far greater than the first stand-alone cost figure corresponding to the transportation of the one good by the existing railroad.[13]

It should be obvious that if this railroad were permitted to charge a price equal to the higher of the two stand-alone costs, it would derive enormous profits attributable exclusively to the monopoly power it holds by having preempted the mountain pass. Clearly, in this case, the second stand-alone criterion is unacceptable.

But there are other cases in which it is to be preferred. Suppose the current supplier is inefficient and that a new firm could supply the affected customer group at a far lower cost. Surely there is no reason the incumbent firm, which by hypothesis possesses market power, should be permitted to extract the costs of its inefficiency from its customers. It would seem to follow that, in principle, the appropriate stand-alone cost figure is the lower of the two.

Granted, for the sake of argument, the acceptability of the stand-alone criterion, whose logic as an inhibitor of monopoly profit is indicated by the preceeding mountain-pass example, let the focus turn last to the measurements it requires. This is obviously no trivial issue since it refers to a hypothetical arrangement which almost certainly will never have been observed in fact. The multiproduct firm simply will not have been observed, at least in recent history, providing any of its products in isolation, and so there will exist no data permitting a direct calculation of stand-alone cost.

One obvious possibility is an engineering calculation, attempting to obtain by simulation an estimate of what would be required to supply one product alone. There are obvious questions about the reliability of such a calculation which the engineers themselves are the first to emphasize. Its cost is also likely to be enormous.

There is a second way of going about this calculation which follows directly from the test of compensatory pricing. Here, the crucial result is due to Gerald Faulhaber (1975) who proved that a firm which earns no more than a normal return on its capital overall is guaranteed to earn no more than its stand-alone cost from the sale of a particular item, if it is also true that the prices of all other products are compensatory in the sense defined in the preceeding section. In other words, the firm can prove that it is not exceeding the stand-alone ceiling over the price of product $X$ by showing that it is earning normal profits in total, and that the prices of its remaining products, $Y$, $Z$, . . ., are compensatory.[14]

The intuitive reason for this result is not difficult to describe. If a firm earns more than the stand-alone cost of item $X$ (including a normal return on the capital involved), then $X$ must, by definition, be contributing more than normal profits to the firm. This must then manifest itself in (at least) one of two ways: it must result in greater than normal profits for the firm overall, or some other product or products of the firm must yield enough of a loss to offset the excessive profit brought in by item $X$. Thus, violation of the stand-alone ceiling on the price of $X$ will always be accompanied either by an observable supernormal profit rate for the entire firm or by noncompensatory net prices for some of its other products. That, of course, is precisely what the Faulhaber theorem asserts.

It follows immediately that a ceiling based on stand-alone costs is required for efficiency and not just for equity. For earlier it was noted that noncompensatory prices lead to inefficiency by preventing the entry of more efficient firms. Thus, violation of the stand-alone ceiling means that the firm must either be earning profits that are inefficiently large and must involve a misallocation of resources (unless the earnings are pure rent), or it must involve uncompensatory and, hence, inefficient prices of some other products. The preceding explanation of the Faulhaber theorem was deliberately loosely phrased, but it is easy to provide a simple proof for the case of the two-product firm to give the flavor of the argument.

Suppose the firm produces exactly two goods $X$ and $Y$, that $P_x$, the price of $X$, is compensatory, and that the firm's revenues just cover its overall costs, including its cost of capital. Then the price of $Y$ cannot exceed the stand-alone ceiling.

Compensatory pricing of $X$ requires by 11.5 and 11.2 that net-incremental revenue of $X = (P_x x + P_y y) - [P_x O + P_y(y + \Delta y)] \geq$ net-incremental cost of $X = C(x,y) - C(O,Y + \Delta y)$, or

$$P_x x - P_Y \Delta y \geq C(x,y) - C(O,y + \Delta y). \qquad (11.6)$$

But if the firm is earning only its normal return, then

$$P_x x + P_y y = C(x,y). \qquad (11.7)$$

Subtracting 11.6 from 11.7:

$$P_y(y + \Delta y) \leq C(O,y + \Delta y) \qquad (11.8)$$

which proves immediately that the total revenue that would be produced by price $P_y$ if $X$ were not supplied (so that the demand for $Y$ would rise to $y + \Delta y$) is no greater than the (stand-alone) cost of $y + \Delta y$. But that is precisely what it was intended to show.

This, then, completes the discussion of an appropriate ceiling formula for products over which the residually regulated firm still retains some market power. No doubt, further analysis of the subject is still needed urgently. But the economic logic of the proposed stand-alone criterion seems clear, and its intimate connection with the criterion of compensatory pricing is one of its attractive features.


## Concluding Remarks

In a sense, the preceding discussion may be characterized as an attempt to do something economists have with good reason attempted to avoid—to provide some substantive content to the discredited concept of just price. But while there may be no unique price which can unequivocally be declared just, it may be possible to determine ranges of prices all of which we will be agreed to be unjust. It is in this spirit that this chapter has sought to deal with floors and ceilings, implicitly using them to define a range of intermediate prices each of which is to be considered acceptable in the weak sense that there appears to be no reasonable way to show it to be unjust.

This chapter must end as it began, by protesting that it has not been its objective to advocate the desirability of price floors and ceilings, even for a small subset of markets in a deregulated industry in which there is no effective competition. The social costs of the associated regulatory process may or may not be justified by the likely benefits. But whatever one's judgment on this score, it seems cleary desirable, if price regulation is to be preserved, to minimize the administrative and resources cost of the process by spelling out the approved range of freedom of entrepreneurial decisions and making as specific as possible the boundary between acceptable and objectionable conduct. That has been the primary purpose of this chapter.


## Notes

1. That is, he concludes that it may not be possible for losses to be eliminated by raising price to full cost as though full cost were an invariant figure. In his parable Cassel has the management of the firm learn by experience, finally deciding to reduce price drastically, which simultaneously attracts many new customers and reduces average cost, and then the firm does at last manage to make a profit.

2. This is not meant to deny that some portion of such common costs will be economically attributable to a firm's individual products. For example, if on launching a particular product the firm hires an additional vice-president, his cost is clearly attributable to that product alone. Even in

more complicated cases partial attribution is possible in principle. Suppose, for example, that a trucking firm takes on the transportation of a product, $X$, which it did not carry before. Suppose, moreover, that $X$ is never carried by itself but is always transported in mixed truckloads. But if, as a result of the increase in traffic, the firm adds three trucks to its fleet, even though these trucks also carry only mixed loads, their cost must be entirely attributable to product $X$ (assuming there are no offsetting changes in the use of other inputs). Nevertheless, there will always or almost always remain a residue of common costs which is unattributable to any individual product because the magnitude of this residue is unaffected by the quantity of any products supplied or sold or even by the decision to inaugurate the supply of a particular product. Such unattributable common costs can constitute a very substantial proportion of a firm's total costs.

3. It can be argued with considerable justice that the public will gain little from such a price reduction if it is offered only so long as the competitor remains in operation and then promptly withdrawn once that competitor is driven from the field. But, surely, the proper cure for this disease is prevention of the subsequent price rise, rather than prohibition of the initial price reduction. Elsewhere (1978) I have proposed a criterion of predatory pricing which is based on this view.

4. Their advocacy of such full-cost prices is often buttressed by a fallacious argument which implies that marginal cost is inevitably lower than average, that is, full cost. Of course, this view could not get by the examination in a freshman economics course, but it is instructive to observe how it is presented. Its advocates imply that marginal cost is not the first derivative of total cost but that it is what may be described as a partially distributed cost from which all common costs and perhaps all capital costs have simply been omitted. To defend themselves from this charge some advocates of marginal-cost criterion have been driven to emphasize long-run marginal cost which, of course, must include all marginal-capital costs.

5. See, for example, *Pacific Engineering* v. *Kerr-McGee* (1977); *Inglis and Sons Baking Co.* v. *ITT Continental Baking Co.* (1978); and *Janich Bros., Inc.* v. *American Distilling Co.* (1977).

6. This conclusion is viewed with considerable suspicion by a number of observers who argue that the social desirability of any particular pricing pattern must be judged, in ways which cannot be specified completely, in terms of the circumstances of each case, and that there are too many ways in which pricing freedom can be misused to permit the adoption of any simple criterion of legality. On this see, for example, Frederic M. Scherer (1976). In reaching this conclusion these commentators have not adequately weighed the costs and benefits of an undefined criterion of illegality in pricing.

7. As a matter of fact, if one is merely looking for an approximation to marginal cost, it should often be possible to do better than average variable

cost. When costs decline with output, marginal costs must lie below average variable costs, and such qualitative information can help to narrow down the zone of ignorance about the true marginal-cost figure. As this was being written, a court decision appeared which seems to have taken a fairly similar view, concluding that in the case in question the use of average variable cost to evaluate a price was illegitimate because there were special reasons for its use in that instance.

8. There seems to be some confusion about the relation between short- and long-run marginal cost. It seems to be believed rather widely that short-run marginal cost will normally be the lower of the two, on the ground that it contains no investment outlays or returns on capital because these are fixed in the short run. But his conclusion about the relative size of the two costs is generally not true. As a matter of fact, short-run total cost will normally be higher than its long-run counterpart. A simple example will make this clear. Suppose a shift in the demand curve leads a firm to expand output by hiring overtime labor at a cost of ten dollars per unit of output. The increase in demand seeming more or less permanent, the firm decides to invest in additional equipment as a substitute for the overtime labor. Why does it do so? Obviously, the explanantion must be that the machines incur a cost below the ten dollar per unit corresponding to the overtime labor. This is the explanation of the act of legerdermain whereby long-run total cost includes capital outlays omitted from the short-run figure and yet manages to be the lower of the two. This relation will hold generally, since capital will be purchased only if it is the more economical means to do the job.

The reason short-run total costs are at least as high as the long-run figures is that short-run costs correspond to an investment commitment based on a particular expected output level, $y^*$. If demand turns out to be just sufficient to elicit this level of output, short- and long-run total costs will coincide. But if output turns out to be larger (smaller) than $y^*$ the plant selected will be uneconomically large (uneconomically small) and so short-run total cost for that actual output must be larger than it would be if the firm were operating in the long run, meaning that it had full freedom of choice in plant design.

From this one can now deduce the relationship between short- and long-run marginal costs. Figure 11-1 depicts the pattern of short- and long-run costs that has just been described, with $y^*$ the output level for which current plant was designed. As one can see several relationships emerge: if the total cost curves are differentiable they must be tangent at output $y^*$, so that at this output level short-run and long-run marginal costs must be equal. For outputs slightly above $y^*$, short-run marginal cost must exceed long-run marginal cost, while the reverse must be true for outputs slightly below $y^*$. For outputs far from $y^*$ one cannot, in general, say which of the marginal cost figures is the larger, though if curvatures do not change, the short-run

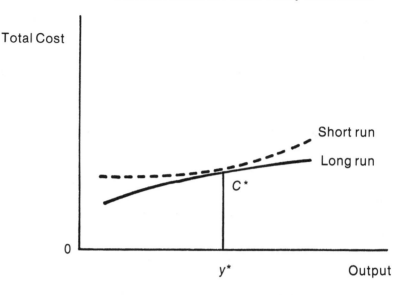

**Figure 11-1.** Relationship between Short- and Long-Run Marginal Costs

figure will be higher for all $y > y^*$ and the long-run figure will be higher for $y < y^*$. Intuitively, the reason $SRMC > LRMC$ for $y > y^*$ is that expansion of output beyond $y^*$ is handicapped in the short run by inadequate plant size so that expensive substitute inputs, such as overtime labor, will be required to make it possible. On the other hand, where $y < y^*$, the usual story about excess capacity and the consequently low cost of expansion becomes valid. I am deeply grateful to Robert Willig and Gerald Faulhaber for correcting a serious error in my discussion of this issue in an earlier draft.

9. Similar points are made by Williamson (1977).

10. I am indebted to Robert Willig for this observation. See also W. Arthur Lewis (1947), p. 22ff.

11. This definition seems first to have been formulated by Panzar and Willig (1976). It is not absolutely certain that Areeda and Turner want to define average variable cost in this way. Suppose there is a product-specific fixed cost incurred in supplying $X$; for example, suppose $X$ represents the delivery of oil by pipeline to a particular city and that this requires the construction of an extension to the company's pipeline system leading directly into that community. Then this investment outlay is clearly incurred exclusively on behalf of $X$ and by either definition 11.1 or 11.2 it constitutes part of its incremental cost. On the other hand, on the grounds that a fixed cost cannot be considered variable it might be decided, quite inappropriately, to exclude this construction outlay from average variable cost.

12. For the original source and fullest discussion of this concept, see Panzar and Willig (1976) or (1978).

13. Of course, if there really were a rival so that the mountain pass had an alternative user, it would carry a rent, and the incumbent's cost advantage would disappear. I deliberately deal with the case in which this is not so in order to be able to consider the appropriate criterion for cases in which the two stand-alone costs do differ.

14. This is not quite true if we define the proper ceiling as the lower of the two stand-alone costs defined before. Since the data in the calculation described in Faulhaber's theorem apply only to the firm whose price is being tested, the stand-alone figure provided by the calculation refers to the cost if product $X$ were to be supplied by itself but by the firm which now also produces items $Y, Z, \ldots$.

## References

Ackworth, William M. *The Railways and the Traders*. London, 1891.

Alexander, Edward P. *Railway Practice*. New York, 1887.

Areeda, Phillip, and Donald Turner. "Predatory Pricing and Related Practices under Section 2 of the Sherman Act." *Harvard Law Review* 88 (February 1975):697-733.

Baumol, William J. "Quasi-Permanence of Price Reductions—A Policy for Prevention of 'Predatory Pricing'," *Yale Law Journal* 89 (November 1979):1-26.

Cassel, Gustav. "The Principles of Railway Rates for Passengers." *International Economic Papers*, no. 6. Translated from *Archiv für Eisenbahnwesen* (1900).

Faulhaber, Gerald R. "Cross-Subsidization: Pricing in Public Enterprise." *American Economic Review* 65 (December 1975):966-977.

Hadley, Arthur T. *Railroad Transportation*. New York and London, 1886.

Hotelling, Harold. "The General Welfare in Relation to Problems of Taxation and Utility Rates." *Econometrica* 6 (July 1938):242-269.

Lewis, W. Arthur. *Overhead Costs*. London: Allen and Unwin, 1949.

Panzar, John and Robert Willig. "Economies of Scale and Economies of Scope in MultiOutput Production." Bell Laboratories Economics Discussion Paper (1976).

———. "Economies of Scope, Product-Specific Economies of Scale and the MultiProduct Competitive Firm." Bell Laboratories Economics Discussion Paper (1978).

Ramsey, Frank P. "A Contribution to the Theory of Taxation." *Economic Journal* 37 (March 1927):47-61.

Scherer, Frederic M. "Predatory Pricing and the Sherman Act: A Comment." *Harvard Law Review* 89 (1976):869-890.

Smith, Adam. *The Wealth of Nations* (1776). New York: Cannan, 1937.

Williamson, Oliver E. "Predatory Pricing: A Strategic Welfare Analysis." *Yale Law Journal* 87 (1977):284-340.

U.S. Court of Appeals, 10th Circuit, 551 F. 2d 790, *Pacific Engineering and Prod. Co.* v. *Kerr-McGee Corp.* (February 28, 1977).

U.S. Court of Appeals, 9th Circuit. 570 F. 2d 856, *Janich Bros., Inc.* v. *American Distilling Co.* (1977).

U.S. District Court, Northern District of California. No. C-71-1906 SW, *Inglis and Sons Baking Co.* v. *ITT Continental Baking Co.* (October 2, 1978).

# 12

## Caveats on Applying Ramsey Pricing

*David R. Kamerschen* and
*Donald C. Keenan*

### Ramsey Pricing

Recently, there has been an effort to introduce into regulatory practice the theoretical device now popularly called Ramsey pricing.[1] This effort is notable since traditionally economic theory has been more successful in developing an understanding of why actual practices occur than in providing new ones. One may easily argue that, typically, interested parties will have long since discovered desirable practices through trial and error without the need to wait for the painstaking process of economic science to obtain them. If this argument is taken seriously, one may, a priori, be skeptical as to the applicability of Ramsey pricing; it is of rather recent origin even within the theory of industrial organization. The seminal work of William Baumol and David Bradford appeared only in 1970.[2] The term Ramsey pricing itself arises from the pioneering work of Frank Ramsey, who only somewhat earlier investigated the mathematically similar but economically distinct problem of optimal commodity taxation.[3] While efforts have been made to relate Ramsey pricing to earlier discussions of discriminatory pricing, Baumol and Bradford themselves point out that the relationship can be more apparent than real.[4]

### The Basic Theorem

The basic theorem known as the inverse-elasticity or simple Ramsey-pricing rule indicates conditions under which even in the absence of externalities prices are required to deviate in a systematic manner from marginal costs for a socially optimal allocation of resources. In the sense of partial equilibrium, Ramsey-pricing analysis demonstrates that under certain strong assumptions quasi-optimal pricing by a multiproduct monopolist operating under a profit constraint mandates that for each product the percentage deviation of quasi-optimal price from marginal costs must be inversely proportionate to its own-price elasticity of demand. If a product is produced

---

Certain portions of this chapter were drawn from the Verified Statement of David R. Kamerschen before the Interstate Commerce Commission, No. 37062 and 37063 (Sub-No.1), Ex Parte No. 357 (May 11, 1981), July 27, 1981), (November 25, 1981) and his article entitled "Unraveling the Mysteries of Telephone Ratemaking," 201 *Telephony* (July 20, 1981), pp. 50-62.

in a market where own-price elasticity of demand is quite low (that is, inelastic), the positive percentage deviation of price from marginal costs should be larger than where a product is produced in a market with a relatively high (that is, elastic) own-price elasticity of demand. Moreover, quasi-optimal prices must yield outputs that deviate by (approximately) the same proportion from those which would result from pricing at the marginal costs corresponding to the quasi-optimal output levels. This solution is called quasi-optimal because it is a second-best solution to the constrained maxi mum problem forced upon a regulatory tribunal by the requirement of adequate revenue. The Ramsey differential rate structure has sparked considerable controversy because its precepts are contrary to the beliefs of some economists, consumer groups, and regulatory bodies. In fact, a number of regulating bodies are required by law to avoid unjustly differential or discriminatory rate structures.

## Basic Assumptions

There are a number of assumptions or conditions required before it is in fact necessarily true that simple Ramsey pricing is both efficient and different from traditional analysis. These include: one, that there are joint outputs with common inputs; two, that there are economies of scale such that marginal-cost pricing would not cover all costs; three, that cost must in fact be covered by the firm using a uniform-pricing schedule; four, that all cross-price elasticities of demand are zero (demands are independent); five, that the regulated firm acts as a price taker for the labor and raw materials it buys; six, that the goods or services do not exhibit consumption externalities (where enjoyment of any of the firm's services by one customer affects other agents); and seven, that the rest of the economy, unlike the regulated firm, must be perfectly competitive. For Ramsey pricing to be applicable accurate estimates of the own- and cross-price elasticities of demand for all goods and services must be available. Moreover, regardless of efficiency, without certain restrictions Ramsey prices can be unsustainable (or vulnerable to attack by a rival firm offering lower viable prices to a subset of the regulated firm's services) or unstable (vulnerable in a dynamic sense, that is, what is commonly called cream skimming or hit and run). No one to our knowledge has shown that all these conditions prevail in any of the traditional areas of regulation.

## Bonbright's Insights

As a number of the other chapters in this book have illustrated, Bonbright, the celebratory doyen of this festschrift, has made a germinal contribution in the field in the area covered by this chapter.[5] He has addressed some of the strong and weak points of the present topic under the heading of value of service pricing.

Let a sampling of four of his comments on this topic suffice:

> The problem of determining what surcharges will impose the least serious harm in the form of curtailments and distortions of use of service when the rates as a whole must yield total revenue requirements is perhaps the most complex and most difficult problem of modern rate theory. Not only does it require for its solution highly involved mathematical analysis; in addition, the application of this analysis depends on a knowledge of cost functions and of demand functions that practical rate makers simply do not and cannot possess. How far these refinements of theory may lend themselves to practical use in the future is a question on which I venture no opinion. But certain elementary aspects of the problem can be discussed without reference to the tools of mathematics; and they will be discussed in Chapter XIX, on rate discrimination.[6]

> Most discussions of the merits and demerits of rate discrimination are not concerned primarily with those discriminatory relationships which are simply unavoidable under any full-cost system of rate making. Instead, they are concerned with that deliberate policy of rate differentiation known as 'value-of-service' rate making or, in railroad parlance, as the practice of charging 'what the traffic will bear'. Here, the apportionment of the burden of covering any excess in total costs over marginal costs (or 'out-of-pocket' costs) is deliberately 'biased' so as to impose on the services in relatively inelastic demand (services of high 'value' in popular speech) higher surcharges, over and above marginal costs, than would be imposed by *any* rule of apportionment based exclusively on cost relationships.[7]

> Even more formidable are the problems raised by the question to what extent, and subject to what restrictions, the practice of this kind of discrimination is in the public interest. Here too, theoretical answers have been offered by recent economists. They take the form of a statement of conditions for "optimum rates subject to a budgetary constraint"—subject for example, to the requirement that the rates of any one company must yield total revenues equal to total operating expenses plus a "fair return" on capital investment. But just as with the problem of price determination for the purpose of securing maximum profits, so with this distinct though related problem, their application would call for unattainable information about elasticities of demand and supply. Moreover, they depend for their validity on the acceptance of highly artificial standards of social welfare. At the present stage of their formation they can hardly serve as practical guides to the rate maker or rate regulator in his attempt to draw lines between 'due' and 'undue' forms and degrees of price discrimination.[8]

After quoting the Ramsey article, Bonbright says:

> The general conclusion, based on simplified assumptions including assumed independent demands for the various services, is that rates should

be proportional to the demand elasticities of the various services at these rates. Applied to utility rates, Ramsey's article implies that the surcharges above marginal costs should diminish in the same proportion as the demand for each service. I take it that these two propositions are essentially the same.[9]

## *Difficulties with Ramsey Pricing*

The present discussion will review some of the outstanding difficulties with Ramsey pricing as an operational rule. Despite concern with application, most of the difficulties with Ramsey pricing have their source in its weak theoretical foundations. The general tenor of this discussion will be that Ramsey pricing, because of its unsatisfactory formulation, remains for the present more of a theoretical curiosity than a workable regulatory rule.

### The Framework for Regulation

The traditional viewpoint of economists is that regardless of decreasing costs a firm should follow marginal-cost pricing. One difficulty with this position is that efficiency will require that there be but one firm in a decreasing-cost industry. However, this one firm will not be motivated to pursue marginal-cost pricing even if it faces threat of entry by other firms. This creates the usual presumption for regulation.[10] Marginal-cost regulation presents its own difficulties, though, since firms with decreasing costs will not be able to generate sufficient revenue. In order to continue operation the firm will have to be subsidized. What is more, if the solution is to be first best, or efficient, these subsidies will need to be raised in a lump-sum manner so that no resulting distortions are introduced into the economy.

The starting point for the Ramsey-pricing literature is the argument that in practice lump-sum taxation is impossible. Thus, the argument goes, the firm should introduce a discriminatory pricing structure in order to raise enough revenue to cover costs. If this is done in a manner judged to best promote society's interests, the result will be a Ramsey-pricing scheme. For a single-product firm this reduces to average cost pricing; for a multiproduct firm, this typically involves raising price above marginal cost more for those goods which have more inelastic demand.

The presumption that lump-sum taxes are impractical is far from clear. Quoting Frank Hahn:

> Somehow the belief has grown up amongst economists that lump-sum taxes and fees, etc., are simply impractical for unexplained reasons. But this is both unsatisfactory and hasty. The Poll Tax Act of 1660 taxed dukes at

£100, earls at £60, baronets at £30, squires at £10 . . . It levied a fee of £100 on archbishops and of £40 on dons. It taxed every £100 worth of land, money or stock at £2 . . . the government has no less information than the 17th century legislators; indeed, it has a good deal more. What is stopping them from using appropriate instruments?[11]

The usual argument against lump-sum taxes is that information on which to base them is unobservable. Further, individuals have an incentive not to reveal such information. However, this would at most prevent some forms of lump-sum taxes; other forms, such as uniform poll taxes, would surely remain available. If there are pure profits within the economy, as there will be with decreasing returns to scale in some sectors, and if these are sufficient to cover the regulated industry's deficit, then the first-best solution can be achieved by a tax on pure profits, or equivalently, by a uniform tax on all goods and factors of the economy. The extent to which certain lump-sum taxes, or indeed any form of tax, cannot be used to subsidize decreasing-cost industries ought to be explained within the model. It is clearly unsatisfactory to impose the ad hoc requirement that the firm must cover its own costs through manipulated prices.

That cost must always be covered is not all that obvious. Presumably, the argument is that sufficient capital cannot be attracted if the rate of return on existing capital is insufficient. But as Kahn points out this hardly applies to sunk capital.[12] Investors realize the distinction and could be counted to offer sufficient funds, provided an adequate rate of return was assured on new investments, regardless of returns to sunk capital. There can be no argument on the grounds of efficiency why overinvestment should be supported, that is, why poor past investment should be rewarded.

Even granting that costs are to be covered from the firm's own revenue, it still remains to determine how a firm should accomplish this. In the Ramsey setup this is done by a linear price scheme. The price of one kind of good remains the same, whatever the amount purchased. However, Willig has shown that nonlinear pricing dominates simple Ramsey pricing, whenever the former is feasible, which requires only that resale be impossible.[13] Thus, Ramsey pricing of the usual sort is itself inefficient, even if one accepts the constraint of revenue adequacy.

**Marginal-Cost Pricing versus Ramsey Pricing**

The most remarkable attribute of the first-best, marginal-cost pricing-cum-subsidy solution is that it permits a separation between the concerns of efficiency and equity. Marginal-cost pricing should be pursued in the interest of efficiency, whatever society's objectives are. Any distributional considerations can be handled via lump-sum transfers. However, if lump-sum taxes are forbidden, as is invariably the case in arguments supporting the adoption of Ramsey pricing, then this separation property is lost. This means that the appropriate Ramsey scheme must then take into explicit account considerations of fairness or equity. Putting it another way, a number of treatments in the theory of the second best deal with one single consumer, so that only the question of efficiency arises. Neglecting the uninteresting possibility that there is but a single consumer, these treatments are meant to refer to the situation where lump-sum taxation is always employed to obtain an optimal distribution. It is then a well-known result that society acts like a single consumer. However, if lump-sum taxation is available, it is difficult to see why it could not be used to cover the deficits of decreasing-cost industries, thus making possible the first-best marginal-cost pricing solution.

If Ramsey pricing is to be interesting, it must occur in a world without lump-sum taxes. But then one must face up to the fact that its application will have a distributional impact which must be accounted for. The difficulty here, of course, is that in reality regulators have little idea what society's distributional goals if any, are. While it seems forgotten in much of the discussion of the simple unweighted inverse-elasticity rule, there is in fact not just one single Ramsey-pricing scheme but rather a whole family of them. Which particular one is appropriate depends on one's distributional goals. The simple unweighted inverse-elasticity rule does not arise from efficiency considerations alone. Efficiency is only a partial criterion and is not up to the task of singling out a particular regulatory rule. The welfare goal in fact used to obtain the simple inverse-elasticity rule is the unweighted sum of producer and consumer surplus. This choice of a goal is essentially arbitrary; there is lengthy economic literature establishing the inappropriateness of consumer surplus measures both at the individual and aggregate levels.[14] This situation is to be compared with that of the traditional first-best solution, which requires no ethical choices on the part of the regulator; marginal-cost pricing is adopted solely from considerations of efficiency. Distributional concerns, such as how the resulting subsidies ought to be raised, need not be the regulators' concern. Under marginal-cost pricing the economic and political roles of government are separated.

The argument is also made that if marginal-cost pricing would provide adequate revenue, Ramsey pricing would reduce to marginal-cost pricing so that in general the former encompasses the latter. This is true only when distributional concerns are absent. But this is reasonable only if other tax instruments are available to obtain the desired distribution. If these instruments are present, they ought to be available to subsidize the decreasing-cost industry. Thus, the Ramsey formulation has been misspecified in any case.

When marginal-cost pricing fails to cover costs, the revenue deficit needs to be filled through Ramsey pricing or a subsidy. As indicated earlier, the interesting cases of Ramsey pricing arise with joint output. It is sometimes argued that with joint output common costs will lead to revenue insufficiency under marginal-cost pricing. The presumed difficulty lies in the fact that common costs cannot always be unambiguously attributed to various outputs. But so long as marginal costs are defined (as they must be for the usual form of Ramsey pricing to be available) and so long as marginal-cost pricing covers costs, the allocation of such shared costs will be irrelevant. John Panzar and Robert Willig,[15] along with Baumol,[16] have extended the usual results for single-output production to multioutput production, where common costs may exist and have shown that marginal-cost pricing is unprofitable when and only when there are locally increasing returns to scale. Thus, common costs affect profitability only insofar as they are associated with increasing returns. Whether many regulated industries such as railroads do in fact experience increasing returns is, of course, a matter of long-standing controversy. For example, Huettner and Landon (1978) opine that electric-utility operations are not subject to increasing returns to scale.

**The Implications of the Inverse-Elasticity Rule**

It is a common observation that Ramsey pricing is mathematically the same problem as optimal-commodity taxation, a topic of much recent research. However, it would be more appropriate to say that it is public-sector pricing which is like optimal-taxation theory; regulation of private industry involves the additional complication that a firm is interested in maximizing its profits, not society's well-being, and so must be given the incentive to produce the Ramsey optimal quantities. Even if the appropriate Ramsey prices are set, a firm may find that it can do better by producing other than the Ramsey optimal quantities. Some examples are presented in Dieter Bos for a single output firm.[17] Richer examples can be constructed using multioutput firms.

Whereas marginal-cost pricing, whenever feasible, represents the first best solution, Ramsey pricing remains a second-best solution. Like many results from the theory of the second best, it is quite sensitive to the assumptions being made. Thus, the great numbers of simplifying assumptions used to obtain the simple inverse-elasticity rule appear quite disturbing. Those assumptions used by Baumol and Bradford in their derivation of the simple inverse-elasticity rule include:[18]

*Assumptions of the Rule*

1. Equal welfare weights: this is equivalent to choosing the unweighted sum of producer and compensated consumer surplus as the social goal.

2. No income effects.
3. Zero cross elasticities of demand.
4. Constant factor prices.
5. Monopoly under no threat of entry.
6. Uniform pricing only, that is, neither nonlinear pricing schemes, such as two-part tariffs, nor any alternative form of taxation to raise revenue are considered.
7. Constant marginal costs.[19]
8. Final goods only, that is, the firm does not produce intermediate goods.

### Complications of the Rule

In addition, they assumed that the remainder of the economy is perfectly competitive. If there are any of the following complications present in the rest of the economy, then the Ramsey-pricing scheme may be seriously affected:

1. Imperfect competition, that is, monopolistic industries.
2. Taxation or other forms of government regulation.
3. A public sector.
4. Pure profits in the private sector.
5. Nonmarket clearing.
6. Intermodal or intramodal competition with the regulated firm.

Outstanding among the difficulties involved in the previous considerations will be the informational requirements that result. Ronald Brauetigam presents a model incorporating the last of the listed complications and obtains a Ramsey solution that is obviously unmanageable.[20] While he proposes an alternate solution, it is based entirely on ad hoc devices and so lacks even the second-best optimality properties associated with true Ramsey pricing.

It is not mere carping to point out the modifications required of Ramsey pricing due to distributional concerns or economy-wide interactions. The presumption created by the long tradition of neoclassical economics is that marginal-cost pricing principles are rather robust. However, the exactly opposite presumption has been created for results of the second best, including Ramsey-pricing principles. Much of this discussion has been within the context of the optimal tax problem, but as pointed out earlier any formal difficulty with optimal commodity taxes must yield a difficulty with Ramsey pricing. In concluding a survey that must be regarded as sympathetic to the optimal tax literature, Anthony Atkinson and Joseph Stiglitz nonetheless state:

A second objection is that the optimal tax literature does not lead to un-ambiguous policy conclusions and that the results depend sensitively on parameters about which we have little empirical knowledge, such as the second derivative of the demand function or the elasticity of the labor sup-ply with respect to the rate of interest. This is a reasonable statement of the position (and indeed we have sought to bring this out), but *it is a misun-derstanding of the purpose of the literature to suppose that it can yield defi-nite policy recommendations.* As we emphasized at the outset, the aim is rather to explore the "grammar of arguments."[21]

## Toward Applications

Baumol and Willig in a discussion oriented toward application suggest that when it is impossible for a firm to obtain sufficient revenue by any system of prices, one should at least allow the firm to maximize its profits, that is, let it act as a discriminating monopolist.[22] This, however, cannot follow from the Ramsey setup. Without any pricing scheme whatsoever that covers cost, one cannot select an optimal scheme. In any event, their claim seems unlikely in light of their own more formal considerations.[23] They show that as permitted profits of a monopolist reach the discriminating maximum, consumer surplus is lost at an infinite rate.

Baumol and Willig go on to argue that regulation may be unnecessary for optimality, since a firm that cannot make profits in any event ought to be allowed to behave as a discriminating monopolist, whereas one that can make profits will choose the Ramsey prices for fear of entry by competitors.[24] This chapter has already contested the first claim; the second holds only under strong assumptions, notable of which is gross substitution.[25] When these strong assumptions do not hold, the interesting possibility arises that Ramsey pricing may lead to cross-subsidization. To prevent this, Baumol and Willig propose a stand-alone test to eliminate such cross-subsidization.[26] However, this proposal is entirely inconsistent with the Ramsey-pricing methodology. One of the more convincing aspects of Ramsey pricing is that it is obtained in a comprehensive manner once the objective has been imposed. Any dissatisfaction with the implications of the Ramsey rule ought to be dealt with through modification of the goals from which it is obtained, not by ad hoc modification of the end result.

In the same vein, Baumol and Willig propose to apply the simple partial equilibrium inverse-elasticity rule to the general setting by arguing that the rest of the economy may be taken as given, as is the case with a competitive firm. But a natural monopolist (the most pertinent case for Ramsey pricing) is not a competitive firm: that is, its actions can be expected to affect the re-mainder of the economy. Further, it is the regulator, not the firm, that must set prices. There can be little rationale for regulators to ignore the fact that the economy consists of more than that one industry. But once this is done, the reasoning that would otherwise lead to simple Ramsey pricing leads instead to economic-wide rules which have little hope of implementation even in principle.

**Notes**

1. David A. Huettner, "Optimal Second Best Pricing of CATV Pole Attachments," *Southern Economic Journal* 49 (April 1982):996-1015, reviews the few attempts to apply optimal second-best pricing rules (Ramsey prices) to existing problems. In addition to his own application to CATV pole-rental rates, applications have been to postal rates [Roger Shermen and Anthony George, "Second-Best Pricing for the U.S. Postal Office," *Southern Economic Journal* 46 (January 1979):685-709]; to journal pricing [Janusz A. Ordover and Robert D. Willig, "On the Optimal Provision of Journals qua Sometimes Shared Goods," *American Economic Review* 68 (June 1978):324-338]; postal and telephone rates [Robert D. Willig and Elizabeth E. Bailey, "The Economic Gradient Method," *American Economic Review* 69 (May 1979):96-101]; to electric utilities [Randy A. Nelson, "An Empirical Test of the Ramsey Theory and Stigler-Peltzman Theory of Public Utility Pricing," *Economic Inquiry* 20 (April 1982):277-290, and David A. Huettner and John A. Landon, "Electric Utilities: Scale Economies and Diseconomies," *Southern Economic Journal* (April 1978):883-912]; and to railway rates [Sylvester Damus, "Two Part Tariffs and Optimum Taxation: The Case of Railway Rates," *American Economic Review* 71 (March 1981):65-79]; also see the Kamerschen, Kahn, and Baumol and Willig Interstate Commerce Commission testimony cited in subsequent footnotes.

Huettner (p. 997, citations added) states:

> While applicable to a wide range of regulatory problems, these principles are yet unused by virtually every regulatory agency in the U.S. perhaps the only effort to implement second best pricing rules has been made by the U.S. Postal Commission and this effort was recently rebuffed by the District of Columbia U.S. Court of Appeals [*National Association of Greeting Card Publications* v. *The U.S. Postal Service*, Civ. No. 75-1856-U.S. Appl. D.C. Cir. F. 2nd, Dec. 28, 1976]. Of perhaps greater concern is the fact that few regulatory economists have discarded traditional pricing rules and adopted second best principles. Indeed, Lancaster has recently suggested [Electric Utility Rate Design Study Report, no. 70, *The Problem of the Second Best and the Efficient Pricing of Electrical Power*, San Francisco: Gordian Associations and Kevin Lancaster, August 7, 1979] the second best principles should be ignored in electricity pricing because of the difficulties involved.

2. William J. Baumol and David F. Bradford, "Optimal Departures from Marginal Cost Pricing," *American Economic Review* 60 (June 1970):

265-283. Also see William J. Baumol, "Quasi Optimality: The Price We Must Pay for a Price System," *Journal of Political Economy* 87 (June 1979):578-599.

3. Frank Ramsey, I.P.A., "A Contribution to the Theory of Taxation," *Economic Journal* 37 (March 1927):47-61.

4. Ramsey, "A Contribution," p. 267.

5. As Bonbright's vita indicates, he has written widely and seminally in the public-utility area. This chapter will concentrate on his imperishable contribution encapsulated in his *Principles of Public Utility Rates* (New York: Columbia University Press, 1961). All quoted material reprinted with permission.

6. Ibid., p. 303.

7. Ibid., p. 378.

8. Ibid., pp. 382-383.

9. Ibid., footnote 25, p. 382.

10. Another presumption for regulation arises because when there is a natural monopoly (that it is efficient for only one firm to operate), inefficient entry by other firms may nonetheless occur in the absence of regulation.

11. Frank H. Hahn, "On Optimum Taxation," *Journal of Economic Theory* 13 (February 1973):106. Reprinted with permission.

12. Alfred E. Kahn, Verified Statement of Alfred E. Kahn before the Interstate Commerce Commission, Ex Parte, No. 347, (Sub-No.1), Coal Rate Guidelines Nationwide, September 28, 1981), pp. 4-14.

In all, Kahn expresses four major reservations about Ramsey pricing in setting railroad rates for shipping coal, and they warrant reiteration (See Kamerschen, Verified Statement):

a. It is not true that unrestricted Ramsey pricing is necessary so long as railroads fail to earn the current cost of capital on their entire net-invested capital (that is, on their historical total book value of their investments). The only costs that economic efficiency requires be reflected in rates is the minimum-incremental-current cost of producing the service(s) in question with new facilities.

b. Economic efficiency does not require that captive shippers contribute to a return on railroad facilities that do not service them if these are costs that would be avoided if other shippers were not served. The exploitation of monopoly by so charging would be more a matter of violating equity or the general social standard of fairness than of efficiency.

c. Ramsey pricing on the basis of differences in the own-price elasticity of demand of various groups of rail customers that are attributable to the presence or absence of intramodal competition from competing transporters raises serious questions about both economic efficiency and equity.

d. The railroads should not be permitted the unrestricted exploitation of captive coal shippers as long as they continue to obstruct or restrict competition through the entry of coal-slurry pipelines into the transportation market.

13. Robert D. Willig, "Pareto Superior Nonlinear Outlay Schedules," *Bell Journal of Economics* 9 (Spring 1978):56-69.

14. It would not be correct to say that simple Ramsey pricing assumes that the initial distribution is socially optimal since it affects what that distribution is.

15. John C. Panzar and Robert C. Willig, "Economies on Scale in Multi-Output Production," *Quarterly Journal of Economics* 91 (August 1977):481-491.

16. William J. Baumol, "Scale Economies, Average Cost, and the Profitability of Marginal Cost Pricing," *Public Urban Economics, Essays in Honor of William S. Vickrey*, ed. R.E. Grierson (Lexington, Mass.: Lexington Press, 1975), pp. 43-67.

17. Dieter Bos, *Economic Theory of Public Enterprise: Lecture Notes in Economics and Mathematical Systems* (Berlin: Springer Verlag, 1981), 188:62-63.

18. Baumol and Bradford, "Optimal Departures," pp. 268-273.

19. Ibid., footnote 8, p. 270.

20. Ronald R. Brauetigam, "Optimal Pricing with Intermodal Competition," *American Economic Review* 60 (March 1970):38-49.

21. Anthony B. Atkinson and Joseph E. Stiglitz, *Lectures on Public Economics* (New York: McGraw-Hill, 1980), p. 456 (emphasis added).

22. William Baumol and Robert D. Willig, (hereinafter Baumol and Willig, Verified Statement No. 1) Verified Statement No. 1 before the Interstate Commerce Commission, Ex-Parte No. 342 (Sub-No. 1), Coal Rate Guidelines Nationwide, May 11, 1981, pp. 32-41.

23. William J. Baumol and Robert D. Willig, "Fixed Costs, Sunk Costs, Entry Barriers, Sustainability of Monopoly" 95 *Quarterly Journal of Economics* (August 1981):423.

24. Baumol and Willig, Verified Statement No. 1, pp. 69-70. However see Trout Rader, "Normally Factors are Never Gross Substitutes," *Journal of Political Economy* 76 (January 1968):38-43 for a discussion of the improbability of gross substitutes in an economy with produced goods.

25. Baumol and Willig, Verified Statement No. 1, pp. 32-41.

26. Baumol and Willig, Verified Statement No. 1, pp. 74-80.

27. Baumol and Willig, Verified Statement No. 1, p. 64.

# Part V
# Rate of Return, Taxation, and the Value of Utility Securities

# 13 Regulatory Lag in an Inflationary Environment

## Milton Z. Kafoglis

The central messages of this chapter are that rapidly rising unit costs in the utility industry call for a reduction in regulatory lag, and automatic-adjustment clauses and future test years are a means for achieving this objective. However, such policies may weaken traditional regulatory procedures and diminish the incentives to efficiency that are a built-in feature of regulatory lag. These undesirable effects can be mitigated by incorporating productivity as an explicit variable in the regulatory process. Over the longer term, greater reliance on incentives generated by market competition is in order. Protective regulatory policies should be abandoned and a positive effort should be made to accommodate new forms of competition.

## The Current Regulatory Issue

Dissatisfaction with commission regulation has increased sharply during the past decade. This dissatisfaction centers around the responsiveness of the regulatory process to the pressures created by severe inflation, insecure and expensive energy supplies, unsettled capital markets, and technological mandates imposed by various federal agencies. For over a decade rate increases have not kept pace with increases in the unit costs of producing utility services with a consequent decline in the rate of earnings and dividend growth.

The impact has been especially severe in the electric and gas-utility industries where the combination of high-interest rates and rapidly rising unit costs has created a squeeze on profit margins and on the availability of internally generated capital. Though demand pressures have eased somewhat recently in response to higher service rates and conservation measures, there remains a serious question about the ability of the industry to finance projected annual outlays of about $40 billion for new plants and equipment. Failure of commission regulation to respond to this problem could lead to deterioration in the quality of service as revenues fall short of the level needed to replace existing capacity and to provide for capacity expansion

The failure of the industry and its regulators to respond effectively is due only in part to the inflexibilities and lags that are inherent in the regulatory process. Marginal-cost, time-of-day, and other efficiency prices were actively opposed by the utility industry (with the tacit support of state commissions) long after the financial markets signaled that the industry was moving from a period of rapid growth to one of slower growth. For example, in 1963, the ratio of market to tangible book value for securities of electric utilities stood at a remarkable 2.5, well above the 1963 all-industry average of 1.5 (see table 13-1). The market signal was for growth and abundance with more of it accruing to the utility sector than to the rest of the economy. Small wonder, then, that the industry and regulators found efficiency pricing impractical and not worth the trouble. However, by 1970, and prior to the oil embargo, the market-to-book ratio for the electric-utility industry had fallen to 1.4 while the ratio for all industries remained virtually unchanged. Notwithstanding these strong market signals, rate making remained growth oriented and promotional. By 1978 earnings growth had declined sharply and market values of securities had fallen below—in some cases far below—book values as a capital crisis began to emerge. Regulatory inflexibility along with an ostrich-like attitude on the part of utility managements had combined to preserve the practices that were already out of tune with market realities.

The reaction at the federal level was predictable. The Public Utility Regulatory Policies Act of 1978 was enacted giving birth to a new federal involvement in state regulatory affairs in an attempt to coerce practices that should have been fairly considered as early as 1970. The continued federal regulation of domestic oil prices and the rolling in of high-priced imports contributed significantly to the problem because it transmitted false price signals to utility managements, regulatory commissions, and other in-

**Table 13-1**
**Ratios of Market to Tangible Book Value per Share, Selected Regulated Industry Groups**

| Industry | 1963 | 1970 | 1973 | 1978 | 1980 |
|---|---|---|---|---|---|
| Sample of U.S. industry | 1.47 | 1.52 | 2.35 | .99 | 1.50 |
| Electric utilities | | | | | |
| East, nonnuclear | 2.61 | 1.40 | 1.12 | .94 | .80 |
| East, nuclear | 2.42 | 1.36 | 1.09 | .89 | .74 |
| Mid, nonnuclear | 2.56 | 1.52 | 1.27 | .98 | .81 |
| Mid, nuclear | 2.48 | 1.28 | 1.15 | 1.01 | .82 |
| West | 2.31 | 1.38 | 1.15 | .99 | .86 |
| Natural gas | 2.14 | 1.39 | 1.37 | 1.03 | 1.44 |
| Other regulated industries | | | | | |
| Railroads | | | | | |
| East | .68 | .50 | .62 | .61 | .90 |
| West | .42 | .46 | .48 | .56 | .94 |
| Trucking | 2.03 | 2.16 | 2.51 | 1.10 | 1.40 |
| Air transport | 1.62 | 1.59 | 1.98 | .81 | 1.20 |

Source: Data compiled from *Value Line* by Oliver R. Grawe, Emory University.

dustries. Recently, there has been a response to market conditions, but it has been slow and lagged at both the commission and industry levels.

## Reduction of Regulatory Lag

Disenchantment with the commission response to higher relative costs has led to proposals that would reduce the time lag between the increase in unit costs and the approval of rate increases. Since initial requests for rate increases must be predicated on a showing that rates of return have actually fallen below an acceptable level, earnings must continue at the lower level until rate increases are put into place. A year and a half of regulatory lag is not unusual for a significant rate revision. The attrition in earnings can be severe during this period and these earnings are lost forever. In an inflationary environment the cycle will be repeated almost immediately with another lump of earnings lost forever.

Automatic-adjustment clauses, future-test years, interim rate increases and inclusion in the rate base of construction work in progress are among the remedies that are being adopted. Some commissions have adopted these remedies as a matter of considered regulatory policy; others have adopted them as a matter of administrative necessity as requests for rate increases came in with increasing frequency and stacked up like airplanes waiting for clearance in a congested airport. These measures are now providing some relief for the industry.

In 1980, for example, electric utilities were granted $6.0 billion in rate increases, more than double the $2.9 billion granted in 1979. During the same period the average length of time to decide rate requests has dropped from eleven and one-half months to less than nine months. In addition, interim rate increases without formal hearings are becoming fairly routine. Though these measures are providing much needed relief, they may encourage new inefficiencies and distortions that might be overlooked, especially in situations where capital shortage threatens the maintenance of service quality and minimum reserve capacity.

It has long been recognized that regulatory lag is necessary for effective regulation; it provides necessary time for careful commission review. The increased participation of consumer groups and third-party intervenors also seems necessary in view of the general trend to encourage regulation in the sunshine and the recent tendency of the courts to expand the concept of due process. Beyond these information gathering, procedural, and political requirements, regulatory lag provides useful economic functions. To minimize the attrition of profits during the lag period management is under continuous pressure to maintain operating efficiencies and to adopt innovative practices and technologies.

Continuous, frequent, or automatic regulatory rate response to rising unit costs removes a major incentive to keep costs down. Economists also have emphasized that traditional rate-base regulation may lead to excessive and redundant use of the factor whose return is regulated. Regulatory lag reduces whatever tendencies exist toward the use of redundant capital and distorted capital-labor combinations in the production process. Easy or automatic flowthrough of costs may also reduce the incentive to bargain aggressively in purchasing energy inputs or in making collective bargaining agreements. There is, then, a legitimate concern about the implications of recent efforts to reduce or eliminate regulatory lag. Zero regulatory lag amounts to the emasculation of the traditional regulatory process since it virtually guarantees earnings subject only to cursory or automatic review and fails to take full advantage of the profit motive as an instrument for attaining economic efficiency. On the other hand, excessive lag leads to rates that are increasingly inappropriate to current cost and leads to serious erosion of earnings, declines in the quality of service, and higher than necessary costs of capital.

During the 1930s and 1940s when input prices were declining and productivity improving, consumer groups advocated what at that time was called continuous-earnings regulation. The shoe was on the other foot, and regulatory lag worked to the disadvantage of consumers. To overcome regulatory lag some commissions sought to turn excessive past returns into current-price reductions and to make up deficiencies in past returns with current-price increases. Under continuous-earnings regulation rate increases or decreases were never final since they were subject to continuous review as the earnings experience of the firm unfolded. Continuous-earnings regulation tended to guarantee returns over the long term with no real incentives for management to minimize costs because any excess profits would be captured by consumers immediately. Moreover, the practice probably encouraged excessive use of capital and rate-base inflation. Efforts to improve the system through sliding scales and other automatic devices—all designed to reduce regulatory lag which at that time penalized consumers—were gradually abandoned. Thus, both theory and experience points out that some degree of lag is a necessary economic and administrative part of effective regulation.

Certainly, the conditions which exist today warrant a reduction in regulatory lag. However, this adjustment should be made with a minimum of loss in efficiency.

## Techniques for Reducing Lag

The major technique for reducing regulatory lag is the use of automatic rate adjustments which permit the flowthrough of certain costs without formal regulatory proceedings. Automatic fuel-adjustment clauses have been used for many years and are now used in almost every state. They now account for about two-thirds of recent electricity rate increases. Though automatic fuel adjustments represent a reasonable response to changes in costs, they may create an incentive to inefficiently substitute fuel-intensive technologies for more capital-intensive technologies. In addition, they weaken the incentive to make efficient decisions relative to choice of fuels. One of the many factors that has contributed to delays in conversion from oil to coal has been the easy flowthrough of fuel costs. The federal government has sought to coerce conversion from oil to coal while regulatory commissions have been relaxing the penalties for the continued use of oil by permitting an easy flowthrough of costs.

Fuel-adjustment clauses also shift a larger proportion of the total risk immediately to consumers, insulating stockholders from inefficiencies associated with fuel-related operations. It seems likely that automatic adjustments for fuel-cost increases may also diminish the incentive to bargain aggressively in an effort to hold fuel prices down. The possibility of these inefficiencies may be mitigated somewhat because rate changes, even when fuel adjustments are made, are lagged to some extent. Thus, inefficiencies will have some negative impact on the profitability of the firm. The possibility of inefficiency can be reduced further by permitting only some fraction of fuel costs to be passed through.

The potential bias as to the input choices of the firm can be reduced somewhat by permitting automatic passthrough of a broader or comprehensive array of costs. For example, the choice between a fuel-intensive technology and a labor-intensive technology will be efficient only if both labor costs and fuel costs are passed forward automatically. But comprehensive adjustment can have other serious disadvantages. The New Mexico plan, for example, permits quarterly rate adjustments to reflect increases in all costs and attempts to achieve a continuous target return on capital. This amounts to the complete removal of regulatory lag as well as to a significant reduction of any built-in regulatory incentives to overall efficiency. Thus, comprehensive adjustment clauses may eliminate one set of inefficient incentives by adding another, possibly more potent, source of inefficiency.

Some efficiency incentives can be preserved if the productivity of the firm is introduced as a component of the automatic rate-adjustment formula. In this connection it merits noting that regulatory problems have been aggravated by a significant decline in the rate of productivity growth in most regulated industries. During the period 1961 to 1973, output per manhour of electric utilities increased at an average annual rate of about 5 percent, well above the economy-wide average of 3.5 percent. During the period of 1973 to 1976 productivity growth in the electric industry had fallen to 0.1 percent, which was well below the subpar economy-wide average of 1.0 percent. The productivity performance of the natural-gas industry has been even worse. The decline in productivity from 5 or 6 percent to almost zero means that utility rates which had declined (in real terms) for many years have ceased to decline. Unless productivity improvements are made, the full brunt of increased energy prices and wage rates must be reflected in rate increases.

Productivity incentives can be incorporated into automatic adjustment formulas by permitting the passthrough of an increasing fraction of the increase in unit costs as productivity is improved. In order to use this technique commissions must determine the price-cost relationship that existed at a time (or during a test period) when productivity was satisfactory. This requires a study of historical productivity relationships and trends for the regulated firm as well as comparative information about the performance of other firms. A firm would be permitted to recover an increasing fraction of increases in its unit costs as its productivity improved relative to some productivity target. In effect the profit margin per unit of output is made to narrow as productivity falls short of the target and to widen as improvements approach (or exceed) the target. This general approach protects the profits of the firm from changes in costs that are beyond its control while at the same time rewarding efficient management with an improved profit margin. The use of a productivity target ensures that consumers will share the productivity improvement. Formula rate making is, of course, imprecise; but the inclusion of some measure of productivity as a formal part of the regulatory process is probably better than the present technique of permitting some totally arbitrary fraction of costs to be passed through. The mere recognition of productivity as a regulatory variable should help.

Automatic adjustment formulas are by no means a total answer to the problems created by rapidly rising unit costs. Nor can the inclusion of productivity targets in such formulas completely overcome the potential inefficiencies of automatic cost passthrough. They do, however, provide an orderly basis for reducing regulatory lag as well as the number of rate hearings. Formal, though less frequent, regulatory proceedings are still in order. Automatic adjustments are superior to the granting of interim rate increases with almost no formal proceedings. Interim rate increases create uncertainty and confusion.

Traditionally, commissions establish rate levels on the basis of cost and demand conditions during a recent test year. A number of commissions have permitted the introduction of estimated future costs and revenue. Practically, this means that proposed rates will go into effect if justified by acceptable forecasts of future costs and revenues. The future-test year procedure raises the specter of contending forecasts. However, carefully employed, the practice seems no worse than interim rate increases or the present method of examining past costs in order to determine future prices. A fair proportion of future costs, especially the escalation of labor costs provided for in collective bargaining agreements as well as fuel costs in long-term energy contracts, are well defined, and there is no obvious reason for not taking them into account, especially when it is known that failure to do so will only lead to a new rate request initiated on the heels of the one just completed.

Though it would be difficult to guess as to the adequacy of current earnings, it seems clear that rising input prices generate a downward bias to earnings calculated according to traditional methods. This downward bias has increased in recent years because regulatory proceedings now permit substantial review by third party intervenors. These intervenors predictably present testimony that favors low estimates of capital costs. The regulatory practice of splitting differences after the introduction of a new and lower third party estimate may have aggravated the downward bias created by inflation.

## The Longer-Term Regulatory Response

Tinkering with regulatory lag in search for some sort of optimal lag cannot come to grips with the assertion that traditional regulation has been a failure. There is real doubt that regulation actually has led to the lowest possible rates. There is even a question as to whether regulation has had any beneficial effects at all. For the longer term, a wide variety of proposals ranging from complete deregulation to government ownership have begun to surface.

One way of dealing with the problem is to abandon regulation altogether. The market power of natural monopolies is easily overestimated. Demands for the services of particular firms may be much more elastic than is commonly supposed. The potential impact of substitutes, new technology, and potential price and geographic competition on the market power of entrenched firms is too easily overlooked. Thus, traditional recommendations for strengthening and improving the quality of commission regulation and public-utility rate making have been replaced by a host of new proposals to reduce or to eliminate commission regulation entirely in favor of regulation by the competitive marketplace.

Today one finds at least as much creative effort devoted to the elimination of regulation as was devoted to its inauguration. Strategies for relying more heavily on market forces to guide the allocation of resources have been extended even to that hallmark of regulation—the natural monopoly. The regulation of natural monopoly can be replaced, one hears, by competitive bidding for franchises, excess profits taxation, the divorcement of generation, and the elimination of barriers to both entry and exit. Overlapping, competing, and duplicating utilities, once viewed with great distaste, are now perceived as benign instruments of market competition.

Most of the proposed market-oriented alternatives are not adequate substitutes for regulation, but it seems clear that the regulatory process has failed to harness what competition is available. Indeed, the history here is one of suppression of fly-by-night and irresponsible competition. Looking far—perhaps very far—into the future, one can imagine the organizational divorcement of generation and production from distribution with the main efforts of state and federal regulators being devoted to the regulation of the rates for the transmission of energy where monopoly seems inevitable. In short, the structure of the market will become an increasingly important consideration in the development of regulatory policy.

One can anticipate a search for market competition that may have been subdued, inhibited, or even precluded by existing regulatory institutions. The technologies that have developed since World War II suggest vastly different industrial structures than existed at the time regulation was established. It is possible that changes in technology have made traditional rate-base regulation obsolete. AT&T, that most natural of monopolies, is now exposed to long-lines and other competition that has, in fact, been available for over twenty years, and important and painful adjustments in rate relationships are in the offing. At the same time AT&T is now free to compete with giants of the nonregulated sector in the communications, data-processing, and related industries.

**Conclusion**

Rapidly rising unit costs in the utility industry require that regulatory lag be reduced. Automatic adjustment clauses and future-test years are an appropriate means of achieving this objective. However, such policies may weaken traditional regulatory procedures and diminish some of the incentives to efficiency that are a built-in feature of regulatory lag. These negative effects can be mitigated by incorporating productivity as an explicit variable in the regulatory process. Over the longer term greater reliance on market competition is in order. Protective policies should be abandoned and a positive effort should be made to accommodate new forms of competition which can supplement, and in some cases replace, traditional regulation.

# 14 Rate-Base Determination, Inflation, and Realized Rates of Return to Electric Utilities

*Chris W. Paul II*

In recent years public utilities have experienced problems in maintaining revenues in relation to expenses and rate base which has caused an erosion in their earnings. For instance, rate increases during 1976 were only 4.5 percent of revenues, well below the 5.7 percent increase in the general price level. Similar discrepancies relative to inflation rates occurred in 1973, 1974, and 1975. This erosion of revenues caused utilities to seek an appropriate offset to maintain their allowed or permitted rate of return. This chapter discusses the general problem of erosion, the more specialized problem of rate-base attrition, and finally some empirical effects of rate-base determination on utility and earnings during inflationary periods.

It is well known that regulatory agencies determine the dollar earnings of utilities by fixing their rate base and allowed rate of return. A number of alternative methods are used to accomplish this end. Some regulatory agencies employ original cost (OC) as their criterion in determining the rate base, while others use reproduction cost (RC). Still others use a value somewhere between original cost and reproduction cost, which, for the purposes of this chapter, will be called fair value (FV). Since the cost of replacing public-utility assets and reproduction cost has exceeded the original cost of these assets and this difference has been especially pronounced in the past fifteen years, a question has arisen whether agencies using the original-cost rate base have compensated for the lower rate base by allowing higher rates of return. In order to understand better erosion and attrition it is worthwhile to review the general characteristics of public utilities.

## Characteristics of Public Utilities

Firms traditionally classified as public utilities, even though they may be privately owned, have two major obligations not shared with other types of firms. First, they must serve all demanders within their exclusive franchise area without undue discrimination, and as a result they are required to expand capacity to meet additional demand. Second, they must sell their services at reasonable rates or prices; in practice this means selling at prices that will provide reasonable earnings under prudent management. To ensure that those businesses affected with a public interest meet these obligations and that utilities act like competitive firms would if competition were feasible, the regulatory authorities in this country have adopted rate-of-return regulation.

Utilities typically are capital intensive, as measured by capital invested per sales dollar generated; have high fixed costs, that is, large contractual obligations such as interest and amortization which are independent of the level of output; and have specialized capital equipment, epitomized by sunk capital, such as a power-generating plant, which has very little alternative use. In addition, the utility's service is generally considered essential. Moreover, because service cannot be stored or produced for inventory for use during peak periods, a utility plant must be designed to meet peak-period demand. Finally, in the past, because of the high fixed costs and rapid technological change, utilities were generally decreasing-cost industries, experiencing decreasing costs as the level of output increased. This cost characteristic no longer seems to hold for all utilities.

These factors also contribute to the constant and recurring need for new capital by public utilities. That is, the capital-intensive nature of utilities, the steady and implacable long-run growth in the demand for utilities services, and the long history of utilities which have made it necessary to refund or revolve past capital obligations have each contributed to the utility industry's high demand for capital.

**Erosion of Earnings**

What does the unique configuration of regulation firms have to do with the problem of erosion? (See David R. Kamerschen and Chris W. Paul 1978, 1981) But what is meant by erosion? Earnings erosion can be explained by disaggregating earnings or rate of return (as a percentage) into three components, that is,

$$\text{Earnings (in percent)} = \frac{\text{Revenue} - \text{Cost}}{\text{Net Plant Investment}}$$

Earnings erosion means that cost and investment are growing faster than revenues so as to produce lower than expected earnings. Thus, erosion does not involve the level or trend of any one of these three factors alone but rather is the interrelationship of the changes in all three factors. Earnings erosion will occur if revenue is held in check because of the regulatory lag while costs and investment outlays are increasing due to inflationary cost increases and the higher costs of capital. While there are numerous internal and external factors which affect revenues, cost, and net investment, in recent years it has been inflation which has been the primary factor causing the erosion of earnings. Each of the components will be examined in more detail.

*Revenue and Costs*

There are a number of factors that can influence the growth rate of revenue, including growth in the number and usage of customers, changes in the quality of service offerings, changes in the approved rate schedules, and internal management forecasting, planning, and implementing of productive capacity needs. The precise effect that a rate change will have on revenue depends upon the own price elasticity of demand.

Costs represent the influence of resource prices and productivity. As with revenues costs depend on both internal and external factors, although it is sometimes difficult in practice to disentangle them. While internal managerial decision making does affect operating efficiency and productivity to some extent, it clearly has a lesser influence on essentially market-determined resource prices. In recent years resource prices like most prices have been rising with the advent of higher inflation rates. Under these circumstances it has not been possible for most utilities to achieve productivity increases—resulting from economies of scale or the introduction of more efficient technological innovations—to overcome these resource price increases.

Economies of scale still exist for utilities but to a lesser degree than in the past. Since the mid-to-late 1960s the gains from advancing technology and increasing plant size have been more than offset by the costs arising from inflation—higher labor and material costs, higher plant investment and other construction costs, and higher capital costs.

The retardation or slowdown in productivity advance in the private domestic-business economy, including the regulated industries, since the mid-1960s has been attributed to a number of factors. Included in these factors are: slower overall rate of economic growth; cost of mandated social programs such as antipollution, health, and safety; and the decreased ratio of research and development outlays to gross national product.

*Net Plant Investment*

Net plant investment is the component which this study has emphasized. It is a public utility's legal duty to be prepared to render service whenever it is demanded. One integral element in the earnings erosion which relates to this service obligation is called rate-base attrition. Rate-base attrition (accretion) is the adverse (beneficial) effect on a utility's percentage earnings resulting from augmentation and replacement of plant which occurs at current marginal-investment cost per unit which is above (below) the average embedded-investment cost per existing unit. Using economic terminology rate-base attrition occurs when the marginal-investment outlay per unit of output added exceeds the average past investment outlay per unit of output in service. So long as per unit marginal costs exceed average costs, assuming per unit marginal revenues do not exceed average revenues, attrition will occur. The greater this cost differential and the longer the interval between test period and implementation of new rates, the greater the attrition suffered by a utility. A utility is never guaranteed that it will earn its authorized fair rate of return. However, if no allowance is made for attrition or the other erosive elements, the utility is effectively denied a realistic opportunity of earning the permitted rate of return.

### Attrition and Inflation

Inflation is singularly the most influential cause of present attrition. Moreover, current and future inflation will accelerate the attritional trend. But present attrition remains even if current and future inflation is arrested or eliminated.

Inflation does not have the same attritional and erosive effects on all firms and all industries. In general, regulated utilities are harmed more by inflation than are firms in nonregulated industries. There are several reasons why regulated firms are less capable of neutralizing or offsetting the erosive and attritional effects. The nonregulated firm can promptly and significantly adjust prices, quantity of output, quality of output, or any combination of these decision variables. A regulated public utility cannot react in any of these ways without the consent of regulatory authorities. Utilities are obligated to provide service to the public when and where demanded. They are not free to curtail or eliminate service to their more costly customers. In addition, capital costs, including embedded-fixed-interest-charge-depreciation charges carrying yesteryear values, are a much greater proportion of a utility's revenues. The utility, therefore, must constantly chase but never quite catch up with today's cost levels.

### Regulatory Lag

The elapsed time between a managerial decision to change some economic variable and the point at which the decision is made effective to customers is relatively long for regulated firms because of the requirements for review and approval that are inherent in the regulatory process. The term coined to describe this situation is regulatory lag, and it simply means that some aspects of the regulatory process prevent rates from reflecting the current costs of providing service. Because of regulatory lag firms in the regulated sector cannot adjust rapidly to inflationary pressures. Assuming costs increased proportionally for regulated and unregulated firms, the regulated firm would not fare as well because its revenues move more slowly. A regulated firm cannot readily adjust its prices to fluid demand and supply conditions. Rate relief often must wait the outcome of a long, deliberate, and sometimes expensive procedural process of regulation. Under conditions of sustained and serious inflation, the regulated sector becomes less attractive to investors because of declining relative profitability that impairs its ability to provide efficient service to its customers. In other words, nonregulated firms generally set prices upon a consideration to retrospective, current, and prospective costs. Utilities operating in jurisdictions where the rate base is determined in original-cost values and where prices are set only in consideration of the past ten years have prices which may be out of sync with current and future costs.

Under most contemporary regulations utilities are obligated to offer service and if necessary build additional capacity, even when the added revenue will not cover the extra cost of the increased investment. Even though current costs per unit exceed embedded costs per unit, additional utility plant, for example, must be built and expanded in order to furnish utility service when and where needed. A utility is not free to curtail and expand output with changes of the business cycle. Moreover, it is expected to forecast anticipated growth with some accuracy to be ever ready to meet it when it arrives.

*Other Factors*

There are other factors which cause inflation to have more deleterious effects on regulated than on nonregulated industries. Utilities are generally highly capital intensive, requiring abnormally large quantities of capital per unit of output or sales revenue. For instance, telephone utilities have a heavy investment in fixed-plant and other assets, such as poles, cable, central office equipment, and so on.

Because utilities tend to be capital intensive with durable plants, changes in capital costs—interest rates and equity charges—are very significant. While many factors affect interest rates and equity cost, inflationary expectations and anticipation during periods of inflation have a profound effect. Sustained inflation of the last fifteen years has impacted on the capital market. Utilities, as large consumers of capital, are especially negatively affected. Additionally, investors tend to shun utilities or demand an uncertainty premium for investing because a large portion of a utility's capital assets, once installed, are fixed or locked into that specific use.

Plant durability has exacerbated the level of attrition and erosion to which utilities are subject. Plant durability extenuates the difference between embedded cost of existing plants and the higher cost of replacement plants. Moreover, because depreciation accounting matches capital recovery with plant life during inflationary periods, funds recovered through historical-cost depreciation are inadequate to replace the retired plant.

Thus, given the historically high inflation during the last fifteen year period and a host of reasons to believe that inflation will persist into the future, a solution through reforming the regulatory system to ensure financial viability for public utilities would appear to be necessary and desirable.

**Empirical Findings**

To ascertain the impact of inflation on the realized rates of return to electric utilities the realized rate of return on equity (ROE) was regressed against time, where the year 1964 equals 1, 1965 equals 2, and so on to 1978 (see table 14-1). The purpose is to derive a measure of the effect of inflation over time on the realized rate of return. The data were also subdivided into fair value (FV) and original cost (OC) jurisdictions. The results reported in table 14-2 demonstrate that for all public utilities, both FV and OC, the realized rate of return has been decreasing over time. For example, in nominal terms the ROE for electric utilities in the sample decreased by an average of .20 percent a year. The decrease was slightly higher for FV jurisdictions and slightly lower for OC. This provides a hint that the rates of return were converging for utilities located in the two jurisdictions. However, one must note that the convergence is a result of FV jurisdictions decreasing at a faster rate than the OC jurisdictions. This is the converse of the finding found by David Eiteman (1962) that the OC jursidictions would converge

**Table 14-1**
**Calculated Nominal Rates of Return on Equity, by Jurisdiction**

| Jurisdiction | 1964 | 1978 |
|---|---|---|
| Fair value (FV) | 14.016 | 11.000 |
| Original cost (OC) | 13.185 | 10.754 |

Source: *Value Line*, various issues; U.S. Federal Power Commission, Jurisdiction and Regulation of Electric, Gas, and Telephone Utilities (Washington, D.C., 1973).

**Table 14-2**
**Nominal and Real Rates of Return Regressed on Time**

| Nominal | | | | Real | | | |
|---|---|---|---|---|---|---|---|
| $ROE^a$ | = | 13.747 − | 0.206 | $ROE^a$ | = | 15.48 − | 0.682 |
| | | (72.26) | (9.88) | | | (98.02) | (39.31) |
| $ROE_{FV}$ | = | 14.248 − | 0.232 | $ROE_{FV}$ | = | 15.945 − | 0.707 |
| | | (50.11) | (7.42) | | | (67.93) | (27.41) |
| $ROE_{OC}$ | = | 13.372 − | 0.187 | $ROE_{OC}$ | = | 15.132 − | 0.664 |
| | | | (6.78) | | | (72.34) | (28.87) |
| $ROK_T$ | = | 7.813 − | 0.103 | $ROK_T^a$ | = | 8.87 − | 0.387 |
| | | (87.30) | (10.49) | | | (60.68) | (8.34) |
| $ROK_{FV}$ | = | 8.087 − | 0.122 | $ROK_{FV}$ | = | 9.112 − | 0.402 |
| | | (60.68) | (8.34) | | | (83.82) | (33.69) |
| $ROK_{OC}$ | = | 7.608 − | 0.089 | $ROK_{OC}$ | = | 8.689 − | 0.375 |
| | | (64.00) | (6.81) | | | (87.94) | (34.54) |

[a]ROE = Realized rate of return on equity.

ROK = Realized rate of return on total capital.

FV = Fair value.

OC = Original cost.

T = Total = FV + OC.

Source: *Value Line*, various issues; U.S. Federal Power Commission, Jurisdiction and Regulation of Electric, Gas, and Telephone Utilities (Washington, D.C., 1973).

Note: Sample size = 66. Table shows regression coefficients with t-ratios in parentheses.

with FV jursidictions by OCs increasing their ROEs relative to FV. The results of the regressions on return to total capital show the same pattern with the change being proportionate to the lower return on total capital.

When the data are deflated by the consumer-price index to show real returns, the effects are even more pronounced. The average ROE decreases for all utilities, and the decrease to firms in FV jurisdiction is somewhat higher than those in OC jursidictions. Again similar patterns hold for the realized rate of return on total capital.

**Concluding Comment**

In peroration, erosion and attrition caused by inflation have been and continue to be serious problems in regulated industries. Utilities deserve a realistic opportunity of earning the authorized rate of return. This does not mean that inefficiency should be subsidized. But if their failure to achieve their approved rate of return is due to erosion or attrition, an allowance or adjustment which is based on accepted economic principles should be considered. And regulators, employing various types of rate-base determinations (see David R. Kamerschen, James B. Kau and Chris W. Paul 1981), should be made aware of the unique problems inherent in each, especially during inflationary periods.

**References**

Eiteman, David K. "Interdependence of Utility Rate Base Type, Permitted Rate of Return, and Utility Earnings." 17 *The Journal of Finance* (March 1962):38-52.

Kamerschen, David R.; Kau, James B.; and Paul, Chris W. "Bills and Rates of Return with 'Fair Value' Jurisdiction." 195 *Electrical World* (May 1981):139-140.

Kamerschen, David R.; and Paul, Chris W. "Higher Earnings Can Lead to Lower KWH Price." 195 *Electrical World* (January 1981):109-110.

Kamerschen, David R.; and Paul, Chris W. "Erosion and Attrition: A Public Utility's Dilemma." 102 *Public Utility Fortnightly* (December 1978):21-28.

# 15 Taxation and the Economic Health of Regulated Utilities in a World of Inflation: Selected Elements

*C. Lowell Harriss*

The attraction for politicians of extracting revenues from people in the form of utility charges must be obvious. If the onus of financing government can be put on public utilities rather than on voting human beings, then utility services are likely to be taxed heavily—property, income, payroll, and sales taxes.

Much of the taxpaying public may in a vague and unarticulated manner prefer to bear taxes in ways not seen—out of sight, out of mind. Who can know whether the public not only condones this practice but in some manner actually approves?

## Hidden Taxes

If consumers and investors really knew about the tax burden incorporated in utility charges—or in reduced net earnings for shareholders—would voters prefer some other method of financing government? The convenience of paying for governmental services in the monthly installments of the telephone, electricity, and gas bills does have attractions. (For many taxpayers, however, there is almost equivalent convenience in the automaticity of property-tax payment in the monthly mortgage installment and of income-tax collection at source on earnings.) But are there not also disadvantages?

Directness and openness in taxation do help to make the public aware of the costs of government. Inevitably, collective choice must be crude. It should be less so, however, if voters have some sense of what they are paying. Such conclusions seem intuitively correct. Yet one must be cautious in going on to assert that any differences in actions are appreciable.

The significance of taxing people indirectly through business firms—and especially regulated utilities—is not confined to the hidden versus open aspect of tax collection. The taxes on the utility may affect both the longer-run provision of utility services and the use in the short run of existing facilities.

Views expressed are the author's and not necessarily those of any organization with which he is associated.

The relation of utility charges to the optimum supply and use of utility facilities presents problems of great complexity. Peak-load needs require capacity that will be unutilized during more than minor portions of the year. Rate discrimination to induce more efficient use of capacity presents challenges familiar to an increasing number of regulators, utility officials, consumers, and academicians. The inclusion in rates of an element of the cost of government along with the specific costs of the services themselves will more likely confuse the calculations than assist in rational adjustment; the resistance to logical discrimination among rates is likely to be more difficult when the level of rates is high (because of taxes) than when the level is more moderate. However, the validity of this conclusion will depend upon factors peculiar to specific conditions; the rise of fuel and interest costs, for example, will alter the relative weight of taxes with results not intuitively obvious.

### Corporate Income Taxes

A few words about corporate income taxes. They are among the costs presumably recognized by regulatory authorities in setting rates. In this connection federal (and state) income taxes have grown increasingly complex, and utilities and their regulators have faced a variety of problems. Although inflation has been largely ignored in computing appropriate deprecation so that taxable income overstates real income, the investment tax credit and accelerated depreciation have reduced current cash outlays for income taxes.

Controversy about the treatment for rate making of the tax results took on different aspects in various jurisdictions. If the tax effects were to be passed on immediately to customers, the stated objectives of congressional actions—notably the stimulation of new investment—would be frustrated. Moreover, the need for tax recognition of inflation gained increasing respect. The present situation, differing from one jurisdiction to another, defies simple description. The checks to government from utilities for dollars to pay income tax are often quite small relative to size of operations—but less clearly characterized as a percentage of earnings because of doubts about the size of profit. Rates charged customers will often relate to longer-run (normalized) cost (and income) as distinct from cash payments to governments. Tax changes voted in 1981 affecting capital recovery (depreciation) that go into effect over a period of years will apparently offset much of the tendency of inflation to tax return of capital as if it were earnings.

### General Property Taxation

The local property tax quite typically bears heavily on utilities. They own and use real and tangible personal property in amounts which are large relative to other measures of their activities. Much property is specialized and hard to value accurately. Regulation has pervasive effects on value, generally in times of inflation depressing true value below the level presumably intended by the assessor.

In normal conditions of the U.S. political scene, overassessment and overtaxation of regulated utilities can be expected—not always and not necessarily egregiously, but rather often. The difficulties of reaching a responsible judgment about magnitudes grow out of the diversity of circumstances over the country and a lack of basis for confident assurance about what would really be correct.

Why any concern for at least moderate excesses of property taxation? If rates charged customers adjust accordingly and if market conditions permit earnings based on the actual taxes imposed, then consumers will bear the extra cost. This form of consumption will have a larger element of property taxation than will exist typically for goods and services. A few percentage points in prices will distort. But will any results be significant? Such questions justify serious attention and corrective response more often than in fact appears.

## Assessment Complications Resulting from
## Dollar's Loss of Value (Inflation)

Inflation complicates the problems of valuation for property tax purposes. This is especially so for public utilities. Frequently the method to be used for utilities is neither a current market as for residences nor a capitalization of earnings as for much business property, for example, office buildings. For utilities replacement or reproduction cost minus depreciation will often, though not always, be used, perhaps in combination with others. In fact, utilities-replacement or reproduction-cost criterion is easily more misleading than helpful.

During inflation, reproduction cost rises, perhaps dramatically. Observers sometimes point to such inflated cost figures in justifying high assessments; if production capacity that cost $10X$ would cost $15X$ to replace, is not the latter a proper benchmark for tax assessment? There is a certain plausibility to the argument—but a greater error. The proper valuation, as professionals recognize, must allow for depreciation and obsolescence—including the economic as well as technological. Economic obsolescence will result from the loss of present and prospective earning power. If management cannot by either reducing other costs of operation or raising the rates charged to boost net earnings in line with inflated construction cost, then the value for property-tax purposes must recognize the economic realities of earnings properly adjusted for rising expense of replacement. True earnings may justify only a tax assessment which is much lower than a figure based on the expense of building today.

This general principle will not be challenged seriously. Yet how frequently in practice is an assessment shaded upward by reference, perhaps unconsciously, to rising construction (reproduction) costs? Case by case analysis is called for.

## Income Capitalization

Prospective earnings must be relied upon heavily. This section comments upon one complexity growing out of inflation. Inflation influences interest rates which results in the discounting of expected earnings in capitalizing a stream of income. If interest (discount) rates of the levels seen in the early 1980s are used in the valuation for property-tax assessment of utilities as they actually receive earnings, the resulting valuations might seem incredibly low. If present earnings are discounted at, say, 17 percent, some utility properties will get assessments well below those recently used. Local government revenues will suffer.

The interest rates have clearly prevailed. They cannot be ignored. But are they appropriate? Is not an average using past rates better? Can one not assume that the income stream will be adjusted to take account of them?

As of assessment day, the current rates of interest will be better than alternatives. The past will clearly be inappropriate. Inflation and uncertainties about its future assure that the past has an unknown obsolescence. Whatever logic once justified averaging annual interest rates for current use has been much eroded by inflation.

Among uncertainties is a question of the allowance being made for the possibilities of utility rate adjustments and for changing market conditions. To what extent are current yields for utilities A to M reflecting expected changes in the income stream to adjust for interest rates? Can similar allowances be made for utilities N to Z?

Overassessment and thus unduly heavy property taxation seem probable from the effects of inflation or interest (discount) rates. Who suffers? Customers? Suppliers of capital? It depends.

## Obligation to Serve

Inflation may or may not add to a problem which property-tax assessment has too often ignored. Valuation for tax purposes should recognize the legal requirement of obligation to provide service. Railroad lines include property which might cost a considerable amount to replace, which might have value in alternative uses, and which must be retained for uses which generate only losses.

A facility, such as a branch rail line, which cannot in fact be abandoned under legal and other conditions may in fact have negative value. The law may require that service be provided even though adequate remuneration is not obtained and losses result. Such property detracts from the worth of the entire line. This negative element can help to explain why a total property—say the railroad as a unit—has less economic value than would ordinarily appear.

Taxation of utilities on a unit basis avoids a problem which can arise with local assessment and taxation. The existence of property may suggest something of value to be taxed. Yet it may have negative value.

Inflation adds complications if only because it changes costs and revenues. Deregulation and new competition, as in communications, will probably create more problem situations than local officials will be attuned to recognize. An obligation to provide service affects value. Explicit recognition of the possibility can help in preventing avoidable error.

### Regulation—and Lags

Excess property taxation of utilities can be expected as a general tendency. Regulation produces part of the total result. Regulation developed in a noninflationary environment is not readily adapted to inflation. Neither is property-tax assessment.

Tension will be a normal condition of utility regulation. Representatives of various groups press their differing interests. In this process, however, taxpayers usually have no obvious spokesmen. Any appraisal of regulation over the years—for railroads and other transport, communications, energy—must involve differences from case to case. These aspects have been handled rather poorly, but other factors have overwhelmed tax matters. (At the margin, however, taxes may tip a balance; in the case of railroads, for example, one should not be cavalier in shrugging off the adverse effects of discriminatory taxation as a factor contributing to distress.)

Presumably, taxes are to be recognized in rate regulation so that suppliers of capital will be properly rewarded. Consumers—not the employees, suppliers of fuel and other supplies, for example, telephone equipment and power generators, landowners, or investors—are expected to pay the costs of government collected from a utility. Regulation as a process takes time; in a world where conditions are generally stable, the parties would generally adjust to produce reasonably satisfactory results over the long run. The real world, however, is one of change of many types, including inflationary increases in costs and rising state-local taxes.

Regulatory lag became part of the reality of the post-World War II period. Taxes were only one of the elements which changed more rapidly than could be accommodated expeditiously by normal procedures. If taxes discriminate between regulated and nonregulated suppliers of essentially the same or closely competitive services, even apparently small tax differences can affect behavior. (For a time after World War II a 3 percent tax on common-carrier freight allegedly led some companies to acquire facilities to transport their own products.)

Where property-tax rates are as high as in much of the country today—exceptions do exist—the delays from regulatory lag must depress the worth of utility property. Do assessments recognize this reality? Actual results vary from case to case, but the political bias will be against utilities, that is, chiefly the suppliers of (equity) capital in the short run and users of service over the longer run when adverse effects on investment returns lead to slower modernization and expansion of capacity.

Inflation, to reword, adds to the risk of distortion and loss from regulatory lag. Costs rise because of inflation during the months of consideration of an application. Property-tax increases due to inflation (as well as other factors) are not always clearly foreseen and allowed for adequately. Where utilities are targets for heavier taxes to help hard-pressed local governments, the direction of results, but not the magnitude, can be predicted. Yet those responsible for setting utility charges will have understandable resistance to making advance adjustment for prospective tax increases and other elements of inflation. The net income for the suppliers of capital is likely to be less than presumably intended.

Where there is uncertainty about property-tax bills, the element of risk due to regulatory lag may be more than trivial in relation to the net amounts remaining for shareholders. Numbers will differ from place to place and may not seem to be more than minor. But where real returns to shareholders are low and under pressure, each element reinforcing the depression of yield has significance. The risk can be substantially reduced by provision for automatic tax adjustment similar to fuel-clause provisions. Some states do have some such protections for utilities. Where market demand will not support the higher customer charge, the tax can remain on shareholders. Where nonregulated suppliers of certain services are taxed less heavily than the common carrier—communications present this situation in some communities today—competitive forces may be accentuated by tax differentials.

**Property Tax Reform**

Property taxation differs greatly among the states and among communities within states. Changes are taking place. Limitations, not only Proposition

Thirteen in California, have been enacted and may spread. Classification of property to differentiate burdens has popular appeal. Residential and farm properties get systematically lower effective rates than do other properties. Utilities are likely to be at the top. (Federal law, however, provides that railroads may no longer be taxed at rates higher than those applicable to commercial and industrial property.)

One possible property-tax change offers an opportunity for utility managements to serve the interests of customers and suppliers of capital as well as the general public. The revision would shift more of the tax to the land element and thereby permit reduction of the burden on other types of real and personal property—on man-made capital.

Assume that the same total revenue is to be obtained from people as owners and users of property—no increase or decline in overall burden. The shift of emphasis away from reproducible capital and on to land would have positive nonrevenue results. These results have been pointed out many times over many years. Capital formation in new housing, plant, and equipment would be speeded by a cut in tax rates on such facilities.

Any actual change in the U.S. environment would represent many decisions about specific elements. Without going to the extreme associated with Henry George's single tax, the public could reduce the burdens on man-made capital while making up the revenue by a heavier reliance on land. Land is one resource which will not move and which will not be reduced by a tax increase; inducements for higher and better use can have beneficial effects. The net benefits over the longer run would include improvements in resource allocation, economic progress, and meaningful aspects of tax equity. The underlying reasoning requires more space than is available in this chapter.

Electric, telephone, and other regulated utilities make relatively heavy use of man-made capital as compared with land. Therefore, their consumers and the suppliers of capital would be affected relatively more than most other groups. By changing the structure of tax-property taxation without an increase in total burden, communities could improve their total well-being.

# 16 The Market Environment for Utility Securities

*Anthony D. Osbon*

Electric utilities represent a sizable portion of the existing debt and equity investments in the U.S. securities market. This utility investment, for several years, has been valued at well below the cumulative original investments. The effects of inflation, high capital costs, and heavy capital requirements for new utility construction, combined with a reluctant, historical cost-minded regulatory establishment have severely reduced the attractiveness of utility securities, especially to institutional funds. Quality is low, and new equity capital needs are high. To attract this capital without further harming the tenuous financial condition of the industry, utilities must earn higher returns on equity than have so far been achieved. Regulators must take steps to enable utilities to actually earn their allowed returns. Rate-case decisions in recent months indicate greater awareness of the problems by regulators. The economic policy of the Reagan administration offers hope for lower capital costs which, if realized, would enhance the outlook for utility investments.

## Historical Comparisons: 1965 and Now

This chapter will concentrate on electric-utility securities because electric utilities tend to do about two-thirds of the external financing of the overall utility industry. And in particular it will concentrate on the equity or common stock market for electric utilities, because of all investors the equity investor is at the greatest risk.

As shown in tables 16-1 and 16-2, at the end of 1980, the long-term capital on the books of the electric industry totaled about $209 billion. Another $7.5-8.0 billion of short-term capital, represented by bank borrowings and commercial paper, was also being used by utilities, so a total of about $217 billion was at work for the industry. Of the long-term capital, $104 billion, or 50 percent, was in the form of bonds, $26 billion, or 13 percent, was preferred stock equity, and $79 billion, or 37 percent, represented the common-stock equity ownership of the electric industry. To put this into perspective, the book equity of the industry is very roughly equivalent to about 9 percent of the book equity of all companies listed on the New York Stock Exchange. Yet the current market equity of electric companies,

**Table 16-1**
**External Financing by Investor-Owned Electric Utilities**

| | 1980 Long-Term Capital | | |
| | Structure in Billions of Dollars | Percent | Outside Requirements in Billions of Dollars, 1981-1985 |
|---|---|---|---|
| Debt | 104 | 49.8 | 47.4 |
| Preferred stock | 26 | 12.4 | 11.7 |
| Common stock | 79 | 37.8 | 25.9 |
| | 209 | 100.0 | 85.0 |

Source: Edison Electric Institute: Donaldson, Lufkin & Jenrette, Inc.

the value that investors now place on owning the industry, is only $61 billion, or roughly 5 percent of the current value of all companies on the New York Stock Exchange.

In 1965, only sixteen years ago, the common stock of the Standard and Poor's (S & P's) 400 industrial companies were valued at 225 percent of their underlying book values, and the electric utilities were selling at 220 percent of book value, or on about the same market-to-book relationship as industrials. At the end of 1980 the S & P industrials were valued at 143 percent of book value, certainly not attractive relative to 1965, but the electric stocks were selling at only 73 percent of book value at the end of last year, far below the industrial stocks. Therefore, one can see that the market environment for utility securities is not good and, in fact, has not been good for a long, long time. This chapter will deal with why this is so and what will be necessary to improve it.

In those halcyon days of 1965, electric stocks were selling at over twenty times earnings, and the average dividend yield was only 3.3 percent. Depending upon what assumed level of expected total return investors were applying at that time, it is not too difficult to justify that there was an expected growth rate for earnings and dividends of at least 6.0-8.0 percent. In fact, during the five years before 1965, the industry's earnings-per-share growth rate was about 8.0 percent and dividend growth had exceeded 7.0 percent.

While the evaluation of the industry may have been overexuberant to a point, there was a general feeling that the industry's potential for continued and sustained growth would be fulfilled, and this was felt with a high degree of confidence. The following quotation is from the textbook which most colleges and universities at one time used to teach securities valuation:

> Public utility common stocks are susceptible, we believe, of valuation for investment purposes within considerably more precise limits than the commons stocks of either railroads or industrial companies. This results from the high degree of stability of utility earnings, the reasonable predictability of growth trends, and the general improbability of any sudden or unexpected developments that might have a marked effect on operations.[1]

**Table 16-2**
**Historical Utility Capitalization and Capital Costs**

| Year | Total Capitalization in Billions of Dollars | Capital Structure in Percent | | | Embedded Rates in Percent | | Year End Return on Equity in Percent |
| | | Long Term Debt | Preferred Stock | Common | Debt | Preferred Stock | |
|---|---|---|---|---|---|---|---|
| 1980 | 209 | 49.8 | 12.4 | 37.8 | E 9.6 | E 7.7 | 10.8 |
| 1975 | 133 | 52.6 | 12.7 | 34.7 | 7.2 | 6.8 | 10.5 |
| 1970 | 76 | 55.3 | 9.8 | 34.9 | 5.2 | 4.8 | 11.2 |
| 1965 | 50 | 51.8 | 9.5 | 38.7 | 3.8 | 4.6 | 12.2 |
| 1960 | 40 | 52.7 | 10.7 | 36.6 | 3.4 | 4.5 | 10.9 |
| 1955 | 28 | 51.0 | 12.3 | 36.7 | 3.0 | 4.3 | 10.6 |

Source: Edison Electric Institute: Donaldson, Lufkin & Jenrette, Inc.

This was written in 1961, before the Viet Nam War, before the Great Society, before national economic priorities made the great shift to a consumption-based economy from a production-oriented one. In the last decade, utility earnings have been neither stable nor predictable, although they have been predictably unstable. The improbability of sudden or unexpected developments became a moot point after Consolidated Edison eliminated its dividend in 1974 and after the Three Mile Island nuclear accident in 1979.

**Construction and Operating-Cost Inflation**

In 1968 the average cost of producing a kilowatt-hour of electric energy stopped falling and began increasing. For thirteen years now the incremental cost of producing electricity has been rising steadily. When a company builds a new power plant today, it will most likely produce more expensive power than the existing plant. Because regulatory procedures and principles are predominantly based on the use of average historical plant costs and dated operating costs to establish revenue requirements and do not give sufficient consideration to the substantially higher operating and replacement costs that now exist, utilities seldom earn their stipulated allowed rates of return.

Part of the reason for the long-term rising trend in costs is technical. Previous economies of scale realized from building larger and more efficient generating units and transmission lines were no longer available to the industry. Most significant though was the onset of higher and higher inflation within the economy in general and within the prices of electric supply equipment in particular. Not only do utilities have to absorb the passthrough of inflation in their equipment purchases, but because well over one-half of their capital requirements have to be financed with new external money, the sharply rising cost of capital has hit the industry with a double dose of inflation. Thus, the end result is a bad combination: the industry is capital intensive, rampant inflation is pushing up costs, and revenues are regulated.

The managements of utility companies were very slow to react to the new reality of utility economics—almost as slow as the regulators' reaction to the reality of the securities markets. The term price elasticity was not in the lexicon of managements. There seemed to be a belief that the demand for electricity would rise in a straight line, regardless of the price, and that, therefore, plans for construction of additional capacity should go on just as it always had. As for the regulatory commissions, no one truly understood the depth of distrust that they had for management at the beginning of the really hard times eight to ten years ago. The industry's efforts to convince regulators of the need for higher rates that would provide sufficient profitability to make utility securities, especially common stock, competitive with those of other industries fell on deaf ears. To be sure, rate relief was given, sometimes in large amounts, but it was not adequate to prevent a drastic decline in the quality and investment attractiveness of utility securities.

**Valuation Measures**

Therefore, as shown in table 16-3 and table 16-4, the important measures that investors used to determine differences in investment quality have all gone through a dramatic deterioration over the years. This deterioration, as previously mentioned, has been sharply illustrated by the typical market-price-to-book-value ratio which fell as low as 60 percent in 1974 and has not gotten above a one-to-one relationship since then, except for a brief period in 1977. That ratio is now about 78 percent.

Another example: the industry's average return on common equity has floundered in the 11.0 to 11.5 percent range since 1975, even though inflation has reached double-digit proportions and bond investors can now realize 16.0 percent or more on their money. By comparison, the S & P 400 industrials were able to offset inflation somewhat by pushing their returns on equity from 12 percent in 1975 up to the 17 percent area by early 1980.

Even the static utility return on equity is misleading because of the methods of accounting required by most regulatory commissions. This refers primarily to the practice of capitalizing the cost of financing construction and then applying it as a credit to earnings. Although the

**Table 16-3**
**Electric-Utility Financial Indicators**

| Year | Common Stock Price to Book Value | AFUDC[a] Percent of Earnings | Pretax Interest Coverage | | Return on Average Common Equity in Percent | | Payout in Percent | |
|---|---|---|---|---|---|---|---|---|
| | | | Including AFUDC | Excluding AFUDC | Including AFUDC | Excluding AFUDC | Including AFUDC | Excluding AFUDC |
| 1980 | 0.7 | 50 | 2.7 | 2.3 | 11.5 | 5.8 | 80 | 160 |
| 1979 | 0.8 | 46 | 2.9 | 2.5 | 11.1 | 6.0 | 78 | 144 |
| 1978 | 0.9 | 40 | 2.8 | 2.4 | 11.3 | 6.8 | 72 | 121 |
| 1977 | 1.0 | 38 | 2.9 | 2.5 | 11.4 | 7.1 | 68 | 109 |
| 1976 | 0.9 | 34 | 2.8 | 2.5 | 11.5 | 7.6 | 67 | 101 |
| 1975 | 0.9 | 35 | 2.6 | 2.3 | 11.1 | 7.2 | 67 | 103 |
| 1974 | 0.6 | 38 | 2.4 | 2.1 | 10.6 | 6.6 | 68 | 110 |
| 1973 | 0.9 | 32 | 2.8 | 2.4 | 11.5 | 7.8 | 65 | 95 |
| 1972 | 1.2 | 29 | 2.9 | 2.6 | 11.7 | 8.3 | 65 | 91 |
| 1971 | 1.3 | 25 | 2.9 | 2.6 | 11.6 | 8.7 | 67 | 89 |
| 1970 | 1.4 | 20 | 3.1 | 2.9 | 11.8 | 9.4 | 68 | 85 |
| 1969 | 1.4 | 14 | 3.7 | 3.5 | 12.2 | 10.5 | 67 | 78 |
| 1968 | 1.8 | 10 | 4.3 | 4.1 | 12.3 | 11.1 | 69 | 76 |
| 1967 | 1.7 | 7 | 4.7 | 4.5 | 12.7 | 11.8 | 66 | 71 |
| 1966 | 2.0 | 5 | 5.0 | 4.9 | 12.7 | 12.1 | 65 | 69 |
| 1965 | 2.2 | 4 | 5.3 | 5.2 | 12.5 | 12.0 | 65 | 68 |

Source: Edison Electric Institute: Donaldson, Lufkin & Jenrette, Inc.
[a]AFUDC = Allowance for funds used during construction.

**Table 16-4**
**Electric-Industry Historical Operating Income Statistics**
*(percentage)*

|  | 1955 | 1960 | 1965 | 1970 | 1975 | 1979 |
|---|---|---|---|---|---|---|
| Revenues | 100.0 | 100.0 | 100.0 | 100.0 | 100.0 | 100.0 |
| Operation and Maintenance | 50.0 | 48.5 | 45.9 | 49.7 | 58.6 | 64.0 |
| Depreciation | 9.2 | 9.9 | 10.9 | 10.8 | 8.5 | 7.6 |
| Nonincome Taxes | 8.7 | 9.7 | 10.0 | 10.9 | 8.7 | 7.4 |
| Income taxes | 12.8 | 11.8 | 11.0 | 6.6 | 5.3 | 5.1 |
| Total operating expense | 80.7 | 79.9 | 77.8 | 78.0 | 81.1 | 84.1 |
| Operating income | 19.3 | 20.1 | 22.2 | 22.0 | 18.9 | 15.9 |
| Allowance for funds used during construction | — | .3 | .6 | 2.7 | 3.5 | 4.7 |
| Other income | .8 | .7 | .2 | .4 | .8 | 1.1 |
| Gross income | 20.1 | 21.1 | 23.0 | 25.1 | 23.2 | 21.7 |
| Interest | 5.2 | 6.1 | 6.4 | 10.1 | 10.7 | 10.1 |
| Net income | 14.9 | 15.0 | 16.6 | 15.0 | 12.5 | 11.6 |
| Less preferred dividend | 1.8 | 1.6 | 1.4 | 1.6 | 2.4 | 2.2 |
| Available for common | 13.1 | 13.4 | 15.2 | 13.4 | 10.1 | 9.4 |

Source: Edison Electric Institute: Donaldson, Lufkin & Jenrette, Inc.

allowance for funds used during construction (AFUDC) may have value over the longer term, it does nothing to help the industry's cash needs today, nor can it be used to pay interest and dividends on securities sold to finance that same construction. Today, this noncash apparition represents one-half of the earnings reported by the industry. It was negligible in the 1960s.

Another example: when stockholder investment deteriorates, investors that lend money are not far behind. Utility bondholders have also suffered along with the equity owners. Moody's and Standard and Poor's rating departments have spent a lot of time in the last decade reducing the credit status of many utilities. The most important measure of debtholder protection, the pretax coverage of interest charges, was well over five times in the 1960s but is now well under three times.

**Financing Pressures**

Perhaps the effect of financial weakness is best exemplified by the ongoing effort to finance construction projects. If future construction and capital requirements are large, a company's earnings will be under greater pressure, and the regulatory commission will be under greater pressure to provide rate relief. To maintain balanced capital-structure ratios under such circumstances usually requires the sale of both bonds and equity. The cost of new bond interest will be included in the cost of service in a reasonably prompt period of time since it is a fixed-cost, known expense. But the cost of common equity is a subjective, much-discussed topic in rate-case determinations. With inflation, it is a moving target. If utilities earned the market-determined cost of equity, then theoretically at least, stock prices would be about the same as book value. Unfortunately, the market-determined cost of equity and earned return on equity for utilities have had little to do with each other in recent years.

Any student of finance knows that if a company sells new stock at a price below the existing book value of the company, future earnings growth will be negatively affected. If a company has to do this year after year, the long-term prospects almost have to be ominous. This is the plight of the electric industry. I recently completed a study shown in table 16-5 of all the electric-utility common stock sales since the end of 1973. In the seven and a half years under study, 567 offerings were made to the public, aggregating some 1.5 billion shares of new stock with gross proceeds totaling $26 billion. In only one year, 1977, did the average price of new shares sold equal the underlying book value per share. For the entire seven-and-a-half-year period, the average proceeds to the issuing companies were only 84 percent of book value. To put this another way, if that stock could have been sold at book value, the number of shares issued would have been about 16 percent less, or 240 million shares less than actually had to be marketed. In truth, if earnings had been sufficiently high enough to bring about a one-to-one relationship between market price and book value, internal funds would have been much higher, and therefore the reduction in new shares sold would have been substantially greater than the 240 million shares.

**Table 16-5**
**Electric-Utility Public Issuance of Common Stock, 1974-1981**

|  | Number of Offerings | Amount in Billions of Dollars | Shares in Millions | Price/Book in Percent |
|---|---|---|---|---|
| 1974 | 57 | 2.0 | 139 | 76 |
| 1975 | 91 | 3.3 | 218 | 84 |
| 1976 | 84 | 3.8 | 207 | 97 |
| 1977 | 69 | 3.8 | 187 | 102 |
| 1978 | 76 | 3.4 | 177 | 95 |
| 1979 | 65 | 3.3 | 191 | 83 |
| 1980 | 82 | 4.1 | 258 | 76 |
| 1981 (6 months) | 43 | 2.3 | 152 | 73 |
|  | 567 | 26.0 | 1529 | 87[a] |

Source: Edison Electric Institute. (Donaldson, Lufkin & Jenrette, Inc.).

[a]Approximately 84 percent based on net proceeds.

In the last few years, utilities have progressively reduced their forecasts of future growth in electric-load demand to the point that now the average expected growth is somewhere between 3 percent and 4 percent. Even so, plant that is planned or under construction to meet that demand is expected to require $135 billion over the next five years, $85 billion of which will quite likely be financed with external funds which will include over $20 billion or more from the sale of new common shares. The big question is if this equity money will also be raised at prices that cause earnings attrition, that perpetuate the lowly financial condition of the industry, and that further increase the need for higher rates to consumers. The answer does not have to be yes.

## Management and Regulatory Response

First, managements in more and more utilities are figuring out ways to reduce their construction burdens—methods that range from extensive and sophisticated conservation and load-management programs, to greater activism through legal procedures against overly restrictive environmental requirements, to greater emphasis on renewable energy resources, and to just flat saying no to building plants when their financial situations cannot afford it.

And second, regulatory commissions seem to be awakening to the reality that although utilities do not have to compete too much for business, they are in fierce competition in the capital markets. Edward Larkin, of the New York public service commission and current president of the NARUC, earlier this year made the following comments:

> At the present time . . . the future of all investor-owned regulated utilities lies in the hands of the regulatory forums of this nation . . . Unless regulators recognize the total needs of the industry and translate that recognition into proper and adequate rates of return, the future of the utility industry will be dubious. It will not be enough for regulators merely to postulate adequate rates of return which, in practice, may not be earned. The real and urgent need is for adequate revenues to make stated return a reality. The time has passed when the result of inadequate earning can be masked for economies of scale . . . interest coverages are at an all-time low and (stock) prices have fallen to economically and financially dangerous levels.[2]

Commissioner Larkin in that statement gave voice to the major concern of utility financial analysts and investors across the nation—the seeming ability of regulatory commissions to identify appropriately the rate-of-return needs of utilities but in practice to not provide the opportunity to earn those returns. In 1980 the average allowed return on equity granted in rate cases was 14.3 percent (see table 16-6), a substantial improvement over the 13.5 percent average allowed return in 1979. Nevertheless, the average earned return on equity in 1980 was 11.5 percent, only slightly above 1979.

All the blame of the industry's financial condition cannot fall on the regulators. Clearly, the national experience with ultrahigh inflation and interest rates has been difficult for practically everyone. However, the regulators are the ones appointed and elected with the purpose of establishing utility rates that are fair to consumers and that also give a real opportunity for utilities to recoup the costs of providing their services. That has not been done.

However, progress is now being made. The average allowed return on equity jumped to 14.3 percent in 1980. On the basis of a study recently completed, shown in table 16-7, the average allowed return on equity in major rate-case decisions during the first half of 1981 was up to 15.4 percent, indicating another quantum jump from just six to nine months ago. More important, the industry's current average earned return on equity is up to 12.2 percent, a significant improvement from last year. In fact, the future industry earnings at this point is that return on equity will reach about 12.5 percent in 1981 and perhaps 13.0 percent in 1982, finally breaking away from the stagnant 11.5 percent area of the last five years.

The higher returns being allowed are showing up clearly in the annual dollar levels of rate relief. According to Edison Electric Institute (EEI) statistics electric-rate relief in 1980 totaled $5.9 billion, which was more than twice as large as any of the past five years. On the basis of my own informal survey, the total amount of electric-rate relief granted so far in 1981 through early July has been about $4.3 billion. Therefore, it appears that 1981 will again be a record year for rate increases. The momentum that has now gathered will last at least until the relationship between stock prices and book values becomes much more favorable.

**The Future**

Given today's very high cost of capital, it will take more than favorable regulatory treatment to bring about a sustained and permanent improvement in the market conditions for utility securities. The direction of economic policy being established by the present administration in Washington is the most positive, politically led effort that has come along. It offers promise for business in general and for utilities in particular. If the administration's goal of significantly reducing the rate of inflation is successful, utilities would quite likely benefit more so than others, just as they have suffered the most as inflation increased. In addition, the administration's emphasis on enhancing capital formation and on improving the cost effectiveness of energy and environmental regulations are promising objectives.

**Table 16-6**
**Electric-Utility Return on Equity Statistics**
*(percentage)*

|  | 1975 | 1976 | 1977 | 1978 | 1979 | 1980 |
|---|---|---|---|---|---|---|
| Average Return on Equity Authorized | 13.2 | 13.1 | 13.3 | 13.2 | 13.5 | 14.3 |
| Average Return on Equity Earned | 11.1 | 11.5 | 11.4 | 11.3 | 11.1 | 11.5 |
| Return on Equity Attrition | 2.1 | 1.6 | 1.9 | 1.9 | 2.4 | 2.8 |

Source: Edison Electric Institute. (Donaldson, Lufkin & Jenrette, Inc.).

The prospects for a period of disinflation mean that the possibility of a significant decline in interest rates is very good. Electric-utility stocks, which have grown more interest-rate sensitive as their earnings growth has diminished, would perform well in such an environment.

Institutions, those professionally managed pools of the savings of countless individuals, have reacted by and large to the financial problems of utilities by employing their capital elsewhere. This is not to say that institutions do not occasionally try to play the utility market in an effort to capitalize on swings in interest rates or increases in dividends, but the point is that institutions have generally avoided new long-term commitments to utility equities on the basis of fundamental growth potential. Instead, individuals have been providing most of the nearly $5 billion of new annual equity capital that the industry has needed. Individuals at this time seem to be satisfied with the high dividend yields and modest growth rates they are receiving.

In summary, the market for utility securities is not good, but has been worse. The chances for improvement seem brighter now than they have been in several years, but there are a lot of uncertainties that must become reality to bring it off: if the new momentum in rate-increase approvals and higher equity returns continues; if the industry can reduce its capital-requirements load; if the inflation rate is reduced significantly; if expensive environmental constraints can be removed; and if new equity can be secured at prices that do not deteriorate the value of the existing equity, the market could improve.

**Notes**

1. Benjamin Graham, David L. Dodd, and Sidney Cottle, *Security Analysis*, 3rd ed., (New York: McGraw Hill, 1962), p. 570.

2. Edward Larkin, Speech at the Edison Electric Institute, Financial Conference, (Palm Beach: October 5, 1981).

**Table 16-7**
**1981 Major Electric Rate-Case Decisions to Date: Comparison of Allowed Rates of Return on Equity, Equity Ratios with Previous Orders**

| Name of Company | 1981 Decision | | | | | Previous Decision | | | |
|---|---|---|---|---|---|---|---|---|---|
| | Date of Order | Millions of Dollars Electric Amount | Test Period Ended | Allowed Rate of Return on Equity (ROE) | Common Equity Ratio | Allowed Rate of Return on Equity (ROE) | Common Equity Ratio | Date of Order | Regulatory Jurisdiction |
| Illinois Power | 7/1/81 | 104 | December 1980 | 15.50 | 39.8 | 12.53 | 36.4 | November 1979 | Illinois |
| Commonwealth Edison | 7/1 | 504 | June 1981 | 17.50 | 33.5 | 13.71 | 33.0 | February 1980 | Illinois |
| Wisconsin Power and Light | 6/18 | 37 | June 1982 | 14.75 | 39.4 | 13.50 | 36.9 | February 1980 | Wisconsin |
| Kansas City Power and Light | 6/17 | 17 | December 1980 | 14.40 | 35.5 | 13.40 | 34.3 | June 1980 | Missouri |
| Southwestern Electric Power (Central and South West Corporation) | 6/17 | 24 | September 1980 | 16.33 | 39.7 | 15.00 | 39.0 | August 1976 | Texas |
| Iowa-Illinois Gas and Electric | 6/4 | 15 | May 1980 | 14.80 | 35.8 | 12.53 | 36.4 | December 1978 | Illinois |
| Public Service Indiana | 6/10 | 113 | September 1980 | 16.75 | 39.4 | 14.00 | 38.3 | September 1978 | Indiana |
| Public Service New Mexico | 5/29 | 14 | December 1980 | 15.50 | 32.5 | 15.50 | 33.8 | June 1980 | New Mexico |
| Wisconsin Public Service | 5/29 | 31 | May 1982 | 14.00 | 38.2 | 13.00 | 41.5 | December 1978 | Wisconsin |
| Arkansas Power and Light (Middle South Utilities, Inc.) | 5/27 | 105 | August 1979 | 15.00 | 32.0 | 13.75 | — | February 1980 | Arkansas |
| Louisiana Power and Light (Middle South Utilities, Inc.) | 5/26 | 156 | December 1980 | 14.90 | 37.0 | 13.25 | 34.0 | December 1979 | Louisiana |
| Long Island Lighting | 5/20 | 184 | April 1982 | 16.00 | 42.7 | 13.70 | 41.0 | May 1980 | New York |
| Oklahoma Gas and Electric | 5/18 | 12 | October 1979 | 14.88 | 39.2 | 12.48 | 35.2 | September 1978 | Arkansas |
| Utah Power and Light | 5/15 | 5 | December 1980 | 15.75 | 40.0 | 14.16 | 37.5 | March 1980 | Idaho |

**Table 16-7** *(continued)*

| Name of Company | 1981 Decision | | | | | Previous Decision | | | |
|---|---|---|---|---|---|---|---|---|---|
| | Date of Order | Millions of Dollars Electric Amount | Test Period Ended | Allowed Rate of Return on Equity (ROE) | Common Equity Ratio | Allowed Rate of Return on Equity (ROE) | Common Equity Ratio | Date of Order | Regulatory Jurisdiction |
| Appalachian Power (American Electric Power Company, Inc.) | 5/8 | 27 | December 1979 | 16.00 | 34.1 | 13.62 | 33.0 | May 1980 | West Virginia |
| Cleveland Electric Illuminating | 5/4 | 141 | December 1980 | 16.22 | 35.6 | 15.00 | 38.4 | July 1980 | Ohio |
| Northern States Power | 4/30 | 56 | July 1981 | 13.50 | 42.2 | 12.90 | 40.0 | September 1979 | Minnesota |
| Philadelphia Electric | 4/24 | 188 | March 1981 | 16.00 | 34.3 | 14.35 | 35.0 | April 1980 | Pennsylvania |
| Northern States Power | 4/21 | 21 | December 1981 | 14.00 | 41.9 | 13.00 | 40.7 | January 1978 | Wisconsin |
| Utah Power and Light | 4/21 | 39 | June 1981 | 16.80 | 39.2 | 16.80 | 37.0 | April 1980 | Utah |
| Mississippi Power (The Southern Company) | 4/16 | 11 | November 1981 | 14.00 | 32.2 | 12.10 | 32.7 | March 1980 | Mississippi |
| Union Electric | 4/15 | 11 | December 1980 | 15.30 | 37.3 | 13.70 | 32.0 | February 1978 | Illinois |
| Carolina Power and Light | 4/10 | 15 | December 1979 | 13.75 | 33.8 | 12.25 | 36.5 | July 1978 | South Carolina |
| New Orleans Public Service (Middle South Utilities, Inc.) | 4/9 | 19 | December 1980 | 15.00 | 30.2 | 12.50 | — | November 1975 | New Orleans |
| Toledo Edison | 4/9 | 65 | December 1980 | 15.30 | 33.4 | 14.77 | 35.1 | February 1980 | Ohio |
| Portland General Electric | 4/7 | 58 | December 1981 | 16.25 | 35.0 | 15.17 | 36.7 | January 1980 | Oregon |
| Pacific Power and Light | 4/7 | 46 | December 1981 | 16.25 | 35.1 | 14.80 | 34.9 | October 1979 | Oregon |
| Indiana and Michigan Electric (American Electric Power Company, Inc.) | 4/3 | 45 | December 1979 | 19.00 | 30.3 | 15.90 | 30.6 | September 1978 | Indiana |

| Company | | | | | | | | | |
|---|---|---|---|---|---|---|---|---|---|
| Ohio Power (American Electric Power Company, Inc.) | 4/1 | 59 | December 1980 | 14.50 | 34.6 | 13.77 | 35.1 | April 1979 | Ohio |
| Central Illinois Public Service | 3/25 | 31 | December 1979 | 15.32 | 37.6 | 12.05 | 36.8 | December 1979 | Illinois |
| Cincinnati Gas and Electric | 3/18 | 51 | October 1980 | 16.12 | 34.4 | 14.39 | 35.8 | January 1980 | Ohio |
| Consolidated Edison | 3/12 | 450 | March 1982 | 14.51 | 46.6 | 12.14 | 42.7 | April 1979 | New York |
| Niagara Mohawk Power | 3/12 | 154 | March 1982 | 16.00 | 39.5 | 14.00 | 38.5 | February 1980 | New York |
| Dallas Power and Light (Texas Utilities Company) | 2/25 | 56 | June 1980 | 16.00 | 42.9 | 14.50 | 41.6 | October 1979 | Texas |
| Florida Power Corporation | 2/20 | 58 | December 1980 | 15.40 | 29.4 | 14.30 | 30.0 | December 1977 | Florida |
| Duquesne Light | 2/20 | 48 | December 1979 | 15.25 | 33.8 | 13.15 | 33.0 | July 1979 | Pennsylvania |
| Ohio Edison | 2/11 | 91 | October 1980 | 15.60 | 32.2 | 13.86 | 34.5 | January 1980 | Ohio |
| Minnesota Power and Light | 1/31 | 61 | April 1981 | 13.47 | 33.8 | 13.00 | 35.7 | April 1979 | Minnesota |
| Pennsylvania Power and Light | 1/30 | 101 | December 1980 | 15.75 | 32.7 | 14.28 | 31.0 | August 1976 | Pennsylvania |
| West Penn Power (Allegheny Power System, Inc.) | 1/30 | 46 | December 1980 | 15.25 | 36.6 | 14.00 | 34.0 | August 1979 | Pennsylvania |
| Delmarva Power and Light | 1/20 | 46 | December 1979 | 15.00 | 35.7 | 14.00 | 35.8 | September 1978 | Delaware |
| Oklahoma Gas and Electric | 1/19 | 78 | March 1980 | 15.25 | 36.3 | 14.00 | 36.2 | November 1979 | Oklahoma |
| Central Illinois Light | 1/7 | 23 | December 1980 | 14.30 | 35.6 | 13.25 | 31.7 | August 1978 | Illinois |
| Puget Sound Power and Light | 1/2/81 | 90 | December 1979 | 15.25 | 36.5 | 13.00 | 35.3 | March 1979 | Washington |
| Average | | | | 15.37 | 36.3 | 13.75 | 35.9 | | |

Source: Edison Electric Institute: Donaldson Lufkin & Jenrette, Inc.; *Moody's Public Utility Manual*, Vol. 1 (New York: 1981).

Note: Controlling corporation is listed in parenthesis after the company name.

**Part VI
Recent Developments
in the Telecommunication
and Electric-Utility
Industries**

# 17

# New Legislation and the Impact on Changing Price Structure of Telephone Service

## William R. Nusbaum

The National Telecommunications and Information Administration or NTIA is the successor agency to the White House Office of Telecommunications Policy and the Office of Telecommunications in Commerce. NTIA's establishment was in response to President Carter's Reorganization Plan No. 1 of 1977. The plan, which represented a new approach to telecommunications policy making in the executive branch, stipulated that a position of assistant secretary for communications and information be created in the commerce department. Henry Geller was the first assistant secretary. He resigned when President Reagan was inaugurated and Bernard Wunder is the new assistant secretary.

One of NTIA's major functions is to serve as the principal advisor to the President and executive branch on matters of telecommunications policy. It is in this policy role that NTIA has been involved in the various proposals to revise the Communications Act of 1934 and in the major common-carrier matters before the FCC. NTIA's role is strictly advisory both in the legislative efforts and in the comments it provides to the FCC.

I work in the Office of Policy Analysis and Development or OPAD in the common-carrier program. In addition to participating in telecommunications policy development and formulation, I am NTIA's principal liaison to the state public utility commissions.

Congress has been attempting to revise the Communications Act of 1934 for the past four years. Many bills have been introduced in both the Senate and the House. Last year, H.R. 6121 got as far as a full committee vote. While there is still not a revised communications act, there has been substantial progress.

Now there is a new bill, S. 898, which was introduced on April 7, 1981, by Senators Packwood, Goldwater, and Schmidt. Hearings have been held, amendments submitted, and markup occurred July 16, 1981. Markup went very smoothly and the full committee passed the bill by a sixteen to one vote. As with previous bills on telecommunications policy, S. 898 has the potential for major impacts on the traditional telephone industry, competitors, the FCC, consumers of telecommunications services, and state regulators.

This bill in general adopts the philosophy that competition is a more efficient regulator than government of the provision of diverse telecommunications services, and as competition continues to develop, deregulation of telecommunications carriers and services should occur.

While the bill promotes marketplace competition, deregulation, and reliance on the private sector to provide telecommunications services, the basic goals of the 1934 Communications Act are stressed as still valid. Thus, S. 898 ensures that basic telephone service, which includes long distance and local telephone service, will continue to be regulated and will be available on a universal basis at reasonable rates. In effect, the bill attempts to balance reliance on the marketplace with the commitment to the traditional social-policy goals enumerated in the 1934 act. While basic services will continue to be regulated, all other telecommunications services, unless they are not subject to effective competition in any geographic area or market, will be deregulated following a transition period.

In determining whether there is effective competition in any particular geographic area or market, the commission must find the existence of a reasonably available alternative service which is the same as or substantially similar to the service offered by the regulated carrier in that area or market. Factors that the Federal Communications Commission (FCC) must consider in determining the existence of a reasonably available alternative service include:

1. The number and size of unaffiliated providers of service or facilities;
2. The extent to which service or facilities are available from unaffiliated providers in the relevant geographic area or market;
3. The ability of such unaffiliated providers to make such service or facilities readily available at comparable rates, terms, and conditions;
4. Whether the service or facilities are necessary to the nation during a state of public peril or disaster or other national emergency;
5. Other such indicators of the extent of competition.

Further, and of particular relevance to residential subscribers, S. 898 provides that prior to deregulation of basic telephone service in any particular geographic area or market, the commission must find that such basic telephone service is subject to effective competition and will continue to be universally and reasonably available.

To carry out the provisions of the act, S. 898 requires the FCC to establish a transition plan designed to foster marketplace competition and to implement deregulation. Part of this plan would include the classification of carriers. Those carriers which are fully subject to regulation by the FCC on the date of enactment of S. 898 and which on the date of enactment were deriving revenues from separations, settlements, and division of revenues will be classified as regulated carriers. The FCC may also classify as a regulated carrier any carrier which offers regulated interexchange services or facilities where the commission determines after a hearing that such services or facilities are not subject to effective competition; that federal regulation of such carrier is required to accomplish the purposes of the act; and the benefits of such regulations outweigh the costs. American Telephone and Telegraph (AT&T) will be further classified as a dominant-regulated carrier. Carriers not within these categories will be unregulated.

A significant number of provisions in the bill deal with AT&T and the structure which is mandated for AT&T to provide customer-premise equipment and competitive services on an unregulated basis. Most of these provisions are similar to those that appeared in previous bills last year to amend the 1934 communications act, such as the requirement that AT&T create a fully separated subsidiary to provide competitive services.

To be more specific, S. 898 modifies the 1956 Consent Decree to allow AT&T to offer unregulated services such as data-processing services and deregulated customer-premise equipment (CPE). However, to prevent the Bell system from exercising unrestrained market power and to prevent the cross-subsidization and anticompetitive conduct, S. 898 provides that any AT&T provision of unregulated services must be through a fully separated affiliate or FSA.

Some of the separations requirements between the parent, AT&T, and its FSA include: the FSA may not have more than one director who is also a director, officer, or employee of AT&T or any other affiliate of AT&T; the FSA may have no officers or employees in common with AT&T, but temporary assignments or transfers from one entity to another are permitted; joint FSA/parent sales or marketing is prohibited except for joint institutional advertising where each party pays its pro rata share; joint ownership of property prohibited; a requirement provides for full separation of books, accounts, and records; and there is a prohibition against the parent disclosing commercial information to the FSA if the information would give the affiliate an unfair competitive advantage.

Further, the bill provides that all dealings between AT&T and the FSA be pursuant to contract, filed with the FCC, and must be on a fully auditable and compensatory basis. In addition, such dealings must be on an arms-length basis and cannot be preferential or discriminatory.

Before AT&T can offer services on an unregulated basis, it must submit a plan to the FCC relating to the creation of an FSA. The plan must demonstrate that AT&T and any affiliate have an accounting system which ensures complete separation between all costs related to services, facilities, and products which are developed, manufactured, or offered by the parent and all costs of any FSA. In addition, the plan must demonstrate that the assets AT&T intends to transfer to an FSA are fairly and properly valued.

With reference to regulatory jurisdiction, S. 898 provides for federal preemption of state regulation of intrastate toll services. The state public service commissions would retain jurisdiction over local-exchange services but must reconfigure those exchange areas in accordance with standards established in the bill.

To promote full and fair competition, S. 898 provides that every telecommunications carrier must provide interconnection of its regulated services upon reasonable request and may not discriminate in an unreasonable or anticompetitive manner with respect to charges, terms, and conditions.

Further, the bill carries forward the requirements of the 1934 act that regulated services be available upon reasonable request and under just, reasonable, and nondiscriminatory tariffs.

Another significant issue addressed by S. 898 relates to exchange-access charges. Earlier bills attempted to spell out in great detail the amount and the structure of access charges. S. 898 takes a different approach. The bill sets out five principle purposes for the establishment of a system of access charges. They are:

1., To achieve equitable treatment among all telecommunications carriers and other customers using services of each exchange carrier through direct or indirect interconnection and to prevent subsidies from exchange services to interexchange services;
2. To assure that payments and assignments of costs relating to exchange access are carried out in a manner which is open to public examination and which ensures accountability to the public;
3. To achieve flexibility in accommodating changes in market conditions and technology;
4. To establish incentives for efficient investment decisions and technological choices;
5. To ensure that exchange carriers are compensated equitably for the costs of providing exchange access in order to ensure the continued universal availability of basic telephone service at reasonable charges.

These are the general principles. In addition, the commission is ordered to adopt a mechanism such as a surcharge on access charges whenever necessary to assure reasonable charges for basic telephone service. The bill requires that the surcharge must ensure that rates for basic telephone may not exceed the national average by more than 110 percent for those companies that receive rural telephone loans. While the surcharge mechanism or safety net is not as explicitly defined as in last year's bills, the inclusion of a provision ordering the FCC to implement such a mechanism is important especially since the bill specifically states that changes in the 1934 act should not be permitted to result in unreasonable charges for basic telephone service.

With reference to implementing access charges, S. 898 directs the FCC to establish a federal-state joint board to ascertain the direct, joint, and common costs of exchange-telecommunications services and exchange access and to apportion those costs between exchange-telecommunications services and exchange access. In makeup the joint board is similar to the 410 (c) type joint board in the 1934 act, that is, it is to be composed of four state commissioners and three FCC commissioners. However, unlike the existing joint board process, the decisions of the access-charge joint board will be binding on the FCC unless the commission determines that any such decision is arbitrary, capricious, or not consistent with the policy or purposes of the act.

The procedures for cost ascertainment and apportionment developed by the joint board will replace the jurisdictional separations procedures in effect at the time of enactment. It is expected that the existing separations manual will serve as the starting point for the joint-board effort. Other revisions will be necessary because the basic dividing lines used in existing procedures will be altered by the enactment of S. 898, which will put intrastate toll under federal jurisdiction. Another factor to be taken into account is the deregulation of customer-premise equipment.

It will be the responsibility of the commission to prescribe uniform procedures by which each exchange carrier will determine its access charge.

Exchange carriers, with certain exceptions, will be required to file with the commission a tariff governing the charges, practices, and conditions for use of its facilities by any telecommunications carrier. To reduce any administrative burden on the FCC, the bill allows for the filing of joint tariffs.

Now for the exceptions. There has been concern that a general requirement for filing individual access-charge tariffs with the commission would be unduly burdensome for very small companies—particularly if a detailed cost-separations study was required for each company as part of the prescribed procedure for calculating and justifying access charges.

The bill contains several provisions that are designed to assure that neither small telephone companies nor the affected regulatory agencies will be unnecessarily burdened by the procedures for regulating exchange-access charges. For example, the state commissions are granted authority to regulate exchange-access arrangement for any exchange carrier not subject to classification by the commission after the state has certified that it has established a program consistent with the act. This provision could potentially relieve more than 95 percent of the independent telephone companies of the requirement of filing access tariffs at the federal level.

These are the major provisions of S. 898. But what are some potential impacts of this bill on pricing structure of telephone services?

First, one of the main purposes of S. 898 is to foster competition and deregulation. As competition increases in the interexchange market, rates for such services should be significantly reduced with prices more accurately reflecting the true costs of providing such services. The same principle will apply to customer-premises equipment.

While basic local-exchange services will continue to be regulated for the foreseeable future, there is certainly the potential for upward pressure on local rates. It must be kept in mind, however, that reductions in interexchange rates will tend to offset on an individual basis increases in local-exchange rates. In addition, it must be stressed that S. 898 specifically provides that local rates must be reasonable and further provides that the FCC must implement a surcharge on access charges where necessary. These provisions will tend to minimize rate increases for local service.

As this chapter previously noted, S. 898 provides for FCC preemption of state regulation of intrastate toll services. By placing all interexchange services under one jurisdiction, toll-rate disparity between interstate toll and intrastate toll will be minimized, if not entirely eliminated. Thus reductions in toll rates will occur for both interstate and intrastate toll services.

Another important provision of S. 898 that will impact upon pricing is the elimination of prohibitions on resale. Resale of telecommunications services will tend to reduce cross-subsidization and move the rates for such services closer to cost-based pricing. As one moves closer to marginal-cost pricing in the interexchange market, the trend will be to adopt such pricing for local service through usage-sensitive pricing. Usage-sensitive pricing methodologies, such as local-measured service, will place the costs of services on the cost causers and will potentially reduce rates for a significant portion of residential subscribers.

Many sections of S. 898 provide for the filing with the FCC of extensive information related to the provision of regulated services. Access to such information by enterpreneurs will tend to promote entry based on correct pricing signals rather than based on false pricing signals that currently exist. This will go far in ensuring that investment decisions by potential competitors are based on accurate market analysis.

Finally, and perhaps most importantly, is the area of access charges. The implementation of an equitable system of access-charge arrangements can have greater potential impact on pricing policies than any other provision of this bill. In looking at the traffic-sensitive and nontraffic-sensitive costs of access, one is dealing with over 50 percent of the total revenue requirements of the telephone industry. The sheer magnitude of this figure demonstrates that changes in the allocation of costs can have a dramatic impact upon rates. Further, the access-charge area deals with more sectors of the telecommunications market than any other single provision of S. 898. The first of these sectors is the competitive interexchange-services market.

Here, proper terms and conditions for local origination and termination services are necessary, not only to assure competitive equity among interexchange carriers, but also to protect against pricing practices that would distort the development of the interexchange sector as a whole.

The second market is that which is served by telephone-exchange carriers. For these carriers the local origination and termination of interexchange traffic is today a major source of revenues. Many of the smaller independent telephone companies now derive significantly more than half of their operating revenues from this source, primarily from conventional long-distance services. In this sector equitable access charges and orderly transitional arrangements are necessary to avoid dislocations which would adversely affect the quality and price of local-telephone service.

The third sector is the emerging nontelephone local-distribution facilities and services market. As substitutes for telephone origination and termination services become increasingly competitive in the years immediately ahead, economically correct access charges will be necessary to discourage new suppliers from entering the market where they would be economically inefficient and to encourage their entry where it would be publicly beneficial.

As one can see, S. 898 has the potential to dramatically impact upon not only the pricing of telecommunications services, but further, on the other significant and diverse issues that face the evolving telecommunications industry. It is important that all interested parties provide input into the process so that the end result allows everyone to take full advantage of the many benefits of a dynamic telecommunications industry.

# 18 The Effects of a Competitive Environment on Local-Service Rates

*Larry R. Weber*

In an industry driven by changes, no changes have had more effect on the industry and its consumers than those demanded by and resulting from the introduction of competition. After a century of growth in an environment where regulation was the substitute for competition, the telecommunications industry has now come full circle; for over ten years it has lived in a new era, an era in which, clearly, competition is to be the substitute for regulation.

The transition to a competitive world has not been an easy one and there are certainly no signs that the journey in the future will be any more smooth. The changes required are far reaching and pose difficulties for the industry, its consumers, and its regulators.

The industry itself will continue to face new challenges in structure, pricing philosophies, and perhaps a fundamental change in its role in society. Consumers will experience changes in the relative rates for industry services, must adapt to the delivery systems of the new environment, and will be presented with a myriad of new service options. Regulators who already share with the industry the burden of price levels pressured by sustained inflation are seeing market forces intrude at a rapid rate on what was once solely their turf. Unquestionably, every aspect of the industry will be affected.

It seems apparent, however, that the most far-reaching effects and most difficult problems lie in the area of basic-exchange service. The status of this fundamental service is rapidly changing and will be markedly different from the past. Competitive pressures and changes in the industry's structure will continue to erode the opportunity for regulators and the industry to shelter local ratepayers from bearing the true economic cost of providing local network access and usage. Carefully created and applied cross subsidies have long permitted basic-service rates to be set below economic cost. Such techniques are not viable long-term mechanisms in the competitive world. As the availability of these subsidies diminishes, it is inevitable that rates for basic service will experience significant increases as they move nearer their cost.

In order to analyze the effects of competition and deregulation on basic service, the unique status it enjoyed in the regulated monopoly environment must be clearly understood. The industry and its regulators embraced the

259

objective of universal service, and to facilitate its attainment, carefully controlled the industry's economics and precisely tuned its rate structure to establish basic service as the benefitted service. By creating revenue support for it through the pricing of other services such as toll and supplemental services, basic service has not shouldered its fair share of the revenue burden. In fact it is common today for basic-service rates to be set without regard to the cost of providing the service, but rather the minimum rate level necessary to satisfy whatever remains of the firm's overall revenue requirement after rates for all nonbasic services have been set.

The support strategy was spectacularly successful. Virtually every household in the United States has a phone and pays a rate unimaginable in other parts of the world. Moreover, the average worker spends less time on the job today to pay for telephone service than at any time in over twenty years.

The prospects for the continued availability of local-exchange service as it has been known in the past at rates which, relative to other goods and services, are quite low are at best questionable. With embedded-inflation rates now judged to be in the range of 8 to 9 percent, no letup in the pressure of inflation on rates can be predicted. Moreover, these inflationary pressures will be a more significant factor in local-service pricing, as means used in the past to mitigate them become unavailable in a competitive environment.

While fundamental economics and competitive pressures in an unregulated environment will move all rates nearer their cost, it is clear that the most significant initial impact of today's transitional changes will focus on the principal sources of basic-service subsidies, toll services, and customer-premise or terminal services. Competitive impact on these services will be the first to flow through the basic service, thereby placing upward pressure on local rates.

Fundamental to the future of subsidies available from toll services is the jurisdictional separations process, a key element in the determination of revenue levels required in both the interstate and intrastate jurisdictions. The nature of telecommunications services and the regulatory structure in which they are provided do not permit ready quantification of that investment to be supported by interstate revenues as opposed to that supported by intrastate revenues. In recognition of the fact that the majority of investment is jointly used in the provision of inter and intrastate services, the fundamental basis for assigning revenue-support responsibility is the relative usage levels of that investment by each jurisdiction's services. In order to permit lower local-exchange rates, interstate services bear significantly more than their share of the revenue-support burden for jointly used plants. Since the 1950s various formulas and factors have been used to relieve the intrastate ratepayer of support responsibility for jointly used plants that usage studies indicate he should bear. Currently, in excess of $5 billion in revenue requirements are shifted to interstate responsibility not based on relative usage but rather on the desire to lighten the revenue requirement on intrastate services. The resulting understatement of intrastate requirements permits rates that fail to generate revenues at the level separation based on usage would require.

In a regulated monopoly environment, the use in rate making of investment bases which reflected social objectives was acceptable. The industry was not harmed so long as investment responsibility was accepted by one jurisdiction or the other. Regulators achieved their objective of flowing subsidies to basic service through reduction of the investment burden intrastate ratepayers picked up. And finally consumers benefitted from exchange rates which were priced lower than would otherwise be possible.

The introduction of competition to previously regulated monopoly markets renders unworkable many of the approaches which have served well in the past. Moreover, the same structures and mechanisms which contributed to local-service rate stability in the past will now reverse themselves and amplify the immediate effects of the transition to a competitive environment.

Customer-premise equipment (CPE) is a case in point. In the order in its second computer inquiry the FCC detariffed customer-premise equipment and removed it from normal regulatory rate-making processes. While the ultimate schedule of removal and the means used to accomplish it may be subject for conjecture, the implications for the local rate payer are clear and significant.

On the surface the effects of removal would seem straightforward: remove all expenses, revenues, and investment associated with the provision of CPE services. Since these services have generally been priced at levels which provide a contribution above their cost which flows to basic service, it is apparent that an adverse effect on basic rates will take place. While the impact varies by jurisdiction, this loss of support is generally at manageable levels.

However, on close examination, one sees that this support is but the tip of the iceberg. Since it is jointly used in the provision of interstate and intrastate services, a portion of customer-premise-equipment investment is transferred through the separations process to interstate responsibility. However, no similar separation of revenues takes place.

Thus when removal is accomplished, state jursidictions will lose revenues which cover 100 percent of true CPE investment, but intrastate investment bases which are understated due to the separations process will decrease by only 70 percent of the amount rates have been set to cover. This disproportionate removal of revenues and investment generates further deficiency in overall intrastate revenues, a deficiency which will, and properly so, become the responsibility of the basic ratepayer.

Turning to the other major source of support for basic service, long-distance service, one sees a similarly dim future for continuation of support through current mechanisms and at current levels. Both interstate and intrastate toll provide support for basic service in today's environment but deliver that support through different means. Interstate rates have been established not to cover economic cost but rather economic cost plus an investment additive which is more properly the responsibility of intrastate.

When the provision of toll service was opened to competition, the results were predictable. In the interstate arena the disparity between rate-making investment and economic investment had resulted in rate levels which provided a price umbrella beneath which competitive suppliers could comfortably price and profitably operate. Microwave technology eliminated dependence on high-cost physical circuits and facilitated entry to profitable high-volume markets. By concentrating on high-density routes, new suppliers were able to avoid the upward pressure on rates of providing service on less profitable, low-density routes. This concentration, coupled with an earnings need to cover only true economic costs, resulted in alternative suppliers establishing rate levels which fell beneath those of traditional common carriers. Since consumers' purchase decisions are founded in true economics, traffic began to move away from common carriers to specialized carriers who offered a price advantage.

This shift to alternative suppliers has great significance to local rate-payers. As interstate traffic leaves common-carrier networks and moves to competitive suppliers, the interstate share of the usage of joint plant will decline, resulting in an increase in the investment assigned to the intrastate ratepayer and the revenues which must ultimately be obtained from basic service.

It should be noted that there has been progress toward equalization of the cost burden borne by suppliers through the provision by specialized carriers of some revenue support to local service. Nonetheless, wide disparity in support levels continues and seems certain to insure further customer movement to alternative toll suppliers.

At the same time, interstate toll services were subsidizing basic service by assuming a disproportionate share of investment, subsidies from intrastate toll were generated. Public acceptance of higher rates for toll services permitted satisfaction of significant portions of overall intrastate revenues by maintaining toll rates at levels well above cost. Generally, intrastate toll rates are equal to or higher than interstate rates which themselves are based on overstated, noneconomic investment bases. Sheltered by a monopoly environment, intrastate as well as interstate toll rates do not reflect primarily cost considerations but rather have been established at levels which will generate support for basic service. Thus, in the intrastate arena one finds a price umbrella similar to that found in interstate. The emergence of alternative suppliers of intrastate interexchange services is a clear sign that present intrastate toll rates will be driven in the direction of cost.

Clearly, the implications for the basic ratepayer of movement to competitive environment are significant. A state and federal joint board has been established to address the problems noted in this book as well as other implications of movement to a competitive environment. This board has before it several proposals which should be noted.

The Bell system has put forth a comprehensive plan which addresses, among other things, the implications of the removal from rate making of customer-premises equipment and movement to economic investment bases in both the interstate and intrastate jurisdictions. The plan provides that the jurisdictional assignment of joint-use plant would be based entirely on usage, and the investment additive which currently takes place would be eliminated. In order to avoid a sudden increase in intrastate revenue requirements, the plan calls for phasing in the changes over a five-year period. At the conclusion of the phase-in period, both intrastate and interstate rates would shoulder their true economic burden and fend for themselves in the competitive arena.

Also before the board is a more narrowly constructed proposal which addresses the loss of support associated with the removal of customer-premise equipment from rate making. It is based on the FCC's latest position on removal of CPE which calls for a gradual movement to a detariffed environment. The plan advocates removal of CPE investment support by interstate services over a five-year period. It does not address the problems currently existing relative to toll rates.

The toll rate and investment problems are the subject of yet another proposal which is under study. Put forth by the FCC, this plan offers support to basic service through an access charge to be paid by all intercity carriers to compensate for their usage of local facilities in rendering intercity service.

There is yet another avenue under study as a solution to the toll problem. As noted earlier, through industry agreement and FCC approval interstate specialized common carriers today are charged for local-network usage in rendering intercity service. This ENFIA (Exchange Network Facilities for Interstate Access) tariff results in specialized carriers currently providing support at a rate of 55 percent of common-carrier support for similar usage levels. There are provisions for increasing this support level to parity with common carriers.

It is apparent that the problems of the changing structure of the telecommunications industry are varied and complex. The solutions will require extensive study and will not be implemented without some pain. However, the fundamental economics of a competitive world will clearly drive the prices of all services nearer their cost. This movement will certainly result in the curtailment if not elimination of major subsidies to basic service and will drive its prices significantly upward from present levels.

# 19 Pricing Telephone Service in the 1980s

*Hunter E. Harvey, Jr.*

This chapter treats the change in local-telephone-service pricing from flat rates to cost-related, usage-sensitive rate structures or local-measured service, as it is called. It also places the current issues and events in telephone rate design in a larger historical context.

Telephone company personnel and their government regulators are no different from the rest of humanity in facing the familiar, persistent problem of losing sight of the forest for the trees. The trees in this case are the problems and arguments grappled with daily in the regulatory arena. My point, of course, is that it is much easier to get from tree to tree without wasting steps if we can keep an eye on the forest we are traveling through. The telecommunications industry is entering a decade of rapid, accelerating change. But insofar as one can keep a larger historical perspective, day-to-day worry and contention will be diminished, not only for those who work in telephone companies and sit on state regulatory commissions but also for the public. Those responsible for the provision of telephone service must make a major effort to explain to consumers what is happening in the industry if they are to navigate this era of radical change smoothly and efficiently and thereby maximize the potential benefits for society.

## Technology, Market Demand, and Competition

There is a profound transformation currently underway in the U.S. telecommunications industry. For several decades now the telecommunications, electronics, and computer industries have enjoyed breathtaking improvements in technology and reductions in costs, and all indications are that this trend will continue. Microelectronics, fiber optics, microwave transmission, and communications satellites are only the most familiar current examples. As a result new telecommunications services have become possible, and the network is being put to new uses. Concurrently, the new technology has made entry into the telecommunications business relatively easy for new firms by lowering the initial investment required to offer specialized services for groups of users with specialized needs. While economies of scale will probably always characterize some parts of the industry, economies of innova-

---

tion and specialization play a growing role in others. Together, technological innovation and the changing nature of demand for telecommunications are destroying the old natural-monopoly character of the telephone industry.

Step by step, the laws and regulations that traditionally governed and enforced the regulated monopoly structure of telecommunications have become increasingly untenable and are being removed. Thus there has been a long series of public-policy decisions such as the Hush-a-Phone decision, the Above 890 decision, Carterphone, Specialized Common Carriers, Execunet, registration of terminal gear, Exchange Network Facilities for Interstate Access (ENFIA), Computer Inquiry II, and Resale and Sharing of interstate services. So far the courts and the FCC have been the main agents in this process of legal and institutional adaptation to the changes in our industry. But faced with the prospect of continued piecemeal change, more and more participants in the public-policy debate are coming to see the need for congressional legislation in managing an orderly and fair transition to a more competitive telecommunications industry. Congress itself is also coming to favor competition more strongly as it comes to see more clearly the significance and extent of the transformation in telecommunications that evolving technology and customer needs have wrought. Even the titles of legislative proposals reflect the trend. Last year's Senate bill was modestly called the Communications Act Amendments of 1980. This year's is entitled The Telecommunications Competition and Deregulation Act of 1981.

No one can predict whether new federal legislation will pass this year, but there can be no doubt that the industry will continue to become more competitive. Competition is already a reality today in the provision of customer-premises equipment and interstate telecommunications transport. According to the current Federal Communications Commission (FCC) schedule, customer-premises equipment will be detariffed in 1982. In some jurisdictions competitors also supply intrastate long-distance service, and there is strong pressure for expanded intrastate competition, including the provision of alternatives to local-exchange service.

In the old regulated monopoly environment telephone companies and their regulators have enjoyed a great deal of freedom in setting prices, which has made it relatively easy for them to pursue public-policy objectives such as universal service. In essence, they were able to price some services above cost and thus generate contributions for the purpose of subsidizing other services. That freedom is fast being curtailed by the growth of competition and deregulation because users of contributory regulated services are gaining the option of turning to competitive suppliers.

## Changes in Costs, Prices, and Rate Design

Once the larger picture of the transformation underway in telecommunications is clearly grasped, the changes in rates and prices it necessitates are fairly straightforward. Basically, the growth of competition in the industry requires that the various services of regulated telephone companies be priced much more closely in line with their costs than they are today.

From the standpoint of local telephone companies and their state regulators, this shift from value-of-service pricing to cost-based pricing will have two very significant consequences. First, it means unprecedented increases in the price of local-exchange service because today local service is the primary beneficiary of the system of contributions and subsidies that has evolved under the traditional regulated monopoly structure of the telephone industry. Many of the cost reductions that have resulted from the wave of technological innovation mentioned earlier have been concentrated in the area of long-haul transmission. By contrast the costs of the end links of the telephone network, that is of picking up and delivering messages to customers' premises, are relatively intractable. This seems to be a general characteristic of many transportation and communication systems. For example, the postal service faces a similar situation in terms of long-haul versus short-haul costs. Under the so-called Ozark separations procedures used in the telephone industry, savings realized in long-haul transmission have year by year swelled the subsidy delivered to local-exchange service so that today there is a major distortion between the prices and costs of different services. Such price distortions cannot be sustained now that competitors to the regulated telephone companies have begun to arise.

Interstate long-distance service currently contributes over $6 billion a year to local-exchange costs through the separations procedures. Intrastate toll rates are similarly overpriced today, providing more than $5 billion this year. These are largely subsidies that do not correspond to costs actually incurred by long-distance usage and so must inevitably fall as competitive alternatives to regulated service spread.

Furthermore, deregulation and growing competition will cause increases in local revenue requirements for several other reasons, which can only be discussed briefly. Contributions to basic-exchange service from customer-premises equipment and enhanced services will no longer be available under the terms laid down in the FCC's Computer Inquiry II and the proposed legislation, neither of which permit subsidy flow between regulated and unregulated telephone company subsidiaries. A competitive marketplace requires accelerated depreciation schedules and that will mean higher local bills, at least initially. The same is true of the expensing of station-connection costs. Currently, capitalized-connection charges amount to about $12 billion. A competitive industry means capital is more at risk and will therefore command higher rates of return. And, of course, competitive carriers will continue to attract more customers, who will thus cease to contribute to the basic network. Add in the continuing cost of inflation with which local-service price increases have failed to keep pace for more than a decade, and one has a rough, overall conception of the magnitude of the transition problems. If this transition is not managed properly, the availability of affordable basic telephone service, that is universal service, will be endangered.

The second and related major consequence of the shift to cost-based pricing has to do with rate design. In most jurisdictions customers in the United States have traditionally paid flat-rate bills for their local-telephone service. In return for a fixed monthly fee, each customer received a basic telephone set, inside wiring, an access line to the local switching center, and unlimited local-exchange usage, including various operator services like directory assistance. In order to implement cost-based pricing and to avoid the adverse social effects of rapidly rising local-exchange rates, local-telephone rate structures must be unbundled so that discrete services can be individually priced in relation to their costs and the market. Hence, each customer's bill will more accurately reflect the amount and nature of the services he actually consumes. This means costs will be distributed among customers more equitably, and customers will gain more freedom to meet their individual needs by selecting from a diverse menu of services. They will also be more able to control their own telephone bills by adjusting the amount and nature of their usage.

There are many parts to this transformation in the design of local rate structures. Service-connection charges will be increasingly disaggregated to reflect and fully recover the costs of establishing, moving, or changing service. This makes possible cost-reducing options for customers who are willing, for example, to pick up and install their own equipment. Charges for directory-assistance calls are being introduced today. In the future it may be appropriate to make greater distinctions between the prices for various kinds of operator assistance, such as requests for credit card, collect, and third-number billing. Telephone sets and other equipment will be fully unbundled from local access and usage. While there are other examples that could be listed, the largest and most important of all these changes in telephone rate design is the implementation of local-measured-service rate structures.

**Local Measured Service**

The measured-service plan itself is really quite simple. The point is to separate the monthly charge for access to the telephone network from charges for the use of the local network. Usage charges are then further unbundled so that they reflect the different characteristics of telephone calls which determine their cost. These are the number of a customer's calls, their duration, distance, and time of day. Of course, usage charges only apply to outgoing calls. Notice that this four-element charging structure for local usage is quite similar to charging practices for long-distance calls today.

Customers sometimes find usage-sensitive pricing of local service complex and confusing because they are accustomed to the old, simple flat-rate structure. But, in fact, they have traditionally paid for long-distance calls on this same basis for nearly a hundred years.

Usage-sensitive-local-service pricing, embodied in the measured-service plan, is the key to preserving the level of universal service achieved in the United States in the face of the massive revenue requirement shifts described earlier. If customers have no option to flat-rate local telephone billing, the less well-to-do will be forced to drop off the network as local revenue requirements rise. Certainly the price of local service has been kept low in relation to the rapidly rising prices of other utility services, and local rates would probably have to increase substantially before significant erosion of universal service takes place. But it must be recognized that for each customer driven off the network by rising flat rates the consequences are very significant indeed. Such customers would be isolated from a society that is becoming increasingly dependent on the telephone system. In an emergency they would have only limited, indirect ways of summoning assistance. In terms of universal service, the loss of one customer is unmeasurably small but to that customer the loss is total. By separating the prices of access and usage and deaveraging the price of local usage, measured service allows one to make available low-priced, low-use service options that will preserve telephone service for those customers who cannot afford to pay higher flat-rate bills.

The plan is to offer residential telephone users a choice among three local-service options: standard measured service, low-use measured service, and a premium flat-rate service. The first two options incorporate the four-element, usage-sensitive charging structure described. Standard measured service, which includes a usage allowance, will for the majority of its subscribers roughly correspond in terms of price to current flat-rate service. So customers who select standard measured service will see no significant change in their bills, at least initially. Low-use measured service, which has little or no usage allowance, is intended to serve as a threshold option. It will be priced well below standard measured service and the remaining flat-rate option and thus will become the entry-level service that assures access to telephone service for everyone.

Notice that this discussion does not include withdrawing flat-rate residential local service. By virtue of the fact that it allows for unlimited calling, it will be priced at a premium level. Indiscriminate increases in the price of flat-rate service will not be sought, but flat-rate price levels will be adjusted as local revenue requirements change. The goal is to price flat-rate service approximately in line with its costs. Because of the changing environment those costs will probably rise substantially, but no one can predict with certainty how rapidly this will occur. By offering customers a choice between flat-rate and measured options, the measured-service plan is designed to address an uncertain future. Measured-service options are intended as a haven for customers who wish to control the level of their own monthly telephone bills. The proportion of customers who elect measured-service options will adjust automatically as current contributions to local exchanges diminish and local rates consequently rise. Measured service will thus grow in response to customers needs and desires. The object is not to force measured service on telephone users but to increase their freedom of choice.

The pricing of local business service, however, is a different matter. In most jurisdictions measured service for business customers has initially been introduced as an optional form of local billing like residential measured service. But ultimately flat-rate options for business customers should be withdrawn. Indeed, measured service is already the only local-service offering available to businesses in five states and the District of Columbia, and measured service is nonoptional for business customers in the major metropolitan areas of six other states.

There are two reasons for this distinctive treatment of business customers. First, in contrast to residential customers, whose telephone calling is primarily social, businesses use the telephone for the purpose of economic gain. The only arguable exceptions in the business class of service are government and nonprofit organizations. The National Regulatory Research Institute did an extensive study of the impact of measured rates on such institutions for the Ohio Public Utilities Commission in 1979. That study stated it was fair to conclude "that over the long run measured service will not affect the quality of service" of government and nonprofit organizations.[1] Likewise, an independent study performed at the behest of the Wisconsin Public Service Commission this spring concluded that local measured-service "rates are unlikely to interfere significantly with charitable activity."[2]

The second reason that business customers should only be offered measured service has to do with the resale of telephone service. In June the FCC lifted the prohibition on resale of interstate telecommunications service, and indications are that resale and sharing will be permitted in all sectors of the market within the next few years. Flat-rate pricing simply makes no sense in an environment where local service can be resold. The resale of flat-rate lines could very quickly generate a new industry of telephone-service middlemen. They could buy quantities of flat-rate-local-access lines and resell them on a measured basis to low users. As fewer and fewer regulated telephone lines are utilized, and usage becomes concentrated on those lines, their price must rise to meet the revenue requirements of the regulated telephone companies. Such price increases would make the reseller's services increasingly popular until conceivably only the heaviest users would remain as direct customers of the regulated companies. Flat-rate service options for business customers must therefore be eliminated wherever resale is permitted.

**Additional Benefits of Measured Service**

Deregulation and the growth of competition in the telecommunications industry, with the revenue requirements shifts they entail, are making measured-service rate structures a virtual necessity. But they ought to be welcomed in any event because they possess many other advantages over traditional flat-rate-local-service pricing. Indeed, those other advantages played a major role in the decision of regulated telephone companies to begin implementing measured service several years ago, when the prospects for deregulation and the growth of competition were not nearly so clear as they have become today. A brief review of those other benefits is important because they remain just as relevant as they ever were.

First, local-telephone usage has grown steadily in the past, and as new and expanded services become available, it is expected to grow more rapidly. With traditional flat-rate local pricing, increasing levels of usage create significant costs for the regulated telephone companies without generating any corresponding increase in revenue. Conversion to measured service means that the generation of revenue automatically responds to changes in usage so that revenues continue to cover the cost of the services provided. At the same time measured service allows increases in cost due to inflation to be spread more fairly, that is, in proportion to the consumption of telephone service.

Second, measured service pricing is desirable because it constitutes a major improvement in the equity with which the costs of local service are distributed among telephone users. There are wide disparities in the ways different people use the telephone and consequently in the costs they cause to the network. Under mandatory flat-rate pricing, the costs of local usage are averaged and all subscribers must bear the burden imposed by heavy users. Figure 19-1 shows how local telephone calling rates are typically distributed among residential users, and it is a graphic picture of the unfairness inherent in flat-rate pricing. One way to describe this usage distribution in words is that the 20 percent of customers who call the most use the telephone nearly ten times as much as the 20 percent who call the least. Clearly, under flat-rate pricing low users are forced to subsidize the local telephone service of heavy users.

There are also wide disparities in the duration of calls among residential customers, which can be seen in figure 19-2. Here, each bar represents thirty seconds. Some customers make strikingly long calls. The longest call in this study lasted two hundred and seventeen minutes, which is over three and a half hours. Since it was made in an untimed area in California, it was billed as a single message unit. The granddaddy of all the calls recorded was between two university campuses in Manhattan on a computer facility: it lasted for eighty-two-and-a-half days, incurring a single-messuage unit

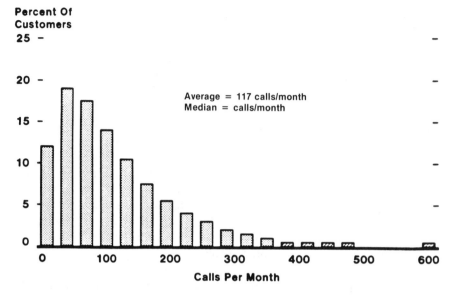

Source: Lawrence Garfinkel and Peter B. Linhart, "The Revenue Analysis of Local Measured Telephone Service," *Public Utilities Fortnightly*, (October 9, 1980). Copyright Public Utilities Fortnightly. Reprinted with permission.

**Figure 19-1.** Residential Monthly Local Calls—Single Party, Flat Rate

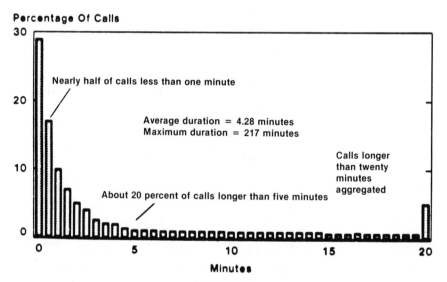

Source: Internal Bell System Study, (New York: AT&T, 1979).

**Figure 19-2.** Call Duration Distribution among Single-Party Flat-Rate Residential Users

charge of a little over eight cents. Such calls are exceptional, but more common than one might imagine. Of course, any single customer makes both short and long calls, but the average duration of different customers' calls varies widely, as shown in figure 19-3.

New and expanded uses of the network will cause the distribution of residential usage to become increasingly skewed, especially in view of the long holding times associated with interactive services. Since not all customers will take advantage of the new services, the only equitable way to recover the costs of this increased usage is from the customers who generate it. With the forced averaging of flat-rate prices this is not possible.

Third and lastly, measured service is desirable because it is the proper way to price services in terms of economic efficiency. Under a flat-rate tariff users have no incentive to conserve because they receive a misleading price signal that suggests local-telephone usage is without cost. To understand how peculiar our traditional system of local-telephone service really is, just imagine how wasteful and unfair it would be if all automobile owners paid the same monthly fee for gasoline regardless of how much they actually consumed.

One may wonder why, if measured service is so logical and has so many benefits, it has not always been employed in the pricing of local-telephone

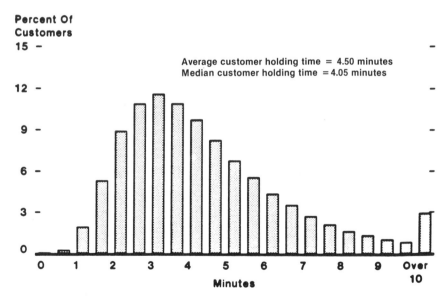

Source: See figure 19-1. Garfinkel and Linhart, "The Revenue Analysis." Copyright Public Utilities Fortnightly. Reprinted with permission.

**Figure 19-3.** Residential Conversation Time Local Calls—Single Party, Flat Rate

service. Quite simply, it was not as practical as it is today because of the sizable costs of measurement in older electromechanical central offices. However, the wave of technological innovation mentioned earlier has led to improvements, such as electronic switching machines and microprocessor-based measuring equipment for the nonelectronic offices that have brought the cost of measurement to an acceptable level. As such new equipment is installed, measured service can be introduced at low cost. That is why telephone companies have been able to begin implementing measured service in recent years.

## Progress and Contention

The implementation of measured service is proceeding on a reasonable schedule and in an orderly manner in most jurisdictions. In just the last six months regulatory commissions in ten states have approved significant portions of the measured-service plan. And many local telephone companies plan filings in the near future. Today, Bell system companies either offer or have the approval to offer some form of local-measured service in thirty-three states. Already, more than half of the Bell system's business customers pay usage-sensitive local telephone bills, and most residential customers served by the Bell system have the option of choosing a usage-sensitive local billing arrangement if they wish to.

It is true that local customers are sometimes suspicious of measured service when first presented with the idea, but studies have shown that their doubts diminish as they become familiar with it. To cite a nearby example, an independent survey conducted in Florida by Peter Merrill Associates concluded that most customers understand and support the fairness of usage-sensitive pricing.[3] This study also showed that the vast majority of customers who subscribed to measured service in a set of experimental pilot exchanges reported that they did indeed like it. Admittedly, Lee Richardson, a consumer advocate, has questioned the methodology of the Florida consumer study, but a rebuttal to his objections is from the testimony of Seymour Sudman, a professor at the University of Illinois and current president of the American Association for Public Opinion Research, before the Florida Public Utility Commission which concluded his testimony by saying,

> The important thing for a user of this report is to distinguish between the methodology and the result. Some readers, such as Mr. Richardson, appear to be unhappy with the results. As a consequence, they may follow this line of reasoning: since I don't like the results the methodology can't be any good . . . I have ignored the substantive results, and looked only at the methodology. The methodology in this study follows well accepted professional practices and, to me, shows no sign of a lack of objectivity.[4]

Despite the fact that Sudman's remarks may seem to deal with a comparatively minor scrap between experts, his observation raises an important point. Although the introduction of measured service is progressing successfully in most areas of the country, it is not without difficulties. Special interests that profit from the averaging of costs intrinsic in flat-rate pricing will have to pay more for local service, and they sometimes actively resist the conversion to measured service. Enough money is at stake to make it worth their while to bring strong pressures to bear in local regulatory proceedings. One can sympathize with their situation, but they are vested interest groups at odds with the majority of telephone users. However, the responsibility of the industry is to price local-telephone service equitably for the benefit of the public as a whole. The growth of competition in telecommunications ultimately leaves no alternative to usage-sensitive local pricing, and the sooner local-measured service is implemented, the less these vested interests will become entrenched behind the flat-rate pricing system.

**Conclusion**

For more than a decade now the telecommunications industry has grown steadily more competitive, and the pace of change will accelerate through the 1980s. Adapting to this transformation will tax the ingenuity of all who are responsible for the provision of telephone service, industry people and regulators alike. Hard work and difficult decisions are inevitable, but if we prepare with foresight now, we can avoid or minimize potential socially damaging side-effects and smooth the transition to a new telecommunications industry, which will not only be more competitive, but much more productive and useful to the public than it already is today. In terms of local-telephone service, the implementation of measured service is the key to a smooth and successful adaptation.

As the noted economist, Alfred Kahn, the former chairman of the New York public utilities commission, in recent testimony on the proposed telecommunications legislation before a Senate committee said:

> Local service is subsidized to the tune of many billions of dollars annually by toll service, as well as residential, by business. This kind of internal subsidization is basically incompatible with competition. Competitors will naturally want to enter the markets where rates are held way above cost, drying up the ability of the regulated companies to serve the unprofitable markets . . . The burden that is thrown by separations procedures on interexchange service is enormous . . . It produces grossly uneconomic results . . . It is practically unacceptable when what is being subsidized is not really basic service, but unlimited placing of unlimited numbers of calls of unlimited length, over wider and wider areas . . . I urge you to make certain that the subsidy is confined to truly basic service, that is simply the ability to receive calls.[5]

**Notes**

1. The National Regulatory Research Institute, *The Impact of Measured Telephone Rates on Telephone Usage of Government and Nonprofit Organizations* (Columbus, Ohio: Ohio State University, 1979), p. 5.

2. R.T. Luke, Testimony before the Wisconsin public service commission (Austin, Texas: Research and Planning Consultants, Inc., June 1981), p. 28.

3. Peter Merrill Associates (PMA), Inc., *Implementation of Local Measured Service in Florida—Survey and Analysis of Residential Sector* Boston: PMA, Inc., 1980).

4. Dr. Seymour Sudman, Testimony before the Florida public service commission, Docket #810035-TP (July 13, 1981).

5. Alfred Kahn, Testimony before the Senate Committee on Commerce, Science, and Transportation, Hearings on the Telecommunications Competition and Deregulation Act of 1981 (June 11, 1981), pp. 152-83.

# 20 Deregulating Electric Generation: An Economist's Perspective

*Joe D. Pace*

For economists, the debate over the deregulation of electric generation is so much cleaner because as professionals all highly trained in a well-defined set of economic principles, they know exactly what they are for and what they are against. They are for competition and against monopoly. They are for unfettered markets and against government interference. They are for prices equal to marginal costs and against subsidies or price controls that tend to push prices away from marginal costs. They are for the achievement of economic efficiency and against kowtowing to political pressures that inevitably run against economic efficiency.

Given this, it ought to be relatively easy to decide where they stand on the issue of deregulating electric generation. Once their studies show that economies of scale have been exhausted in electric generation—that is, the optimum generating-plant sizes are not large relative to the size of the market—and that they see no evidence of the existence of economies of vertical integration, it ought to be clear that a competitive market is feasible in generation and that economists should be for it. Moreover, they know that despite all the doomsayers, deregulation worked in the stock-brokerage industry, it is working in the airline industry, and it is going to work in the trucking industry. The only thing that clearly is not working is the present regulation of the electric-utility industry.

But before they finally decide what it is they are for, they need to determine what *it* is. There really are two *its* that need to be addressed: what is it that they are attempting to deregulate and what is it that deregulators are offering to accomplish this?

Consider the first problem: what are the pertinent economic characteristics of the industry they are seeking to deregulate? First, the nature of the generating-plant investment is unique or very close to it. The construction of electric-generating units requires extraordinary amounts of capital and very long lead times. A conservative estimate would be that the minimum efficient generating-unit size is 300 megawatts and that an efficient plant requires at least two units.[1] At today's prices, such a plant could be expected to involve a capital outlay of one billion dollars. Beyond this, it currently takes eight to ten years at a minimum to bring a major plant into service. This means that investors must wait a decade before beginning to recover their capital. Also, an important characteristic of this investment is its lifetime. The physical life of a generating unit is thirty to fifty years. Finally, in the language of the vertical-integration literature, a generating plant is a very idiosyncratic asset. A generating plant can produce only one product at one place for sale only to a directly connected customer. If market conditions change, one cannot vary the product mix, one cannot accumulate inventories for a future time, and one cannot put it in a truck and ship it to a foreign market.[2] For investors to deal with such risk, they must either have long-term assurance of a market at prices varying to reflect cost changes, or they must anticipate being able to price at levels providing quick investment recovery and large risk premiums, or they must hire extremely perceptive forecasters who can see the next forty years.

Second, the operations of generating units must be closely coordinated with one another on a second-to-second basis. It is not electrically possible to operate generating units independently if they are connected to a single-transmission grid. Nor is it economically feasible for the dispatch of individual units to be uncoordinated.

Third, it is necessary for generation and transmission planning to be optimized jointly and for the operation of generation and transmission to be coordinated on a second-to-second basis.

Finally, because as a general proposition electricity cannot be stored, because all demands placed upon the system at a given point must be met (or interrupted) in order to avoid system collapse, and because holding excess capacity is so expensive, a mechanism must exist for closely coordinating load and capacity plans in the long run and for equilibrating load and capacity on a second-to-second basis.

What this brief review reveals is that for a deregulation scenario to be both technically workable and economically feasible, it must provide a mechanism for calling forth the necessary investment, coordinating the operation of generating units, jointly optimizing generation and transmission, and matching load to capacity. In addition, transition problems need to be addressed—assuming that one knows where the promised land is and how to cultivate it, how does one get from here to there? Finally, of course, it is helpful if a deregulation scenario at least offers some prospect of being politically feasible.

Now let us consider the second problem: what is it that the deregulators are proposing? This is not an easy question to answer for there are as many deregulation scenarios as there are deregulators, and none of them is the one you would find most attractive—that is, regulators just go away, to be replaced by highly competitive markets yielding lower prices, greater efficiency, an end to capital-attraction problems, and heightened responsiveness to consumer needs for varying prices and qualities of service. No deregulation scenario offers a fully competitive market structure. Instead, all scenarios envision continued regulation of the rates paid by end users and regulation or government ownership of local distribution systems and regional monopoly transmission entites. Nevertheless, the attractiveness of the system they describe is not to be underestimated. It promises in one fell swoop to:

1. Replace regulation with competition at the generating level, putting pressure on power producers to build the most efficient plants possible and operate them at lowest cost;
2. Give distributors and their customers an opportunity to buy power from the cheapest source by changing sources easily, or, at minimum, by benefitting from competitive offerings of long-term contracts;
3. Encourage entry into the generating business by anyone who feels he can make money offering power at competitive rates;
4. Discourage construction of unneeded plants, as no one would have an assured outlet for his power;
5. Eliminate the costs and delays associated with regulation.

This is, it must be conceded, a formidable set of hypothetical advantages. Indeed, it promises to deliver everything economists are for and it promises to remove at least a large part of what they are against.

Can they deliver? To address this, one must look more closely at what the deregulators are proposing. At the risk of oversimplifying, all deregulation scenarios can be placed into one of two categories—traditional deregulation scenarios and the Massachusetts Institute of Technology (MIT) scenario.

**The Traditional Deregulation Scenario**

The traditional deregulation scenario envisions an industry composed of: independent competitive generating companies, free to sell at unregulated rates and maximize profits; regional transmission monopolies that are government owned or regulated; and local distribution monopolies, also government owned or regulated. The traditional approach would rely upon a combination of long-term contracts and substantial central control to achieve the integration of functions that now are performed by large horizontally and vertically integrated utilities. Competitive generating companies and the buyers would negotiate long-term contracts aimed at providing the seller with adequate assurance of a market to permit raising capital at reasonable costs (thus replacing the present economic function of franchises) and providing the buyer with an assured source of supply (replacing the present public-service obligation). The day-to-day operations of generating plants would be coordinated by the transmission entity which would centrally dispatch all generation in the region. Beyond this, in some traditional scenarios the transmission entity would make load forecasts for the whole region, contract for all needed generating capacity, and sell at uniform rates to all distributors in the region. In other less well-defined traditional scenarios, individual distributors or groups of distributors are envisioned as shopping for their own power supplies, while the transmission firm simply coordinates operations and conveys purchases to individual distributors.

The proposition this chapter suggests is that the traditional deregulation scenario either will not work, or if it is patched up enough to make it work, it will not offer much in the way of economic benefits. Consider how this scenario handles each of the economic problems faced by the electric-generating business. First, how is the investment in generating plants called forth? Answer: through the use of long-term contracts with comprehensive price escalators. No financial analyst has stated that capital can be raised to finance a billion-dollar plant (coming on line a decade later, subject to substantial environmental controls, and capable of producing only a single output) without vertical-ownership ties or full payout (generally long-term) take-or-pay contracts. But such contracts present several economic problems. If the price escalators are comprehensive enough—that is, if cost-plus contracts are used—then the incentives to construct a generating plant efficiently are destroyed. Beyond this, it is extremely difficult to imagine specifying a contract fully enough to control all critical dimensions of generating unit performance—its capital costs, thermal efficiency, outage rates, fuel flexibility, and load-following capability. Ask the following question: if such contracts could be adequately specified and if investors stood willing to finance generating plants on any basis other than cost plus, why are they not now in the marketplace? Presumably, the architect-engineering firms that design and construct power plants and the equipment manufacturers that supply the turbines and boilers are competitive, profit-maximizing entities. Why do they not offer to construct and operate plants for existing utilities on a competitive contract basis? Capital-starved utilities could hardly be expected to turn them away. And regulators should be anxious to approve at least some such contracts in order to create yardsticks against which to measure the performance of regulated utilities.

Second, how does the traditional scenario handle the problem of coordinating the operations of individual generating units? Answer: it either assumes that contracts among competing generators would accomplish the coordination or that the transmission entity would centrally dispatch the system.[3] Contracting would provide an excellent vehicle for collusion among generating companies, would provide for endless disputes among companies (a magnification of the conflicts that occur today within power pools), and would destroy the incentives to solve day-to-day operating problems in the optimal way from a system point of view. Central dispatch by the transmission entity, combined with a scheme to allocate the savings resulting from such dispatching, presumably could solve the coordination problem but only at the expense of a competitive operating market.

Third, how does the traditional deregulation scenario solve the problem of jointly optimizing generation and transmission planning? Answer: it does not. Moreover, it never even addresses it. To deal with this problem, one could create a central-planning agency to designate how, when, and where generation and transmission facilities will be built. In theory, this coordination also could be achieved if it were possible to set transmission prices equal to marginal costs and to engage in an elaborate scheme of side payments among generating companies. For reasons too complex to delve into,[4] no one has yet figured out how to set such prices.

Fourth, how does the traditional deregulation scenario solve the problem of reasonably matching electric load to generating capacity? Answer: it does not pay too much attention to this problem. The transmission entity may be assumed to forecast load and acquire capacity for the whole region. Alternatively, it can be assumed that individual distribution companies will make their own load forecasts and plan for their own capacity to meet load. But to achieve accurate load forecasting requires the integration of all load data in the region. To match capacity to load requires a set of arrangements to permit individual companies to rely upon one another's capacity to meet unexpectedly large demands. In the end, at the very least, one would expect large numbers of distributors to band together into joint-load forecasting and purchasing agencies.

In sum, when one plays out the traditional deregulation scenario, the result is not a very appealing market structure. Competition would have very little room in which to operate. Regional authorities or joint agencies would be created to make such crucial decisions as how much and what general type of capacity must be acquired, what reliability standards must be met, how the transmission system will be designed, and how generating companies will be operated. Indeed, at the bulk-power level, it is not clear that individual decision making would have any role to play. A consensus would be necessary to support any large-scale generating project. At most, the distributor's decision would be limited to which of several groups to join in contracting for capacity. Regulation or government ownership would continue to prevail at the distribution level, unaided by any substantial competition among distributors. There is nothing to suggest that the interaction of distributor groups with individual generating companies would unleash the forces of competition. The industry structure would be one in which a small number of groups of regulated or government-owned distributors faced a small number of closely coordinated generating companies in an environment where long-term cost-plus contracts and guaranteed passthroughs are financial necessities. Such is not the stuff of which effective competition is made.

### The Massachusetts Institute of Technology (MIT)
### Deregulation Scenario

The MIT deregulation scenario clearly is the most innovative approach to be suggested in years.[5] It differs from the traditional scenario in that in lieu of contractual and regulatory control, it relies to a great extent on market forces and consumer and producer responses to varying prices.

In the MIT scenario, a regulated or government-owned regional transmission company would purchase energy from competing, separate generating companies and would sell to all distributors in the region. The transmission entity would not contract with generating companies for long-term capacity commitments. Instead, it would purchase energy on a spot basis at prices varying every five minutes. Computers would allow continuously floating price signals to be communicated to generating companies. Large customers and distributors, for whom sophisticated metering is economically feasible, would pay the varying generation spot price plus the necessary transmission markup.

How would spot prices be determined? The transmission system would set a single price during each five minutes just high enough to induce the desired amount of generation.[6] The transmission company would try to set price equal to the marginal running cost of the marginal generating unit at the desired level of production. All else being equal, a profit-maximizing generating company would bring its unit on line any time the spot price rose above its incremental start-up and running costs. As a result, economic behavior by individual generating companies should mimic central dispatch.

A generating-unit failure would drive up the spot price instantaneously, thus calling forth higher cost, hitherto idle, generation. If demand threatened to exceed supply at a price high enough to call forth all available generation, the spot price would be raised to whatever level was required to depress demand to the acceptable level. Since generating companies and customers face the same spot price (aside from the transmission and distribution markup), high prices needed to discourage demand mean high prices paid to generating companies and thus high profits for generating companies. This means that when capacity generally is tight and demand frequently presses upon available supply, the generation business becomes very profitable and firms should be induced to build additional generation. It is this profit lure that should guide investment behavior. Those entrepreneurs who guess capacity needs correctly and build cost-effective units will earn high profits; those who guess wrong may go bankrupt.

Under this plan large industrial customers and distributors would pay continuously varying spot prices, curtailing less essential uses as the spot price rises. Prices would, of course, be much simpler—there would be no demand charge, no customer charge, no backup charge, and no customer classes.[7] The MIT scenario also envisions the existence of various independent middlemen and brokers who would package unit entitlements, like mutual funds, for investors and offer long-term contracts to customers who want firm prices.

Does the MIT scenario offer us a workable alternative to the traditional deregulation approach? Engineers who have looked at the proposal have been unable to suggest any reason why the complex moment-to-moment and day-to-day coordination problems presented by a modern electric-power grid could not be handled in the MIT scenario. Due to lack of knowledge about competitors' scheduling plans, some inefficiency may creep into the daily commitment of units to generate and into maintenance scheduling; but the economic cost of such inefficiency may be very low. Aside from this, if one assumes that a large enough number of generating companies will exist in a region to assure independent action, then the MIT approach should lead to economic dispatch of units and provide a strong incentive for individual generating companies to operate their units efficiently, all the while leaving those companies free to design and operate their own units. This represents a potentially major improvement over the traditional deregulator's approach to coordinating operations.

But whether the system will expand in an optimal way over time seems less clear. Consider first that the MIT scenario depends critically on unimpeded entry into the generating business. If environmentally acceptable sites are in short supply or if need for power hearings continue to be required, free entry will not be possible and the MIT system will not operate.[8]

Second, because generating investments under the MIT scenario would be extraordinarily risky (there being absolutely no assurance of a market), investors would demand large risk premiums, thus significantly increasing the industry's capital costs. The high spot prices needed to call forth marginal investment would create a grave political danger of reimposing regulation to control risks and returns. Alternatively, unless such contracts were prohibited, buyers and sellers both could be expected to seek long-term contracts in order to minimize risks. Particularly, it might be expected that regulated transmission and distribution entities would opt for the quiet life offered by long-term contractual relationships, thus undermining the MIT scenario. Further, the high cost of risky capital could be expected to lead to major shifts in the types of units built, tilting toward units with lower capital costs, shorter lead times and higher operating costs. Unless the market is assumed to handle risks efficiently, such changes would not necessarily be optimal.

Third, fuel markets would be adversely affected. Generating companies would find it very risky to offer long-term take-or-pay contracts to fuel suppliers in order to support the opening of a new mine, for example. Correspondingly, without the assurance of a long-term source of a specific fuel type, generating units would have to be designed to handle a wider variety of fuels.

Fourth, the industry described in the MIT scenario would seem to possess many characteristics ascribed to destructively competitive industries, including very high fixed costs and demand subject to fluctuations over the business cycle but extremely inelastic in the short run.[9]

Beyond this, the MIT scenario does share several problems with the traditional deregulation approach. It is not clear that transmission prices can be formulated so as to promote joint optimization of the generation and transmission systems. Moreover, the absence of central planning to match capacity additions to requirements inevitably will lead to inefficiencies. During the times of excess capacity, the cost of those inefficiencies will be borne largely by private-generating companies, but when capacity is short, the customer will pay.

**Political Feasibility and Transition Problems**

There are several key problem areas. First, any deregulation scenario hinges upon preempting a substantial piece of state regulatory authority over the electric-utility business. The political feasibility of doing that in the near future seems remote. Second, an ever-growing portion of the electric-generating capacity in this country is owned by state and local governments or by cooperative utilities, each utilizing subsidized capital to finance generating-unit construction. Any realistic deregulation scenario would have to shut off those sources of capital and perhaps even attempt to prevent state and local government authorities from constructing new generation (or condemning and taking over regional transmission facilities). Third, most deregulators concede that under deregulation, prices would rise and perhaps very substantially, at least in the near future. Implementing any deregulation plan thus involves selling the concept of higher prices to the same political establishment that now is financially starving the industry in order to hold rates down. Finally, any effort to vertically and horizontally disintegrate the present industry so as to move quickly toward deregulation will involve massive income transfers. Utilities owning hydroelectric, nuclear, and efficient coal-fired units would tend to be big gainers, while utilities dependent upon oil would be big losers.

**Conclusion**

In sum, as the ideas have evolved thus far, the deregulators do not offer us the promised land. Instead, the choice is as follows: a scenario that will work, but is not deregulated, not very competitive, and not politically feasible, or a scenario that is more completely deregulated, is potentially more competitive, but leaves us at this point with grave questions regarding its workability and political feasibility.

What then should economists be for? They should return to their principles and see what can be accomplished without restructuring. Specifically, they should be for the following policy initiatives.

1. The elimination, at least at the margin, of the tax- and capital-raising subsidies conveyed to government-owned and cooperative electric utilities. There can be no excuse for continuing a program of massive subsidies that results in significantly underpricing the electricity received by one-fourth of the population without regard to their need, stimulates those consumers to utilize 20 percent more electricity than used by the average customer not so subsidized, leads to ever-expanding government ownership of electric facilities, and thus creates an industry structure extremely resistant to change. There undoubtedly are many ways of approaching the subsidy problem. The industry should consider replacing all present federal taxation of electric-utility income and payments to security holders with a uniform excise tax designed to raise the same amount of revenue. This tax would be levied on every kilowatt-hour sold to retail customers, regardless of whether they are served by a privately owned, government-owned, or cooperative utility. Not only would this go far toward eliminating the subsidy enjoyed by government-owned and coopertive utilities, it would greatly simplify accounting by and regulation of privately owned utilities by eliminating controversies over treatment of accelerated depreciation, investment tax credits, and the like.

2. The complete deregulation of the prices charged to large new industrial customers. New industrial customers have many options. They can choose among various locations for a new plant, they can select electrical equipment for their plant that offers varying combinations of price and electrical efficiency, they can alter production processes to utilize fuels instead of electricity, and they can more effectively implement conservation measures. In addition, they could be given the right to have power transmitted in to them from an adjacent supplier if it offers more attractive terms and conditions. With so many options available to the large new customer, why not let the market, rather than a regulator, determine the rate?[10]

3. The full marginal-cost pricing of electricity, immediately and with an excess-profits tax, if thought necessary for political acceptability. Such fundamental questions as how much additional generating capacity must be built in the next ten years and are large scale capital-intensive generating plants really economical will continue to plague the industry until prices are permitted to do in this industry what they do best—allocate resources by subjecting consumption and production decisions to a market test.

4. The expansion of the small producer provisions of the Public Utilities Regulatory Policies Act (PURPA). Under PURPA, utilities are compelled to purchase power at avoided costs from qualifying cogenerators and small power producers. If administered correctly, this should assure that the vertically integrated structure of the existing electric-utility industry does not impede the introduction of small-scale technologies that offer lower marginal costs. Perhaps the industry should periodically raise the size of qualifying small generators from the present eighty megawatt limit (as well as removing limitations on the types of units built) as experience accumulates with integrating output into the system.

5. The creation of monetary incentives for utilities to operate their existing units at maximum efficiency.[11] For example, one admittedly imperfect approach would be to permit utilities to keep as profits, say, 10 percent of all savings realized as a result of short-term (economy) energy transactions with neighboring utilities.

6. The development of mechanisms for tapping the sources of capital that the deregulators promise are out there. If investors will come forward to construct a generating plant on the promise of being able to sell power at short-run system marginal cost as the MIT scenario suggests, they should be encouraged to show up with their plans. Given the current financial condition of the industry, it would be difficult to imagine any utility or regulator turning them away. Beyond that, one should try to tap the capital source the traditional deregulators promise is there. If investors will support plants on anything less than a long-term cost-plus contract basis, and if contracts can be specified fully enough for the buyer to know what he is buying, then let the contracts be presented. If the regulator will approve such a contract, it is difficult to imagine that capital-starved utilities would shy away from it.

**Notes**

1. Some analysts believe that competitive entry by very small power producers using unconventional technologies is feasible. See Roger W. Sant, *The Least-Cost Energy Strategy* (Pittsburgh: Carnegie University Press, 1979). If it were to turn out that small scale noncapital-intensive, short-lead time units were the economically optimum choice, much of the argument found in the remainder of this paper would not follow.

2. This is not to deny that generation tied into a regional transmission grid might not economically be transportable over, say, a three hundred-mile distance. Even so, the scope of this market is much more limited than typically would be the case for major capital-intensive industries.

3. The transmission company thus would be responsible for meeting load, providing proper reserves, regulating voltage, maintaining system

stability, and coordinating maintenance. This would require that the transmission entity not only dictate when units would operate, but in addition, have some control over the design of units.

4. For a more complete discussion of this problem, see Joe D. Pace, "Comments Prepared For the California Public Utilities Commission Workshop on Electric Generation Deregulation," (July 30-31, 1981), pp. 5-8.

5. Bennett W. Golub, Richard D. Tabors, Roger E. Bohn, and Fred C. Schweppe, "Deregulating the Electric Utility Industry: Discussion and a Proposed Approach," MIT Energy Laboratory Working Paper No. MIT-EL81-043, (July 1981).

6. Spinning reserves and kilovars would be purchased via separate spot prices. Also, some geographic price differentiation would be introduced in order to maintain proper voltages and minimize line losses throughout the transmission system.

7. Because of high metering and communications costs, continuously varying spot prices would not apply to residential or small commercial customers.

8. Such hearings require the proposed constructor of a generating unit to demonstrate that enough demand exists to require the addition of capacity and that the particular unit being proposed is the best among available alternatives for meeting the requirement.

9. See Frederic M. Scherer, *Industrial Market Structure and Economic Performance* (Chicago: Rand McNally, 1980), pp. 212-220.

10. In fairness, I should point out that there are drawbacks to this proposal. Charging market-determined rates only to newly locating industrial customers may tend to discourage mobility. Also, the industrial customer would have to make a relatively long-term arrangement with the supplier in order to protect itself against rate changes imposed after it committed to locate in a given area. Finally, it would be unrealistic not to recognize that politically sensitive state legislators and regulators desirous of attracting new industry may interfere indirectly in the rate-setting process.

11. For a discussion of recent evidence relating declining generating-unit availability to low allowed rates of return on capital, see the expert report by Marie Corio, "Heat Rates and Availability: The Use of Econometric Analysis in Comparing Electric Generating Unit Performance," (New York: National Economic Research Associates, Inc., Summer 1981).

# 21 Issues in Deregulation of Electric Generation

*William R. Hughes*

Increasing dissatisfaction with the present system of electric-utility regulation and a sense of urgency concerning the weakened financial condition of the industry have led to a search for workable approaches to deregulation of electric generation. This chapter relates the goals of deregulation to the problems it seeks to solve, examines some critical problem areas, and relates them to feasible deregulation structures.

In designing a program of deregulation it is necessary to consider much more than the expected workability of the deregulated market once it becomes established. Transition is important: divestitures and other major adjustments raise complex issues, require years to implement, are costly to reverse, and involve steps which must be taken before deregulation benefits occur. Credibility is also important; even if experts reach consensus on the workability of deregulation, legislators and practitioners must also be convinced. There is also the question of risk: because the consequences of any deregulation program are not completely certain, methods of reducing risk are important.

To select and design the deregulation programs that are most likely to succeed, it is important to understand the issues bearing upon how each program will work in practice. For each deregulation program, it is necessary to understand as well as possible how the generation market will work, what legislative or regulatory changes are to be involved, how transition is to be accomplished, and where the greatest risks or problems lie.

## Goals of Deregulation: Motivating Problems

Before analyzing deregulation alternatives, it is important to have a clear understanding of deregulation objectives. Specifically, what problems of the industry have motivated the proponents of deregulation to recommend it, and what criteria should be used either to determine whether deregulation will succeed or choose between two alternative approaches to deregulation.

Advocates of deregulation include some prominent regulators and civil servants; lawyers, economists, and engineers in universities; and electric-utility executives. It should not be surprising that individual proponents

289

differ greatly over just what the problem is. Indeed, advocates of apparently similar deregulation schemes have very different reasons for wanting the same results. Taken as a whole, there appear to be six interrelated goals of deregulation: relief from the industry's financial distress; resolution of regulatory dilemmas concerning risk bearing; improved incentives for investment decisions; improved reliability; improved allocative efficiency more generally; and additional benefits of competition.

## Financial Relief

The current wave of deregulation can be attributed in large part to the financial crisis of the electric power industry, abetted by double-digit inflation and other sources of cost escalation that have increased the cost of service more rapidly than regulators have been willing or able to allow increases in rates. If the root problem were strictly financial, then the obvious remedy would be to allow higher rates of return. Deregulation, once in place, is one means of achieving this. A quicker, more direct method would be for regulators to allow rates of return high enough to attract capital, either directly or through the aid of modifications in rate-making conventions, such as inclusion of construction work in progress (CWIP) in the rate base. Advocates of deregulation are characteristically skeptical of rate reform or more enlightened rate regulation as a solution. They point to the very strong pressures on regulators to hold rates down; to public skepticism of the legitimacy of rising costs, especially when associated with cost overruns or abandonment of partially completed facilities; to the short duration of the commissioners' terms of office; and to the tendency of commissions to select rates that resolve uncertainties over cost of service in a generally downward-biased direction. These patterns appear strongly entrenched: reform would effectively require a change of heart for regulators (and their successors as terms expire) in many, perhaps most, states.

## Risk Bearing

In principle, public-utility regulation allows rates high enough to provide a fair return (in effect, the cost of capital) for any investment prudently made. In times of stability such as the 1950s and 1960s, virtually any major investment by a utility that was not an obvious mistake was assured of becoming part of the rate base, and the associated operating costs would become part of the cost of service. Beginning in the 1970s, the costs of generating facilities became increasingly out of control. Lead times for nuclear units more than doubled from 1965 to 1980; for coal-fired units they may have tripled. Retrofits of plants under construction or already in operation were often imposed for environmental and safety reasons. Reduced growth in demand and rapidly escalating costs led to cancellation of plants under construction. Regulators found themselves faced with decisions concerning who should bear risks of unneeded facilities, whether cancelled or not, and of making judgments as to whether all the costs of new generating units with large overruns were prudently incurred. For the regulator, this sort of decision is a no-win situation. If the cost is disallowed, he aggravates the utility's financial difficulty and may thereby threaten its ability to provide reliable service over the long run. If the cost is routinely allowed, he will sometimes be imposing costs on the ratepayer that would not be part of a competitive market price. Regulators such as John E. Bryson, president of the California public utility commission, emphasize that there is nothing in their training or background that gives them or anyone else the ability to resolve the question of who should bear the applicable risks on a case-by-case basis.[1] Deregulation of generation is attractive as a solution to risk bearing, because the operation of a well-working generation market, if feasible, would provide an objective and economical process for sorting out the bearing of risks of investment in generation. The owner of a generating facility with costs out of line with general best practice would suffer a commensurate loss, just as industrial firms on unregulated markets have to absorb their overruns. At the same time, if factors outside the industry's control [such as the Nuclear Regulatory Commission (NRC) and environmental regulation] are raising the industry's costs and risks, the general level of those increases will be reflected in competitively determined rates.

### Incentives for Investment Decisions

Particularly in the context of a financial squeeze that makes new investment decisions unprofitable, the utility's incentives to add to, modify, or replace its facilities may be distorted. Replacement or major modification of old oil-fired equipment may often be thwarted because its present high operating costs are readily flowed through to rates, but the investment in new equipment to burn coal could not be expected to earn as adequate return. The electric-power industry has entered an era of moderate growth, much lower than the accustomed rate of the last twenty years. During this period, decisions to retire, replace, and modify old plants will be as important as decisions to add new facilities. Deregulation offers an attractive means of providing incentives for economically efficient retirement, replacement, modifications, and capacity expansion decisions, provided that deregulation can successfully create a pricing environment with the performance characteristics of the competitive market.

*Reliability*

Under regulation, reliability or continuity of service is a public good. Interruption of service or apparent shortages of capacity are the subject of regulatory investigation. For the most part, ratepayers are not offered a variety of options combining different levels of reliability with appropriate rates. Instead, they buy electricity at the offered rate on the assumption that service reliability will be at the accustomed standard, typically one designed to make service interruptions very rare events. Actual reliability criteria and reliability planning reflect a mixture of rules of thumb adopted by power engineers, regulatory influence, and the utility's perception of its own business self-interest.

Prior to the 1970s, when electric utilities were able to sell their equity at prices in excess of book value, the incentives operating on utilities favored high levels of reliability. By planning for reliability levels at least as high as the regulators' standard, they could minimize regulatory criticism, and they could also earn a profitable return on the capacity needed for reliability.

In a regime of persistent high inflation and allowed returns persistently below the cost of capital, the incentives for reliability operate differently. Regulatory pressure for high reliability is tempered by a desire to keep down rate increases. More important, utilities' ability and incentives to make new investments are seriously hampered. Either because they cannot raise the needed capital, or because new investments would further dilute the equity of the stockholders, utilities seek to economize on investment. One of the means of economizing on new investment is to rely more extensively on conservation, load management, and lower reserve margins. In addition to the tendency to reduce reserve margins, the weak financial condition of utilities induced by regulation can lead to a deterioration of the condition of an existing plant as retrofit and maintenance outlays are deferred and an old plant is utilitzed more intensively.

Resolution of the financial crisis of utilities by regulatory means would also lead to higher levels of reliability. Deregulation, if it led to effectively competitive generation markets, would also eliminate the present threat to reliability. The level of reliability would reflect the amount of capacity that could profitably be provided in the competitive generation market. That level need not be the same as experienced under regulation in times of utility financial health. Different deregulation schemes have different implications for reliability. There is a need for rigorous analysis of the reliability implications of different deregulation schemes.

*Allocative Efficiency*

Whereas regulators, utility executives, and other practitioners in the utility fields have emphasized specific financial and regulatory issues in their advocacy of deregulation, the economists proposing deregulation have emphasized economic efficiency. Economic efficiency is a global concept. Its purview includes all of the aspects of incentives, reliability, and risk bearing discussed. There are also additional aspects of economic efficiency that are pertinent to deregulation. The most important of these concern the relation between generating costs and rates over time and also for utilities serving nearby service areas.

Under the present regulatory structure, retail rates are typically based on average embedded costs. The operation of original-cost regulation results in a front-end loaded time path of rates. That is, the recovery of costs of an investment occurs quickly. In an inflationary period, the cost of service of old equipment does not rise; in real terms, it declines. If that same equipment were producing for a competitive industry, the price would rise over time under comparable conditions. This front-end loading phenomenon of original-cost regulation leads to distortions on the time path of electricity prices over long periods and has been an important contributing source of the financial crisis being experienced by electric utilities.

The spatial pattern of electricity rates is also out of line with allocative efficiency and the geographic pattern of pricing that would occur with a competitive market. In a competitive market the geography of prices reflects transportation costs and production costs in different areas. Large discrepancies in price between adjacent locations are rarely feasible. Utilities, pricing on the embedded costs of their own facilities, frequently show large discrepancies because of differences in access to old facilities, particularly hydro, with low embedded costs, because of different degrees of dependency on natural gas, and, it seems likely, because of differences in managerial efficiency. The recent radical increases in the cost of new nuclear and coal-fired facilities and the very high prices of oil since 1979 have led some very large rate discrepancies for neighboring utilities. The effect of a deregulated market for generation would be to create a unified price structure. Because utilities and power pools already dispatch and interchange most of the country's electric energy on a least-cost basis, it is doubtful whether there are any major allocative inefficiencies in the geographic pattern of generation directly associated with the retail rates, and retail customers would probably be little affected in their location decisions. However, very large rate effects would occur and the effect of deregulation in the direction of rate equalization ought to lead to more rational energy-conservation decisions.

Perhaps the most important aspect of the impact of deregulation on retail cost-price relationships is the effect of replacing the present embedded average cost of generation with its market price, which is effectively a marginal-cost price. With 60 percent or more of the total cost of electricity at retail being priced at wholesale on a competitive basis, one can expect a strong incentive to design retail rates and service offerings or take advantage of the prices and (in all probability) variety of service offerings that would be presented by the competitive market.

*Additional Competitive Benefit*

A final goal of deregulation, perhaps the most important, is to open up generation markets to the freedom and vigor of competition. Advocates of deregulating electric generation make much of the notion of the free market as an invitation to innovate and take risks, as a spur to better managerial efficiency, and as a generally buoyant and exciting business environment. Regulation at its best prevents excessive earnings, but it can do little in providing positive incentives.

This chapter discusses some key issues in the context of two prototypes, a vertically disintegrated arrangement requiring a major reorganization of the industry and a more incremental partial-deregulation arrangement. These are broadly representative of the two basic approaches taken in proposals for deregulation.

## Prototype Deregulation Structures

A fully developed deregulation arrangement involves a complex combination of legal, regulatory, and organizational factors. To analyze how a particular deregulation arrangement would work, it is necessary to identify the relevant factors and understand how they would affect the market. The two prototype structures discussed here—vertically disintegrated structures and structures that involve incremental change—are described in terms of some of the main factors affecting the operation of deregulated markets. To preserve focus this chapter does not go into a number of relevant factors, such as the tax status of publicly owned and cooperative electric systems, the public-power preference laws and the Public Utility Holding Company Act. Table 21-1 presents some of the elements of a deregulation structure that should be considered in a reasonably complete analysis.

The vertically disintegrated structure has been popular among proponents of deregulation, mainly because it isolates the generation stage, where competition is feasible, from the other two stages, which are generally understood to be natural monopolies. Transmission and distribution would also be separately owned under this structure; this separation would help assure competition among distributors in the generation market.

The vertically disintegrated prototype is the favorite of deregulation proponents whose starting point is an ideal structure. The prototype has

**Table 21-1**
**Elements of a Deregulation Structure**

*Status of rate regulation for generation*

All generation deregulated.
Partial deregulation.
 All new facilities deregulated.
 Deregulation of cogeneration and small generating facilities.
 Allow entry by generation or distribution entities into cogeneration, solar, and other
  small decentralized sources as long as rates paid are comparable to avoided-cost rates
  paid to outside sources.
 Limited deregulation, for example, of unit contracts.

*Regulatory status of licensing and entry*

Retailer must show need to include purchased generation in cost of service.
Generating entity must meet general environmental and health criteria but no showing
 of need.
Same previous criteria except that generating entity must show evidence that output can
 be marketed.
Same previous criteria except that generating entity must show need.
In combination with the three previous cases: deregulate electric-utility entry into
 cogeneration and decentralized sources.

*Regulatory status of transmission rates and access*

Reorganization to regional publicly owned or regulated common carriers.
Ownership of existing lines unchanged, common-carrier requirement for existing capacity.
Present structure regulatory status of access to transmission.

*Vertical organization*

Existing structure: vertically integrated systems use transfer prices for generation at
 market level.
Incremental modification of existing structure by deregulating only those generating
 facilities not owned by the transmission or distribution entity.
Complete vertical disintegration: specialization in generation, transmission, distribution.
Partial vertical disintegration. Compulsory exits from generation by transmission or
 distribution entities.

*Status of public and cooperative entities*

No changes.
Reduce or eliminate tax and preference advantages of publics and cooperatives.

*Status of restrictions of utility diversification*

No changes in Public Utility Holding Company Act (PUHCA), National Energy Act
 (NEA).
Remove or reduce restrictions on electric generating or distribution companies.

many variations, but for the most part these variants have the same major
problems and issues in common. The incremental approach trades off additional regulation of transmission for deregulation of generation. Its point of
departure is the present structure, and its objective is to introduce deregulation without a radical overhaul of the industry's organization.

*Vertically Disintegrated Structure*

A sample of proponents who have set forth proposals for vertically disintegrated deregulation structures includes an engineering-economics group at MIT, the president of a major utility, an attorney, and two academic economists.[2] There are important differences in specific features of the individual proposals, but they all share the essential features of vertically disintegrated deregulation.

In this structure there would have to be a sufficient number of generating firms to assure competition. It appears that the number of potential competitors nationally is more than sufficient. In addition to the generating organizations spun off by the major utilities, the engineering construction firms and others are potential entrants. As long as entry is kept free, this large number of potential competitors would assure competition even though only a few firms might be operating major plants in any given region.

Transmission would be controlled by a single entity in each region: either an investor-owned public utility or a publicly owned entity. The transmission entity would act as a middleman between generating firms and distributors, coordinate the operation of the network and, of course, provide energy transportation from generating sites to distribution points.

The essence of how the generation market would work under vertically disintegrated deregulation is in the role of the transmission entity. Proposals for deregulation differ in the mechanics of how the market would work and in the specific middleman role of the transmission entity.

In the system developed by Golub, Tabors, Bohn, and Scheweppe at MIT, the transmission entity orchestrates a spot market that operates on a near-instantaneous basis.[3] By posting the market-clearing price at which it will buy or sell, separated by a differential which is the price of transmission, the transmission entity sends the market signals generators and distributors need to make their supply and demand decisions. In its management of the market the transmission entity also orchestrates decentralized decisions by generators and distributors to maintain load-frequency control, schedule planned maintenance, and provide operating reserves. Implementation of the system would require sophisticated electronic systems utilizing homeostatic control. Years of testing and trial implementation are likely to be needed before homeostatic control can be considered a proven system for commercial application to large scale regional networks.

A significant feature of the MIT deregulation structure is that the transmission entity engages exclusively on spot market and futures transactions. Contracting for intermediate or long-term transactions would arise only as an activity of middlemen who would act as packagers for generating firms or distributors who preferred long-term arrangements to dealing directly in the spot market.

At the other extreme is the deregulation proposal made by Matthew Cohen.[4] Cohen's transmission entity provides bundled retail service to distributors and leases and operates generating facilities owned by generating firms. The emphasis is on central management and long-term arrangements. Other proponents of vertically disintegrated deregulation opt for an intermediate mixture. The transmission entity buys, sells, or acts as a broker for a spectrum of arrangements that include both term contracts and spot transactions.

The vertically disintegrated deregulation proposals all have several virtues. First, they would assure arms-length transactions between distributors and generating firms. Arms length would help assure competitive choices by buyers and also reduce the likelihood of regulatory review at the retail level that would, in effect, regulate generation. Second, the vertically disintegrated structure would avoid difficulties in the use of transmission that occur whenever the owner of transmission is also a competitor of other buyers or sellers of generation. Third, by breaking up the dominant position of existing electric utilities in generation, vertical disintegration could assure a relatively unconcentrated market for generation.

The virtues of vertical disintegration would be purchased at a very high price in the cost and difficulty of transition, and there would also be efficiency losses in the coordination of transmission and generation planning and development. There would have to be extensive exchanges of property that might require a decade or more to effect. There would be difficult problems of compensation, valuation, and rate treatment of divested assets. There could also be some transitional windfall losses by utilities whose current retail rates are above the level implied by deregulation, though these losses could be mitigated by phasing deregulation. The difficulty of implementing vertically disintegrated deregulation carries with it a dilemma. On the one hand, the extreme changes called for are likely to be adopted only in response to extreme events calling for extraordinary action. Continued deterioration of the financial condition of the industry may well be such an event. Yet on the other hand, the time required to bring vertical disintegration into effect suggests that deregulation would be unlikely to bring much financial relief to electric utilities for at least five and perhaps more than ten years.

*Structures Involving Incremental Change*

In view of the difficulties of implementing far-reaching reform, it makes sense to examine alternatives which involve less radical change and which could be implemented fairly quickly. Well-developed proposals of this type are rare. To be workable, a deregulation plan must cope with the problems that led to vertical disintegration proposals: access to transmission by all generators and distributors, assurance of competitive prices accepted by retail regulators, and assurance that distributors will be willing to buy from the most economical generating source, no matter who owns it.

Incremental deregulation on a very limited basis poses few problems and no severe ones. One proposal, championed by former Federal Energy Regulatory Commission (FERC) commissioner George Hall, is to eliminate FERC regulatory review of unit contracts among utilities within a designated size range. The rationale is that in these interutility transactions, the balance of bargaining power among the parties does at least as good a job of moderating the terms of trade as FERC's time-consuming review of the details, which leaves the parties in uncertainty until the transaction is approved, modified to meet FERC's approval, or disapproved. This reform would require only a FERC rule making and would reduce regulation without increasing it elsewhere. However, the benefits would also be very limited: incentives to coordinate or transact would be improved, and the process of consummating coordinated-capacity additions would be slightly eased, but there would be no noticeable impact on the problems that lie at the heart of the interest in deregulation.

Another incremental change that has received wide support is to allow electric utilities the same privileges with respect to cogeneration and small scale or decentralized generation that is now available to others under section 210 of the Public Utility Regulatory Policy Act (PURPA).[5] A variant to this approach is to enlarge the size limits for small generation to increase the amount of deregulated generation. In either event electric utilities would be free to enter into cogeneration or small-scale generation and sell to themselves at a rate based upon and presumably close to the electric utility's avoided costs. The rationale behind this form of deregulation is that it stimulates the supply of cogeneration and small-scale generation and acts to reduce the marginal cost (avoided cost) of the utility as the deregulated supply displaces higher cost sources. The magnitude of actual effects depends on the elasticity of supply of cogeneration and small-scale generation. Most informed observers of the power industry and cogeneration believe that only a small proportion of the industry's generation is likely to be accounted for from cogeneration or small sources as presently defined by PURPA.

To have a substantial impact, the PURPA approach would have to be extended to include a much larger size limit. A number of proponents of vertical disintegration, including Richard Tabors, have recommended extensions of the PURPA approach as a natural transition to full deregulation, but they have not been very specific about how the market would work under the transitional structure before vertical disintegration could be accomplished. It is notable that even deregulation skeptics or opponents have suggested that if deregulation is to be accomplished, extending PURPA avoided-cost approaches is the natural direction in which to develop.[6] The partial deregulation scheme developed at the end of this chapter is at least first cousin to an extension of the PURPA approach, and it uses a generation-pricing approach that is extremely similar to the pricing approach recommended by Tabors and his colleagues at MIT.

If the deregulated generation were small scale and involved little interconnection effort, as is the case with most generators presently covered by section 210 of PURPA, there would be no serious problems of the sort that motivate recommendation for vertical disintegration. However, to obtain material benefits from deregulation, the scope of included generation must be large enough to induce an elastic supply at prices reasonably close to an efficient utility's own costs of expansion with equipment of efficient scale. Once the scope of deregulated generation is increased to that point, all of the problems that vertical disintegration approaches to deregulation were designed to solve would appear. In other words, to gain material benefits from deregulation without vertical disintegration, it is necessary to devise alternative solutions to the problems of arms length and access to transmission so that markets for generation would exhibit adequately competitive performance.

In general, advocates of deregulating generation without vertical disintegration have embraced added regulation as a substitute for structural changes that would assure competition. Two main threads run through the suggestions for added regulation to achieve the incremental or partial deregulation; one is to use common-carrier regulation of transmission to increase access to transmission. The other is to broaden the approach taken in the cogeneration and small-generation provisions of PURPA, where each utility must purchase this unregulated generation on a price based on its avoided cost. The prices and purchasing rules need not be the same as those used in PURPA, but the basic approach is similar.

Common-carrier status for transmission addresses the ability of competing generating sources to participate in the market, and the PURPA prices standard is designed to prevent the purchasing utility from controlling the price of generation. It also would provide an objective price for the utility's own generation. Adding extensive new regulation runs the danger of creating new regulatory problems as serious as the old ones they are intended to solve.

Before examining the partial deregulation approach further by developing a particular scheme, it is helpful to discuss some key issues which bear upon the workability of deregulation: entry into generation, the relation of generation to retail regulation, transmission issues, and the handling of long-term commitments.

## Licensing and Entry

Freedom of entry helps assure effective competition by providing independent competitive alternatives to the offerings of existing sellers. The potential for entry is essential to effective competition in markets that are relatively concentrated, as markets for electric generation are likely to be under any deregulation scenario that does not include extensive divestiture of generating properties. Entry is particularly important if deregulation is confined to new generating facilities. Given the moderate rates of demand that are expected in most regions, only a few major base-load units will be added in the 1980s or 1990s in the typical regional market. Competition would come mainly from firms that compete for the chance to build and operate these few units, most of which would not actually construct their proposed units. Nationally, the generating market can support a relatively large number of firms. These firms would be potential entrants in any region.

In view of the importance of entry conditions, the licensing of new generating facilities for environmental purposes deserves much more attention than it has received in deregulation discussions. Licensing of facilities for environmental, health, or safety purposes affects many industries generally viewed as effectively competitive or at least sufficiently competitive to enjoy deregulated status. Whether or not licensing is compatible with effective competition in a particular case depends on the behavior of the licensing authority and the licensing criteria which are applied. If the criteria are completely objective and unambiguous, then all entrants meeting the standard would compete with one another, and licensing would not impair the competitive process. The regulation of taxicabs in the District of Columbia is a case in point: every potential driver who can pass a proficiency test may obtain a license, and the market is highly competitive.

Application of a simple, objective, unambiguous test to the licensing of electric-generating facilities is likely to be practically impossible. The nearest parallels to power-plant licensing are in the regulation of sites for large industrial facilities with substantial environmental impact: smelters, chemical plants, or coke ovens. In these cases, as in a power-plant siting, the decision is typically one of making a judgmental tradeoff of the potential environmental harm against other public-interest considerations. For the industrial facility, the public-interest benefit of a plant is its impact on the local economy: jobs and expenditures to local business firms. The question of local need for the industrial product is often irrelevant because the product is sold competitively in broad regional, national, or international markets. If licensing decisions in one state restrict new supplies, other states or foreign sources provide the incremental supply.

In electric-power siting decisions the public-interest consideration that receives the most attention is that of need for electricity, focusing especially within the licensing state. In effect, a public-interest judgment concerning local need versus environmental impact is applied. In the absence of the countervailing pressure of local need, there is a strong tendency to deny the sites: utilities have had difficulty in obtaining out-of-state sites except where local utilities also have a share in the facility and benefit from the combined venture.

Competition and entry take on a very different character in a regime of licensing based on need from a regime that grants licenses to all applicants meeting an objective standard. In a regime of licensing according to local need, the licensing authority must decide which among the available applicants is to build what will often be the only needed new facility in the area within a period of several years. If a deregulated generation market were combined with needs licensing, competition would have to take the form of convincing the authority that one site and plan were superior to another. The licensing authority's judgment would, in effect, replace that of the market in equilibrating supply and demand. As a result licensing on the basis of need would weaken the competitive force of free entry and necessarily politicize the selection of entrants.

It is likely to be difficult to supplant need as a licensing criterion, because it is the main public-interest offset to the environmental disbenefit associated with any large facility. Without such an offset the licensing process would tend to reject license applications. The challenge to licensing reform is to find ways of implementing a need test that would be compatible with an unregulated generating market and would minimize the politicization that would occur when the licensing authority decided which plants should be built. Present tests of need emphasize the retail market for the applicants, which generally have a public-utility responsibility to serve. In an unregulated generating market it is desirable for competition for scarce licensing slots to occur in the market place rather than through administrtive processes. One possibility is to require each applicant to produce a credible marketing plan and to accept letters of intent from buyers to contract for, say, 70 percent of the output or the facility as a conclusive indication of need. This solution would not be feasible for the deregulation structures that operate wholly on a spot basis.

## Relation of Generation to Retail Regulation

Most proposals for deregulating generation leave retail distribution regulated because of its natural-monopoly characteristics. Since the primary rationale for deregulating generation is to alleviate problems arising in retail regulation, the relationship between the generating market and retail regulation is particularly important.

Ideally, prices of generation determined in an unregulated market would be accepted by regulators as part of the cost of service just as the costs of fuel and other purchases are now accepted. For example, the typical regulatory treatment of coal contracts is to ascertain whether they are reasonably in line with prevailing market values for similar coal under comparable conditions. If price is found to be in line with market value, the full cost of the coal is allowed as part of the utility's cost of service. Essentially the same market-value criterion is applied for coal purchases at arms length and purchase from a coal-producing subsidiary of the electric utility. However, there is a general presumption of reasonableness for arms-length transactions, whereas purchases from subsidiaries typically receive much closer scrutiny.

In the case of electric generation it is reasonable to expect the market-value test to prevail in the case of arms-length purchases, at least once the generating market becomes established. In the other extreme of generation directly owned by the retail utility, it is likely that regulators would continue to subject the costs to closer scrutiny and reflect them in rates much as they do today, with the added complication of questioning whether the utility's own generation is the best available source. Thus, it appears that the effective reach of deregulation would likely be limited by whatever portion of the total generation is owned by retail utilities unless some alternative for regulating generating prices were to provide the retail regulators with an objective standard. Generating subsidiaries of retail companies are regulated by FERC and then accepted as part of the cost of retail service by state regulatory agencies. If FERC jurisdiction were abandoned under deregulation, it is likely that there would be a tendency for states to fill the vacuum by questioning the rates of electricity purchased by the retail utility from itself and entering into a de facto cost of service determination.

The key to successful resolution of the arms-length problem under partial deregulation is to substitute objective standards that either promote market competition or simulate market results for the discretion of regulators or utilities in the market place. Specifically, these standards would have to eliminate the distributing utility's control over the price of generation purchased from independent sources, objectify the transfer price of its own generation that would enter into its retail cost of service, and eliminate the discretion of the utility to refuse to deal with potential suppliers of generation who meet objective quality-control requirements. The extended PURPA approach discussed earlier is an attempt to apply an objective pricing standard and compulsory purchase requirement to the arms-length problem. To deal with the problem fully, an additional increase in regulation would be required so that potential generating sources would have access to transmission. In other words, to be workable the extended PURPA approach would require common-carrier status for at least the purchasing utility. In many instances the requirement would have to be extended to surrounding utilities for potential generating sites to have access to the logical buyer.

Given that retail rates are regulated by state commissions having jurisdiction over the treatment of the utility's own generation in its cost of service, implementation of an objective generation-pricing standard along the lines of an extended PURPA approach would require either state-commission adoption of the standard or creation of generating subsidiaries with sales subject to FERC jurisdiction. In the latter case utilities would have a choice of remaining wholly regulated by the state commission, putting all of its generation in the subsidiary subject to avoided-cost pricing rules, or dividing its generation among the two groups. Creation of new generating subsidiaries might be encouraged by new legislation providing an exemption of generating subsidiaries from Securities and Exchange Commission (SEC) jurisdiction under the Public Utility Holding Company Act.

**Transmission Issues**

Transmission arrangements are particularly critical to the operation of a deregulated generating market, because transmission is both an essential means of transportation and a focal point in the coordination of the market. In addition, management of transmission relates closely to provision of the systems-optimization aspects of bulk-power supply: economic dispatch, optimization of reserves, maintenance scheduling, and load-frequency control. Economies of scale and utilization of right-of-way make transmission a natural monopoly.

At present most transmission is controlled by vertically integrated utilities. These utilities use the facilities mainly to transmit their own generation. They also coordinate with one another, sometimes in formal power pools, in carrying out the systems-optimization aspects of bulk-power supply. Under deregulation generating entities would need access to the transmission network on comparable terms to compete effectively with one another and deliver their product to retail buyers. Similarly, the deregulated structure would have to allow for effective performance of the systems-optimization functions.

The common-carrier approach recommended for incremental deregulation builds on the existing pattern of ownership of the transmission network and would rely on existing utilities and pools to carry out systems-optimization functions. The vertical-disintegration approach would create new regional transmission entities which would provide transmission services and oversee the accomplishment of systems-optimization functions.

Under the common-carrier approach owners of transmission would be required to make transmission available to all prospective users willing to pay regulated rates and comply with regulated conditions of services. Provision of sufficient transmission capacity to service expected or planned uses would be part of the obligation. In practice this approach has many complexities and pitfalls. The history of cases involving access to transmission under the antitrust statutes, under the Federal Power Act, and under the Atomic Energy Act attests to many practical difficulties connected with the regulation of transmission rates and access. Supply and demand for transmission are rarely in balance. Where the owner also is a major user of a line, it is difficult to administer a mandate that all users have access to transmission. Furthermore, market-clearing prices are usually incompatible with conventional cost-of-service rate making. The common-carrier approach in effect trades increased regulation of transmission for reduced regulation of generation. Despite its administrative difficulties, which are considerable, the common-carrier approach appears to be the only available alternative to vertical disintegration as a means of reconciling deregulation of generation with the natural-monopoly status of transmission.

Deregulation proposals featuring vertical disintegration would establish regional transmission organizations, regulated or publicly owned, to plan and operate the transmission network and to act as a middleman between generators and retailers. In some proposals, the middleman is effectively a broker. In others, the middleman's role is larger, involving leasing of generating facilities and resale of bundle electricity to retailers. In all instances, the transmission organization orchestrates system optimization.

The complexity of transmission pricing would be greatly reduced in a vertically disintegrated arrangement. A regional transmission organization could employ a simple tariff that would recover its total cost and allow for some of the main cost-influencing factors. The rate structure need not be very refined because transmission is typically less than 10 percent of the total cost of electricity whereas generation is over 60 percent. The delivered prices of generation and competition among generating sources will be largely unaffected by differences in transmission rates over a reasonable range.

Under vertical disintegration no retail buyer or seller in the generating market would control the means of transportation, which would avoid a source of thorny problems in the common-carrier approach. Taken as a whole the vertical-disintegration approach, once implemented, would provide a simple and cleaner solution to the transmission-access problem than the common-carrier approach. However, massive divestiture and reorganization would have to occur before its benefits could be realized.

**Long-Term Commitments**

In general the most important problems and issues in deregulating generation involve investment decisions and long-term commitments rather than shorter-term issues. The importance of long-term decisions necessarily follows from the high-capital intensity of the industry, the long lead times for new base-load generation (twelve to fifteen years), and the durability of generating plant (service lives upwards of thirty years). A new base-load generating plant usually involves a commitment of billions of dollars. The magnitude of the investments and the length of the lead times substantially exceed those of any industry in the unregulated private sector.

A controversy has arisen over the feasibility of an unregulated generating market relying entirely or mainly on short-term or spot transactions. The dispute hinges on two considerations: whether competition or objective pricing standards are compatible with extensive long-term contracting and whether base-load generating facilities can be financed without the visible assurance of a market provided by advance contractual commitments. The view that long-term commitments are necessary is widely held by utility practitioners and members of the financial community.

Concern over whether long-term contracts would inhibit competition in generation stems partly from the fact that once a commitment is made, the contracted generation is effectively moved from the marketplace. The longer term the contractual arrangements that characterize the market, the smaller the percentage of total generation open to active competition at any time. However as long as buyers and sellers each have independent, active alternatives at the time of commitment, then competition will be present. Moreover, as long as buyers and sellers are free to enter into short-term transactions when they profit from doing so, the presence of the short-term alternative limits the ability of sellers (or buyers) to push risks in long-term contracts on to the buyers (or sellers) or extract excessive prices.

The issue of whether or not long-term arrangements are essential to a viable generating industry under deregulation cannot be resolved by debate or by observing the present regulated pattern. Indeed, it is not necessary to resolve the issue as long as participants in generating markets are free to contract over the full spectrum of contract lengths, escalation provisions, and other contractual arrangements. In any reasonable competitive market the participants will select the mix of transactions they prefer. In existing unregulated markets it is normal for a wide range of contractual arrangements to coexist. Long-term, highly escalated contracts are particularly common where long lead times and large capital investment are involved.

The relevant question for deregulation so far as long-term contracts are concerned is not whether they will be needed or not but how a deregulated structure can accommodate them if buyers and sellers show a preference for them. In a vertically disintegrated structure accommodating long-term contracts would be straightforward. The transmission utility, whether a broker or a buyer, simply schedules all contracted deliveries in much the same ways as contracts are scheduled in the interchange market of a power pool. After contracts are scheduled, spot-market transactions clear the market for the residual supply and demand.

A regime of deregulation without vertical disintegration is also potentially compatible with long-term contracting, but the issue is more complex than in the case of vertical disintegration. To begin with, establishing competitive markets is more difficult with vertical integration. The principal buyers start with large market shares in generation and occupy strategic positions in the ownership of transmission. By reducing the portion of the market open to arms-length transactions in any one year, long-term contracts reduced the portion of the market open to competition and may add to the effective degree of market concentration.

Deregulation without vertical disintegration confronts another problem with long-term contracts: conflict with the need for a simple, objective pricing rule. Whereas relatively simple, objective pricing rules are feasible for short-term transactions, they are not feasible for long-term contracts. Any price or formula applied to term contracts for purchased generation is sufficiently complicated to invite regulatory scrutiny of each contract and extensive regulatory proceedings for establishing, updating, and interpreting standards. One way to mitigate this problem would be to deregulate contract prices for generation purchased at arms length while preserving the seller's option for short-term sales (in the absence of a signed contract) at a rate based on an objective incremental cost-based pricing standard. The purchasing utility would thus retain its option to purchase its own generating based on the incremental cost-pricing rule.

There appears to be a viable place for long-term contracts in incremental deregulation as long as a solution can be found to the basic problems of transmission access and willingness of integrated utilities to purchase from other generating sources. If potential buyers and sellers want to transact and have the short-term option, the addition of a long-term contract option does not render the market noncompetitive.

### Partial Deregulation: An Example

Given the amount of time and change required to implement a vertically disintegrated structure and the high cost of reversing the reform once it is undertaken, ambitious methods of attaining some of the benefits of deregulation without such massive change need to be explored. The approach developed here, still not fully worked out, is presented in an exploratory spirit. It illustrates the potential use of an objective pricing standard as a device for achieving partial deregulation without comprehensive reorganization of the industry. It can also be viewed as an approach to transition to a vertically disintegrated deregulation structure. The emphasis is on discovering how partial deregulation could be made to work and on highlighting the problems it would encounter.

In essence the approach outlined here provides the utility with the option of partial deregulation of its generation, provided that it also accepts other conditions designed to encourage competition. The key provisions are the use of an objective pricing benchmark for generation which is based on the price behavior of an ideal competitive market and provisions for compulsory purchase of generation offered at the benchmark price. The essence of the approach is contained in the following provisions.

First, freedom to generate and sell electricity at the benchmark price based on the buyer's incremental costs would apply potentially to all new generating sources, including large units and units owned by the utility itself if federally regulated. Potentially, the restriction to new units only could be relaxed.

Second, the incremental-cost benchmark to be applied would be based on the *short-interval marginal cost ($\lambda$)* used for economic dispatch by the relevant utility or regional pool at the time of delivery. This benchmark would become, in effect, the market-clearing price.

Third, any utility opting to buy its own electricity at the $\lambda$-based price would have to purchase from any other source offering electricity to it.

Fourth, any utility opting to purchase its own electricity at the $\lambda$-based price would have to make a reasonable effort to provide transmission for competing sources of generation for its own loads or for the benefit of other distributors.

Fifth, prices of term contracts with generating sources other than purchasing utility would be exempt from rate regulation. The short-term benchmark price would not apply.

*The Pricing Benchmark*

The pricing benchmark is effectively the market-clearing price for the spot transactions that would be achieved in a perfectly competitive market. In the electric power-industry, $\lambda$ is routinely measured by utilities and power pools to optimize the allocation of output among available generating units (economic dispatch) and as part of the determination of interchange prices. The values of $\lambda$ for particular locations are routinely recorded. The measurement of λ is much more objective than most cost determination, because the marginal cost consists largely of fuel and both the applicable heat rate and fuel costs are known with high level of accuracy. It would be necessary, however, to be assured that all relevant costs are included in λ used for deregulation so that the price level is unbiased.

The pricing benchmark would indeed be simple and objective if λ as conventionally measured always equalled the relevant marginal costs. However, in practice, a benchmark equal to a conventional measure of marginal-operating costs would often generate insufficient revenue to justify investment in new base-load capacity. For example, the marginal-operating costs of a coal-fired system averaged around the clock are below the unit cost of a new coal-fired facility. By including price premia for peak hours and years when expected reserve margins are low, the price benchmark can be made to clear the market with adequate capacity. However, the introduction of price premia introduces a major element of regulatory judgement into the determination of the price benchmark.

There are two strong reasons for adopting λ rather than a longer term pricing standard. First, a λ based price is in complete harmony with the pricing characteristics of an effectively competitive market over the short and long run. If demand and capacity are in optimum balance, the price benchmark would just equal the long run incremental cost (LRIC) of expanding (or contracting) system capacity and output. If capacity shortage is anticipated, the expected levels of the price, properly averaged for investment decisions, would exceed expected LRIC. If capacity were expected to be in surplus, the expected price, properly averaged, would be below LRIC. Second, λ is a much more objective, simple benchmark than any alternative system that would provide, as λ does, a reasonable approximation to economically efficient price signals. The λ-based benchmark does it with a simple price to guide both long and short-term decisions, and the price is derived mainly from operating data that are easy to audit and maintain without much intervention of the regulatory process. This is an essential feature for any partial deregulation scheme. Otherwise, deregulation would merely change the form of regulation or even increase it.

## Statutory and Legal Requirements

The deregulation system set forth here would require some legislation to implement, but it appears that the required legislative and regulatory changes would be few. The key areas of legislative requirement appear to be establishing the pricing standard and providing a legal base for facilitating FERC (rather than state) regulation over generation owned by the distributing utilities. Legislation would almost certainly be required to establish a λ-based price as the pricing standard for generation. One feature of the λ-based standard is that all the rents from intramarginal sources would go to the seller. Of course, what appear as rents in the short run are often simply the reimbursement of capital outlays and the cost of capital. In *American Electric Power Service Corporation et al.* v. *Federal Energy Regulatory Commission* the District of Columbia struck down the provisions in FERC's rules under section 210 of PURPA that permitted and encouraged rates for cogneration and small generation equal to full avoided cost.[6] In essence the court's rationale was that the cogenerators and small power producers would accrue all of the rent while the utility's customers would get none. The court suggested that an alternative standard based on a stated percent of avoided costs would be acceptable.[7]

Clearly, λ could not be used in deregulation without a legal foundation accepting it. A standard of, say, 90 percent would not be workable because it would discourage expansion of supply to meet load growth. In effect the capacity shortage would take the form of a λ that is 111 percent of its efficient level, because no one would voluntarily commit to new capacity knowing that the revenues would be less than its total cost. Of course, the PURPA standards reviewed by the court involve long- and short-term measures. Nevertheless, it is unlikely that FERC or other regulators would risk an adverse court ruling by implementing a λ-based pricing system without explicit legislative endorsement.

The second area of probable legislative need is less essential than legislation establishing the pricing standard. Presently, FERC and state commissions divide the applicable jurisdiction. Sales by a generating subsidiary of a utility system, such as New England Power Company, or the reverse pyramid generating companies with multiple owners are regulated by FERC. Because of this regulation, the rates of these companies are legitimated as part of the cost of service and are rarely disallowed by state commissions in setting retail rates of the owning utility systems. Generation produced by the distribution utility is regulated directly by the state commissions, which determine the applicable return on capital and the measurement of costs.

Clearly, the natural path to implementing partial deregulation on a wide scale would be to set up the system through FERC. System implementation would require enlarging the proportion of total generation that is subject to rate regulation by FERC. There appear to be two possibilities. The first is to make no legislative changes but simply let the appeal of partially deregulated status act as an incentive to forming new generation subsidiaries under present law. The second involves making generating subsidiaries more attractive to utilities by amending the provisions of the Public Utility Holding Company Act so that a permanent exemption is available to utilities, not otherwise subject to SEC holding-company jurisdiction, which form generating subsidiaries.

Generating subsidiaries exist today, and some utilities are forming them. Northern States Power Company, for instance, is establishing a generating subsidiary. Unlike most of the utility systems with wholly owned generating companies, Northern States is basically an operating company engaged directly in the electric-utility business rather than a holding company owning electric-utility subsidiaries. If utilities view partial deregulation of their generation as attractive, it is reasonable for such subsidiaries to become widespread despite potential regulation under the Holding Company Act. However, there are a substantial number of combination electric and gas utilities. Any such utility which formed a generation subsidiary and was subsequently decided by SEC not to be exempt would be required to sell all of its gas properties. Consequently, there is little doubt that holding company act reform would improve the potential effectiveness of deregulation of generation without vertical disintegration.

*Operating Decisions*

The distributing utility, typically vertically integrated, must purchase whatever is offered at $\lambda$ at each particular time of day. As a practical matter many transactions would be scheduled in advance based either on long-term contracts or on one-day forecasts need for off-line dispatch. There remains, however, a problem of matching the real-time generation level with the load and determining how much each competitor should produce. The MIT scheme uses homeostatic control to give real-time price feedback. Under PURPA the purchasing utility is responsible for the balance; the unregulated sources supply what they want, and the utility adjusts to preserve an overall balance between generation and load, including appropriate operating reserves. But under PURPA only a small portion of the generation is deregulated. Under the approach discussed here, how would generation be controlled? In practice, the problem appears substantial but also tractable. Each utility being offered generation at $\lambda$ would have to accept the indicated quantity and would also require appropriate dispatching authority to see that delivered quantities follow prior commitments.

At least initially most generation would continue to be owned by integrated utilities. Some of this old and some new generation would continue to be regulated; utilities not wanting to have to purchase from others would continue to sell. The value of $\lambda$ would be based on the operating costs of the utility's highest cost unit in operation at the time in question, typically a relatively old fossil-fueled unit or a peaking unit. Generating firms considering whether to invest in a new generating facility would know that they could sell the output of the facility at a price related closely to the actual $\lambda$ prevailing on the system at each time energy is transferred to the buyer. By comparing forecasted values of λ with its expected costs, the generating firm would determine whether the prospective facility would be profitable. The higher the value of expected λ, the more profitable it would be to expand and enter. As plans for new units were announced and commitments were made, expected λ would be correspondingly reduced. A situation of equality between the present value of the applicable expected prices and the present value of all costs of a prospective facility is directly comparable to a state of long-run equilibrium in a competitive market. The incentives provided by expected λ would thus lead to corrective action in the market to keep the price in equilibrium.

How would investors in new generating projects tell whether a new generating facility were likely to be profitable? The answer depends on two kinds of considerations: the predictability of the various elements in the revenue-cost calculation and the degree to which risks can be hedged. Consider first the revenues. These depend on a λ, which in turn has two main components: fuel price and heat rate. Because λ follows the actual price of the fuel used by the marginal unit the revenues are effectively hedged against fuel-price changes. This is a good hedge for new units of similar design. For example, a peaking turbine would have an almost perfect hedge if it used the same fuel as the existing unit. For a new base-load unit the marginal fuel is likely to be different and would exert a much higher leverage on λ than on the costs of the new unit: nevertheless, there is a partial hedge. The other component of λ, heat rate, is highly predictable. Heat rates and ages of existing units are well documented and available to investors. Further, the groups of generating units that are likely to be marginal for a range of future scenarios can be readily identified. Their heat rates tend to cluster within a close range.

The real uncertainties for decisions on new generating facilities would come on the cost side in differences between actual and expected capital outlays. Fuel costs, as noted, are at least partially hedged. There is also a partial hedge on capital outlays, best illustrated by an example. Suppose a competent generating firm encounters unexpected cost increases resulting in a lifetime cost per kilowatt-hour 25 percent higher than assumed when construction was begun. As news of the cost overrun and its causes surfaced, other generating firms would defer or cancel plans for new capacity which would raise expected λ. The remaining risks would be unhedged, but it is important to note the self-limiting nature of the problem. If investors in λ large new generation projects perceived the risk of cost overruns as too high to justify investment, then less new capacity would be built and λ would rise. Eventually, the higher expected λ would justify more construction, and allow a margin for overrun contingencies. That process may not yield as efficient results as one in which generating firms and utilities would be free to contract at prices geared to the actual after-the-fact costs of the new generating unit and which would usually be lower but sometimes much higher than a λ-based price. An exemption for long term contracts is provided to allow this sort of pricing where the utility does not own the generating facility, but it is difficult to see how such contracts could escape regulatory scrutiny when actual cost greatly exceeded original estimates. It is reasonable to expect cost overruns for purchased generation under contract to be disallowed by the retail regulators to about the same degree under partial regulation as they are under the present regulatory structure. That is, the distribution utility may not be able to pass on all of its supplier's overruns.

Long-term contracts can survive in the partial deregulation arrangement described here only because the ceiling of λ would not apply to arms-length purchases in term contracts. The λ-based ceiling should be viewed as based on the integral of prevailing λs, weighted by the quantity generated and appropriately discounted to obtain a present worth or levelized cost over the life of the contract. If the ceiling were universal, then the seller could always do as well by simply selling on a spot basis. Yet for generation owned by the distribution utility, some objective standard is needed for the price, and λ serves that purpose.

### Reserve Capacity and Operating Reserves

To maintain reliable continuity of service despite outages or sudden increases in load, operating reserves are necessary: equipment warmed up or otherwise ready to go on short notice. The purchasing utility could buy or provide its own reserves, and it could pool its reserves through agreements with neighboring systems much as electric utilities do today. Some thought would have to be given to operational detail, but it appears the system could be made to work.

Reserve capacity under partial deregulation system developed here would be determined by the long-run market-clearing function of the price. If capacity were expected to be short, then the λ-based price would be relatively high, and the present worth of expected revenues would make it profitable to expand. If capacity were expected to be in excess, expected λ would be low, discouraging expansion. The market-clearing balance of supply and demand would include some reserve capacity. The implicit standard of reliability would be derived from retail-market demand.

Retail service is at regulated rates, and current standards of reliability are based on the utility's judgment, rules of thumb for outage probability that have gained acceptance, and regulatory pressure on public-interest grounds. The resulting standard of reliability does not enter directly into the capacity-demand balance of the λ-based system. The standard enters into the λ-based system indirectly through what the retail customers are willing to buy given the regulated rates and the levels of reliability they have come to expect through their experience with electric service. With a few exceptions involving interruptible service, customers do not make a market choice between different combinations of reliability and rates.

Effectively, the market would provide a somewhat different reliability standard from the present regulatory system. Regulation tends either to discourage reliability, as under present conditions, or to encourage it beyond what a competitive market would provide.

Effectively, reserve capacity would be provided up to the point where the owner of standby equipment could recoup the cost of operating and maintaining that equipment by infrequent sales at $\lambda$ during emergencies. The implied level of reliability depends crucially on how $\lambda$ is measured and on the price set during shortages when all available generation is insufficient to meet the total loads. In that event, the relevant market-clearing price should not be simply the cost of operating the highest cost unit but that amount plus a premium to reflect the value of additional generation needed to meet the shortage. By setting this premium, regulators of the buying utilities can influence the overall reliability of supply to each utility. In general, a premium over conventionally measured operating cost is likely to be needed so that price provides an adequate incentive for investment in new capacity.

## Deregulation of Old Generation

The partial deregulation arrangement outlined previously might limit deregulation to new generating facilities, principally to avoid the problem of creating an abrupt change accompanied by large rate increases and windfalls to the utilities affected. However, limiting the scope of the partial deregulation to new facilities has some weaknesses. First, deregulation of new facilities would offer virtually no financial relief to utilities. The costs of prospective facilities are not very different from the $\lambda$-based price: in equilibrium the two should be the same. Moreover, the new facilities will be few, and any price differences would not show up until output is produced; deregulation offers no CWIP. Second, the old-new dichotomy would aggravate resource misallocation just as it has in the regulation of field prices of natural gas and oil.

One virtue of a $\lambda$-based system for all units is that incentives for replacement or modification of old units and for addition of new units are all in harmony with one another. In an era of slow growth much of the efficient adjustment of electricity supply is likely to take the form of modification or replacement of old equipment rather than expansion through new facilities. Consequently, if partial deregulation is to be attempted, there is much to be said for deregulating old equipment as well as new.

The potential windfall effects or different vintages differ greatly. Original-cost regulation returns capital-related costs quickly in the early years of an asset's life, and new equipment has relatively high embedded costs because of inflation. Very old equipment has very high operating costs, and, particularly if oil-fired, is largely depreciated in the rate base. These two classes of equipment, the oldest and the newest, also provide the main tradeoff margin in retirement or expansion decisions. Because of the characteristics just described, these classes of equipment would not provide large windfalls in a $\lambda$-based price system. Equipment of intermediate vintage has relatively low embedded costs, and its operating costs for any given fuel type are similar to those of new equipment. The largest deregulation windfalls are likely to be in this category of equipment. This equipment rarely provides serious candidates for immediate retirement.

*Deregulation as an Option*

The partial deregulation approach discussed previously would provide an opportunity for utilities to deregulate, but if deregulation were offered as an option, not all would take the opportunity. In particular, the utilities with high embedded costs relative to $\lambda$-based pricing would find it unprofitable to opt for deregulation. There may also be cases where utilities prefer to avoid the complexities of the requirement that they provide transmission to competing sources of generation. The virtue of making deregulation an option, at least for an initial period, is that the reform would avoid harsh side effects on individual utilities. In addition, the response of utilities to the deregulation offer would be an instructive source of information on the practical problems to be encountered in implementing deregulation on a broader scale.

*Assessment of Partial Deregulation*

Partial deregulation as outlined in the previous section would be likely to achieve some desirable results, but it would also have some drawbacks and encounter some difficulties. Its main accomplishment would be to build a competitive market standard into the price of generation and to inject some of the dynamics of competition into the price. Incentives to add generating equipment would be economically efficient if old equipment were deregulated. The incentives would be efficient for all generating decisions: new capacity additions, refinements, and operation. However, to obtain these benefits, some kinds of regulation would be materially increased. Power-pool and system-dispatching operations, now largely self-regulated, would come under increased regulatory scrutiny, accelerating a trend already evident under PURPA. Transmission line access, already one of the most nettlesome, complex, and lag-prone areas of regulation, would be the center of very tough issues that would undoubtedly involve a high level of regulatory activity. Because of the complexity of determining what comprises providing for transmission on reasonable terms, resolution of transmission issues is virtually doomed to a lengthy case-by-case process where one party would usually have a strong incentive to delay. Finally, the partial-deregulation arrangement, by virtue of its reliance on a short-term pricing benchmark, may not offer enough flexibility for long-term commitments, though the preservation of deregulation as an option and the exemption of purchased power under long-term contracts should mitigate the problem.

**Conclusions**

Deregulation of electric generation has been advanced both as a means of remedying the industry's current financial distress and as an instrument for improving the industry's long-term performance. This chapter has analyzed some key issues in deregulation, focusing on two deregulation prototypes: a vertically disintegrated prototype representative of several proposals for restructuring the industry and a partial-deregulation prototype. In the latter case, this chapter developed a specific deregulation scheme to examine the problems and issues associated with an ambitious approach to partial deregulation.

Deregulation has been proposed as a potential solution to the industry's financial crisis; as a means of resolving regulator's dilemma over risk bearing; as a way of providing proper incentives for decisions to retire, replace, or modify existing facilities or to add new ones; as a way of achieving optimum reliability of service; as a way of eliminating additional resource misallocation caused by regulation; and as a way of introducing more freedom and competition into the industry. Skeptics of deregulation have questioned whether workably competitive generating markets could be established, whether long-term contracting and financing would be adequately provided for, and whether deregulation would deal effectively and realistically with issues relating to public-power competition, licensing of generating facilities, problems of divestiture or manipulation, and other institutional questions.

Would deregulation achieve its stated goals? This analysis suggests that deregulation can achieve most of them, but only if considerable care goes into the design and implementation of deregulation. Moreover, deregulation is likely to show few positive results during its first several years: implementation is likely to be a long, difficult process.

With respect to the financial crisis, certainly the most important motivator for practical efforts to achieve deregulation, deregulation offers a long-term means of preventing future financial squeezes, but deregulation cannot provide much relief to financially distressed utilities during the next three to five years. Clearly, deregulation cannot be viewed as an alternative to more direct methods of attacking the financial problem. Rather, it can supplement direct approaches to financial relief and help establish an environment in which similar financial crises would be unlikely to occur in the future.

Why is it that deregulation cannot provide financial relief for the electric-power industry within the next several years, even if the necessary legislation could be passed immediately? Vertically disintegrated deregulation would have an extremely long setup time with little benefit in the interim because of the time required to effect divestiture and reorganization. If it were accompanied by a transitional scheme, then its benefit and problems during transition would effectively be those of the partial-deregulation scheme used for transition. In partial deregulation, substantial amount of capacity would have to be deregulated before much financial benefit could show, and it would take time to bring that about. Note also that financial relief requires rate increases, and taking the political step of accelerated deregulation to achieve them could be just as difficult as effecting similar rate increases by other means. With respect to the other goals, the ability of deregulation to attain the performance hoped for by it advocates depends largely on whether an effectively competitive market for generation can be established.

The vertically disintegrated approaches to deregulation seek to assure an effectively competitive generating market by restructuring the industry. Arms length in purchase of generation and free access of all generators to transmission and markets would be assured by segregating all generation and distribution. Coordinated planning and operation of bulk-power systems would be accomplished by regional transmission utilities. This chapter's analysis of this prototype indicates it could include long-term contracting compatibly with structures that have worked effectively in other industries, the vertically disintegrated approach would avoid major problems associated with the present industry structure.

Vertically disintegrated deregultion has a number of potential problems. One problem is that it has never been tried. Although the structure meets every logical test of a well-working market, there is a risk that unforeseen problems would arise in practice. Moreover, there are some known problems. For example, licensing, as pointed out, may continue to function on the basis of need and operate as a serious impediment to market entry. However, the principal drawback to vertically disintegrated deregulation are the problems associated with establishing it: property valuation and compensation for divested assets, organization of the regional transmission firms, establishing the necessary operation practices, and reshaping regulatory practice at the state and federal level. It appears unlikely that legislation will embrace such a massive restructuring of the industry unless they can see very large, tangible benefits and have a strong base of political support. Once a massive reorganization were begun, it would be costly to reverse.

The foregoing considerations suggest the wisdom of a more incremental or experimental approach that could be abandoned or reversed if results were discouraging but could also become a vehicle of transition to full deregulation with or without vertical disintegration. Comparatively little work has been done to design partial-deregulation schemes and analyze how they will work. The analysis of a partial-deregulation scheme developed in this chapter is designed to surface the key issues associated with partial deregulation and stimulate alternative suggestions for how it may be accomplished.

Deregulation without vertical disintegration must contend with two issues associated with vertical integration. The first is the arms-length problem: if retail regulators are to accept deregulated rates for generation owned by the retail utility, there must be some objective market or regulatory standard for the price of generation. The second issue is that of access to the retail utility by generating entities other than the retail buyer. This has two aspects: access to transmission and willingness of the retail utility to buy from the most economical sources of generation regardless of ownership.

To get around the problems of arms length and market access, increased regulation appears the only feasible path. If the increased regulation is not to negate the benefits of deregulation, it must be very specifically directed to the problem areas and framed in terms that are compatible with a competitive generation market subject to a minimum of regulatory intervention.

A complete scheme of partial deregulation requires three ingredients to assure a sufficiently competitive generation market and a solution to the arms-length/retail regulation problem. First, there must be an objective pricing rule for generation, probably sanctioned by federal regulatory authority. Second, there must be a requirement to purchase from all sources offering generation at the designated price; and third, all generating sources must have access to the buyer's transmission. As discussed earlier, every one of these ingredients is in practice difficult to effect. Regulation of transmission access is likely to be a particularly difficult area.

The particular partial-deregulation scheme developed and analyzed in this chapter employs a pricing rule based on system $\lambda$ which closely simulates the operation of a competitive market and has the virtue of being much more objective than alternative price measures. This scheme does not, of course, get around the difficulty of deregulating transmission access, and it also may be difficult to sell to the legislators or regulators who must enact and effect reform. If the cool reception regulators have given marginal-cost retail pricing is a relevant indication, there may be resistance to reform using a pricing benchmark for generation with a marginal-cost base.

The problems with deregulation are much too serious to justify moving ahead rapidly with any of the major deregulation schemes advanced thus far. At the same time, the stakes involved in electric-utility reform are much too high to abandon serious consideration of the deregulation alternative and operational analytic development of the most promising approaches. Local or regional experiments and small-scale partial-deregulation are needed to build experience, assess the problems, and plot more expansive approaches. The objectives must be long term, as the benefits of the process will not be realized quickly, and efforts to deregulate should not be a diversion from direct efforts to increase electric-utility revenues in the near term.

## Notes

1. John E. Bryson, "Remarks to the Commonwealth Club of California," May 15, 1981, p. 7. See also Statement of John E. Bryson before the Committee on Energy and Commerce, Subcommittee on Energy Conservation and Power, United States House of Representatives, (April 6, 1981).

2. Bennett W. Golub, Richard D. Tabors, Roger E. Bohn, and Fred C. Schweppe, "Deregulating the Electric Utility Industry: Discussion and a Proposed Approach," MIT Energy Laboratory Working Paper MIT-EL 81-043, (July 1981). William W. Berry, President of Virginia Electric and Power Company, Remarks at National Economic Research Associates (NERA) Deregulation Workshop, (June 5, 1981). Matthew Cohen, "Efficiency and Competition in the Electric Power Industry," *Yale Law Journal* 88 (1979):1511. John H. Landon and David A. Huettner, "Restructuring the Electric Utility Industry: A Modest Proposal," in *Electric Power Reform: The Alternatives for Michigan*, ed. William Shaker (Ann Arbor: University of Michigan, 1976) p. 217.

3. Golub, et al., "Deregulating the Electric Utility Industry."

4. Cohen, "Efficiency and Competition."

5. 16 United States Code 796 (17)-(18), 824 a-3, 824i, 824k, (Supp. III 1979).

6. United States Court of Appeals, District of Columbia Circuit, *American Electric Power Service Corporation, et al., Petitioners*, v. *Federal Energy Regulatory Commission, Respondent*, Decided January 22, 1982, No. 80-1789.

# Appendix:
# Works by
# James C. Bonbright

## Books

*Railroad Capitalization; A Study of the Principles of Regulation of Rail-road Securities.* New York: Columbia University Press, 1920.

_____. Orgel, Lewis, eds. *Valuation Under the Law of Eminent Domain.* Charlottesville: The Michie Co., 1936.

*Valuation of Property,* 2 volumes, (New York: McGraw Hill, 1937).

*Principles of Public Utility Rates.* New York: Columbia University Press, 1961.

*The Valuation of Property; a Treatise on the Appraisal of Property for Different Legal Purposes.* Charlottesville: Michie Co., 1965.

_____ and Means, Gardiner C. *The Holding Company: Its Public Significance and Its Regulation.* New York: McGraw Hill, 1932. Reprinted New York: A.M. Kelley, 1969.

*Public Utilities and the National Power Policies.* New York: Columbia University Press, 1940. Reprint. New York: Da Capo Press, 1972.

## Articles, Reports, and Testimony

"Depreciation and Rate Control: A Further Discussion." *Quarterly Journal of Economics* 30 (May 1916):546-548.

"Basis of Railroad Capitalization." *Political Science Quarterly* 35 (March 1920):30-53.

"High Finance on the Railroads." *Nation* 111 (December 1920):637-638.

"Earning Power as a Basis of Corporate Capitalization." *Quarterly Journal of Economics* 35 (May 1921):482-490.

"No-par Stock, Its Economic and Legal Aspects." *Quarterly Journal of Economics* 38 (May 1924):440-465.

"Depreciation and Valuation for Rate Control." *Quarterly Journal of Economics* 41 (February 1926):185-211.

"Progress and Poverty in Current Literature on Valuation." *Quarterly Journal of Economics* 40 (February 1926):295-328.

"Economics in the Business Curriculum." *Journal of Political Economy* 34 (April 1926):233-242.

"Value of the Property as the Basis of Rate Regulation." *Land Economics* 2 (July 1926):276-281.

"Depreciation and Valuation for Rate Control." Published Simultaneously in *Quarterly Journal of Economics* 4 (February 1927):185-211 and *Columbia Law Review* 27 (1927):113-131.

"The Economic Merits of Original Cost and Reproduction Cost." *Harvard Law Review* 41 (1928):593-622.

"Railroad Valuation with Special Reference to the O'Fallon Decision." *American Economic Review* (Supplement) 18 (March 1928):181-205.

*Report of Commission on the Revision of the Public Service Commission*, New York State (Albany, 1930), Minority Report of Messrs. Walsh, Bonbright, and Adie, New York Legislature, Docket No. 75, pp. 52-55.

"Regulation of Stock Ownership in Railroads." House Committee on Interstate and Foreign Commerce. Washington: U.S. Government Printing Office, 1931.

"Should the Utility Holding Company Be Regulated?" *Public Utilities Fortnightly*, 7 (February 19, 1931):195-203.

"Evils of the Holding Company," *Annals of the American Academy of Political and Social Science* 159 (January 1932):1-6.

"Can We Curb the Holding Company?" *New Republic* 72 (November 2, 1932):322-325.

Chairman Round Table Discussion: "Rate-Making Problems of the Tennessee Valley Authority." *American Economic Review* (Supplement) 2 (March 1935):7-8.

_____ and Means, Gardiner C. "What a Holding Company Is and How It Operates." *Congressional Digest* 15 (October 1936):233, 256.

"Valuation of Property Review." *Quarterly Journal of Economics* 52 (November 1937):155-178.

"Public Ownership and the National Power Policy." *Yale Review* 28 (September 1938):36-49.

"Major Controversies as to the Criteria of Reasonable Public Utility Rates." *American Economic Review* (Proceedings) 31 (May 1941):379-389.

"Power Aspects of the St. Lawrence Waterway." *Canadian Journal of Economics and Political Science* 8 (May 1942):176-185.

"The Depreciation Reserve as a Measure of Actual Accrued Depreciation." *Land Economics* 20 (May 1944):98-100.

"Contributions of the Federal Power Commission to the Establishment of the Prudent Investment Doctrine of Rate-Making." *George Washington Law Review* 14 (December 1945):136-151.

"Original Cost as a Rate Base." *The Accounting Review* 20 (October, 1945):441-447.

"Memorandum of Income Tax Allocation Submitted to Arthur Andersen & Co." Chicago: Arthur Andersen & Co., 1946.

"Rate-making Policies of Federal Power Projects." *American Economic Review* 36 (May 1946):426-434.

"Utility Rate Control Reconsidered in the Light of the Hope Natural Gas Case." *American Economic Review* (Papers & Proceedings) 38 (May 1948):465-482.

"Public Utility Rate Control in a Period of Price Inflation." *Land Economics* 27 (February 1951):16-23.

"Interest during construction," submitted to Arthur Anderson & Co. (August 15, 1952), included in Arthur Anderson's brochure *Principles Underlying the Capitalization of Interest during Construction* (March 1, 1953).

Commonwealth Edison Company, Testimony and Exhibits Presented by Dr. James C. Bonbright, in Illinois Commerce Commission cases 41120, 41207-41214 inclusive, consolidated (1953), and case 44391 (1957).

"Status of GATT Agreement and Protocols." *U.S. Department of State Bulletin* 33 (November 21, 1955):860-861.

"Two Partly Conflicting Standards of Reasonable Public Utility Rates." *American Economic Review* (Supplement) 47 (May 1957):386-393.

"Fully Distributed Costs in Utility Rate-Making." *American Economic Review* (Supplement) 51 (May 1961):305-312.

"Public Utility Financing as Affected by Rate Regulation." *Public Utilities Fortnightly* 69 (May 10, 1962):649-659.

_____ et al. "The Role of Cost in the Minimum Pricing of Railroad Services," *Journal of Business* 35 (October 1962):357-366. "The Role of Cost in the Minimum Pricing of Railroad Services: Statement of Clarification." *Journal of Business* 36 (July 1963):348-351.

Treatment of Investment Credit Statements in Revenue Act 1963, Part 4. Case Clearing House (1963), pp. 1863-1868.

American Telephone and Telegraph, Testimony and Exhibits Presented by Dr. James C. Bonbright, in Federal Communications Commission, Docket No. 16258 (1966).

# Index

# About the Contributors

**William J. Baumol** is professor of economics at Princeton and New York universities. He received the B.S.S. from the City University of New York (1942) and the Ph.D. from London University (1949). He has taught at Princeton since 1949 and at NYU since 1971. He is past president of the American Economic Association, the Eastern Economic Association, and the Association of Environmental and Resource Economists. Among his publications are *Welfare Economics and the Theory of the State* (1952), *Business Behavior Value and Growth* (1959; 2d ed., 1966), *The Theory of Environmental Policy* (with W.E. Oates, 1975), and *Contestable Markets and the Theory of Industry Structure* (with John Panzar and Robert Willig, forthcoming).

**Edward H. Clarke** is an economist with the Office of Information and Regulatory Affairs, U.S. Office of Management and Budget. Dr. Clarke has worked in state and federal government for the last twelve years on state finance and federal regulatory reform. He received degrees from Princeton University and the University of Chicago.

**Gregory B. Enholm** is an economist with the Public Service Commission of Wisconsin and a Ph.D. candidate in economics at the University of Wisconsin—Madison. He also serves as staff assistant to the Ad Hoc Committee on Utility Diversification of the National Association of Regulatory Utility Commissioners (NARUC). He received the B.S. in business administration and the M.A. from the University of Florida in 1975.

**Leigh H. Hammond** currently serves on the North Carolina Utilities Commission. He received the B.S. from Clemson University, the M.S. from the University of Tennessee, and the Ph.D. from North Carolina State University. His many roles include that of vice-chairman of the Committee on Electricity in the National Association of Regulatory Utility Commissioners; chairman of the board of the National Regulatory Research Institute in Columbus, Ohio; member of the National Advisory Panel of the Sea Grant College Program; and member of the Joint Council on Food and Agricultural Sciences.

**C. Lowell Harriss** is professor emeritus of economics at Columbia University and executive director of the Academy of Political Science. He is also an economic consultant to the Tax Foundation, Inc., and an associate at the Lincoln Institute of Land Policy. He received the B.S. in economics from Harvard University and the Ph.D. from Columbia University. He has written numerous articles and books in the field of regulatory economics.

331

**Hunter E. Harvey, Jr.**, is director—Tariffs and Costs at American Telephone and Telegraph Company. He was assistant vice-president—Rates at New Jersey Bell Telephone Company from 1974 through 1979. He received the B.S. in management from Rutgers—The State University and received the M.A. in industrial management as a Sloan fellow at Massachusetts Institute of Technology. Mr. Harvey joined New Jersey Bell as a customer sales representative in 1955 and has held various positions in the engineering, marketing, commercial, traffic, and data-systems departments. He was appointed general manager of the central area in 1970.

**William R. Hughes** is president of Charles River Associates (CRA). He has been with·CRA since 1969, serving previously as vice-president. He received the B.A. in business administration from the University of Maryland and the M.A. and Ph.D. in economics from Harvard. He also held the position of assistant professor of economics at Boston College and has written several books in the regulatory area.

**Milton Z. Kafoglis** is John H. Harland Professor of Economics at Emory University where his current research interest is with the impact of inflation on the regulatory process. He received the Ph.D. from The Ohio State University. His publications include several books and many articles dealing with regulation and public finance. He has served as a senior economist on the staffs of the Council on Wage and Price Stability and the Civil Aeronautics Board.

**Alfred E. Kahn** was appointed by President Carter to serve as Advisor to the President on Inflation and as chairman of the Council on Wage and Price Stability. He left those positions to return to his chair in economics at Cornell University. At the time of his appointment, Dr. Kahn was serving as chairman of the Civil Aeronautics Board. He had previously been serving as chairman of the New York State Public Service Commission. He is a Special Consultant to the economic consulting firm, National Economic Research Associates.

Dr. Kahn received the B.A. and M.A. from New York University and the Ph.D. in economics from Yale University. He also has honorary LL.D. degrees from Colby and Ripon colleges and the University of Massachusetts.

Throughout his career, Dr. Kahn has served on a variety of public and private boards and commissions, including: the Attorney General's National Committee to Study the Antitrust Laws (1953-1955); the President's Council of Economic Advisors (1955-1957); the Economic Advisory Council of American Telephone and Telegraph Company (1968-1974); the National Academy of Sciences Advisory Review Committee on Sulfur Dioxide Emissions; the Environmental Advisory Committee on the Federal Energy Administration; the Public Advisory Board of the Electric Power Research Institute; the Executive Committee of the National Association of Regulatory Utility Commissioners; and the National Commission for the Review of Antitrust Laws and Procedures. He is a member of the Board of Directors of New York Airlines, Inc. He is also a Fellow of the American Academy of Arts and Sciences, and has been elected vice-president of The American Economic Association.

Dr. Kahn's publications include *Great Britain in the World Economy*, (1946, 1978); *Fair Competition, The Law and Economics of Antitrust Policy* (coauthored, 1954, 1970); *Integration and Competition in the Petroleum Industry* (coauthored, 1959, 1971); and *The Economics of Regulation* (1970).

**Donald C. Keenan** is assistant professor of economics at the University of Georgia. He received the B.A. from Carnegie-Mellon University and the D.Sc. from Washington University. His interests are microeconomic theory and its applications, and he has published research in these areas.

**John B. Legler** is professor of banking and finance and director of the Georgia Economic Forecasting Project in the College of Business Administration at the University of Georgia. He received the B.A. from Allegheny College and the M.S. and Ph.D. in economics from Purdue University. Dr. Legler has done extensive research and publishing in the areas of state and local finance and regional economics. He has served as a consultant to state and local governments and has appeared as an expert witness before the public service commissions of several states and the Nuclear Regulatory Commission.

**J. Robert Malko** is chief economist at the Public Service Commission of Wisconsin. He received the B.S. in mathematics and economics from Loyola College and the M.S. and Ph.D. in economics from Purdue University. From 1978 to 1980 he served as program manager of the Electric Utility Rate Design Study of the Electric Power Research Institute. He has also served as chairman of the Staff Subcommittee on Economics of the National Association of Regulatory Utility Commissioners. Dr. Malko has taught public-utility economics at the University of Wisconsin—Madison and at Stanford University, carried out consulting assignments for state and local governments, and appeared as an expert witness on electricity-pricing issues before various regulatory commissions. He has written several articles on electricity pricing.

**John R. Marks III** has served on the Florida Public Service Commission. After receiving the B.S. from Florida State University, he entered the Florida State University College of Law and graduated in 1972. In addition to his commission duties, he serves on many committees and organizations and writes a column about the Florida Public Service Commission, which appears in fifteen weekly newspapers and monthly magazines.

**William R. Nusbaum** is associate counsel with Bank of America—San Francisco. He formerly was communications policy specialist with the Common Carrier Program, National Telecommunication and Information Administration, U.S. Department of Commerce, and worked for the Bank of America. He received the B.A. from City College and a law degree from the New England School of Law in Boston. He is a member of the District of Columbia Bar.

**Anthony D. Osbon** is a vice-president and utility investment analyst for Donaldson, Lufkin and Jenrette, Inc., a major New York securities firm. He received the B.B.A. from the University of Georgia and attended the New York University Graduate School of Business Administration. During his thirteen years of association with the utility industry, he has written many articles and research reports on the investment appeal of utility securities. Mr. Osbon is an active member of several utility-analyst groups including the New York Society of Security Analysts where he recently was chairman of the utility-program committee.

**Joe D. Pace** is senior vice-president of National Economic Research Associates, Inc., where he previously served as vice-president. He received the B.A., M.A., and Ph.D. from the University of Michigan. He has written articles and delivered speeches in the regulatory area.

**Chris W. Paul II** is associate professor of economics at the University of Alabama at Huntsville. He received the Ph.D. from Texas A&M University. Dr. Paul has published studies concerning the structure and impact of regulation on motor carriers and electric utilities. He has held positions with the Federal Energy Administration and Texas Transportation Institute and served as consultant to the Civil Aeronautics Board.

**Charles F. Phillips, Jr.**, is the Robert G. Brown Professor of Economics, Washington and Lee University. He received the B.A. from the University of New Hampshire and the Ph.D. from Harvard University. He is also a member of the board of editors, *Atlantic Economic Journal*; president, Institute for Study of Regulation; and a member of the board of trustees of Omicron Delta Epsilon. He has testified on rate of return or rate structure in some ninety utility cases before twenty-five state and three federal commissions. He is a member of the faculty, Public Utility Executive Program, at the University of Michigan and takes part in the semiannual financial seminars sponsored by Irving Trust Company and by Kidder, Peabody & Company. He is the author of *The Economics of Regulation* (1965, 1969); editor of seven books on regulatory issues, including *Regulation and The Future Economic Environment—Air to Ground* [1980]; and author or coauthor of numerous articles in professional, business, and legal journals.

**William G. Shepherd** is professor of economics at the University of Michigan. He received the B.A. from Amherst College and the M.A. and Ph.D. from Yale University. He is the author of many articles and books, including *Public Politics toward Business* (with Clair Wilcox); *The Economics of Industrial Organization; Public Enterprise: Economic Analysis of Theory and Practice*; and *The Treatment of Market Power*; and is coeditor of *Economic Regulation*, a book in honor of James R. Nelson.

**Roger Sherman** is professor of economics at the University of Virginia. He received the M.B.A. from Harvard University and the M.S. and Ph.D. from Carnegie-Mellon University. He has written numerous articles and books in the field of regulatory and public-utility economics.

**Ford B. Spinks** has been president of Tifton Tractor Company since its founding in 1955. He was elected to the Georgia Senate from the ninth senatorial district in 1962 and to four consecutive terms. In 1971 he resigned to accept appointment to the Georgia Public Service Commission (GPSC). He was elected in 1972 to fill the remaining four years of Commissioner McDonald's term and reelected in 1976 to a six-year term. Mr. Spinks is chairman of the board of directors of both Dealers Equipment Credit Company and South Georgia Banking Company.

**Jim J. Tozzi** has been the deputy administrator for Information and Regulatory Affairs in the U.S. Office of Management and Budget (OMB) since January 1981. Dr. Tozzi's varied background includes the B.S. in chemical engineering, the M.A. in retailing, and the Ph.D. in economics and business administration from the University of Florida. He oversees the President's regulatory reform program, the reduction of federal paperwork, and the acquisition and utilization of information systems within the federal government. Before assuming his present position, he was the chief of the Environmental Branch of OMB.

**Harry M. Trebing** is the director of the Institute of Public Utilities and professor of economics at Michigan State University. He received the B.A. and M.A. from the University of Maryland and the Ph.D. from the University of Wisconsin. He is a past chairman of the Transportation and Public Utilities Group of the American Economic Association, and a past president of the Association for Evolutionary Economics. His recent publications include *Issues in Public Utility Regulation* (ed.), "Equity, Efficiency, and the Viability of Public Utility Regulation," and "Structural Change and Regulatory Reform in the Utilities Industries." Professor Trebing served as chief economist, U.S. Postal Rate Commission, and as chief of the Economic Studies Division, Federal Communications Commission. He currently serves on two advisory panels for the Congressional Office of Technology Assessment, the Comptroller General's Panel on Regulatory Accounting, and is a public member of the board of directors of the National Regulatory Research Institute at The Ohio State University.

**Robert G. Uhler** is vice-president, National Economic Research Associates, Inc. He attained the B.Sc. and the A.B. from Ohio University and the M.A. from The Ohio State University. He has served as chief of the division of economic studies at the Federal Power Commission and was an assistant professor of economics at the U.S. Military Academy. He has published articles in the public-utility field including several in *Public Utilities Fortnightly*.

**Larry R. Weber** is assistant vice-president of Southern Bell Telephone and coordinates the firm's activities before regulatory agencies. He has been associated with the Bell system for twenty years and has worked principally in the area of finance and data systems. He is a graduate of the University of South Carolina.

**Ronald P. Wilder** is a professor of economics in the College of Business Administration of the University of South Carolina. He received the B.S. and M.S. in economics from Rice University and the Ph.D. in economics from Vanderbilt University. His teaching and research interests are in the areas of industrial economics, regulation, and energy economics. He has been consultant to the South Carolina public service commission and South Carolina Electric and Gas Company.

# About the Editors

**Albert L. Danielsen** is professor of economics at the University of Georgia. He received the B.S. from Clemson University in 1960 and the Ph.D. from Duke University in 1966. He recently authored a book entitled *The Evolution of OPEC* and has written numerous articles and research reports on energy markets. He has also served in the U.S. Department of Energy as special assistant to the deputy assistant secretary for international energy research.

**David R. Kamerschen** is holder of the Chair of Public Utilities in the Department of Economics at the University of Georgia. He received the B.S. and M.A. in 1959 and 1960, respectively, from Miami University and the Ph.D. in 1964 from Michigan State University. He has served as an expert witness in approximately sixty antitrust and utility-regulation cases for both private and public bodies. He has also presented testimony before numerous state and federal public service commissions. He served as an appointed member to the advisory committee to the Consumers' Utility Counsel for the state of Georgia. He has written more than 110 professional articles and has authored six books. Dr. Kamerschen also has appeared on public television as a panelist on regulatory economics.

DATE DUE